THE COMPLETE
mothercare
MANUAL

Consultants
Rosalind Y. Ting, M.D., M.P.H.
Herbert Brant, M.D.
Kenneth S. Holt, M.D.

THE COMPLETE
mothercare
MANUAL

An illustrated guide to
pregnancy, birth and childcare through age five

FIRESIDE
F
SIMON &
SCHUSTER

CONTENTS

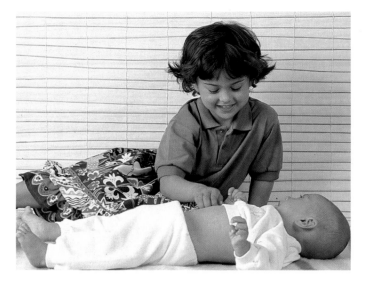

Conceived, designed and produced by
Conran Octopus Limited
Copyright © 1986, 1987 by Conran
Octopus Limited

FIRESIDE
Simon & Schuster Building
Rockefeller Center
1230 Ave. of the Americas
New York, NY 10020

First published in 1987 by
Prentice Hall Press
A Division of Simon & Schuster, Inc.

This paperback edition published in 1992

Fireside and colophon are registered
trademarks of Simon & Schuster, Inc.

Originally published in Great Britain
in 1986 by Conran Octopus Limited

Library of Congress Cataloging in
Publication Data

Ting, Rosalind Y.
  The complete mothercare manual

  includes Index.
  1. Pregnancy. 2. Childbirth.
3. Children – Health and hygiene.
4. Children – Care. I. Brant, Herbert A.
II. Holt, K. S. (Kenneth Sunderland).
III. Title. (DNLM: 1. Child Care –
popular works. 2. Infant Care – popular
works. 3. Labor – popular works. 4.
Pregnancy – popular works. WQ 150
T588c) RG525.T56 1987 618.2 87-
12556
ISBN 0-671-78978-3

Typeset by Dorchester Typesetting Ltd
Printed and bound in China

10 9 8 7 6 5 4 3 2

FOREWORD

The American edition of *The Complete Mothercare Manual* which originated in London and now has been revised and edited with the help of Dr Cynthia Cooke, my distinguished colleague at The University of Pennsylvania School of Medicine, is a timely gift to any parents or would-be-parents anywhere in the world. This book touches upon all the essential aspects of parenthood from preparation for conception to identifying the readiness of your child to enter kindergarten. It covers a wide scope such as the A-Z of common ailments and simple common first-aid treatment.

The presentation with vivid photos in each section makes this book an attractive, valuable and reliable guide for contemporary families. For all new and expectant parents this book will help to relieve some doubts and frustrations, meet the challenges in parenthood and capture every moment of the immense joy in your child's development. The list of references with up-to-date telephone numbers will also come in handy.

Babies are individuals who command our recognition and respect. They never stop amazing us, so let us enjoy and learn from being parents and be enriched by such experiences.

Rosalind Y Ting M.D.

**Rosalind Y. Ting
MD, MPH**
Senior Physician, The Children's Hospital of Philadelphia
Professor Emerita, University of Pennsylvania School of Medicine

Dr Ting joined the Children's Hospital of Philadelphia 30 years ago and has been the senior staff member in the Division of General Pediatrics. She is mainly responsible for teaching Developmental Pediatrics and has been chief investigator in various research projects relating to child development. She also established a model infant daycare center affiliated with the Division of General Pediatrics in the Children's Hospital of Philadelphia for clinical teaching and research for senior resident physicians. During the last 15 years Dr Ting has also been the Honorary Consultant at the Beijing Children's Hospital and Institute of Child Healthcare in Beijing, China.

**Cynthia W. Cooke
MD FACOG**
Clinical Assistant Professor of Obstetrics and Gynecology, University of Pennsylvania School of Medicine. She has been active in women's health issues for many years. She is the author, with Susan Dworkin, of the *Ms Guide to a Womans Health* (Doubleday and Berkley Books).

About the contributors:

Herbert Brant
MD, FRCS (Ed), FRCOG, FRCP(Ed)
Consultant, Pregnancy and birth
Professor Brant qualified in New Zealand, where he had a medical practice for several years. He is presently Professor of Clinical Obstetrics and Gynecology, and Consultant Obstetrician at University College Hospital and Medical School, London. For many years he has taken an active part in prenatal education and communication in obstetrics. He is the author of several books about pregnancy, childbirth and contraception, the most recent being *Childbirth for Men* (Oxford University Press).

Kenneth S. Holt
MD, FRCP, DCH
Consultant, childcare
Professor of Developmental Pediatrics, Institute of Child Health, University of London, and Honorary Consultant at the Hospital for Sick Children, Great Ormond Street, London. He joined the Institute of Child Health twenty years ago to plan and establish the Wolfson Center (for the research into, and teaching of, disabled children), and the Department of Developmental Pediatrics.

Margaret Brant
Pregnancy and birth
Coordinator of the prenatal education program at University College Hospital, London, Mrs Brant qualified in health education and physical education in New Zealand. She has wide experience in teaching midwives, health visitors, medical students and doctors about the patient's view-point in pregnancy and childbirth, and is the author of *Having a Baby* (Macdonald).

Claire Burns
A-Z of common ailments
Dr Burns has worked in hospital pediatrics (she was Senior Registrar at the Hospital for Sick Children, Great Ormond Street, London) as well as in child health clinics. She spent four years in Australia, where she worked for a time as a flying doctor. She has one child.

Sheila Gregory
Growing and learning
Sheila Gregory is an educational psychologist, working with children up to the age of 16, their parents and teachers. She specializes in seeing pre-school children and has worked closely with a unit for children who have language difficulties. She has two children.

Ann Henderson
Play and toys; Pre-school play and learning
Ann Henderson has been involved in teaching playgroup supervisors and tutors, as well as working in playgroups herself. She is the co-author of *Pre-school Playgroups – A Handbook* (Allen & Unwin), and has also edited and written for several childcare magazines. She has two children.

Maggie Jones
Child health clinic; Some common worries; Safety around the house; Emergencies; First aid treatment
As a freelance editor and writer, Maggie Jones has written widely for newspapers and magazines, and is the author of a book on overcoming the problems of infertility and child loss. She was a consultant to the World Health Organization on health and family planning. She has three children.

Sarah Litvinoff
You and your baby/child; Sleep and bedtime; Your day together; Your family life
Sarah Litvinoff is a freelance writer, specializing in health and child-related subjects. At present, she is writing a handbook for working mothers, to be published in 1987. She is a single parent with one child.

Diane Melvin
Growing and learning
Diane Melvin is a Senior Clinical Psychologist presently working at a London teaching hospital. She has worked as a counselor to parents of young children, and is particularly interested in the study of behavioral problems and learning difficulties in young children. She has three children.

Elisabeth Morse
Feeding your baby/child
Elisabeth Morse was the Senior Scientific Officer at the British Nutrition Foundation and editor of the BNF Nutrition Bulletin. The author of two leaflets 'Healthy Eating for Your Children' and 'The Overweight Child' she has also contributed to books published by Mitchell Beazley, Penguin Books and Marshall Cavendish. She has two children.

Heather Welford
Newborn baby; What your baby/child will need; Diaper changing, potty training and bathing
As a writer, Heather Welford specializes in childcare and family life and is actively involved in postnatal support. She is the author of *The illustrated Dictionary of Pregnancy and Birth* (Allen & Unwin). She has three children.

Reader's note
We have used the pronouns "he" and "she" in alternate chapters throughout the book to reflect the fact that the text applies equally to male and female children. Where, occasionally, this is not the case, the appropriate pronoun has been used.

PREGNANCY AND BIRTH

Weeks of waiting and wondering will finally culminate in the moment of birth. This is a period of change – physical change as the baby develops and grows in the womb and emotional change as the idea of a new life becomes real.

Your pregnancy and delivery

A tremendous sense of well-being can add to the enjoyment of being pregnant.

Having a baby is both exciting and demanding, rewarding and frustrating, worrying and yet emotionally satisfying and fulfilling. There is now plenty of opportunity to read about pregnancy, childbirth and parenthood and to talk to friends and professional advisers. Efficient methods and techniques help with pain and with any problems in labor. Be optimistic, be realistic and retain your sense of humor as you approach this very important period of your lives.

Taking the trouble to be prepared in advance and to plan your future is never more important than when you are having a baby. A little forethought can reduce your worries during pregnancy and in the months of babycare that lie ahead. Think about your welfare as a family and especially about what steps you can take to give your baby the best possible start. Having children is a privilege which can enrich the lives of a couple in many ways, but children do bring obligations and responsibilities. Undoubtedly the future happiness and compatibility of children is shaped by the family in which they are brought up.

You should discuss as a couple how you think your lifestyles may be affected by pregnancy and a baby – talk with friends who have been through the experience. Being three is never the same as being two. Your relationships and personal freedom change and you will both need to adjust and think about the future.

Pre-pregnancy health

If you are planning to become pregnant it is worth considering some aspects of your general health even before you conceive. Although there is not yet always good evidence to support this advice there are certainly some advantages for you, and probably for your baby too, in looking after your health before you conceive as well as during your pregnancy.

If you have been taking an oral contraceptive pill you will usually be advised to wait three months after stopping the pill before you conceive. This is because of the pill's possible influence on the development of the baby.

Try to give up smoking as evidence is accumulating about the problems of smoking during pregnancy. Babies of mothers who smoke tend to be smaller and may develop less well. Women can be more at risk if other problems, such as high blood pressure, develop during pregnancy. It is possible, too, that the quality of the man's sperm can be adversely affected if he smokes or drinks alcohol excessively in the weeks before conception. Since there is evidence that even small amounts of alcohol can be harmful in pregnant women the best advice is to give up alcohol before becoming pregnant.

It is important also to avoid taking any drugs that aren't absolutely necessary before conceiving. Fertilization and the early development of a baby are controlled by delicately balanced chemical processes. It is quite easy to understand,

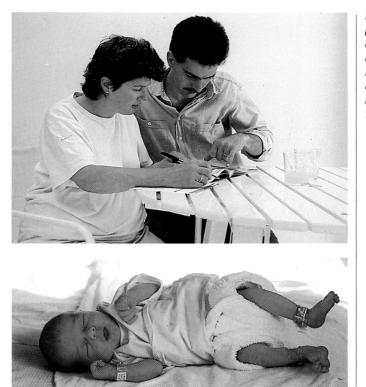

Left *Pregnancy is a time of preparation for parenthood – you can plan things together and choose what your baby will need.* **Below left** *Here at last! and you can begin to get to know the new being who has been part of you for so long.*

therefore, how any additional chemicals entering the body as medication or in any other way could disturb development. Although very few drugs are definitely known to harm the baby none can be guaranteed completely safe. It is a good principle to check with your doctor about the continued use of any drugs or long-term medication. Self medication should be avoided and this, of course, includes all herbal and over-the-counter remedies.

Before starting a pregnancy it is wise to have your immunity to German measles (rubella) checked by a blood test. German measles can be disastrous for the fetus, causing severe handicap, when contracted during the first four months of pregnancy. If you are not immune, you can have a rubella vaccination. You should then use contraception for three months to allow the vaccine virus to be cleared from your blood. If you and your partner are of eastern European Jewish ancestry, Tay-Sachs testing should be done.

There are very good reasons for eating a good diet before as well as during pregnancy. Don't just assume that the addition of vitamin pills will solve any problems. Make sure you're having plenty of fresh fruit and vegetables with additional fiber in the form of whole-grain cereals. You should also ensure that you are having enough protein but try to restrict fats and avoid too much refined carbohydrate.

If you are overweight, try to get into better shape before pregnancy. Exercise and a good diet should help.

Although there is no good evidence that physical fitness is required for labor, if you are fit you are more likely to recover quickly after your baby is born.

Knowing you're pregnant

For most women the first and most obvious sign of pregnancy is when they miss their regular menstrual period. This is not always a reliable sign, particularly for those women whose periods normally come at irregular or infrequent intervals. You should remember also that pregnancy is not the only reason for a missed period – it could, for instance, be due to anxiety of some kind, often about whether you are, or are not, pregnant.

Sometimes, instead of being completely missed, the period may just be much lighter than usual. In other words, there may be slight bleeding at the time of the first missed period. This can be quite misleading but it does not affect the continuing pregnancy. Apart from causing confusion about dates it can be ignored. There are other signs of pregnancy in the early weeks (*see* left), but you may not experience all or even any of them. Although you may suspect you are pregnant if you have some or all of these signs, you cannot be sure until it has been confirmed by a pregnancy test or by your doctor's examination.

Confirming your pregnancy

A pregnancy test is not usually reliable until about two weeks after your period was due or four weeks after conception (*see also* page 14). The test works by detecting, in a sample of the urine you pass first thing in the morning, the hormone produced by the developing placenta. Pregnancy testing can be done by your doctor, a family planning clinic or a pregnancy advisory service. You can also buy a do-it-yourself testing kit from your druggist. Read the instructions carefully but don't be surprised if you are not sure about the result. Some more expensive kits can now diagnose pregnancy just a few days after your period is missed. An even more sensitive blood test has been developed and it is widely available.

For the urine test you need to collect a sample of the first urine you pass in the morning as this is the most concentrated. It is important that you use a clean container which is free of soap or detergent. A laboratory container is provided by places that do the testing. Although test results are almost always correct, it is possible not to be pregnant when a result is positive or, more commonly, to be pregnant when a result is negative. Don't hesitate to have the test repeated after a week if it is not as you expect and if you continue to think you may be pregnant.

Seeing your doctor
Go to your obstetrician/gynecologist as soon as you think you are pregnant. He or she may wish to examine you or to arrange a pregnancy test or other tests as indicated, so it's a good idea to take an early morning urine sample with you. Once your pregnancy is confirmed he or she will discuss with you arrangements for your prenatal care and delivery (*see* page 22).

THE FIRST SIGNS
- Your period is overdue or was unusually light.
- You feel queasy or are sick, not just in the morning but at any time of the day.
- You have your usual premenstrual feelings which may last for several weeks.
- Your breasts feel tender and heavy and the nipples tingle.
- You feel inexplicably tired or moody.
- You lose your appetite for certain foods and drinks, e.g. coffee, tea or alcohol. You no longer enjoy smoking and may have a strange metallic taste in your mouth.
- Your normal vaginal discharge may increase, without any itchiness or soreness.
- You need to pass water frequently both day and night. You may be constipated.

Calculating your delivery date

Your expected date of delivery is called EDD for short. To calculate it you need to know the date on which your last period began and also how many days there are in your average monthly cycle.

Your EDD is calculated from the first day of your last period. The calculation is based on a regular 28-day cycle and assumes that pregnancy lasts 280 days – or 40 weeks – from the beginning of your last period or 266 days from the presumed date of conception or ovulation (*see* page 14). The chart below can help you to work out your EDD.

The varying length of pregnancy

Eighty-five per cent of normal pregnancies end within the range of two weeks before and two weeks after the EDD. In other words, it is quite usual for a pregnancy to last between 38 and 42 weeks. So, for example, if your last period started on January 8, with a 28-day cycle your EDD is October 15 but you could regard yourself as delivering on time if your baby came anytime between October 1 and 29.

Difficulties in calculating an EDD

If you have not had three normal cycles after a previous pregnancy (whether this was a normal pregnancy, a miscarriage or a termination) or after stopping an oral contraceptive pill, the first day of your last menstrual period cannot be relied on to predict the date of your delivery. In these circumstances an estimate of your EDD will depend on other evidence, such as your doctor's examination of the size of the uterus or an ultrasound scan of the fetus.

Menstrual calendar
Below This shows a regular 28-day cycle. Your pregnancy is dated from the first day of your last period although you conceived about two weeks later.
EDD chart
Bottom To find your expected delivery date (EDD), look for the first day of your last period. Your EDD is given underneath, based on a 28-day cycle.

Week 1							Week 2							Week 3							Week 4							
28	1	2	3	4	5	6	7	8	9	10	11	12	13	14	15	16	17	18	19	20	21	22	23	24	25	26	27	28	1

First day of your last monthly period — Ovulation, conception — 4 weeks pregnant

JANUARY	1	2	3	4	5	6	7	8	9	10	11	12	13	14	15	16	17	18	19	20	21	22	23	24	25	26	27	28	29	30	31		JANUARY
OCTOBER	8	9	10	11	12	13	14	15	16	17	18	19	20	21	22	23	24	25	26	27	28	29	30	31	1	2	3	4	5	6	7		**NOVEMBER**
FEBRUARY	1	2	3	4	5	6	7	8	9	10	11	12	13	14	15	16	17	18	19	20	21	22	23	24	25	26	27	28					FEBRUARY
NOVEMBER	8	9	10	11	12	13	14	15	16	17	18	19	20	21	22	23	24	25	26	27	28	29	30	1	2	3	4	5					**DECEMBER**
MARCH	1	2	3	4	5	6	7	8	9	10	11	12	13	14	15	16	17	18	19	20	21	22	23	24	25	26	27	28	29	30	31		MARCH
DECEMBER	6	7	8	9	10	11	12	13	14	15	16	17	18	19	20	21	22	23	24	25	26	27	28	29	30	31	1	2	3	4	5		**JANUARY**
APRIL	1	2	3	4	5	6	7	8	9	10	11	12	13	14	15	16	17	18	19	20	21	22	23	24	25	26	27	28	29	30			APRIL
JANUARY	6	7	8	9	10	11	12	13	14	15	16	17	18	19	20	21	22	23	24	25	26	27	28	29	30	31	1	2	3	4			**FEBRUARY**
MAY	1	2	3	4	5	6	7	8	9	10	11	12	13	14	15	16	17	18	19	20	21	22	23	24	25	26	27	28	29	30	31		MAY
FEBRUARY	5	6	7	8	9	10	11	12	13	14	15	16	17	18	19	20	21	22	23	24	25	26	27	28	1	2	3	4	5	6	7		**MARCH**
JUNE	1	2	3	4	5	6	7	8	9	10	11	12	13	14	15	16	17	18	19	20	21	22	23	24	25	26	27	28	29	30			JUNE
MARCH	8	9	10	11	12	13	14	15	16	17	18	19	20	21	22	23	24	25	26	27	28	29	30	31	1	2	3	4	5	6			**APRIL**
JULY	1	2	3	4	5	6	7	8	9	10	11	12	13	14	15	16	17	18	19	20	21	22	23	24	25	26	27	28	29	30	31		JULY
APRIL	7	8	9	10	11	12	13	14	15	16	17	18	19	20	21	22	23	24	25	26	27	28	29	30	1	2	3	4	5	6	7		**MAY**
AUGUST	1	2	3	4	5	6	7	8	9	10	11	12	13	14	15	16	17	18	19	20	21	22	23	24	25	26	27	28	29	30	31		AUGUST
MAY	8	9	10	11	12	13	14	15	16	17	18	19	20	21	22	23	24	25	26	27	28	29	30	31	1	2	3	4	5	6	7		**JUNE**
SEPTEMBER	1	2	3	4	5	6	7	8	9	10	11	12	13	14	15	16	17	18	19	20	21	22	23	24	25	26	27	28	29	30			SEPTEMBER
JUNE	8	9	10	11	12	13	14	15	16	17	18	19	20	21	22	23	24	25	26	27	28	29	30	1	2	3	4	5	6	7			**JULY**
OCTOBER	1	2	3	4	5	6	7	8	9	10	11	12	13	14	15	16	17	18	19	20	21	22	23	24	25	26	27	28	29	30	31		OCTOBER
JULY	8	9	10	11	12	13	14	15	16	17	18	19	20	21	22	23	24	25	26	27	28	29	30	31	1	2	3	4	5	6	7		**AUGUST**
NOVEMBER	1	2	3	4	5	6	7	8	9	10	11	12	13	14	15	16	17	18	19	20	21	22	23	24	25	26	27	28	29	30			NOVEMBER
AUGUST	8	9	10	11	12	13	14	15	16	17	18	19	20	21	22	23	24	25	26	27	28	29	30	31	1	2	3	4	5	6			**SEPTEMBER**
DECEMBER	1	2	3	4	5	6	7	8	9	10	11	12	13	14	15	16	17	18	19	20	21	22	23	24	25	26	27	28	29	30	31		DECEMBER
SEPTEMBER	7	8	9	10	11	12	13	14	15	16	17	18	19	20	21	22	23	24	25	26	27	28	29	30	1	2	3	4	5	6	7		**OCTOBER**

The reproduction cycle

This is usually called the menstrual or monthly cycle as the monthly period, or menstruation, is the most obvious feature of the woman's cycle. The first day of the monthly period marks both the end of one cycle and the start of the next. When your period starts, the output of the hormones that control the next cycle is already rising. These stimulate the growth of the ovum, or egg, in the ovary. Fourteen days later (in a 28-day cycle) an ovum is released from the ovary. It is at this time, which is called ovulation, that a woman is most likely to conceive.

After ovulation, hormones prepare the lining of the uterus so that it is ready to receive and nourish the egg if it becomes fertilized and then implanted.

If the fertilized egg does implant, the production of more hormones prevents menstruation and the next period is

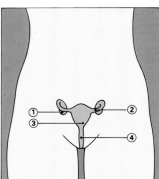

Female reproductive organs
1. Ovary   2. Fallopian tube
3. Uterus   4. Vagina

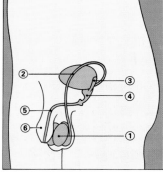

Male reproductive organs
Sperm travel from the testes (1) through the vas deferens (2) and are stored in the seminal vesicle (3). The semen produced mainly by the prostate gland (4) and the seminal vesicle passes at ejaculation along the urethra (5) through the penis (6).

SPERM REACHING THE EGG
Sperm, manufactured continuously in the male testes, are stored close to the bladder in seminal sacs. At the climax of sexual intercourse the semen (containing about 200 million sperm) is deposited in the upper vagina near the cervix. At ovulation the mucus around the cervix increases so that sperm can enter the uterus more easily. They swim upwards and along both fallopian tubes in search of an ovum. They arrive at the ends of the tubes a few hours after intercourse. They remain able to fertilize the ovum for at least 24 hours and maybe up to three or four days.

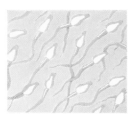

missed. If the egg is not fertilized, the monthly period starts (about 14 days after ovulation) and the thickened lining of the uterus is shed with the bleeding. If you take your temperature in bed when you first wake in the morning, you will find that it is a little higher during the second half of your cycle. This rise in temperature shows that ovulation has taken place.

1. OVULATION

Ovulation is the release of the ovum from the ovary. Usually each month only one ovum escapes, on day 14 of a 28-day cycle. The release is random from either ovary; there doesn't seem to be any arrangement to alternate! It is not certain how long an ovum remains fertilizable after its release from the ovary – probably 24-48 hours.

2. FERTLIZATION

Fertilization takes place in the outer part of the fallopian tube, usually within a day of ovulation. It happens when a sperm fuses with the ovum. Of the many sperm only one succeeds in penetrating the outer covering of the ovum. As soon as this sperm has entered, the surface of the ovum changes so that it cannot be penetrated by any other sperm. The sperm and ovum fuse.

7. IMPLANTATION

About six days after ovulation the ball of cells burrows its way into the lining of the uterus. Once it has become securely implanted, its outer cells start connecting with the mother's small blood vessels to form the placenta, or afterbirth. The inner cells develop to form the embryo and the surrounding membranes.

3-6. CELL DIVISION

Within a few hours of fertilization the ovum begins to reproduce itself by dividing in two. The process of cell division is then repeated an enormous number of times. Each division is more specialized so that the cells form individual organs and characteristics. By the time it reaches the uterus, four days after ovulation, the fertilized ovum has become a solid ball of several hundred cells. It drifts about in the uterus for another couple of days before implantation.

You and your growing baby

As doctors and midwives tend to talk in weeks rather than in calendar months, the development of your baby and the progress of your pregnancy is described below in intervals of four to six weeks, starting from the first day of your last period rather than from the date of conception.

There are three phases in your baby's development. The ovular phase is from ovulation in week 2 until the fertilized egg is safely implanted in the uterus two weeks later. From week 4 until week 12 your developing baby is called an embryo. Thereafter, until he starts his separate existence at birth, he is referred to as a fetus.

Weeks 0-4

The baby This period (described on page 14) ends with the fertilized egg's implantation within the lining of the uterus. The ovum's outer layers are forming the placenta, which is starting to develop a blood supply from your blood vessels. The inner cells are beginning to form into three layers. These grow into three different parts of your baby's body, making him a complete and individual human being.

You As this ovular phase ends at the time your next period would be expected, you may not even realize you are pregnant. You may, however, notice some of the early symptoms of pregnancy (*see* page 12).

Weeks 5-8

The baby In these weeks the principal organs and nervous system are formed. At the end of week 8 the embryo is recognizably human and would fit inside a small plum. He floats weightlessly within a pool of fluid – the amniotic fluid – contained within a double layer of membranes – the amniotic sac. As pregnancy progresses, this fluid protects the embryo like a shock absorber – a fall on the stomach, for instance, or sexual intercourse does not damage the embryo or fetus.

The heart has been beating since week 6 and is pumping blood around the embryo and out along the umbilical cord to the placenta. By week 8 the head is almost half the size of the embryo. The site of the ears is evident and the eyes are developing and have some color. The face is recognizable and there is a mouth and tongue. The limbs are changing from simple flippers and have elbow and knee joints; the hands and feet take shape with the beginning of fingers and toes.

An ultrasound scan can detect the bag of fluid in week 6. Soon the embryo can be picked up on the ultrasound screen as a small blob. In week 8 the heart can be seen beating.

You You begin to suspect you are pregnant. There is a rapid rise in production of hormones from the placenta and ovary. These are beginning to adapt you and your body for

FROM OVUM TO EMBRYO

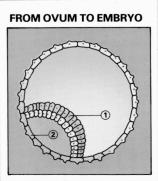

The inner cells (**1**) of the implanted ovum gradually form three layers which develop into the embryo (**1**, below). The outer cells (**2**) of the ovum grow into the mother's tissues and form the placenta (**2**, below) for exchange between the mother's and the baby's blood.

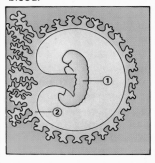

pregnancy. You may begin to have some nausea or vomiting. By week 8 the uterus has softened and enlarged enough for a doctor to confirm by internal pelvic examination that you are pregnant.

Weeks 9-12

The baby In week 9 the soft cartilages of the skeleton have started to change to bone. At birth this process is well advanced but is not finally completed until growth ceases towards the end of adolescence.

By week 12 all the major internal organs – the heart, lungs, kidneys, liver and stomach – have been formed and are working. The embryo has ears, a nose and recognizably male or female external genital organs. The eyelids have formed and closed over the eyes which are continuing

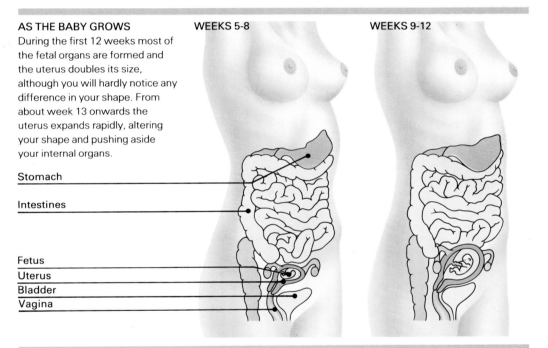

AS THE BABY GROWS
During the first 12 weeks most of the fetal organs are formed and the uterus doubles its size, although you will hardly notice any difference in your shape. From about week 13 onwards the uterus expands rapidly, altering your shape and pushing aside your internal organs.

WEEKS 5-8

WEEKS 9-12

Stomach

Intestines

Fetus
Uterus
Bladder
Vagina

to develop. Nails are growing on well-formed fingers and toes.

The embryo is now quite active and moving freely. He can curl and fan his toes, squint, frown and open his mouth. Most of the time he is in a curled up (flexed) position with his chin down and knees drawn up. By week 12 he weighs about 1 ounce and measures approximately 3 inches.

You Now that you've missed two periods you are in no doubt about being pregnant. You may notice increased skin pigmentation on various parts of your body. A brown line (the linea nigra) may begin to appear up the mid-line of your abdomen.

Nausea may persist for a few more weeks and you may still feel tired and subject to moods.

MILESTONES IN YOUR BABY'S DEVELOPMENT

● By week 6 of pregnancy (4 weeks after fertilization) the heart is beating. 1 week later the earliest movements of the arms have started.

● By week 8 most of the baby's important organs are formed.

● In week 9 the soft cartilage of the skeleton starts to change to bone.

● By week 12 the baby's eyelids are closed over the eyes, finger and toe nails are present and the sex organs are identifiably male or female.

● After week 12 the form of the organs is finally completed and they gradually increase in size and become capable of functioning.

At the end of week 7 this fetus has an easily recognizable eye and the head is beginning to lift up. Five fingers are faintly visible and the umbilical cord has formed.

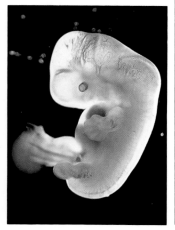

Weeks 13-18

The baby At this stage the fetus is fully formed. From now on it is a question of all the organs growing and improving their activities. The kidneys are producing urine which is discharged from time to time into the amniotic fluid. Amniotic fluid is also continually added to by seepage through the surface of the placenta and from the fetal surfaces. The fetus swallows the fluid which is absorbed through his intestine. The fluid is thus being changed continually. The fetus is now practicing breathing movements. A fine downy hair (lanugo) begins to cover him. He is developing eyelashes and eyebrows and has a bridge to his nose. Teeth are beginning to form in his gums, and the finger and toe nails are more definite.

He is very active. By week 18 he weighs nearly 7 ounces and measures about 7 inches.

You You will notice a definite rounding of your lower abdomen. You may have backache and sometimes quite sharp, fleeting pains or an ache low down in the sides of your abdomen.

Many women have an increased sense of well-being and peace; their hair and complexions glow and they have a welcome return of energy. An unlucky few do not experience this mid-pregnancy radiance and many continue to feel unwell throughout. Feeling generally unwell like this does not in any way imply that the fetus isn't thriving.

Between weeks 17 and 20 most first-time mothers start to feel the fetal movements – it may be a couple of weeks earlier for those having their second baby. You may feel a faint fluttering like a butterfly or a faint bubbling or tickling or strange little movements like gas. You may not notice them again for a few days but as they become stronger they are more definite.

You may notice a little cloudy secretion from the nipples. This is colostrum – the fluid on which the baby feeds before the production of milk on about the second or third day after the birth.

Weeks 19-24

The baby The fetus is active and has well-developed lanugo hair over his body as well as hair appearing on the head. His weight reaches approximately 1 pound and he measures about 12 inches. He is able to react to loud noises and may be able to sense the rhythm of music. If he is born prematurely at 24 weeks there is a small chance that he might survive in a special care baby unit.

You Your stomach becomes progressively more prominent and you may start to develop stretch marks (*see* page 38). As the fetus becomes stronger you will recognize the movements of his limbs as he kicks. At about week 24 the doctor is usually able to hear your baby's heart with a fetal stethoscope depending on how the baby is lying, how much fluid you are carrying and whether the placenta is on the front or back wall of the uterus.

Weeks 25-28

The baby As well as periods of great activity the fetus often seems to have quiet (possibly sleeping) periods. His skin is prevented from shriveling in the amniotic fluid by a smearing of greasy material called vernix. This now becomes thick and white. By week 26 his eyes are open. They are usually blue and will not change to their final color until some weeks after the baby is born. A few babies, however, are born with brown eyes. He has finger prints now and a grip that is strong enough for him to be able to support his own weight.

By week 28 he weighs about 2 pounds and is approximately 16 inches long. His lungs are still rather immature but he has a good chance of survival should he be born now and looked after in a special care baby unit.

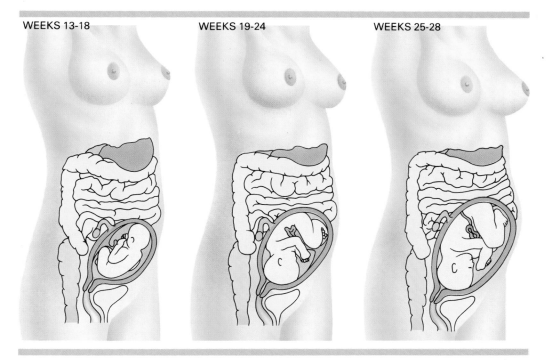

WEEKS 13-18   WEEKS 19-24   WEEKS 25-28

You You will probably continue to feel well. You may, however, be troubled by leg cramps, especially in bed at night. Heartburn may also be a problem as the top of the uterus presses on your diaphragm. You may feel occasional tightenings around the abdomen. It will seem more prominent and when you touch it will feel rather hard for up to a minute. These tightenings are called Braxton Hicks' contractions. They are the early activity of the muscles of the uterus and they will finally develop into the strong and continuing contractions of labor. You may also notice a rhythmic beating low in your abdomen – perhaps like a pulse or a knocking – which may last for as long at 15-30 minutes. This is a bout of fetal hiccuping, a habit often continued after birth especially after a feeding. The doctor may ask you if you'd like to listen to the baby's heartbeat.

Weeks 29-32

The baby By week 32 the fetus has usually settled into a head-down position ready for delivery. He takes up this position in the lower part of the uterus largely because there is more room in the upper uterus for the bulkier bottom (breech) and bent up legs. By the end of pregnancy less than 4 per cent of fetuses are still presenting breech first (*see* page 44).

The fat layer under the skin is still relatively thin but accumulates rapidly during the last eight weeks. It not only serves as an energy reserve but also helps to maintain body temperature after birth by reducing heat loss. The volume of fluid relative to the volume of the fetus is at its greatest at about 28 weeks. Thereafter it diminishes so that it becomes easier for you to feel your baby's arms and legs and if you watch your abdomen carefully you will see the movements. However, there is still sufficient fluid to protect him.

He continues to practice for his life outside and sometimes, for instance, passes the time by sucking his thumb. He loses most of the fine downy hair (lanugo) from his body. If born at this stage his lungs, heat control and digestive system are all immature. With expert pediatric care, however, he has more than a 90 per cent chance of survival. He is now very vigorous. He weighs about 3¼ pounds and is about 18 inches long.

You You will be starting to feel rather more heavy and cumbersome. The upward pressure of the growing uterus on your diaphragm means that you may at times feel you can't breathe properly.

Many women stop work now as they become excessively tired. You may also find yourself becoming a bit forgetful.

Weeks 33-36

The baby Growth is rapid and your baby is getting plumper as he gains extra fat. His skin is smoother and less wrinkled. He now weighs about 5¼ pounds and measures about 20 inches.

You If you are a first-time mother your baby's head may have engaged in the pelvis by week 36. The lower uterus has softened and the baby's head has moved down into the bony part of the birth canal. This is called the lightening. Because it reduces pressure on the diaphragm you feel lighter. Sometimes engagement doesn't occur until week 40 or until labor is well under way.

The head is now squashing your bladder and therefore you have to pass urine more often and may have to get up several times in the night. Your pattern of sleep may be disturbed and you may get increasingly tired. It can be difficult to get comfortable in bed and using extra pillows to support your belly (*see* page 39) may be helpful. If you laugh, sneeze or cough unexpectedly you may lose a small amount of urine. This problem usually disappears within a few weeks of the birth, especially if you do your pelvic floor tightening exercises (*see* page 47).

This 4½ month fetus seems to be happily sucking his thumb. This is probably due to the rooting reflex which causes him to turn to anything touching his face.

Weeks 37-40

The baby Growth often slows towards week 40 when the placenta's reserves begin to run down. Most babies do not grow much more if pregnancy continues past the due date.

Breathing and sucking reflexes are well established so that he can feed well if born at this stage. He has gained immunity to a wide range of infections by the transfer of antibodies from your blood. As he hasn't so much room to move about in the uterus the movements may seem less. But he is strong enough to push the uterus and your tummy wall so that his limbs stick out as recognizable bulges.

At birth the baby's head may appear a little elongated with the forehead sloping backwards. This is because the head is often molded to the shape of the cylindrical bony part of the birth canal. The shape is often further

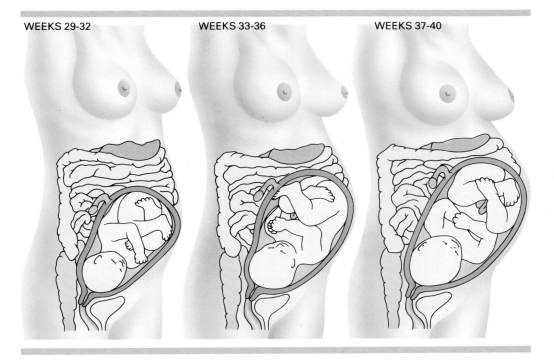

WEEKS 29-32   WEEKS 33-36   WEEKS 37-40

exaggerated by a swelling of the leading part of the scalp. This is called a caput. As the baby emerges he is covered in the white sticky creamy vernix, although this is less if pregnancy has gone beyond week 40.

You Throughout pregnancy your tissues have been softening and becoming more elastic so that the vaginal opening can gradually yield and stretch to let the baby out. The ligaments which bind the bones to your pelvis have also softened to allow expansion of your birth canal so there is extra room for the baby to pass.

Inevitably you will become impatient towards the end of pregnancy, especially if you have to wait beyond your EDD. Remember that delivery is still "on time" even if it comes two weeks late.

Prenatal care

Prenatal care covers all the attention, examinations, tests and treatment you receive in pregnancy up to the time you start labor. To ensure the best chance of remaining healthy and having a healthy baby, you should see your doctor as soon as you think you may be pregnant. Once your pregnancy is confirmed, your doctor will make arrangements for your prenatal care. With the development of new techniques for the detection of any problems it is increasingly important that prenatal care starts early.

Choices in prenatal care

There are a number of alternatives available in this country for prenatal care and delivery. Where you go for your prenatal care depends on where you choose to deliver your baby. Consider all the options carefully before deciding on a hospital or maternity center. If you are going to have a hospital delivery you may decide to have all your prenatal care at the hospital clinic. This care is usually provided by staff physicians, resident physicians (at teaching hospitals) and nurse midwives or nurse practitioners.

The most common option when choosing hospital delivery is to use a private doctor (or group of doctors) who delivers babies at the hospital you have chosen. If you make the choice primarily on the basis of the doctor, the choice of hospitals is made for you if the doctor has admitting privileges at only one place. Some doctors, however, use more than one hospital so you may have a choice. If you decide to have a private physician for prenatal care and delivery, the prenatal visits are made to the doctor's office. This may be located in the hospital or outside.

Also available in many areas of the country are birthing centers, which are usually located near full-service hospitals. The prenatal care as well as the assistance during labor is frequently performed by nurse midwives with obstetricians available for back-up.

Home delivery is an option available in some areas of the country.

Making the choice

A number of factors will influence your decision on the type of maternity care you want and where you would like to deliver your baby. These factors include the state of your general health, the types of deliveries you may have had in previous pregnancies, the availability of help at home and your medical insurance coverage. If you have any health problems such as heart disease or diabetes, a hospital delivery is essential, because you and your baby are at greater risk for complications. If you have a mild health problem check with your physician when deciding where to deliver. Also, if a previous delivery has been difficult or has ended in Cesarian section, hospital delivery is the better choice. On the other hand, if you have had one or two previous deliveries which were fast and uncomplicated, you would be able to choose a maternity center or home delivery.

The final decision, ideally, should not be made because of financial considerations, but, unfortunately, the type of insurance coverage may limit your choice of delivery. Check your coverage early in pregnancy, or before conceiving. Some coverage will pay hospital fees but not physicians'. Other policies such as HMOs require you to deliver with certain doctors at certain hospitals.

Since facilities vary in different parts of the country, you will need to get as much information as you can from your family physician. The National Association of Nurse Midwives (*see* Useful Addresses, page 298) may also be able to provide you with information on what's available in your area. It can be helpful as well to check local and women's newspapers.

Hospital delivery

If you decide to have your baby in a hospital you will be looked after by a team of doctors and nurses. If you have a private obstetrician, he or she will be in charge and perform the delivery. After delivery you may go home as early as several hours postpartum or you may stay for several days.

The advantage of a hospital delivery is that all the equipment and expertise is immediately available if there is any problem with you or your baby. The disadvantage of hospital delivery is that there is a cold, impersonal atmosphere, on occasion, which is contrary to the desired warmth and happiness which should accompany the delivery of a child. Many hospitals are reacting in a positive way to these criticisms and are giving more attention to the individual needs and requests of mothers and fathers.

Birth centers

These centers, which are options in many parts of the country, combine the advantages of both home and hospital delivery. They are usually located near hospital facilities so that emergency care is available if necessary. However, the atmosphere is more nearly that of a home delivery with both midwives and physicians available. Again, if there are any indications of increased risks for mother or baby before labor, hospital delivery should be the choice.

Home delivery

Although home delivery is a choice you do have, only a few women in this country use this option. If there is any medical complication of the pregnancy, or if there is *any* high-risk factor, such as a previous problem pregnancy, women should not deliver at home. Problems are less frequent with second and third deliveries when the first pregnancy and delivery has been uncomplicated. You have to balance the risks of any unforseen problems occurring against the advantage of being in your own familiar surroundings.

If you do wish to have a home delivery, you should talk to your doctor. If he or she does not do home deliveries, he may be able to recommend a doctor who does. Midwives are available for home deliveries in some areas of the country.

Prenatal care

Whether you are having your prenatal care at a hospital clinic or in a private office, the pattern of visits is similar. The record that is kept of your prenatal visits resembles the one shown in the chart below.

Screening

Your first visit to the prenatal clinic, sometimes called the screening appointment, usually takes place when you are between 8 and 12 weeks pregnant.

You will be seen by a physician or nurse who will ask you about any previous pregnancies and deliveries. She will also ask about any illnesses you've had, about any medication you take and whether there is any family history of illnesses such as high blood pressure or diabetes.

WEEKS

This is the number of weeks that you are pregnant, calculated from the first day of your last menstrual period. Term or T refers to your expected date of delivery.

DATE	WEEKS	HEIGHT OF FUNDUS	WEIGHT	PRESENTATION ENGAGEMENT	POSITION	REMARKS
18.6.86	12+	12	52·5	╱	╱	Ultrasound at r
16/7/86	16	15	54.25	╱	╱	All well
13/8/86	20	20	55.5	ceph	╱	
10/9/86	24	23	56·75	ceph	╱	Progressing well

HEIGHT/FUNDUS

This is the measurement of how far the top of the uterus (fundus) is above the pubic bone. The doctor or midwife can feel the uterus by gentle external pressure on your abdomen. The fundal height, or size of the uterus, may be recorded in centimeters or in weeks. In weeks it should be roughly the same as the number of weeks calculated by your dates (see above), although small discrepancies may not be too important.

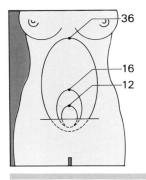

PRESENTATION/ STATION

The presenting part of the baby means the part that is coming first. Head downwards is recorded as Vtx (vertex). Bottom first is recorded as Br (breech).

Station means how far the presenting part of the fetus has dipped into the pelvis. This is measured by feeling for the bony spines of the pelvis during a vaginal examination and determining if the head (or bottom) is above or below these spines. The head is **engaged** if it is at the level of the spines (zero station) or lower (plus one, plus two, etc.) Above the spines (minus one, minus two) the head

is not engaged. Engagement may occur several weeks before the delivery or not until after labor has started.

POSITION

This describes the way the baby is lying. It records the position of the crown (occiput) of the baby's head in relation to the mother's body. The baby's head may be to the left or right (L to R), pointing to the front (A for Anterior), side (T: Transverse or L: Lateral) or backwards (P: Posterior).

Thus LOP (Left Occiput Posterior) means the back or crown of the baby's head is to the left of the mother pointing towards her back. ROT (Right

At this first visit a sample of your urine will be tested, you will be weighed and measured and your blood pressure will be checked. You will also have a blood sample taken and tested for your blood group, for immunity to German measles (rubella), for anemia, for syphilis and, in women other than of West European origin, for other problems such as sickle cell disease or trait.

A doctor will give you a general examination which includes listening to your heart, examining your breasts and feeling your abdomen. You will probably have an internal examination to check your pelvis and cervix and the doctor will do a cervical smear (PAP) test.

Asking questions The nurse or doctor will talk to you about your prenatal care. At this and later visits, do ask the doctor or nurse questions and express your own views and anxieties. You may find it helps to make a note in advance of what you want to ask.

LATER VISITS

You will probably have a prenatal check once a month until the last two or three months when you are seen every two weeks and then once a week.

The pattern of visits may vary according to your needs but checking weight, blood pressure and urine and feeling the size of the uterus are standard at each visit. You will be asked to note when you first feel the baby moving. The fetal heart will be listened to after about 26 weeks.

	BP	Hb	FH	OEDEMA	URINE	NEXT VISIT	SIG
ppointment	125/65	╱	╱	nil	NAD	GP4	KSL
	130/65	╱	╱	NIL	NAD	4/52	Pl
	120/65	╱	╱	nil	NAD	4/52	KSL
	120/60	╱	H	Nil	NAD	4/52	Pl

FETAL HEART

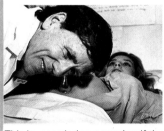

This is recorded as a number if the doctor has heard the fetal heart.

EDEMA

This means swelling and usually appears in the ankles and fingers. A certain amount of swelling is normal but if it is extensive and there is also a rise in blood pressure or protein in the urine, then rest and observation are needed.

URINE

A specimen is tested for sugar and for the protein albumin (Alb). N means negative.
+ or tr means there is a trace or small amount. Repeated presence of sugar can indicate diabetes. Protein can indicate a urinary infection or toxemia (*see* page 29).

Occiput Transverse) means the back or crown of the baby's head is to the right and pointing to the side.

BLOOD PRESSURE (BP)

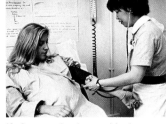

If after starting lower this rises to or above 140/90 and stays there, it may indicate a problem.

Hgb

This is short for hemoglobin, the red pigment in blood, which is tested to check for anemia.

ROT   LOT   LOA

ROA   ROP   LOP

Other prenatal tests

As part of your prenatal care you may have an alpha-fetoprotein test and an ultrasound scan. In addition your doctor may suggest other prenatal tests which mean that more can be learned about your unborn baby. New techniques for finding out more about the fetus are being developed so that many serious abnormalities are now detected at a much earlier stage.

The ultrasound scan

In this test low energy sound waves are passed into the mother's body, building up a picture of the fetus and placenta which is reflected back on to an electronic screen. You can actually see the baby and sometimes identify her different limbs moving and see her heart beating. A scan may detect abnormalities which, fortunately, are rare. Most mothers find the experience of seeing their baby on the screen for the first time an exciting and reassuring moment.

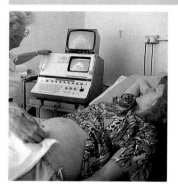

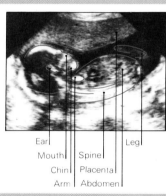

Ear | Leg
Mouth | Spine
Chin | Placenta
Arm | Abdomen

HAVING A SCAN

As the scanner is passed over your stomach it produces pictures on a television monitor. Although these may be indistinct, the doctor or radiographer doing the scanning is usually able to point out at least the head, the heart beat, the limbs and the spine.

TWINS

If you are expecting more than one baby this is usually confirmed by an ultrasound scan. Your experience of pregnancy and delivery, and indeed of childcare, will be different if you are expecting a multiple birth. You will receive special care and advice and there are several books on the subject which you may find helpful. You may also find it useful to contact a local Twins Club.

Often fathers are encouraged to attend a scan so that they can share this experience.

Having a scan done is completely painless. You will probably be asked to come with a full bladder as this helps to get a good picture. A little oil is rubbed on your stomach and then a scanner is passed lightly over it as you lie flat on your back.

If there is any doubt about it, the age of the baby can be checked by measuring the circumference of her skull. Scans may be repeated later in pregnancy and the results compared to this first age check to make sure that the baby is growing properly. A scan is useful in detecting the presence of twins and can also determine when the placenta is attached too low in the uterus (*see* placenta previa, page 29).

Many millions of women have been tested in this way and a great deal of information helpful to the health and safety of both mother and baby has been obtained. There is no satisfactory evidence that it is harmful either for you or your baby, but the test should not be considered routine.

Alpha-fetoprotein

If the mother wishes, a sample of her blood can be tested between 16 and 18 weeks to find out whether the fetus has an abnormality in development of the head or spine (spina bifida). When the test shows raised levels of alpha-fetoprotein (AFP) there is a possibility that the fetus has these abnormalities. A detailed ultrasound scan or amniocentesis is then done to check the result, as you can have a perfectly normal baby with a raised level of AFP.

Amniocentesis

Amniocentesis is used to diagnose Down's syndrome (mongolism), especially in women over 38-40 years of age, when the likelihood of a Down's syndrome baby increases. It is also used to diagnose rare types of family disorder, such as Tay-Sachs, and as a further check when the level of AFP is raised.

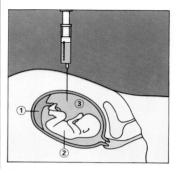

Amniocentesis
You will have an ultrasound scan which enables the doctor to avoid the placenta (1) and the fetus (2) and to find the best pool of amniotic fluid (3) for sampling.

If you are offered an amniocentesis, you should think carefully before deciding to have one. The test does carry a slight risk of miscarriage and this must be balanced against the possibility of abnormality in the baby. Amniocentesis is performed when you are between 16 and 18 weeks pregnant and you have to wait three to four weeks for the result. If an abnormality is detected you then have to decide, at a fairly advanced stage of pregnancy, whether to have an abortion.

The test itself is almost painless. You have an ultrasound scan first to show the position of the baby and the sac of amniotic fluid. A fine needle is passed through your abdominal wall into the amniotic sac. A sample of fluid is then drawn out for analysis. The test can detect the sex of your baby, but if you don't want to know you can say so.

Occasionally amniocentesis is done towards the end of pregnancy to find out whether the baby would have breathing difficulties if delivered early or to estimate the severity of a Rh blood group problem.

Fetoscopy

A very fine telescope is passed into the uterus under local anesthetic and ultrasound control to check for a developmental abnormality or to take a sample of the fetal blood. Fetoscopy is being superseded by skilled ultrasound examination and by chorionic villus sampling.

Chorionic villus sampling (CVS)

This technique is largely replacing amniocentesis and fetoscopy in prenatal screening, and is done under ultrasonic control between the 9th and 12th weeks. A very fine tube is passed through the cervix or abdominal wall into the uterus to obtain a small sample of placental tissue for analysis. As this tissue is formed from the fertilized egg, its cells have all the same characteristics as those of the fetus. It is now possible to detect many disorders much earlier than with an amniocentesis.

Complications in pregnancy

For most women pregnancy is quite straightforward. However, for those who do have problems it can be helpful to understand what is happening.

Ectopic pregnancy
In this rare condition the fertilized ovum becomes implanted in the Fallopian tube or elsewhere in the abdominal cavity. The main symptoms are vaginal bleeding after a missed period, sharp pain on one side of the lower abdomen and feeling faint. You should see your doctor without delay as this type of pregnancy has to be terminated.

Miscarriage
If you lose your baby before the 20th week of pregnancy this is described as a miscarriage (often referred to medically as an abortion). Most miscarriages happen in the first three months. They are nearly always due to a chance error in the very complicated process of fertilization and early development. This leads to a defect which may be in the embryo or fetus or in the placenta. Occasionally miscarriage may be due to illness in the mother.

It is natural to be very upset if you miscarry and to imagine that you have somehow brought it on yourself. Miscarriage is, however, almost always an indication that the pregnancy has gone wrong and was therefore bound to be lost. Grieving and eventually coming to terms with your loss may take some months and it can be helpful to talk it over with your doctor, partner and friends. The next time you become pregnant there is no increased chance of miscarrying. Unless your doctor tells you otherwise there is no reason to rest in early pregnancy or to avoid any activity, including sexual intercourse.

A miscarriage usually starts with vaginal bleeding which continues. You then have a central lower abdominal pain like a period pain. Contact your doctor if you have either of these. You may pass clots but you may also notice larger liver-like lumps. You should save these to show your doctor as he can decide whether or not they are part of the placenta. After a miscarriage you may need to go into the hospital for a day for a D and C (dilatation and curettage). This ensures that any remnants of placenta can be removed to avoid any further bleeding or infection.

Threatened miscarriage
This is when bleeding starts in the first part of pregnancy. You may be advised to stay in bed. If you are going to miscarry you usually do so in the first two or three days after the bleeding starts. If the bleeding stops and the pregnancy continues, then it is likely to be quite normal.

Missed abortion
Occasionally a woman finds that she no longer feels pregnant. On examination, if the doctor finds the uterus to be smaller than expected, an ultrasound scan is used to confirm that the fetus is absent or no longer alive. If this is the case, the contents of the womb are removed by D and C under anesthetic.

Incompetent cervix
From time to time, miscarriage occurs later in pregnancy because the cervix is not tough enough to stay closed. This may be discovered in a vaginal examination, in which case a small operation is done to stitch the cervix to keep it closed. If the incompetent cervix has caused a miscarriage in an earlier pregnancy, the stitch is put in at about 14 weeks in the next pregnancy.

Prepartum hemorrhage

This is bleeding through the vagina after the 28th week of pregnancy. Any bleeding after this time should be reported without delay and is usually treated by bed rest in the hospital.

Placenta previa If the bleeding is from a placenta growing too close to the opening of the uterus, this is called placenta previa or placenta coming first. The danger here is that there may be a lot of bleeding.

If an ultrasound scan after about 28 weeks confirms a definite placenta previa (as opposed to a low-lying placenta), the woman is kept in the hospital until delivery. This is often by cesarean section.

LOW-LYING PLACENTA

An ultrasound scan in the early weeks may pick up a placenta lying low in the uterus (**1**). This may resolve itself as the placenta is taken up by the expanding uterus and settles in an acceptable position (**2**). Alternatively it may be identified later following further scans as a definite placenta previa (**3**).

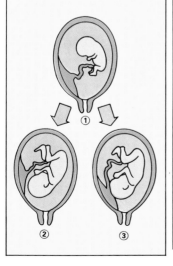

Anemia

Anemia in pregnancy is usually due to iron deficiency. During pregnancy more iron is needed to meet the mother's and baby's growing needs. Extra iron tablets can be prescribed during pregnancy. If a woman is very anemic her system is less able to cope with a hemorrhage that can occur unexpectedly in late pregnancy or at delivery.

Diabetes

Diabetes can lead to a number of problems in pregnancy and must be carefully controlled throughout. It may be diagnosed for the first time during pregnancy or may arise because of pregnancy. Babies of diabetic women may be delivered a little early to overcome any problems.

Rhesus factor (Rh)

Most women in this country have Rh positive blood groups; only 15 per cent have Rh negative. Problems arise only when a Rh negative mother has already given birth to a Rh positive baby. In the next pregnancy there is a danger that the mother's defenses may recognize the Rh factor in her baby's blood as foreign and she may manufacture antibodies that could destroy his blood cells, causing severe anemia. Sometimes the unborn baby is given a transfusion in the uterus.

Almost all Rh negative women are now given an injection containing Rh antibody within 48 hours of delivery, miscarriage or termination of a first pregnancy. This largely prevents Rh factor problems in subsequent pregnancies. The same injection is also given at 28 weeks of pregnancy to women at risk of Rh sensitization.

Toxemia of pregnancy (pre-eclampsia)

Toxemia occurs in pregnancy when there is a sustained rise in blood pressure, accompanied by protein in the urine and swelling and puffiness in various parts of the body.

A woman with toxemia is usually admitted to the hospital for extra rest. Early delivery by induction or by cesarean section may be necessary.

Once the baby is born, blood pressure returns to normal. If it recurs in a subsequent pregnancy, it is likely to be milder.

Early (premature) rupture of the membranes

Occasionally the membranes break a number of weeks before the baby is due. There may be quite a large and sudden escape of waters or just a constant slight trickle. In either case it is important to report to the hospital immediately and the mother is usually admitted because infection may develop. If the waters continue to leak, labor may be induced early.

Stillbirth

Fortunately, this tragedy happens in less than one per cent of pregnancies. It may be due to a developmental abnormality of the fetus or failure of the placenta in its function of keeping the fetus alive. Much of the effort of prenatal care and monitoring in labor is to try to detect any evidence of placental failure. There are other occasional causes of stillbirth, such as high blood pressure, toxemia, hemorrhage from the placenta and diabetes. Your first warning that something may be wrong is a marked reduction or absence of fetal movements. If you do not feel them for six to eight hours, you should report to your doctor or hospital clinic so that the baby can be checked. Most times it's a false alarm. If, undoubtedly, the baby has died you will be told so that you know about it before delivery. Doctors and nurses will explain as much as they can about what may have gone wrong.

Fortunately it is quite rare for a woman to have more than one stillbirth.

Enjoying pregnancy

Many women, particularly in the middle months of pregnancy, look and feel really good.

Pregnancy is for most women a time of ups and downs. Try to make the most of the ups and go along with the downs. Your emotions and moods change more often and to a greater extent. You may well have times of great happiness and excitement, alternating with other times of doubt and anxiety. Knowing how you may feel and also what to expect both in pregnancy and labor can be a great help.

Changing moods

While some women remain even and calm, others may be given to sudden irritability or bursting into tears for no apparent reason. There are extra pressures for you to cope with now – natural fears about whether the baby will be all right, about labor and delivery, and about looking after the baby, as well as hormonal changes that are taking place in your body. These gradually adapt the functions of your body to the needs of pregnancy. Inevitably this means that your outlook changes as the pregnancy progresses. At first it can seem unreal. As time passes you will become more confident and will find yourself thinking of your baby as a developing person.

Fathers

Pregnancy is a time when couples need to give each other as much support as possible. Your partner may find it difficult to adjust to the prospect of becoming a father, particularly for the first time. You will need to involve him from the earliest stages so that he can understand all the things that are happening to you and share with you the anxieties as well as the joys of pregnancy. One of the decisions you will have to make together is whether he will be present at the birth. Like many fathers he may overcome earlier reluctance or misgivings and share the experience of his baby being born. This may well deepen his commitment to you and the baby. However, being at the birth is not for all men and he should not be unduly pressured to be present.

Other children

If you have other children you may be tempted to share the news about the new baby as soon as you know. However, it is usually better to delay telling them for a number of months or at least until your shape begins to look different. Whatever the age of your child you cannot expect the anticipation to survive nine months. How children react to a new brother or sister will depend very much on how you talk to them about the baby beforehand. Try to be prepared for their questions and to answer them simply and straightforwardly. There are several children's books with stories about a new baby in the family and it can be helpful to read and talk about these with your children. They will

See Family life, page 221, for preparing children for a new baby.

be more ready to welcome the baby home if you have included them in all the preparations, such as choosing equipment and clothes and deciding where the baby is to sleep. Talk to them about their own babyhood – they will love to see their baby photographs – and make sure they feel involved and important.

Sex in pregnancy

Unless your doctor tells you otherwise, there is no reason why you should not continue having sexual intercourse throughout pregnancy. You need have no fear that the penis can either damage the baby or break the waters.

Sometimes in late pregnancy you may find that an orgasm sets off Braxton Hicks' contractions of the uterus. Although these may be uncomfortable while they last, they are in no way harmful to the baby.

If you have had a previous miscarriage you may choose to avoid intercourse for the first three to four months. The evidence that sexual intercourse can cause miscarriage during this period is not proved but some doctors still feel that it is safer to abstain in those circumstances. If you are at all anxious about this, talk to your doctor or midwife.

You may find that the discomforts of early pregnancy and the awkwardness of late pregnancy discourage you from having sex. Some couples choose not to have intercourse at all and prefer to find other ways of making love during pregnancy. Whatever your feelings and worries are about sex, it is important that you and your partner feel able to talk to each other about them.

To make sexual intercourse easier for you it may be a good idea for you to experiment with different positions. Certain positions, particularly with the pressure of the man on top and deep penetration in late pregnancy, can be uncomfortable.

Working in pregnancy

How long you continue working is a very individual decision. If you are fit and healthy you will be limited only by how long your energy lasts, how long you continue to do your job satisfactorily and how easily you are able to work in other commitments. You will need to consider a number of questions, such as how much you need the money, how much you enjoy working, whether your job is physically demanding and whether your boss and fellow workers are co-operative and accommodating. Look into your rights regarding maternity leave and maternity pay.

If you have a medical complication during pregnancy or delivery and need to take more time off than your employer allows, you will need your physician's help in applying for disability payments. Laws and policies are changing rapidly in the area of maternity benefits, so keep yourself informed through the benefits office at your job. Also, many employers are now allowing fathers to take maternity leave.

If you are planning to go back to full-time work fairly soon after the baby's arrival, the arrangements for the care of your baby will need a lot of thought.

See Family life, page 174, for going back to work.

Traveling when you're pregnant

There is no reason not to travel in a normal pregnancy but remember that labor can start prematurely so do not travel where you cannot get good care. Sitting in a cramped position for any length of time may cause the blood to clot in the veins of your leg. You should therefore try to wriggle your toes and if possible, stop and walk about every one or two hours. Most airlines won't take pregnant women after 35 weeks so check this if you're planning to fly.

Looking after yourself

It's important to take care of yourself during pregnancy both because this will help you to feel fit and well and because it may help the baby's development.

Diet You should keep to a normal healthy diet with plenty of fresh fruit and vegetables, whole grain cereals, legumes, beans, lentils, peas and nuts. Try to avoid too many sugary calorie-laden foods (sugars, candy, cookies, cakes), saturated fats (butter, cheese and fatty meat). Cook vegetables just for the minimum time in a very little water as this will help to preserve their vitamins and minerals.

Protein is the basis for the growth of new tissues in the baby. It is found in whole grain flour, wheat germ, milk, in milk products such as cottage cheese and yogurt, and in eggs, lean meat, fish and dried beans. You will also need the vitamins and minerals contained in these foods as well as in fresh fruit, vegetables, liver and kidneys. Try to drink plenty of water and cut down on tea and coffee.

Weight gain There has been much debate over the years on what is the ideal weight gain during pregnancy. At present, most studies show that babies and mothers are healthiest when the mother gains between 24 and 28 pounds during pregnancy. This is assuming that the mother is of average weight to start. Underweight women should gain more and overweight women should gain less. This does vary from woman to woman and there is no need to become obsessive about weight gain. Under no circumstances should a woman attempt to lose weight during pregnancy, since a weight reducing diet will not supply

Pregnancy checklist
Use this chart to remind yourself of when to apply for benefits, to attend your prenatal clinics and classes, and to make the necessary preparations for your baby and yourself.

Pink: prenatal care; yellow: preparing for your baby; green: your own preparations

Weeks:	12	16	20	24	28	32	36	40

First visit to prenatal clinics. Then regular monthly checks, and more frequently in final weeks.

Make arrangements to attend prenatal classes.

Make an appointment for a dental check-up.

Make sure you've got all the basic equipment and clothing your baby will need.

Check you've got everything that you'll want in the hospital.

Make arrangements for your other children while you're in the hospital.

Pack your suitcase ready for going to the hospital.

enough nutrients to the developing baby. At three months your weight won't have increased if you have had trouble with nausea and vomiting, but it's likely to rise rapidly in mid-pregnancy as your appetite returns. One to two pounds per week for a while should settle back to one pound a week or thereabouts.

Looking after your breasts If you wish to breastfeed, don't be put off because you have small breasts. This has nothing to do with the capacity to produce milk.

The breasts are supported by ligaments attached to the underlying chest wall. In pregnancy these tend to soften so that they can stretch more easily. To keep the shape of your breasts, wear a good supporting bra throughout pregnancy. You may also need a sleeping bra at night.

When your breasts start producing colostrum the skin of the nipples may tend to crust. Wash this away gently each day, using only a little mild soap, and then you may like to apply a cream such as lanolin.

If your nipples tend to go inwards when you squeeze the edges of the surrounding brown area between your finger and thumb then it can help to get them used to being handled and so prepare them for feeding if you roll the nipples between your finger and thumb for a few minutes each day.

Taking care of your teeth You may get excess plaque when you're pregnant and this can lead to gum problems. Dental care is fine during pregnancy so visit your dentist at least twice – in early and in late pregnancy. Avoid general anesthetics for dental work during pregnancy.

Your skin and personal hygiene If you find that you are sweating more and your skin becomes oily, regular tepid baths and the use of a mild soap will help. If you have dry skin you can use a mild skin moisturizer or body lotion. Some women find that their skin becomes itchy; see page 38 for advice.

Exercise and sport The simple rule is to continue any exercise or sport you normally participate in for as long as you feel fit and able. Special exercises aimed at increasing the mobility of the back should be avoided, as the softening of the ligaments during pregnancy can sometimes lead to back problems.

Physical fitness helps you feel better and recover more quickly after birth. Do as much as you feel like.

Sleep and relaxation When you are pregnant you are expending energy just in meeting the demands of your growing baby. While some women experience a sense of calm and relaxation, others feel tense and seem to need more sleep. Try to get to bed early and sleep as late as you can on week-ends.

Don't be surprised if you have rather vivid and frightening dreams in late pregnancy. These are quite common. You may find that the relaxation and breathing techniques you have been learning for labor will help you get off to sleep. In late pregnancy you should put your feet up whenever you get a chance. Try to nap for about an hour or two in the afternoon to help conserve your energy. If you don't have time to nap, you should try at least to take things rather more gently and avoid getting overtired.

Things to avoid

There are certain things which you should avoid because they are harmful to your baby and to you.

Alcohol It has been traditional to advise moderation in drinking alcohol but research is now suggesting that you cannot rely on even small amounts of alcohol being entirely safe for the fetus, even though there is no clear evidence for this view. It is well known that large amounts of alcohol can seriously affect the development of the baby's brain and other organs, and it now seems likely that small amounts may sometimes do the same thing to a lesser degree. If you cannot stop drinking alcohol altogether, then the less you have the better. Whatever you have enters the baby's bloodstream as well as yours.

Drugs Because some drugs are known to be harmful to the growth and development of your baby, you should avoid taking any pills or medicines without your doctor's advice. This includes over-the-counter and herbal remedies. In certain cases, such as diabetes or epilepsy, drugs are prescribed throughout pregnancy for the safety of the baby. The occasional acetaminophen tablet for a headache or a mild sleeping tablet for sleeplessness in late pregnancy may be necessary but you should always check with your doctor or pharmacist before taking any medicine bought over the counter.

Smoking Smoking is bad for you and for your baby. Now that you have your baby's health to think about, you should try to give up the habit.

Looking good

It's not as hard as you might think to look good when you're pregnant. Stylish maternity wear, plus the natural pregnancy "bloom" many women are lucky enough to have, can combine to make you look better than you ever have!

Choosing underwear

Being comfortable when you're pregnant is an important priority and the first garment you'll need to buy will probably be a bra. Even if you don't normally wear one, you may well need extra support during pregnancy – and many women find their breasts are noticeably larger from as early as the second month. You may find you need to change your bra size several times as your pregnancy progresses. It's a good idea to get specially fitted for a maternity/nursing bra at about seven months. Make sure the fastenings and straps are adjustable as you could increase in size again, and anyway the size of your breasts will vary during the day if you are breastfeeding.

Most women don't need a maternity girdle, but remember it can help with backache or with less than well-toned tummy muscles. You can buy maternity underpants but you may find that your normal briefs will be quite adequate; they'll simply sit under your belly in the later stages. You can get maternity pantyhose or buy normal pantyhose in an extra-large size and wear them back-to-front. Support

DRESSES
There is a great choice of styles in dresses that are flattering and comfortable.

SHIRTS
Shirts or blouses which are loose and long can be worn under jumpers or over slacks.

SLACKS
Slacks may have a drawstring waist or a front flap with adjustable fastenings to allow for expansion.

T-SHIRTS/BLOUSES
Large tops are comfortable, useful and enable you to ring the changes in combination with a basic jumper and slacks. You can also wear them after the baby is born.

pantyhose are helpful if your legs get tired. If you have varicose veins you may be able to get maternity support hose or stockings with a doctor's prescription. If you find you're bothered by moniliasis ("yeast") or other vaginal infections (not uncommon in pregnancy) wear cotton underwear for preference and stockings or open-crotch or cotton-crotch pantyhose.

Adaptable clothes
Most of your normal clothes will probably fit you until the fourth month or so (though tight waistbands may be out sooner than this). Many looser unstructured styles may look fine for even longer. The chances are, though, that you'll need to buy some specifically maternity wear – and nowadays the choice is wide and the style is fashionable. You'll get extra wear after the birth if you try to choose separates or front-opening clothes that lend themselves to breastfeeding. Jogging suits are stretchy, stylish and comfortable; drawstring-top slacks and skirts will grow with you as well. In summer large-sized tee-shirts are cool and fashionable and in winter you can wear extra-big sweaters and sweatshirts.

Choosing shoes
Shoes do need to be comfortable. Ligaments soften as a result of hormonal changes, so a well-fitting shoe that's not too high will help avoid stress or strain (you may need to buy a size or half-size larger than normal as even feet can get slightly bigger in pregnancy).

Your skin and hair
The bloom of pregnancy isn't just a myth. Skin and hair in particular can appear in tip-top condition, especially in the middle months. If your skin feels rather drier than normal however, and even tight and itchy at times, make sure you're lavish with moisturizing creams. A good cut will make the most of your hair. In fact, keeping up your usual beauty routines can help a lot when the pregnancy glow is hidden under feelings of tiredness, discomfort or anxiety.

CHOOSING A BRA
Look for a bra with firm support, broad shoulder straps and adjustable back fastening. Buy a bigger size as your breasts enlarge.

Measure under your breasts for the bra size and around the fullest part for the cup.

A nursing bra should open easily in the front.

Some common discomforts

Most women experience some sort of physical discomfort during their pregnancy. It can be reassuring to know that, however irritating, the problem is quite normal and usual. In some cases there is little that can be done but it can be a relief to know your discomfort is not a major problem so never hesitate to mention these things to your doctor. In other cases there are treatments that can help. Just occasionally a minor discomfort can be a sign of something more serious, so it can be useful to be aware of this possibility.

Aches and pains

Minor aches and pains are common in pregnancy. They can be in the chest or back, beneath the ribs, in the abdomen, around the pelvis or down the legs. The main reason is that the tissues everywhere tend to soften and stretch more easily. The main purpose for these tissue changes is to allow the uterus to grow and the opening of the uterus and vagina to become more stretchy and elastic to let the baby through. Because the ligaments soften, bones can move a little and pinch nerves so that the pains can be quite sharp and shooting in character. Avoid any stretching exercises and bend your knees when you lift something. Talk to your doctor if any pain is worrying you. (*See also* Backache, below.)

Anal fissure

This is a split in the skin around the anus, caused by constipation. It makes bowel movements painful and you may also have some bleeding. Your doctor will suggest creams or jellies to help and you should follow the suggestions given below under Constipation. The split will heal in about four to six weeks if you keep your bowel movements soft.

Anemia

(*See* page 29.)

Backache

This is a very common complaint. It is often due to alterations in your posture as your belly enlarges. Your ligaments also soften throughout pregnancy and this means that the muscles have to work harder to maintain

If you have backache it may help to sit in an upright chair and put your legs up as well. You may find this is a comfortable position for general relaxation whenever you feel tired or tense.

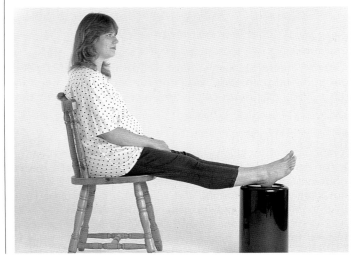

posture. Try to stand tall, bend your knees rather than your back when you're lifting and try to have extra rest. (*See also* Aches and pains, opposite.)

Bleeding gums
This is due to extra growth of the gums during pregnancy and additional plaque forming on the teeth. It helps to brush your teeth regularly and carefully, to use dental floss regularly and also to massage the gums.

Blocked nose
The lining of the nose, the upper windpipe and the back of the throat thicken during pregnancy. The nose may seem stuffy and blocked and you may have a tickly cough as though you have hay fever or a mild cold. Treatment is not usually required although a humidifier or a steaming inhalation can help last thing at night.

If you sleep on your back you may find that your partner complains of your snoring. It usually helps if he nudges you over onto your side.

Breathlessness
In late pregnancy you sometimes get the panicky feeling of not being able to get your breath. In fact your capacity to take a deep breath is very little different but you can lose the rhythm of your breathing. Take one or two deep sighing relaxing breaths and the rhythm of your breathing will quickly come all right again.

Constipation
In pregnancy the muscle of the bowel is more sluggish and you may get constipated. To avoid this, increase your intake of water and of roughage found in fruit, vegetables, salads, whole grain cereals and whole-wheat bread. Sprinkle extra natural bran on your food, or eat a high bran breakfast cereal, and have prunes from time to time. Make sure you have enough exercise.

Emptying the bowel at much the same time each day or taking two large glasses of very cold or hot water as soon as you get up stimulates natural emptying. Don't fuss if you don't have a bowel movement every day. Your doctor may be able to prescribe a mild laxative if this becomes necessary.

Contractions
In the last 10 or 15 weeks of pregnancy you may from time to time feel your belly getting quite hard and you may also have an associated ache in your lower abdomen. This can happen at half-hourly intervals. It is due to the uterus practicing for labor and is sometimes called Braxton Hicks' contractions.

Cramps
Cramps in the legs and feet usually come on at night and can be very painful. Pull your foot up with your hand or get up and walk about. An attack can be brought on by sudden stretching or by getting too hot in bed. There are no satisfactory medicines but many women swear by calcium tablets. As they are harmless to your baby they may be worth trying.

Cravings
You may find yourself consuming large quantities of sweets, chips or pickles or wanting to eat something more unusual such as strawberries or avocados. There is no known explanation for this and it is sometimes known as pica. Occasionally women may crave bizarre things such as clay, paper or starch. These, of course, are dangerous.

Falls
In late pregnancy your center of gravity is gradually changed, so it may be difficult to regain your balance if you trip.

Wear low-heeled shoes and take care when you are walking down stairs. Although you may hurt yourself if you fall, the baby is well protected inside you by the surrounding waters.

Feeling faint
The reflexes that control the circulation of blood to your head are less efficient in pregnancy. If you stand up or get out of bed quickly, you can feel faint or see spots in front of your eyes. This is more likely if you are hot. It is better to change your position slowly. If you have to stand for any length of time, keep wriggling your toes and tightening your legs. Keep the window open when you're working and go outside for some air or sit down as soon as you start to feel faint. Don't have too hot a bath or shower and be careful to get out of the bath slowly.

Frequent urination
The tendency to pass water more frequently in early pregnancy may lessen in mid-pregnancy but usually comes back as the baby's head settles into the pelvis. This is something you will have to put up with; don't be tempted to reduce your intake of water.

Headaches
For some headache sufferers pregnancy is a good time, while others find them more troublesome or get them for the first time. Try to take things easy.

Although it is better to avoid medication if possible, you could take a couple of acetaminophen tablets from time to time if you need to. Migraine sufferers should not take ergotomine tablets during pregnancy.

Headaches that start for the first time in the second half of pregnancy can be due to raised blood pressure. Have this checked if you haven't recently had a prenatal visit.

Heartburn and indigestion
Heartburn is a burning pain behind the breastbone often associated with burping and bringing up a little acid-tasting fluid into the back of the mouth. You may get heartburn because of the upward pressure of the uterus and because your

digestive system works less efficiently in pregnancy.

Try to avoid fried and fatty foods in particular and any other items which you suspect are causing your indigestion. It is better to eat a small amount more frequently, eat slowly and chew your food well, and avoid having a meal last thing at night. A drink of milk can help. Don't stoop or lie flat. Try raising the head of your bed 6-12 inches on blocks or piles of books and supporting yourself on extra pillows at night. Your doctor may suggest antacid tablets to chew on or a powder or mixture containing magnesium trisilicate.

Hemorrhoids

Hemorrhoids, or piles, are prominent veins on the edge of the anus. They feel like smooth lumps and you may notice them especially after straining to pass a bowel movement. They can be very itchy and may also bleed at this time. Occasionally they can become swollen and acutely painful; this is more likely to happen after the birth. The best way to prevent hemorrhoids is to avoid getting constipated (see Constipation, above). Your doctor can prescribe local anesthetic creams which are soothing. Hemorrhoids are not serious or dangerous.

Itching

Generalized itching can be very tiresome. It is quite common for pregnant women to find their skin is itchy, particularly over the stretched abdomen. The itchiness may sometimes be due to dry skin. Try using a mild moisturizing cream or body lotion. Use a mild soap and don't add bath salts or essences to your bath water. Wear light loose-fitting clothes and try not to get too hot, especially at night. Keep your bedroom cool.

If you have itchiness in the vagina or a rash anywhere on the body, you may need to consult your doctor.
(See also Rashes, below)

Leaking urine

Some women can find that they have a sudden spurt of urine when they laugh, cough or sneeze. This is due to softening of the tissues and sometimes continues after pregnancy. It is important to keep practicing your exercises for tightening the muscles of the pelvic floor (see page 47).

Nausea and sickness

If these are troublesome in early pregnancy they usually settle by the time you are three to four months pregnant. Occasionally they persist throughout pregnancy and can be tiresome, although they don't harm the baby. Heartburn (see above) may sometimes cause vomiting in later pregnancy.

Nosebleeds

The thickened lining of the nose bleeds more easily in pregnancy. A nosebleed can be stopped by pinching the soft part of the nose just below the bones between finger and thumb and holding firmly for a good 5-10 minutes. Then continue to breathe through the mouth and don't blow your nose for a couple of hours, and then only gently.

Palpitations

Harmless variations in the rhythm of the heartbeat are more likely to occur in pregnancy and can seem quite alarming. Don't hesitate to mention them to your doctor who will almost always be able to reassure you. When you feel these palpitations, try to relax and focus your attention on something else and they will pass.

Rashes

Towards the end of pregnancy itchy rashes can appear. They may start on your abdomen and spread to your arms and legs.

These are harmless but can itch intensely. They are likely to be worse when you are warm so wear cooler clothes, use fewer bedclothes and make sure your baths are tepid. You

may find a moisturizing cream or calamine lotion helps. If the rash persists, see your doctor.

Skin blemishes

Small red marks sometimes appear on the upper half of the body, including the face. You may notice a red dot in the center which is a stretched blood vessel, and fine vessels spreading out from it like the legs of a spider. These marks usually disappear after pregnancy.

Any brown spots on your skin are likely to darken and new brown patches may appear, especially on your face. Sometimes quite large patches of prominent fine skin veins appear, most commonly over the thighs. These are not necessarily associated with varicose veins. The patches usually tend to fade after pregnancy, though they can sometimes persist.

Sleeping problems

Difficulties in sleeping are common in pregnancy. If you have trouble in getting to sleep, try not to fuss about it. Worrying will only make the problem worse. You could practice some of the relaxation techniques you have been taught and try to make yourself as comfortable as possible. Sometimes it is helpful to read a book or to make yourself a hot drink. If you find you have several successive nights without sleep, particularly in the later months, your doctor may be able to prescribe a mild sleeping pill to help you over a bad spell.

Frightening dreams and nightmares are common in late pregnancy and simply reflect natural anxieties. There is no need to be worried by them.

Snoring

(See Blocked nose, above)

Stretch marks

These red marks occur when the deeper layers of the skin have split to reveal more of the underlying pink blood vessels. In other words, the skin has become thinner over these splits. They can appear over the abdomen, the breasts and on the thighs and buttocks.

Some women just seem unfortunately to have skin that is less stretchy. There is no effective way of preventing stretch marks, though putting on extra weight doesn't help. Many women are lucky and don't get stretch marks. Creams may make your skin more soft and supple but are unlikely to prevent these marks. After pregnancy, stretch marks gradually fade to pearly-white marks.

Sweating

All the activities of the body increase in pregnancy so you may find you are sweating more. If so, wear lighter, preferably non-synthetic, clothing, reduce your bed covers and keep your room cool. Avoid coffee, tea and spiced foods which stimulate sweating.

Swelling

A small amount of swelling of the ankles, feet and fingers is quite normal in pregnancy, especially in hot weather and towards the end of the day. The swelling is due partly to increase in skin circulation and partly to accumulation of fluid in the tissues. Rest your limbs as much as possible. Provided your blood pressure remains normal and the urine test doesn't show protein, you have nothing to worry about. However, you should always have your blood pressure checked in case the excessive swelling is part of a blood pressure problem.

Tingling fingers

In the second half of pregnancy you may get numbness and tingling of the fingers and thumbs, and perhaps pain up the arm. This is most likely first thing in the morning and the feeling improves as you move about. The problem, known as carpal tunnel syndrome, is due to compression of a nerve in the wrist. Raising your hand on a pillow and not getting too hot at night can help.

Tiredness

Some women become very tired and lacking in energy during pregnancy. This doesn't usually indicate that anything is wrong, but mention it to your doctor if it seems excessive. Sometimes tiredness lifts as pregnancy progresses, though it can persist throughout.

Vaginal bleeding

You should always consult your

SLEEPING POSITION

Try using extra pillows to get comfortable at night. Put one between your legs as you lie on your side and another one behind your back.

doctor if you have any vaginal bleeding. In early pregnancy it could indicate the start of a miscarriage (*see* page 28). Later in pregnancy (after week 28) it should be investigated in case you have placenta previa (*see* Antepartum hemorrhage, page 29).

Vaginal discharge

The normal amount of vaginal discharge tends to increase in pregnancy. Wearing cotton underpants or a stick-on mini pad and frequent washing with a mild soap are the best ways to deal with the problem. You should not use vaginal deodorants, sprays and douches or strong soaps, as these can irritate the skin of the vulva.

If you have troublesome itching or a more profuse smelly discharge, consult your doctor. You may have moniliasis ("yeast") or another local infection which can be treated.

Varicose veins

Pregnancy hormones alter the walls of blood vessels so that they stretch to accommodate the 30 per cent increase in your blood volume. In varicose veins the walls have stretched too much for the valves to close effectively and therefore blood collects in pools. The tendency for veins to become varicose runs in families. The most common sites for varicose veins are the legs and vulva. If you do suffer from varicose veins, avoid standing for prolonged periods, sitting cross-legged or wearing anything tight.

Special elasticated support stockings or pantyhose may help to relieve aching legs. Resting with your legs up will relieve both legs and vulva. Varicose veins of the vulva are not usually troublesome after pregnancy. Leg veins usually improve markedly over a few months after delivery, but the problem can sometimes persist, in which case it may need treatment.

Preparing for the birth

As well as looking after yourself and keeping healthy during pregnancy, you should spend some time preparing for the arrival of your baby. This means not only attending clinics or having regular check-ups with your doctor, but also going to prenatal classes (*see* below) where you can find out as much as possible about what to expect in labor and delivery and how to look after and care for your baby. If you understand what is involved, you will be more confident and better able to cope with labor and the birth.

What is labor?

Labor is the process by which the baby is pushed down and finally out of the birth canal by the contracting uterus. There are three stages in labor.

The first stage

The first and longest stage of labor is taken up with the opening of the cervix. At the beginning of labor the cervix is usually closed. The effect of contractions by the uterus is gradually to draw the cervix upwards over the baby's head while at the same time squeezing the head lower into the uterus. The wall of the uterus is a very strong muscle. When it contracts, it pulls the cervix up, making it thinner and shorter. Between contractions the uterus rests before pulling up the slack with the next contraction. It is the opening (dilating) and stretching of the cervix which gives rise to pain. The pain of a first stage contraction feels rather like a wave, gradually rising to a peak then dying away. When the cervix is fully dilated – about 10 centimeters (4 in) in diameter – the baby's head can pass through.

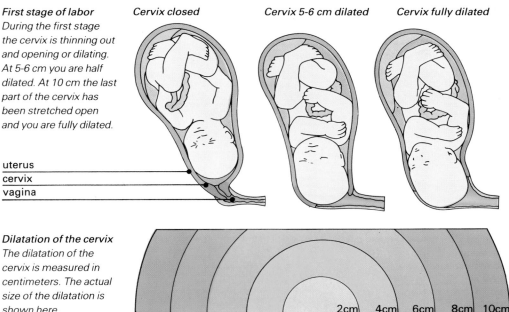

First stage of labor
During the first stage the cervix is thinning out and opening or dilating. At 5-6 cm you are half dilated. At 10 cm the last part of the cervix has been stretched open and you are fully dilated.

uterus
cervix
vagina

Cervix closed   Cervix 5-6 cm dilated   Cervix fully dilated

Dilatation of the cervix
The dilatation of the cervix is measured in centimeters. The actual size of the dilatation is shown here.

2cm   4cm   6cm   8cm   10cm

The second and third stage

The second stage, which is usually much shorter, is when the baby's head emerges through the fully dilated cervix and is pushed down towards the opening of the vagina. The cervix is no longer holding the baby, who is pushed a little further down with each contraction of the uterus. You also help by pushing down with the contractions. This stage ends when the baby is delivered. The third stage of labor is when the placenta or afterbirth is expelled. This usually happens within minutes of the baby's birth. The placenta is just a soft lump and most women hardly notice this stage as they are concentrating on the baby.

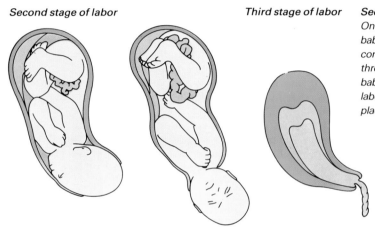

Second stage of labor

Third stage of labor

Second and third stages
Once the cervix is fully dilated the baby is pushed with each contraction down the birth canal through the vagina. Once the baby is delivered the final stage of labor, which is the delivery of the placenta, takes place.

Prenatal classes

These vary in what they offer, although they generally aim to provide information on all aspects of pregnancy, labor and birth, as well as to teach you how to look after and care for your baby. Most include breathing and relaxation techniques for labor and exercises for keeping your muscles in tone during and after pregnancy. Fathers are encouraged to attend and one or two evenings sessions are usually arranged to make this possible if they cannot attend a whole course. Classes provide an opportunity for discussion and information. You will be able to meet other parents with whom you can discuss your experiences and share your worries. You will also be able to ask questions and get advice about things that are bothering you.

In some areas you may have a variety of prenatal classes from which to choose. There are usually classes in the hospital and there may be others run by local midwives, birthing instructors or the Childbirth Education Association (CEA). If you have already had a baby, you may be able to attend a couple of refresher classes to remind you of breathing, relaxation and pushing techniques and to prepare you for the easier labor you will probably have. If you are having your baby in a hospital, it is usually possible to have a tour of the labor and delivery rooms and this can be very helpful.

Changing attitudes to childbirth

Attitudes to childbirth are subject to some extent to fashion. The debate about natural childbirth, and in particular the different positions that can be adopted, has exerted its influence both on mothers and on doctors. As a result hospitals and their staff have a more flexible approach and recognize that individual choices and needs should be accommodated as far as is compatible with the safety of mother and baby. Efforts are being made, for example, to see that labor and delivery wards are less impersonal and clinical. You are now likely to be encouraged to move around during the early stages of labor and to adopt any position that is comfortable. This, of course, will be subject to any monitoring, intravenous fluid or other necessary restrictions (*see* below).

The only position which is unfavorable for the progress of labor is lying flat on your back. As upright positions have no particular advantage over lying on your side, try to move about and adopt the position you find most comfortable. This usually means changing your position from time to time.

In general, most doctors and indeed women themselves prefer, for the second stage, the more usual semi-upright position of the bed supported by a wedge and pillows at your back. This is in effect a squatting position without having to bear your own weight. For the actual delivery you slip down a little so that the baby's emergence is more easily controlled and it is easier to see whether or not an episiotomy is needed.

Birth chairs and birth stools are being introduced and developed in the hope of improving the efficiency of bearing down in the second stage. They are available in some hospitals and you may like to try them at least for a while, although many women seem to find them rather uncomfortable. The true squatting position is too difficult for most women to maintain and does obscure the area where tears tend to occur. Some women have tried a position where they are held up from behind, but this requires strong supporters and doesn't seem to have any particular advantage.

For a forceps, breech or twin delivery (*see* page 44), you are likely to be on your back in a semi-reclining position, tilted a little to one side. Your legs are bent and supported in stirrups so that the lower end of the bed can be removed for the delivery.

Induction and stimulation of labor

Induction means starting labor artificially. It is used when it is likely that the mother of the baby will be at risk if the pregnancy continues. This may be if the baby is overdue or if for some reason the placenta is showing signs of failing. Because it is planned, you have time to discuss the reasons for being induced with your doctor and to ask any questions about what it will involve.

There are several methods of induction. In some centers, if the cervix isn't already soft and open, suppositories or gel are placed in the vagina around the cervix. They contain a substance (prostaglandin) which softens the cervix and may start labor. Once the cervix is softened, the membranes of the amniotic sac of waters surrounding the baby can be broken more easily. If the cervix is already soft, the membranes are broken without the preliminary use of prostaglandin. To do this, the doctor or nurse/midwife makes a small hole in the membranes. You cannot feel the actual breaking of the membranes but the stretching of the cervix which is sometimes necessary first can be quite painful and you may need some pain relief for this.

If labor doesn't start after breaking the waters, a hormone (oxytocin) drip is run into a vein. The rate is regulated so that labor contractions occur at the same rate as in normal labor.

When labor starts normally but is proceeding too slowly it can be speeded up to a normal rate by this same oxytocin drip. This is called augmenting labor.

Intravenous (IV)

This is when a solution is run directly into a vein in your hand or arm. Having it put in can be painful but once it is in you don't feel much. Your range of movement is usually reduced to just getting up and sitting in a chair. An IV may be used for oxytocin (*see* Induction, above) or for giving you glucose or a similar solution. You always have an IV if you have an epidural, an anesthetic or a twin delivery.

DELIVERY ROOM
A typical delivery room would have (from left to right) a baby resuscitation unit, a crib, a chair, a blood pressure gauge, a delivery bed, an overhead light, a gas and oxygen machine, an electronic fetal monitor and an IV stand for setting up an intravenous drip.

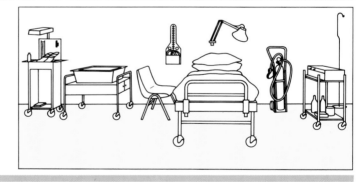

Monitoring

This refers to the use of special equipment for more careful and reliable observation of the contractions and the fetal heart rate. Monitoring is used to detect early evidence that the baby is not getting enough oxygen from the placenta and is therefore at risk.

The monitor may be held in place by a belt strapped around your abdomen or a minute metal clip may be attached to the baby's scalp.

You may just be monitored for half an hour or so at a time or the monitoring may be used continuously. When you are being monitored you can't move very far unless the more unusual wireless monitor (the telemeter) is being used.

EMERGENCY DELIVERY

If delivery does happen
unexpectedly, just accept it
and remember these basic
points. If you have time, call
for an ambulance.

● Get onto the floor and try
to relax.

● Try to pant rather than
push and let the baby come
naturally.

● Once delivered, hold the
baby with his head lower
than his body for a few
moments.

● Do not pull on the cord.

● Wrap the baby up to keep
him warm and make sure
he's not in any draft.

● If the placenta is delivered
keep it, to be checked.

● There is no need to cut or
tie the cord.

● Keep mother and baby
warm and send for help.

Complications in delivery

It is sometimes possible to anticipate a complication in delivery, when the baby is stubbornly breech, for example, or if there have been problems in pregnancy leading to a planned cesarean section. Sometimes however, the course of labor is not straightforward and either a vaginal delivery has to be assisted with forceps or a vacuum extraction, or a cesarean has to be performed.

Forceps delivery

The two most common reasons for forceps delivery are the failure of progress in the second stage, often because the uterus is not contracting sufficiently strongly, and the baby becoming short of oxygen (fetal distress). For a simple forceps delivery, local anesthetic is used to numb the lower part of the pelvis and the vaginal opening. Then forceps, which are specially shaped thin metal blades, are slipped gently around the baby's head to assist delivery as you push with the contraction. An episiotomy (*see* page 54) is usually made just before the baby's head emerges. Although they sometimes leave a slight temporary red mark on the face, forceps should not harm the baby.

Vacuum extraction

This is used as an alternative to forceps. A suction cup is applied to the baby's head so that the doctor can pull while you push. It does no harm to the baby.

Breech delivery

This is when the bottom end of the baby is coming first. As it is more likely that a baby presenting bottom first will be delivered by cesarean, the doctor may have tried to turn the baby's head first by pressing on the abdomen. This is usually done about the 36th week of pregnancy. If this has been unsuccessful then the doctor, with the aid of ultra sound and X-rays, will decide what form of delivery is advisable.

If you have a vaginal delivery, labor proceeds as for head first babies but an epidural is more likely to be advised. You deliver with your legs supported in stirrups and forceps may be used to make the head deliver slowly.

Cesarean section

There are many reasons for having a cesarean which is performed for the safety either of the mother or of the baby. Some of the more common reasons are that the mother's pelvis is too small, that the baby needs to be delivered quickly as he is becoming short of oxygen (fetal distress), because of the risk of hemorrhage in placenta previa (*see* page 29) or because of a previous cesarean.

The baby is delivered by an operation which opens into the uterus through the lower abdomen. Usually a cut is made horizontally along the top of the pubic hairline.

You are often given a general anesthetic but in many hospitals you may be able to choose to have the operation with an epidural. One of the advantages of this is that you are conscious when your baby is born and can participate in the excitement of his arrival.

Pain relief

Most women, especially with first babies, need some sort of anesthetic, or pain relief, to help them cope with the pain of first-stage contractions. Although you will learn breathing and relaxation techniques in your prenatal classes, it is a good idea to consider in advance the various forms of pain relief available to you as it is difficult to think about unfamiliar ideas when you are in the middle of labor pains. Remember that if pain relief is accepted before the pain becomes unbearable and before you start to lose control, it is more likely to help. Above all, don't regard labor as a test of cowardice or courage. You will cope better with it and have a much more positive experience if you have a more flexible approach.

Narcotics and tranquilizers

These are given in the form of an injection either into your buttock or your IV tubing. They usually start to work in 15 minutes and may last for two to three hours. You may need a repeat dose if it isn't giving adequate relief in 45 minutes. A few women feel rather dizzy or are nauseated for a while, but most find that they can then manage their breathing and relaxation better. If you have had narcotics within an hour before delivery, there is a possibility that your baby could be slower to breathe well. For this reason, another method of pain relief is used toward the end of labor.

Paracervical block

This is a method of pain relief in which local anesthetic is injected into the cervix during the first stage of labor. It provides pain relief for one to two hours. There have been reports of changes in the baby's heart rate after injection of the anesthetic, so this should be monitored carefully.

Epidural block

This is a local anesthetic injected into the lower back. It acts on the nerves from the lower part of the body so that messages passing through the spinal cord to the brain are blocked. For most women an epidural means that the lower half of the body goes numb; pain ceases and they then find themselves able to relax.

An epidural is usually given by an anesthesiologist and most hospitals have anesthesiologists available all the time.

You lie or sit curled up and your lower back is numbed with local anesthetic. A fine tube threaded through a needle is then passed between the bones of your lower back. The needle is removed and the tube left in so that the anesthetic can be topped up as needed at two or four hourly intervals. After about 15 minutes you will notice your legs going numb. You will probably lose most sensation in the lower part of your body. Once you have the epidural you have to remain on the bed, but there is no difficulty in getting comfortable as the worst, if not all, of the pain has usually gone.

Sometimes the epidural is not entirely effective. It may,

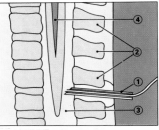

Epidural nerve block
The needle (1) carrying the tube through which the epidural anesthetic solution is given is inserted between the vertebrae (2) into the epidural space (3) below the spinal cord (4). The needle is then removed and the tube left in position.

for example, block sensations down one side of your body only. In this case it can be repositioned but you may continue to have some pain. Sometimes an epidural can cause a fall in blood pressure. This is usually corrected by turning you on your side or tilting the bed so your head is lower. An epidural can mean that you are not able to push so effectively in the second stage. This makes a simple forceps delivery more likely. If you wish and if there is time, the epidural can be allowed to wear off in the second stage so that you are more likely to push the baby out.

Epidurals are sometimes used instead of a general anesthetic for cesarean deliveries (*see* page 44).

Pudendal block

This is a local anesthetic used to numb the external skin and the lower vagina for delivery and episiotomy, if necessary. The anesthetic is injected into the region of the pudendal nerves which are just inside the vagina. The numbness lasts one to two hours.

Spinal anesthetic – saddle block

This anesthetic is administered into the lower back in the same area as the epidural block. There are several important differences. The spinal anesthetic is administered in the sitting position. It is also administered into the spinal fluid so there is usually more complete paralysis of the muscles. The contractions frequently stop, or get very weak, so the spinal anesthetic cannot be given until just before delivery when the baby's head is very low. Also there is a significant risk of severe headache afterwards.

How you can help yourself

At your prenatal classes you will be taught techniques for breathing and relaxing in labor. It is a good idea to practice these at home so that you, and your partner if he's going to be there, are thoroughly familiar with them.

Breathing and relaxation

The first stage contractions of labor are not only painful but can also lead to a feeling of being overwhelmed by some remorseless process. Learning how to breathe and relax can help you to cope with the pain of contractions and any sense of panic you may have.

In labor your aim should be to deal with one contraction at a time. Keep in mind that contractions always wear off and don't last more than one and a half minutes. Each contraction coped with is one contraction nearer delivery.

Being aware of and consciously controlling your breathing calms you and gives you something to concentrate on. Try to breathe as you feel you need – not too fast and not too deeply, always thinking about the breath out. As labor progresses and the contractions become stronger, your breathing usually becomes more shallow. You may find it helpful to take shallow breaths in groups of three when contractions are very strong – especially in the later part. Switch to breathing in threes when it is difficult to keep up ordinary, slow breathing.

As tension makes you feel worse, you should also try to

BREATHING

As a contraction starts, open your eyes, focus on a spot and breathe in and out through your mouth – not too fast and not too deep. When contractions get stronger, try shallow puffs through your mouth in groups of three.

RELAXING

Take a deep sighing breath and let yourself go loose all over. Relax one arm and then the other, then your legs and finally all over. You may find it more comfortable to practice with pillows.

PUSHING

As the contraction starts, take a couple of breaths. Then take a moderate-sized breath (not too deep) and hold it, using the air to push down on the baby. Try not to screw your face up and keep your eyes open. Let your pelvic floor go and get the feeling that you are opening out. Hold the breath for five to seven seconds and then let it out through your mouth. Breathe quickly in and out and then take another moderate breath and push again. As the contraction wears off, take a few sighs and then relax.

relax between contractions. This is another focus for your concentration. You may find it better to keep your eyes open and to fix on a spot during a contraction – this stops you from retreating too much into a world of your own.

In the second stage you push down towards your back passage as though having a bowel movement and at the same time you let go.

Exercises

You will learn a pelvic floor tightening exercise to help reduce the tendency to lose urine in late pregnancy. You will need to do it afterwards too, as it strengthens those muscles which have been stretched by delivery. Those who are used to keeping fit or doing exercises can usually continue exercising in pregnancy. It is better to avoid stretching exercises – especially those involving the back.

How others can help

During labor the presence of another person can be a great comfort to you. Usually this is your partner but this may not always be possible. Hospitals can seem rather strange and even frightening and you may be in the first stage of labor for many hours. So it is as well to have someone with you who can help pass the time.

If your partner has attended prenatal classes he will be better be able to help you. He can alert you to the start of the next contraction – especially if contractions are being recorded on a monitor. He can remind you to start breathing in plenty of time to establish a rhythm before the peak of contractions and make sure you relax between contractions. He can help you get comfortable and encourage you generally.

In the second stage he can relay instructions from the doctor or nurse/midwife and tell you when to push. More importantly, he will be there when your baby is born. For many parents the shared experience of the birth is something that they will never forget.

PELVIC FLOOR EXERCISE

Imagine you have a tampon in the vagina which is about to fall out. Try to keep it in by tightening your vagina and anus. Do not hold your breath or pull your tummy in at the same time. Tighten as hard as you can hold and then let go. Try to do this three times a day, each time repeating the exercise ten times. You can do it sitting, standing or lying down. Remember that this exercise is not the same as trying to stop yourself passing urine.

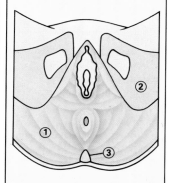

This exercise helps to strengthen the pelvic floor muscles (**1**) which are between the pelvic bone (**2**) and the coccyx (**3**).

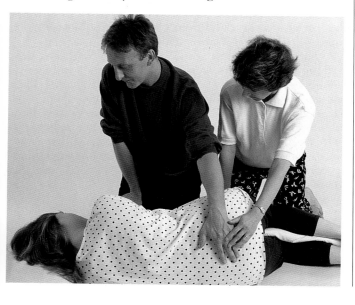

Prenatal classes
Your partner can learn how to massage your back to help relieve any back pain in pregnancy and during labor.

Preparing for your baby

You don't have to buy everything your baby is going to need all at once – but some items of equipment and clothing are wanted right from the start of your baby's life. In the last weeks of pregnancy, it's a good idea to make sure you're prepared. You'll probably be extra busy *and* extra tired during the first days and weeks after the birth – and not really in the mood for unnecessary shopping trips.

First essentials

Essential items for the first two weeks or so include somewhere for your baby to sleep (plus bedding) and something to transport him in outdoors (plus again, bedding). If you have a carriage, bassinet carryall (*see* page 76), the purchase of a crib can wait. Or if you already have a crib for your baby you could put off buying his stroller until later, and carry him outdoors in a baby carrier (*see* page 78). Remember also that the only safe way to transport your baby in a car is to put him in approved car safety restraint equipment *see* page 78). It is also advisable to invest in a baby monitor, especially if you have a large house. Consisting of a transmitter placed by your baby's crib and a receiver which you carry with you, it enables you to hear when your baby is distressed.

You'll need to buy diapers (*see* page 102) before the birth too. If you intend using traditional cloth diapers, you'll also want waterproof pants, liners, pins, and bucket. At least one box of disposables could prove useful, whatever you intend using long term, and you'll find a changing mat useful right from the start. If you want to bottlefeed, you will need bottles plus sterilizing equipment. Remember to sterilize them before you use them the first time, too. For details, *see* page 92.

Although a baby bath isn't essential at first, you will need a towel for your baby and plenty of absorbent cotton. As time goes on you'll be able to make your own mind up about what you find useful for change and bath times. *See* pages 79, 104 and 108 for more details.

Although you won't need all your baby's first-size clothing at once, do remember that the first days and weeks of your baby's life are often the wettest and sickest! This can lead to more from-the-skin-up changes of clothing than you'd think – so don't try to make do on fewer than four complete changes (stretchsuit, undershirt and sweater is a good basic outfit). Winter babies do need a hat (and possibly mittens) for outdoors and you'll want to wrap them up warmly in a blanket bag, or a shawl, with extra covers if it is really cold. Receiving blankets are useful and can double as bedding. *See* page 80 for more information.

What you'll need in the hospital

Opinions differ as to when you should have your suitcase packed and ready to go to the hospital. Some women spend much of the first stage of labor at home, so packing your bag

---

BABY'S BASICS

Use our checklist to prepare for baby's needs in the first week at home.
- bassinet/crib *or* carriage (plus bedding) *or if no carriage* baby carrier
- Undershirts
- Stretchsuits
- Sweaters
- Receiving blanket, blanket bag *or* shawl
- Hat
- Mittens
- Toiletries
- Diapers

and if not using disposables
- Pins
- Liners
- Waterproof pants
- Diaper bucket
- Diaper wipes

if traveling by car
- Infant car seat

if not breastfeeding
- Bottlefeeding equipment
- Formula milk
- Sterilizing equipment

See What your baby will need, page 70; Feed..ig your baby, page 92; Diaper changing, page 102; Bathing your baby, page 108.

can be one constructive way of passing the time. However, you may feel happier knowing weeks beforehand that your bag is ready-packed. Do check in advance that what you intend to take to the hospital is available and in the house even if not actually packed.

You'll need to take at least two nightdresses (with deep front openings or slits if you want to breastfeed) plus a robe and your slippers. Take in several pairs of old underpants you won't mind having to throw away (rather than launder) if need be. You may need two or three changes of pants a day at first to keep clean and fresh. Take at least three bras with you – you may like to buy specially designed nursing bras that give you good support and make breastfeeding much easier. You'll also need a large quantity of sanitary pads. Most hospitals provide these but check before you take in your own.

PACKING FOR HOSPITAL

Try to get all that you'll need in the hospital organized and packed well in advance. It's a good idea to put the things you'll need during labor and immediately after your delivery in a separate small bag or at the top of your suitcase.

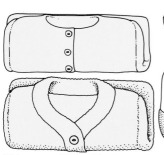

Things you'll need in the hospital

Things for after your delivery

Take your usual toiletries and make-up. Don't forget money for newspapers, reading/knitting/writing paper and pen and anything else for afterwards. If your stay in the hospital is likely to be longer than a day or so, there's no need to take everything in at once. Visitors can bring you clean things and nightwear – and your partner can bring in your day clothes (plus the baby's going home outfit) on the day you are discharged.

It's a good tip to take in a smaller bag with everything you need for the actual labor, birth and immediately after. Include in it a small natural sponge for moistening lips and cooling your face, two washcloths, a nightdress, underpants and bra. You might also like to pack a camera to record your baby's first moments.

Women attempting "natural" childbirth à la Lamaze take a "Lamaze bag" to the hospital containing lollipops, ice packs, tennis balls and chopsticks.

GOING HOME THINGS

Remember that you will need to have clothes brought into the hospital for you to wear home. Choose something loose fitting, as you won't regain your shape immediately, and which will be suitable if you're breastfeeding. Don't forget pantyhose, shoes and a jacket. You'll need clothes for the baby too – a diaper, undershirt, stretchsuit, sweater, hat and a blanket.

Labor and delivery

Labor is recognized by feeling contractions and timing their frequency. Contractions can be felt like a tight gripping ache in the lower back or lower abdomen or perhaps like a period pain or a form of constipation. Occasionally the pains are in the upper thighs.

There are many patterns for the start and early part of labor and no agreed rule for recognizing the onset of labor. Don't hesitate to contact your doctor if you are unsure about anything.

When to go to the hospital

With your first baby you are probably in labor when you have had contractions every 10 minutes, or more frequently, for two to three hours. This is the time to go to the hospital.

If you are having a second or later baby, contractions are likely to remain quite mild and fairly infrequent until labor is quite advanced. Then they can quite suddenly change to strong long contractions which fairly rapidly complete the labor. You should therefore go to the hospital when you think you are in labor, even though contractions may be weak and only at 10-15 minute intervals.

Other reasons for going to the hospital

If the waters break: The waters usually break towards the end of the first stage of labor but it may happen at the onset of labor or even many days or weeks before labor. It may come as a slow trickle or as a sudden rush. Breaking of the waters is always an indication to go to the hospital as an infection of the uterus is more likely and, with sudden loss, the umbilical cord may have come down below the head.

If there is bleeding: Bleeding in the latter part of pregnancy is always a reason for consulting your doctor or for going to the hospital if you can't contact her.

Bleeding should not be confused with the show. This is the passage of slightly blood-stained jelly-like material (mucus). A mucus plug has filled the cervix during pregnancy as a protection and is released as the cervix starts to open. It may be released after the start of labor or a few days to a week before its onset. It alone is *not* a reason to report to hospital. Labor can begin before this show.

Admission routines

These vary from institution to institution but follow a general pattern. When you arrive at the hospital you will be taken to the admission room. If your labor is quite advanced you will probably be taken straight to the delivery room. Otherwise you will go through the following procedures.

Progress report and examination

The nurse asks you about the time of onset of contractions and their nature and frequency, how you feel about any pain you are having, whether the waters have broken and whether you have had bleeding or a show. She then checks your chart. If there is anything needing urgent medical assessment she will call the doctor to come and examine you.

The nurse takes your blood pressure and may test your urine. She examines your abdomen, noting the size of the baby, whether it is lying straight up and down, whether the breech or head is coming first and whether this presenting part is engaged in the pelvis. She listens to the fetal heart rate and rhythm.

Internal examination

The nurse or doctor first looks for any blood or other liquid draining from the vagina. She then passes two fingers into the vagina to see how long the cervix is and how open (dilated). If it is open enough she feels for the intact bag of waters and checks for cord pulsation through it. If the membranes have broken she checks whether the umbilical cord can be felt. If the cervix is sufficiently open she may feel whether the back of the head is to the front or back.

You will find the vaginal examination less uncomfortable if you push down as the doctor or nurse is inserting her fingers, and then relax as much as possible and do your breathing. Tell her if you feel a contraction coming, as it is better if she doesn't try to examine you while you are concentrating on the contraction.

Shaving

It is now unusual to be shaved other than perhaps the small area underneath where you may need stitches. If you are to have a cesarean it is usual to shave hair away from the line of incision.

Enema or suppositories

These may be used to empty the lower bowel if it is full enough to hold up the progress of labor and to save you the embarrassment of passing feces in the second stage. Anxiety about this can be a factor in you holding back from effective pushing.

Bath or shower

You may find a bath or shower quite comforting but the water shouldn't be too hot as you could feel faint. You shouldn't sit in a bath if you have ruptured membranes.

Settling into the labor room

You will now go to the labor room where you may also be delivering. You may be joined by your partner if he hasn't remained with you throughout.

The nurse or doctor will discuss any views you have on pain relief and of course organize any that is already nec-essary. She will start regular checking of you and the baby and make an initial electronic recording of the baby's heart beat using an external monitor. Depending on how far your labor has progressed and the regulations of your particular hospital, you may then get up and walk about, sit in a chair or lie in bed on your side or propped up, as you wish. If you have elected to have an epidural the anesthesiologist will insert it when it is clear that labor has been established.

THE SHOW

A sticky plug of mucus (**1**) seals the cervical canal (**2**) during pregnancy. When the cervix (**3**) begins to stretch this plug is dislodged. When this happens you may notice some blood-stained, jelly-like discharge which is called the show. This doesn't mean that labor has started although it does indicate that your cervix is opening a little. The plug may not come out until labor is well under way.

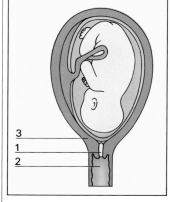

3
1
2

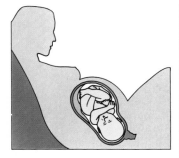

The first stage of labor

The first stage can last anywhere between about 2 and 24 hours but for first babies lasts on average between 10 and 12 hours. For later babies it is a little less and usually the difficult, painful part of labor is much shorter. Your doctor or nurse/midwife will observe your progress by checking how often and how strongly the uterus is contracting. They will also feel the lower abdomen to see how the baby's head is moving down into the pelvis. They'll examine you internally to check how dilated your cervix is and how far down the baby's head has come. Sometimes they will rupture your membranes, if this has not already happened naturally, when your cervix has dilated to about three to four centimeters.

Most labors start gradually. Once you are in the hospital you may like to be up and about to begin with. Between contractions you can sit or lean on a chair or walk about for a while, leaning on something or someone when you get a contraction. Later you may find you want to lie down, get on your hands and knees or find some other position to relieve the pain. The only position that doesn't help the progress of labor is lying flat on your back. What helps most is to be able to move and change positions. All the time you can try to put into practice a breathing pattern and relaxation. Whether you take pain relieving drugs depends on how much pain you are having with contractions. The doctor or nurse can give you some idea of how you are doing and how much progress has been made. However, labor can be much shorter or longer than predicted. Just try to be patient and cope with one contraction at a time. Deciding when the first stage is ended can be confusing. For some women it can seem endless, while for others the change from first to second stage is dramatic. Always tell the doctor or nurse when you feel a sudden need to push.

The experience of labor in this first stage varies enormously. For some it can be long, dreary and painful. Others are lucky and have more rapid labors in which pain is within bearable limits. Don't have unrealistic expectations; every woman and every labor is different.

The transition

Especially with first babies there is often a time at the end of the first stage when the feeling of wanting to push is developing but the cervix is not fully open and therefore pushing is inappropriate. This is sometimes called the transition. It often lasts for about half an hour but may last much longer. You may get an attack of the shakes, or vomit or feel more out of control and unable to cope much longer. You should not push until the desire is overwhelming and even then examination may show that you are not in second stage. Breathing shallowly in groups of threes can help to resist the urge and usually second stage is not far away. Some women suddenly find themselves in the second stage by feeling a lump down near the opening and the doctor may soon get the first glimpse of the baby's head.

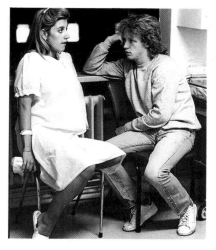

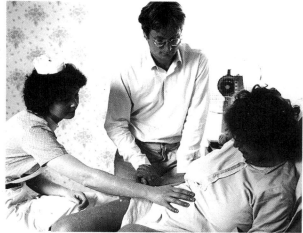

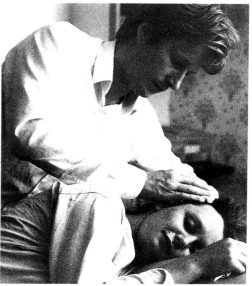

Top left Moving about and changing position is usually helpful at least in early labor.
Top right Your doctor or nurse can feel when your uterus is contracting by putting her hand on your belly.
Left Your partner's presence is reassuring and he can help in many ways, such as wiping your brow.
Below left An irresistible urge to push usually signals the start of the second stage.

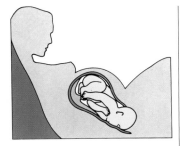

The second stage of labor

The second stage for a first baby usually only lasts up to two hours and is often much shorter than this for second babies. In contrast with the first stage, the second stage can be very satisfying and even enjoyable.

The first feeling is usually one of pressure – often as though wanting to have a bowel movement. This is because the baby's head is squashing the bowel as it moves down the vagina. You will now be encouraged to let go and to push with the contractions. You need to be confident in yourself and in your doctor. Try to go with the contractions and not to hold back. You push down through your lower abdomen towards your anus. At the same time, try to relax and let go down there; concentrate on feeling as if you are opening out.

As the baby's head comes lower you may feel it as a large lump. Then you usually get a stretching feeling which can become so strong that you may feel as if you are splitting. Usually you only have this sensation during contractions until just before delivery when the baby may no longer be slipping back between contractions. Provided you know this is normal and it won't be long before your baby is born, you will cope. The harder you push, the better it tends to feel. You may have some pain between contractions but you don't usually feel this when you are pushing.

If the tissues seem likely to tear, the doctor will tell you and make an episiotomy. This is a small cut in the perineum, which is the area between the vagina and the anus.

The word "crowning" is still sometimes used to indicate that the maximum diameter of the baby's head has delivered. At this point you may be able to feel the head or to see it in a mirror.

When the baby is just about to emerge you will be asked to pant. You should take fairly superficial breaths slowly through your mouth. This tends to stop you pushing with the last one or two contractions, so that the baby is delivered more slowly and gently as the uterus alone is pushing. If the baby isn't quite out when the contraction wears off, you may be asked to give another push even though you haven't got a contraction.

As the baby's head emerges you get a sense of relief. The shoulders soon follow, feeling like another lump, and then the rest of the baby slithers out.

The third stage of labor

This is the delivery of the placenta, or afterbirth, which you will just feel as a soft lump emerging. It is usual for the doctor or midwife to assist its delivery after waiting a few minutes for the uterus to contract. If the delivery of the placenta is delayed it can be trapped in the contracting uterus. The doctor or midwife places a hand on your lower abdomen and pulls steadily on the cord. She may get you to give a push at the same time to help expel the placenta. It

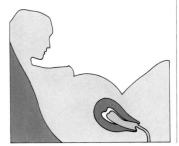

will slip out so smoothly that you may not even notice its delivery. The doctor will keep the placenta carefully to be examined as it is very important to check that it has emerged complete.

After the placenta has been delivered you will be given medication to cause the uterus to contract and limit the amount of bleeding.

Meanwhile, provided your baby is well, you will be nursing her and beginning to relax. The cord will by now have been clamped and cut.

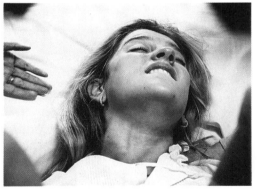

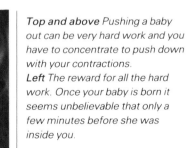

Top and above Pushing a baby out can be very hard work and you have to concentrate to push down with your contractions.
Left The reward for all the hard work. Once your baby is born it seems unbelievable that only a few minutes before she was inside you.

After delivery

The birth of your baby, after all the months of waiting and the experience of labor, can be quite an overwhelming moment. Hearing her first cry as she is born can seem really miraculous. You may find that you are moved to tears, or you may simply be overwhelmed by a sense of relief that the whole thing is safely over. If your labor has been painful and difficult you may find that you feel both physically exhausted and emotionally drained. Not all first-time parents feel an immediate surge of love for their newly arrived baby; emotional bonds usually develop gradually as parents become familiar with their baby in the coming weeks. So don't be surprised if your baby seems a stranger at first. Unless you are prepared you might even be disconcerted by her appearance. But you may hardly notice how she looks in the thrill of seeing her for the first time.

You are usually given your baby to hold immediately after delivery or, if you wish it, she can be delivered onto your abdomen. If she is slow to breathe, blood and mucus are quickly sucked from her nose and mouth. She may need a few puffs of oxygen from a mask and occasionally a tube is placed into her windpipe to help her get started. Sometimes she may be wiped and wrapped up before being given to you to hold. As babies are born wet, they have to be dried off and covered so that they don't lose body heat too rapidly. If you are going to breastfeed you may want to put the baby to the breast soon after. Some suckle readily; others may take a day or two to get the idea but will appreciate the warmth and closeness of your body.

If you have had an episiotomy, you will need some stitches. For this your legs will be supported in stirrups and you will be given a local anesthetic. Some women find the procedure uncomfortable and it does take a little time. You will then be washed and changed into your own nightdress and your blood pressure and pulse will be checked. Before you are taken to the postpartum floor you and your partner can usually have some time to yourselves with your new baby.

Your baby's appearance

When they are first born babies are usually covered by vernix, a greasy white substance, and may also be smeared with some blood. They are usually bluish in color and sometimes their head may look a little elongated due to the molding of the shape as it passes through the birth canal. The face may be a little swollen and even bruised. All this is quite normal and provided you expect it you will hardly notice your baby's rather messy appearance in the excitement of your first sight of her. Over the next few days any swelling or bruising will gradually subside.

Checking your baby

A number of routine checks are made on your baby following delivery. The most important is to see that she

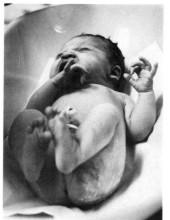

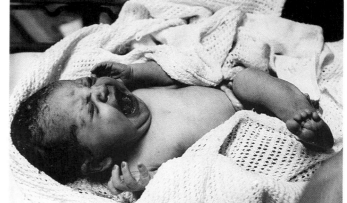

Above Your baby will probably be smeared with white vernix and often greets the world with loud crying.
Left You and your partner can wonder at her birth and spend some time getting to know this new person. She will enjoy the warmth and comfort of being held by you.

establishes breathing and that she is a good color. Her body temperature is checked regularly. If her temperature falls, she is likely to be a little blue – especially in the hands and feet.

At one and five minutes after birth your baby's general vigor is usually recorded in what is called the Apgar score. Up to a total of ten points are awarded for color, breathing, heart rate, general body tone and reactions to stimuli. This provides a useful rough guide to her general condition, and especially to whether she has been short of oxygen before delivery.

Your baby is weighed and her length and the circumference of her head are measured. Her appearance and organs are also checked. If all seems well, this first examination is often followed by a more thorough check by a pediatrician or other doctor sometime in the next day or two (*see* page 61). If there are any problems at any time, a pediatrician is called to examine your baby.

Babies needing special care

If your tiny baby needs to be looked after in a special care unit, you will be encouraged to spend as much time as possible with her and help with routines such as changing diapers.

Babies who are ill at birth or shortly after birth need special care. This is most commonly because the baby is premature, small for dates, has a serious physical deformity or withdrawal symptoms from a drug addicted mother. These babies will usually be looked after in a special care baby unit.

The special care baby unit

Most hospitals have a special facility with extra skilled nursing care and pediatricians for small babies and those with problems needing special attention. These units are equipped with incubators which have their own source of heat as well as a range of monitoring devices to keep the staff aware of what is happening. The length of stay in a special care baby unit will depend on the baby's problems. As soon as the pediatrician is confident that the baby can cope without special care and attention, he will be moved to be with his mother or in the newborn nursery. Mothers and fathers are encouraged to come into the unit to hold, cuddle and feed their babies whenever possible. Just sitting by an incubator and touching your baby can be a comfort.

Premature or pre-term babies

These are babies born before week 36 of pregnancy. The smaller and younger babies in this group are almost always taken into the special care unit. These babies often have difficulty with breathing because of the immaturity of their lungs. At first they may have to be fed continuously through a fine tube passed through their nose and down into their stomach. Sometimes nourishment is given indirectly into a vein. The baby may at first be fed a special fluid formula and later he may have expressed breast milk. Before he goes home he will be feeding from a bottle or the breast and his mother gradually takes over his care under the supervision of the nurses.

Small-for-dates babies

These are babies which are below the weight expected at the time they are born. For instance, full-term babies who have a birth weight below 5½ pounds are considered small for dates. These babies usually need attention as they haven't the normal body reserves of nourishment.

Twins and multiple births

Twins and other multiples tend to be born prematurely, or early. This is partly just because an overstretched uterus tends to start in labor sooner and partly because of other problems, such as toxemia, which are more common with multiple pregnancies. In addition to being premature the babies are more likely to be small for dates. They are therefore usually looked after in a special care unit.

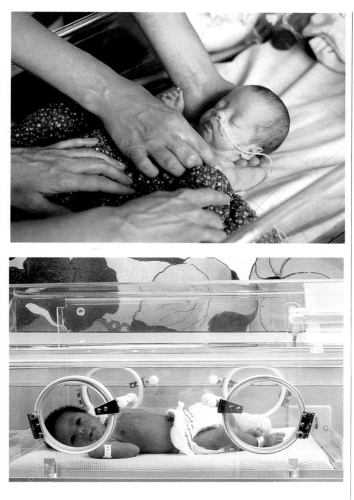

Just touching and stroking your new baby will be a source of comfort for both of you.

Jaundice is common and may need to be treated with ultra-violet light. This baby has just finished his treatment and has had his eye protectors removed, ready for his next feed from his mother.

Jaundice

Slight yellowness is quite normal and occurs in 30-40 per cent of all babies. It has little effect, apart from sometimes making the baby a little sleepy and slow to feed, and usually clears after a few days. Sometimes it may need to be treated by using ultraviolet light. The baby usually stays on the postpartum ward for this treatment. Very occasionally the jaundice is so severe that the baby needs to have his blood changed by a special type of transfusion. The baby would be taken into a special care unit for this.

Handicapped babies

A few parents are unfortunate enough to have a baby born handicapped. This may be because something has gone wrong in the baby's early development or there may have been trouble during labor or at delivery. You and your partner will feel sad, angry and disappointed and somehow guilty that you haven't produced a perfect baby. Try to talk about it to each other and to your doctors and nurses. There are many self-help organizations (*see* page 298) which can offer support and advice.

The first few days

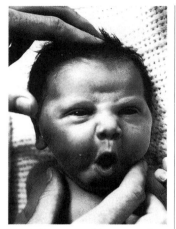

This baby may well be wondering what is going on as the doctor checks his fontanelle to see that it isn't too tense.

You and your baby will spend the first few days, whether at home or in a newborn nursery gradually getting used to each other. Your baby will be adapting to a strange new world and you will be learning to understand her and to care for her.

Your baby's appearance

Normal babies vary considerably in size and appearance. You will probably find yourself exploring your baby minutely and watching how she changes in the very early days. Remember that many of the superficial marks and swellings are normal and will soon disappear.

Her head You will notice that your baby's head makes up a surprisingly large proportion of her body. Although the brain of the newborn baby is well developed it continues to grow until it reaches adult proportions at the end of the second year.

Swellings and bruises The back of the head and parts of the face may be swollen and even a little bruised because of labor. This soon settles and the bones of the skull slide back so that the head shape becomes more normal.

The fontanelle In the newborn baby the bones of the skull are not completely fused. This allows the shape of the skull to adapt to the shape of the birth canal as the baby is born. It also allows the skull to expand as the growth of the brain is completed in the first two years. The bones at the top of the baby's skull are attached to each other by very tough membrane. This area, which is about the size of a quarter, is called the fontanelle. Although it seems quite vulnerable – you can see a pulse beating there – you needn't worry about touching it or about it being damaged by normal handling or hair washing. The membrane of the fontanelle is quite tough enough to protect the baby.

Her skin Your baby's skin may be quite blotchy and even wrinkled at first. She may have a little rash or a few spots but these usually disappear in the early days or weeks.

Birthmarks Some babies are born with pink areas on their forehead, eyelids or round the back of their neck. These are called stork bites and they fade over the first few months. Another type of birthmark is the red "strawberry" mark which also usually fades with time. Port wine stains are more extensive and may need treatment. Some darker-skinned babies have "Mongolian patches" which are areas of increased bluish pigmentation.

The umbilical cord A short stump of cord is left where it was cut at the navel. This is clamped with a plastic clip. You will be shown how to clean around the cord which gradually shrivels and drops off in about a week.

The breasts and sex organs These are often surprisingly prominent in newborn babies, due to the influence of the mother's hormones and the effects gradually fade. Female babies may even have a small amount of vaginal bleeding or emit milk from swollen breasts, also normal.

What your baby can do

Even before she is born your baby will have heard your heartbeat and been aware of the noises around you. Now that she is part of the outside world she has to communicate her needs to you. Her principal needs are for comfort and closeness and to satisfy her strong sucking instinct. Your baby is likely to spend much of her first few days sleeping but even then you will be fascinated to notice some of the movements you felt when she was inside you. She may suddenly start or shiver; bouts of hiccuping are common and she may cough or sneeze. Her breathing pattern can be irregular but this is quite normal.

Your baby's senses

At birth your baby can see and her senses of smell, taste and hearing are quite well developed. She is most responsive to touch and to pressure.

Sight If you hold your baby about eight inches away she will look directly into your eyes. She seems to be able to see and to focus on things at this close range. Very soon she will be able to recognize you by sight. At first her eyes may move independently but by three months this lack of coordination has usually disappeared.

Hearing Babies react best to soft soothing noises and will be startled by sudden loud noises. Your baby will be quite aware of your voice, which will comfort her. She will even appreciate rhythms of simple songs and nursery rhymes.

Smell and taste These are strongly developed and instinctive. Your baby soon recognizes your individual smell.

Touch, pressure and movement Your baby responds to you cuddling, stroking, holding and rocking her. These are important ways of comforting and communicating with her. If you are unhurried and gentle your baby feels secure and relaxed. Soft clothing and warmth also make her feel comfortable. The more time you spend holding and nursing her at first, the more secure she will feel and the more your own confidence will increase.

Emotions Anger, frustration, hunger, desire to suck and discomfort are all expressed by crying (without tears at this stage) but your baby can also look contented and happy.

Reflexes

These are your baby's inborn responses to certain signals or stimuli. Some of these will be retained and develop while others will be lost.

The sucking reflex Newborn babies suck in response to pressure on the palate just beyond the upper gums.

The rooting reflex When lightly stroked on one cheek the baby turns in that direction, her lips pursed ready to suck.

The grasp reflex The baby's early grip is remarkably strong. Her hand will close firmly around your finger.

Swallowing This is well developed as the baby has been practicing by swallowing the fluid in the womb.

The walking reflex A baby held upright makes walking movements as soon as her feet touch a firm surface. This reflex is lost after a few days.

CHECKING YOUR BABY
Sometime in the first couple of days your baby will be given a thorough check by a pediatrician. This will probably be done while you are there to watch. She will be given a complete physical examination to make sure that all her limbs and organs are functioning. The pediatrician will also check her reaction to stimuli.

The baby's head is measured to record the greatest circumference.

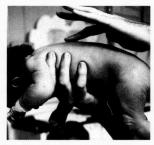

The back is examined from the neck right down to the base of the spine.

The legs are bent up and the movement of the hips checked for any dislocation.

A nurse will help you and your baby to get used to breastfeeding in the early days.

On the maternity floor

During the first few days after delivery you are likely to experience a jumble of feelings and emotions. At first you will probably be tired, yet too excited to sleep. Having your baby beside you gives you a wonderful feeling of satisfaction, but despite this you may at times find yourself feeling physically uncomfortable and unaccountably low.

The after effects of birth

Most women have some discomfort after their delivery and stitches and hemorrhoids can be acutely painful for a few days. A doctor or nurse will examine you every day for the first few days or so to make sure your uterus is contracting to its normal size and to check that any stitches are healing.

Stitches If you have had stitches they can often be very uncomfortable and painful at first. Sitting on an air ring or using an ice pack can help by relieving the pressure and by soothing. It can also be comforting to bathe the stitches in a sitz bath.

Constipation and opening the bowels It may be several days before you have a bowel movement and not surprisingly you will be worried about this if you have hemorrhoids or stitches. It can feel as though your stitches will burst although this doesn't happen. It is wise to do everything you can to make sure the first bowel movement will be soft. Drink plenty of water and have as much roughage – fruit, vegetables and extra bran – as you can manage. You may be offered medication to soften the bowel movement.

Bleeding You will continue to lose blood from the vagina for a few days – rather like a heavy period. There may be a few large clots. The loss gradually settles and changes to a brownish color, and this may continue for several weeks. Wear a sanitary pad, not internal tampons. If at any time you are worried about the bleeding, call your doctor.

After pains Low crampy period-like pains are common and more likely with second and later babies. They wear off after a few days, meanwhile pain relievers help.

Breast engorgement Although your baby gets a little fluid (colostrum) right from the start, your main milk supply doesn't start until the second or third day. At this time the breasts swell and feel hard and are often quite painful. Bathing them with warm water is soothing and letting your baby have frequent small feedings can help. Fortunately this initial swelling settles in a few days.

Hospital routine

You may have to adjust to hospital routines to some extent but in general it is better to follow your own and your baby's needs rather than stick to a schedule. Talk to the doctor or head nurse if you have any worries or requests.

It is now unusual for babies to go to the nursery routinely at night but this may be helpful if you are feeling particularly tired. If your baby does go to a nursery at night you can usually ask to be woken to feed her.

Caring for your baby

You may be quite surprised to find that in some hospitals you are expected to look after your baby almost immediately. Ask the nursery nurses to show you how to change her diaper. You will also be shown how to give her a bath.

Feeding

Many babies take readily to sucking on the breast or bottle but your baby may not seem to know what to do and you may feel inadequate. Don't despair too soon as both you and she will gradually improve in ability and confidence. If you are breastfeeding remember that she has very little need for food in the first few days but usually needs lots of sucking. Some babies drop off to sleep quite quickly after starting to suck while others suck for some time. Your baby may wake up frequently for a while but then sleep for several hours. Expect her to lose weight and not regain her birth weight until the second week. Don't hesitate to ask the nursery nurses or pediatrician for help and advice.

Postpartum blues

In the first week or so you may at times feel tearful, miserable and unable to cope. Tiredness and soreness don't help. These "baby blues" may take you by surprise but are not at all uncommon. It is important to try to talk to someone about how you are feeling.

Visiting times provide an opportunity for your partner to share in the wonder of new parenthood.

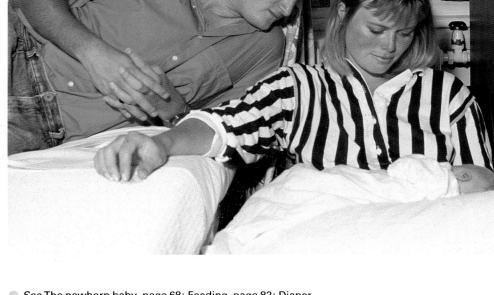

● *See* **The newborn baby, page 68; Feeding, page 82; Diaper changing, page 102; Bathing, page 108; Family life, page 131.**

THE YOUNG BABY

*Once your baby is born she rapidly transforms
your life and inspires your love. As the months pass,
your tiny dependent newborn changes rapidly
as she grows and becomes stronger and more aware.
The excitement and the exhausting chaos of the early
weeks settle down as you grow used to the demands,
and the rewards, of your baby.*

You and your young baby

The passing months deepen your relationship with your baby as you get to know him and all his changing moods.

The months of waiting are over and your baby is here. Immediately you are plunged into one of the most hectic periods of your life, physically and emotionally. This tiny helpless baby, dependent on you for every single thing, has nonetheless managed to change your life forever.

The first few weeks are exhausting, bewildering, sometimes scary and often wonderful. You have to come to terms with your new role as a parent and learn to care for your baby at a time when you are tired and catching up on sleep seems a near impossibility. However, the love for the new member of your family is instinctive and grows with contact, caring and familiarity. From the very beginning you will be surprised by the strength of feeling this little person can engender in you. Picking up a hot damp crying bundle and feeling the sobs subside into contentment against your shoulder can fill you with an overwhelming rush of love. A gentler feeling of emotional satisfaction may be experienced when watching the happy sleepy eyes of your baby feeding. And you can't fail to be moved by the way your baby increasingly regards you, your face and your voice as the most fascinating things in the world.

There will also be the bad moments, when your baby won't stop crying and you find yourself feeling intensely frustrated and even angry. Not knowing what to do to make things better can make you feel rejected by your child and a failure as a parent. And there are times, too, when you may bitterly resent being pulled all ways by too many people, with never a moment to yourself.

Settling down

After the first few weeks things do begin to settle down. You are more confident now that you have got to know your baby better; you are starting to feel a little less tired, and a routine is beginning to emerge. You don't have to think carefully every time you change a diaper, prepare a bottle or give your baby a bath – you now know what you are doing, and caring for your baby comes more easily.

As the weeks pass the pleasures increase – as do the frustrations. Being treated to his irresistible smile is a compensation for the fact that the more he gets to know you the more he wants you all to himself – to spend time playing, chatting, and laughing.

Making progress

The speed at which he develops and gets stronger can be disconcerting. Your once helpless little baby soon learns to roll and shuffle his way into danger, so you have to keep a very close eye on him. In the same way, changing diapers, once a problem of technique, now becomes cause for tact and speed as he waves his arms, bicycles his legs, or simply insists on putting his toes in his mouth.

Once he starts his first tastes of solid foods it can be very funny to watch him try new flavors and textures with all the serious concentration of a judge. First he will slurp desperately at the spoon, then pause and consider his reaction: sometimes his face will pucker with outrage and dismay, or with eager pleasure he will signal his desire for more. He may frustrate or amuse you as he simply opens his mouth, smiles – and lets it all dribble out again, or spits and blows it all over you.

Starting to play

As he gains more control over his movements, he will be interested in toys to hold, shake, and chew. As he nears six months he'll be sitting up with a few cushions to support him, but a sudden movement can make him topple over. He'll give all his concentration to a toy – then drop and forget it instantly when he is offered something else.

But his great love is people – particularly you. You may have long conversations – his contribution may only be babbling, but the urge to communicate is there. Any game that involves talking, laughing and singing will captivate him. In his boisterous moments he'll like to bounce up and down on your knee; in quieter moments he'll love staring into your eyes and touching your face – or molding your nose like a bit of playdough! Towards the end of the six months you may look back and remember with amazement the tiny helpless creature he was as a newborn.

YOU AND YOUR YOUNG BABY

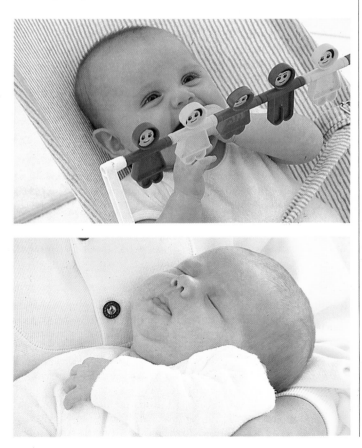

Left You'll find yourself joining in when she chuckles – her increasing sense of fun is irresistible.
Below left He's oblivious to everything but his own contented need for sleep.
Below You can enjoy a good chat with your small baby who'll love being the focus of your attention.

The newborn baby

Coming home from the hospital with your new baby is a big moment, and you will probably feel a mixture of emotions. You may find it a relief to get home, but the knowledge that from now on this little person is in your care can make you rather nervous. It's not just first-time parents who wonder if they will be able to cope: your life with a new baby will inevitably be quite different from before, even if you already have another child or children.

It would be nice if you could arrange for some extra help when you come home. You will benefit from having around someone who can assist with the household routine and, to a certain extent, with the baby as well to give you a chance to rest. If your partner could be at home with you in the early days he would probably enjoy sharing in and learning about the care of your new baby. Your mother, mother-in-law or other relatives would also be ideal. But do make sure that they are really going to be there to help you. If you wish you may even call the Visiting Nurse Association and request a visiting nurse to come to your house. They are experienced in baby care skills, and can show you how to make up formula milk, change diapers, bath your baby and also answer your many questions. Occasionally, you may prefer to hire a private nurse for a few days to help in taking care of your baby's needs so that you may have more time to rest or spend just enjoying your baby while recovering from the childbirth.

During the last two months of your pregnancy, at your prenatal visits, you will have been given the names of pediatricians, the community child health centers and the children's hospitals. Many of you may have already chosen a pediatrician whom you will have met and begun to trust. Your baby's first visit to the doctor will normally take place when he is about two weeks of age.

The early days

Even if you don't have any particular worries (for yourself or the baby) you will probably feel under pressure to begin with. Very few newborn babies are predictable in their feeding and sleeping habits and your baby will probably be no different. Many babies seem to sense the difference between the hospital and home, and they may be unsettled for a few days (and nights!). Try to accept that your baby's somewhat unpredictable, and at times unhappy, behavior is normal, unless you think that he might be ill. Do your best to comfort him when he needs it, but don't imagine that you are at fault in any way for not producing a perfectly contented baby. The early days and weeks are really for you and your baby to get to know each other and your relationship is bound to have its ups and downs, particularly as a baby can only communicate his needs by crying.

It may sometimes appear to you that everyone has set ideas about how you should look after your baby. All new parents have to cope with conflicting advice from profes-

BIRTH CERTIFICATE
Your baby's birth must, by law, be recorded with state authorities. You will be asked, soon after the delivery, for the relevant information including parents' names and citizenship and the baby's name and birth weight. An application will be filed on your behalf with the state central registry. You will then be sent a certified copy of your baby's birth certificate.

See Your day together, page 114; Your baby's health, page 126; Your family life, page 133, for sexual problems after the birth.

sionals and members of the family whose own experiences may mean a lot to them. These people are generally very well-meaning, but ideas and practices do change from one generation to another. You can listen to what people tell you and ask questions, but in the end you must do what you feel is right for you and your baby. So long as you use your common sense and seek advice when you need it, you will be able to cope perfectly well.

Coping with tiredness

All aspects of looking after your baby – washing, feeding, cuddling, and comforting, together with your feelings of responsibility – are much harder to cope with when you're tired. But tiredness is perfectly normal and understandable. You need some time simply to recover from the physical effects of giving birth, especially if you've had a long or difficult labor, or perhaps a cesarean section. Broken nights and exhausting days just add to the problem. Firstly, don't try to be "supermom." Make life easier for yourself by avoiding any housework that is not essential; stick to simple meals and accept any offers of help from your partner, relatives and neighbors. Secondly, grab the chance to rest if you can, and when your baby is asleep during the day use the time to catch up on your own sleep too. It may take time for you to feel relaxed in your new life.

If you're on your own with the baby during the day, make an effort to go out and see people. You may love your baby, but he won't be the most interesting companion all the time – you do need adult company too. Joining a new-parent group is a good way to meet other parents living nearby who have babies of about the same age. They are offered through local Ys, child-development departments of colleges, and some local schools. They are often advertised in local newspapers.

If you ever have the feeling that the problems of new parenthood are outweighing the joys, never try to struggle on bravely. Share your feelings with your partner, parents or a sympathetic friend, and seek professional help if you feel you need to.

WHO CAN HELP?
The La Lèche League has a network of breastfeeding counselors who give practical advice on breastfeeding, *plus* postnatal support groups throughout the country offering friendship within the group or on a one-to-one basis (for useful addresses, *see* page 298).
Mother and baby/mother and toddler groups are often linked with pre-schools, churches and local Ys, or organized independently. Ask your childbirth-preparation instructor or other mothers about these groups.

THE NEWBORN BABY

HOW TO PICK UP YOUR BABY

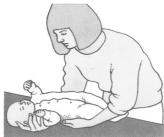

1 Slide one hand underneath your baby's neck and head, and support his back and bottom with your other arm.

2 Continuing to support his head and back, lift the baby very carefully and gently.

Always hold your baby close to your body, as this will make him feel more secure. Be careful that his head doesn't loll back.

What your baby will need

Although your new baby is small, you'll find that all her equipment takes up a lot of space in your house. It is a good idea to do a bit of planning ahead of time so that you feel more organized when your baby arrives. You will probably find that you can throw away many accumulated things. Remember that your baby also needs a clean, smoke-free environment.

Shopping for equipment

Unless you are well informed about the equipment available you may find it difficult to choose wisely and decide what items you really need. There is a difference between a nonessential extra, or luxury item, and one that might not be of any use at all. Make the occasional trip to your local shopping center so that you can see what there is before buying any major pieces of equipment. You can also ask friends and family what they found useful.

Shopping for baby equipment can be quite enjoyable. Manufacturers aim to combine practicality and safety with smartness and style, and this means that you can pick items that you'll feel happy to look at as well as use every day. Even if you can't afford to buy co-ordinated equipment and accessories, you could buy some fabric to cover items so that they complement the decor of your baby's room.

The most expensive equipment you can afford is not necessarily the best. The price of nursery goods reflects more than just the quality of craftsmanship. You may also be paying for fashion styling, range of colors, clever design, practicality – even exclusivity. You will need to assess which aspects of the item are important to you and your lifestyle, as well as your budget. However, if you intend having more than one child, you should also think about whether the cheapest in a range of goods will see you through and remain in reasonable condition.

Your baby's room

Although it is traditional to have a nursery for a newborn baby, few people these days have a large enough house with a spare room to transform into a bedroom-playroom for a child or children. In most families, a new baby either has her own small bedroom or a corner of her parents' room, which is her base for the first few weeks or months. Whether your baby sleeps in your room or her own, it's useful – though not absolutely essential – to have a place for changing her diaper near to where she sleeps, as well as somewhere to store diapers and clothing.

Planning and decorating

Of course it's fun to decorate your baby's room, but don't worry if you don't get around to it. Babies are not concerned with smart new wallpaper or paint. The main thing is to make sure her room is clean, warm and free from drafts.

If you have time and want to make the baby's room look attractive, you can choose from a wide range of papers and soft furnishings which are available at reasonable prices. You can buy matching fabrics and wallpapers in pastel or primary colors, which look bright and fresh and will suit your child better as she grows up than large prints of bunnies or teddies. You could paint the woodwork in pastel or primary colors too, as a change from white.

Plain white paint can look very effective on the walls, or you could choose a white paint with just a hint of color. This makes a good background for any pictures or wall borders you put up. Paint is easier to keep clean than wallpaper and this is worth considering, as the wall nearest the crib is bound to get marked once your baby is able to stand up and touch it. You can get washable wallpapers, although these are usually more expensive. *Always* use lead-free paint for a child's room, and check that other surfaces are nontoxic.

Whatever decor you decide on, don't forget to take into account the colors of your baby's bedding. If it has a bold pattern which is a decorative feature in itself, it may be better to keep walls and other accessories plain.

It is worth considering washable tiles for the floor, which give a good flat surface or an easy-to-shampoo carpet for your baby to play on later when she becomes mobile.

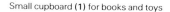

Small cupboard (**1**) for books and toys

Comfortable chair (**2**) or rocking chair for you to sit on

Brightly colored wall border and pictures (**3**)

Toy box with lid (**4**) for large toys

Crib mobile (**5**)

Sturdy crib (**6**) with safe drop-side mechanism

Table (**7**) for night-light or lamp

Open-shelf unit (**8**) for keeping baby creams, tissues and other toiletries

Low chest of drawers (**9**) for clothes and diapers, and as a stable surface for changing your baby's diaper

Right Your baby's bedroom may be where you change her diaper and bath her too. In any case it makes sense to keep all her things in one place. Simple storage units – spanned by a washable worktop – are a good idea in the nursery, and can be adapted to suit the needs of your growing child.

● *See* What your child will need, page 183, for the toddler's room.

NURSERY ACCESSORIES
You can brighten up your baby's room with a colorful peg board, a decorative border, a mobile or a nursery lamp.

Lighting
Make sure that the baby's crib and changing area are not directly under an overhead light. It is a good idea to have a dim bedside lamp or wall light, so that you can feed and change your baby at night without disturbing her too much. A light that is operated with a dimmer switch might be useful here.

Heating
A newborn baby is not able to regulate her own body temperature very well. You need to make sure that her room is kept warm during the day and night, and that when she is asleep she has sufficient bedding to help her maintain her body warmth. From the beginning the room temperature needs to be maintained at about 68°F for a baby of average weight, say between about 5 and 8 pounds. After a few weeks, when the baby is better able to regulate her own temperature and is beginning to get a layer of fat to help her keep warm, the temperature of the room she sleeps in can go down to about 60°F.

If you use an electric or kerosene heater, or you have an open fire, you must use a fireguard. Don't ever wash your baby or change her diaper in a room that is not warm enough – taking her from a cosy crib to the colder air could chill her rapidly. It is far better to take her – and any washing or changing equipment that you need – to the living room or kitchen if it is warmer there.

Storage
The baby's equipment can rapidly clutter up the room if you don't think about where to put it when it's not in use. You can buy a baby dresser with drawers (*see* page 79), but a small chest of drawers is also ideal for a baby's room. If you paint it to match the color scheme of the room, it can look very attractive. You could also mount a few shelves on the wall and use them to store toiletries and other small items in regular use.

A wardrobe is rather a waste of space for young children, whose clothes are usually small enough to fold (on shelves or in drawers) rather than hang. If drawer space is short, you can put garments on hangers and string them up on a cloth line held between two wall hooks. Storing toys doesn't usually present a problem immediately, but as your child gets older you will have to think about it.

● *See* Safety around the house, page 290, for other safety points.

Daytime

After the first few weeks your baby will appreciate being somewhere that is comfortable and where she can see what is going on around her. A mobile attached to the side of her crib, or a row of toys strung across her carriage or bouncing chair, will give her something to focus on and play with. You can, of course, carry a small baby around with you in a sling (*see* page 78), but it is not always practical to do this.

It is not a good idea to prop up a young baby on a sofa or chair unless you're going to stay with her the whole time to make sure she doesn't fall or slump. An essential item at this stage is some kind of baby chair or bouncing cradle, but remember that the floor is the *only* safe place to put your

Low chair
A versatile adjustable chair like this, with a removable tray, can be used once your baby is a month old. With its own stand it converts to a swing or a smart and practical highchair (*see* page 143). Your baby will need a separate harness to strap her in.

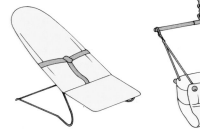

Bouncing cradle
From about three weeks old babies may enjoy reclining in a bouncing cradle. If you rock the cradle gently for your baby, she will soon learn that by kicking she can make it bounce too. You can also buy a clip-on toy for your baby to play with. Some cradles can be adjusted from reclining to almost upright.

Baby bouncer
This is an extra which may help to keep your baby amused. It can be hung up in a doorway from its own steel clamp and your baby can bounce in it for short periods. Don't put a baby in a bouncer before she has good head and back control, and *never* leave her unattended.

Playpen
The traditional playpen is the square wooden type (shown here). It should have a built-in floor, so that the baby can't move it around. Mesh-sided playpens, circular or rectangular, are light and easy to assemble. They have a raised floor and a padded rim. Both types of playpen can be bought in a folding design and used indoors and outside. Be sure to check for built-in safety features.

baby in one of these (*see* Safety, right).

After a couple of months your baby will enjoy the freedom of lying on a rug or mat on the floor, kicking her legs and waving her arms. Once she can wriggle and roll over, it's not safe to leave her on her own. Her newly developed skills make her surprisingly mobile and she could get herself into an uncomfortable position.

Some of the equipment on this page can only be used for a short time as your baby will grow out of it in a matter of months. You should bear this in mind when you're deciding what to buy. A chair or cradle is the most necessary item, but you may find a playpen useful as your baby becomes more mobile. Baby bouncers and walkers can be fun but not all babies like them.

SAFETY
● Never use bouncing cradles or baby chairs on a raised surface, such as a table or worktop.
● Never leave a baby unsupervised in a baby bouncer.
● Make quite sure that your baby is properly strapped into any baby chair or bouncing cradle.

See Feeding your baby, page 92, for bottles and sterilizing equipment.

Somewhere to sleep

Young babies are not fussy about where they sleep, so take advantage of this in the early days and let your baby sleep in her crib, bassinet or carriage, wherever she is happiest during the day. In the first few months, your baby is quite safe sleeping in a port-a-crib or carriage during the day and night, as she won't be able to fall or climb out. You may decide to have her in your own room at night as this makes feeding easier for you, particularly if you are breastfeeding. However, you might find that you sleep better if your baby is in her own room right from the start. If you are worried that you won't hear her, you can use a baby alarm – an intercom system that enables you to hear when she starts to cry. A compromise is to share your room with her while she's still small enough for a bassinet or port-a-crib, and then move her into her own room when she is ready to graduate to a full-sized crib. By this time she may need a little less attention and comfort at night.

Some parents aim to make a distinction between day and night right from the beginning by using the port-a-crib or

Baby's first bed
You may prefer to put your newborn baby into a bassinet, cradle or baby basket for cosiness. These "first beds" can be taken from room to room without disturbing the baby. A portable bassinet (or carriage top) serves this purpose too. Rocking cradles, wicker bassinets and baby baskets have a particular charm for some people. You can buy a stand for your baby basket, but make sure it fits. Do remember to check safety points on cribs and cradles that are second-hand (see above). Carriage bedding fits most of these "first beds," but you may have to buy a mattress.

Cribs
Cribs vary greatly in price. The more ornate ones tend to be the most expensive, and though they may look more attractive, there is little difference in the quality if you buy a reliable make. A drawer (or drawers) underneath the crib is a useful extra, or you can buy a separate drawer that will slide under most standard cribs. A crib with an adjustable base height means that you can use the mattress at its highest position

when your baby is very young. This position is also useful as a changing and dressing top for the baby, saving you too much bending down. Once the baby is more active – and before she can sit up – you should lower the base of the crib to its full depth so that she cannot easily climb out.

Many cribs also have a drop-side mechanism, which allows one side to be lowered for lifting the baby in and out, and to make it easier to make the crib up.

Mattresses
Make sure the crib mattress you buy is waterproof, at least on one side. A sprung interior mattress with bound edges is more expensive than a basic plastic-covered foam rectangle, but it has the advantage of lasting longer. You can also buy a crib mattress which is reversible (both sides are waterproof) and has air vents at one end. Most cribs and mattresses are of a standard size, but you will need to be quite sure you are buying the correct mattress for your crib, especially if it is second-hand. Check that there is no gap between mattress and frame where a baby could trap an arm or leg.

carriage as a "day bed" and putting the baby into a bassinet or crib at night. This will not necessarily encourage the baby to make the same distinction – and therefore sleep longer at night – but the arrangement may suit your family. It is also useful when you need to go out of the house: a sleeping baby who is already in the portable bassinet or carriage need not be disturbed – you can wheel or carry her right outside.

You may find a port-a-crib useful if you go visiting regularly, or have guests with babies staying. They are light, easy to carry and can be folded flat for packing. Most of them include a mattress.

Choosing a crib

All full-size cribs made in the United States must meet mandatory safety standards issued by the Consumer Product Safety Commission in 1973 (see Crib safety, left). If your baby's crib has been passed down within the family, or bought second-hand, you need to check certain safety features carefully. The crib should not have any horizontal bars (for example, with playbeads on them), which could be used as "steps" by an older baby who tries to get out of her crib. The drop-side mechanism on the crib is not safe if it is the old-fashioned sort with a large round-headed screw at the top – older babies and toddlers could get their clothes caught on it and there have been tragic cases where a child was strangled as a result. Make sure also that your baby cannot operate the drop-side mechanism herself. Check that the bars on the crib are close enough together to prevent the baby's head from getting stuck in between them, but wide enough not to trap limbs – and that all bars, particularly on a well-used crib, are firmly attached to the frame. Paintwork should be nontoxic, and there should be no decorative transfers on the inside of the crib.

You can buy a larger crib that converts to a child-sized bed. This can be a good buy, but if you plan to have another child, bear in mind that you will need to buy another crib for the new baby because your first child will be using the crib as a bed.

Bedding for the crib

Crib sheets can be made from old bed sheets, but if you are going to buy new ones you may feel it's worth paying extra for fitted sheets. You can get fitted stretch sheets which make bed-making easy and give your child a smooth and comfortable surface to lie on. A machine-washable comforter is a good buy as it's both warm and lightweight and you don't need a blanket with it. If you do use blankets, choose machine-washable ones for convenience. The covers for comforters come in very attractive prints and colors, although you may prefer to choose your own fabric and make a cover yourself. You can buy Velcro tape (for the open end) in the fabric department of a large store. Crib bumpers (*see* right) can be bought or made. If you make one yourself, check that the padding you use is clean and washable. A young baby should not have a pillow to sleep on; wait until she is at least a year old.

WHAT YOUR BABY WILL NEED

CHOOSING BEDDING

Sheets You will need at least half a dozen crib sheets. Sheets are available in cotton, cotton mix and flannel. Fitted sheets that give a neat finish on the bottom are also available in stretch terrycloth.

Blankets/comforters In winter your baby will need two blankets – or a blanket and comforter – to keep her warm. You'll need spare blankets for when they need washing.

Duvet A crib comforter and cover make a good alternative to blankets and quilts. You'll need at least two covers for the comforter.

Crib bumper This is a slim cushion which lines the insides of the crib and protects a baby from drafts and from banging her hands or head if she moves around in the crib.

MAKING UP A CRIB

If you are using a duvet, your baby will need just a bottom sheet. Very small babies may like to be wrapped in a receiving blanket, with a comforter on top. A crib bumper will protect your baby from bumps and drafts.

Out and about

When presented with the wide range of baby transporters available, prospective parents often wonder which is the best choice. Some kind of carriage or stroller is obviously a necessity for your baby and, since it's also a major item of expenditure, give it careful thought before you go out and buy one. Basically, the choice lies between a carriage (or carriage body plus detachable chassis) and a fully reclining lie-back stroller. If you choose a carriage, it can double as a bed for the baby during the day at least. It's worth noting that a carriage or portable bassinet can be made warm and cosy very easily – the high sides protect the baby from the wind and drafts, and this could be an important consideration if you're expecting a baby in the winter. You can also buy a portable bassinet that clips onto a reclining stroller (*see* 3-in-1, right).

Later on, when your baby is too big for the carriage, you'll need a stroller. This is lighter and more maneuverable, and all types can be folded down for carrying or fitting into the trunk of a car. Strollers that are fully reclining, or those that have their own clip-on bassinet bodies, can be used for very young babies (who need to be laid flat), so you could use this instead of a carriage (*see* safety note, left). Strollers that don't recline fully should be kept until your baby is able to sit up.

It is a good idea to test the different types of carriages or strollers in the shop. Wheel them across the floor, checking that the height of the handle is comfortable for you. You should also check the safety harness (*see* right). Make sure the brake is secure: it should be a safety brake controlling two wheels.

If you choose a stroller with swivel front wheels, make sure it has a dual-link brake so that both rear wheels brake together (this prevents the stroller from swinging round and tipping over). Try folding the stroller: it should be simple, and have a primary and secondary safety mechanism to prevent the stroller from folding up accidentally with your child in it. An extra safety precaution is reflective discs on the wheels to make you conspicuous in bad light.

Bedding for carriage and portable bassinet

A mattress is normally included with the carriage or portable bassinet that you buy but, if not, you can buy one separately. Your baby must not have a pillow to sleep on, but you may want one for her to lean against when you prop her up. You can buy or make your own carriage sheets: you'll need at least three or four – more if your baby uses the carriage or portable bassinet to sleep in all the time. You may need a waterproof sheet if the carriage mattress doesn't have a waterproof cover. You can fold crib-sized blankets to fit the carriage or simply buy carriage blankets. You'll need at least two, including a top cover or quilt. A carriage comforter serves the purpose of both blanket and top cover and should be quite warm enough on its own most of the time, especially if you also wrap your baby in a receiving blanket when she is very small.

WHAT YOUR BABY WILL NEED

Carriage and chassis
A carriage with detachable body and carrying straps, or a portable bassinet plus transporter, is the modern alternative to the traditional hard-bodied coach-built carriage. The bassinet can be used separately, and the transporter folds down for carrying and storing. When buying, make sure that the body fits securely onto the transporter, and that it has harness rings. If you need to separate top from bottom regularly check that it is not too heavy to carry.

3-in-1 stroller
The combined carriage/bassinet/stroller is excellent value. You can use the bassinet for your baby and then move her into the stroller seat when she is older. With some models, the stroller seat can be adjusted from upright to fully reclined, facing backwards or forwards, whichever is the preferred position.

Reclining stroller
This type of stroller folds down easily and can be carried and stored rather like an umbrella, which makes it very convenient when you're traveling. Check the width of the seat (the wider it is, the longer your child will be able to use it in comfort). It can be reclined for the sleeping baby and is suitable for a younger baby who is more comfortable lying back. Although this stroller is quite expensive, it may be worth the cost if you plan to use it often.

Basic stroller
A basic one-position fold-up stroller like this is an inexpensive alternative to the more sophisticated models. Despite its lack of extra features it is perfectly adequate. It has a safe folding action and can be useful to keep in the trunk of the car, or at the grandparents', if you need a spare. You can buy a hood and visor for this stroller.

Maintenance
● All strollers should be checked regularly – tighten screws, nuts and bolts if necessary.
● Lubricate all moving parts sparingly.

Carriage and stroller accessories
Although many of these items are nonessential extras, you may find them useful. You'll certainly need a carriage net to protect your baby from animals and insects, especially if you put her carriage outside in summer. A canopy – for carriage or stroller – is not essential, but it does help shade your baby from the sun. If you have a stroller, an alternative is an umbrella that clips onto the frame or seat.

You may be able to get a shopping tray or basket for your carriage or stroller, and this is a much safer way of carrying heavy shopping bags than over the handles. A carriage seat can be practical if you have an older child, but do make sure it fits your carriage model as it could upset the carriage if it's not secure. Check that it has rings for a safety harness too. A plastic play and feeding tray can be bought for some strollers. For wet weather protection you will need a hood and visor (or zip-up cover) for the stroller, and a small blanket around her legs will keep your baby cosy.

SAFETY HARNESS
This is an essential item and you may need more than one – for the highchair, carriage and stroller.

Safety in the car

When you take your small baby out in the car she should travel in her own child safety seat. There are three major types: infant, convertible, or booster.

Either an infant or a convertible seat (not to be confused with a toddler seat, *see* page 141) is suitable for a very young baby. In the car the infant or convertible seat can be fitted on the front passenger seat or on one of the rear seats, anchored to the car by the car's safety belt. (NOTE: No car seat – no matter what type or model – should ever be used in the front seat of cars equipped with two-point automatic safety belts. As of 1988, cars with those types of automatic belts must be equipped with a special hole to permit the easy installation of a lap belt.)

Whether it is being used in the front or rear of the car, the infant seat always faces the rear. The convertible type seat faces rearward in a reclining position until the baby is old enough to sit up. Then the frame should be adjusted upright and the seat turned to face forward. Convertible seats can be used from infancy until the child weighs 40 pounds. Purchasing a convertible seat can save you the expense of buying both an infant and toddler seat. Toddler seats are for children between 20 and 60 pounds, depending on the type of seat you buy (*see* page 141). (NOTE: Safety experts advise buying or renting only seats made after January 1, 1981.)

Baby carrier/sling
A sling or baby carrier is very useful for carrying your baby around, both indoors and out. She will enjoy being close to you and feeling the warmth of your body. A tiny baby will need a carrier with a head support, but this can be detached as she grows and can hold up her head.

When your baby is in a carrier, make sure that she's well wrapped up in cold weather.

Backpack
When your baby can support her own head you can either wear the baby carrier on your back, or use a "kiddy" carrier. This is worn like a backpack and even quite heavy toddlers can be carried in it. Check that it has rings for a separate safety harness.

When buying any sort of carrier, make sure it is comfortable for you and your baby, and is easy to put on and take off.

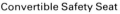

Convertible Safety Seat
This can be used for babies from birth up to 40 pounds in weight. Convertible seats come in several basic models: the primary difference between them being the design of the harness. The simplest and easiest to use are generally those with a harness/

partial shield. These have a small pad joining the shoulder belts and require only one buckle to secure your child. It is vital that the straps fit snugly over your child's shoulders. The safest place for your child's car seat is in the center position of the back seat.

Bathing and changing

You will need to think about equipment for bathing your baby and changing her diapers. A baby bath is not absolutely essential because you can use the big bath, even for tiny babies, but it is probably easier and more comfortable for you and the baby if you use something smaller. A large plastic basin on the table or the floor is a possibility to begin with and when your baby has outgrown this, you can move her to the big bath. By this time you'll be more confident in your handling of her, and bending over to wash a small wriggly baby won't be quite so difficult. The majority of people do opt for a baby bath tub and use it for the first five or six months, or until the baby can sit up by herself. There are several types of baby bath tub to choose from. One of the most popular is made of rigid plastic, molded to support the baby's head and back, and with a slip-resistant surface. Placed on a solid surface (perhaps in the kitchen where it is also warm) you can bath your baby at a comfortable height.

For diaper changing, you'll need almost the same equipment, whether you choose to use cloth diapers, disposables or both. However, if you are using cloth diapers, you will need at least one bucket for soaking them.

It makes life easier if you have everything you need to change your baby's diaper in one place. A neat and useful piece of equipment is a baby dressing and storage unit (which includes a changing mat). Bear in mind, however, that you may not be able to use the changing top for very long. As your baby gets bigger, and more active, you may prefer to change her on your lap or on the floor on a separate changing mat.

WHAT YOUR BABY WILL NEED

SAFETY
● Never leave your baby alone in the bath, even for a few seconds.
● When changing your baby on a changing top, or on any raised surface, have everything you need at hand, so that you don't need to turn away from her. She could roll or slide off and be harmed.

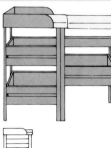

Dresser
A flat-topped unit with drawers can be used for changing your baby's diaper and for storing her clothes. It folds up when not in use.

Changing mat
For changing your baby's diaper on the floor or on a raised surface, a waterproof wipe-clean changing mat is useful. It can also be used when you are sponge bathing (see page 111) your baby or for her to kick on after the bath.

Bathtime accessories
For face washing and for sponge bathing you can use a small bowl with two compartments for water – one for the face and one for the body – or you can fill one with water and put the used absorbent cotton in the other. Buckets with tight fitting lids are needed for soaking soiled cloth diapers.

See Diaper changing, pages 102-107, and Bathing your baby, pages 108-111.

First clothes

You'll be quite surprised at the amount of clothing a newborn baby will need. In addition to this, it's not unusual to have to give a new baby two, or even three, changes of clothes a day, because her diaper has leaked or she has been sick or spit up.

For a basic layette (new baby's wardrobe) you really do need at least four of everything – undershirts or bodysuits, stretchsuits, sweaters or jackets, and nightgowns if you wish. If you do decide on a nightgown for night wear, you will need a couple of pairs of booties too (unless you buy a nightgown with a drawstring hem). This basic wardrobe is suitable for a winter or summer baby, although on very warm days your baby won't, of course, need a sweater on top of her stretchsuit.

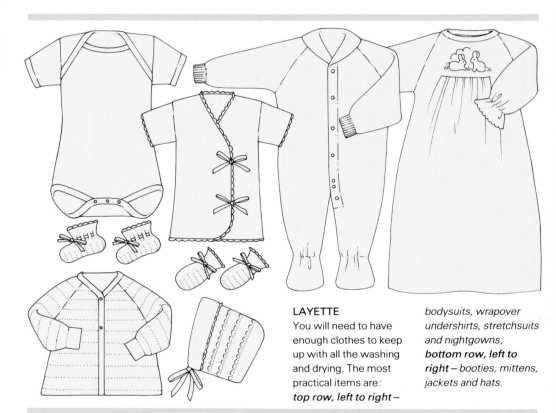

LAYETTE
You will need to have enough clothes to keep up with all the washing and drying. The most practical items are:
top row, left to right – bodysuits, wrapover undershirts, stretchsuits and nightgowns; ***bottom row, left to right** – booties, mittens, jackets and hats.*

In addition to the basics, you'll need waterproof pants (if your baby is wearing cloth diapers) and again you'll find that four is the minimum number. The quality of waterproof pants is reflected in the price you pay – the more expensive kinds always last longer. You may also find a blanket handy; many new babies like to be snuggled up in one when carried or laid down to sleep.

For outside wear your baby will need at least one warm hat. You may or may not need booties and mittens for her as it depends on what else she has on. If your baby is going to wear a stretchsuit most of the time, her feet will be warm enough without booties (except when she is in a carrier or stroller) and, similarly, if you choose stretchsuits with turn-over cuffs you'll only need one pair of mittens rather than two. You could choose a hooded bunting or blanket bag (which zips up the front and is easier to use for a small baby than a snowsuit), or a warm wool jacket with tights or leggings.

Any additional clothing comes under "welcome extras." New babies can wear the same clothes day and night, so you don't need to buy nightgowns. Although playsuits and pretty dresses look attractive, leave it to other people to buy them as presents if you want to save money.

Dressing and undressing

Most young babies dislike having clothing taken over their heads, so garments that fasten down the front (as opposed to ones you pull on or which fasten at the neckline or shoulder) are less trouble. Undershirts that tie at the side are best for tiny babies. Slightly older babies can wear over-the-head type undershirts but, for preference, choose those with an envelope neckline. Zippers or other openings down the front of a garment should be generous enough so that you don't have to bend the baby's legs double to get her into it. Pull-up garments with legs, such as playsuits, are easier to put on your baby if they have a row of snaps up the inside of each leg, so that you don't have to take the whole thing off every time you change her diaper.

Growing into new clothes

By the time your baby is three to four months old, she will probably need some new clothes. It's not just that she will have outgrown some of the garments that seemed so big for her when she was just born; the season may well have changed, too, and she may need clothes that are more suitable for the time of year, especially as she will be spending more time awake and out of her crib or carriage. A blanket (which the growing active baby simply wriggles out of) will have to be replaced by warm garments in cold weather. A snowsuit is a good buy for autumn and winter, and she'll need mittens (if you haven't already bought some) and socks and/or booties if her snowsuit doesn't have feet. A sunhat is important in hot weather, and lightweight short-sleeved or sleeveless dresses or rompers are cooler in summer than stretchsuits (though do be careful – your baby's delicate skin will burn very easily in hot sun).

By the time your baby is about four months old, she will almost certainly have grown out of her first-size undershirts and will need some larger ones (again, four is the minimum number). Although her stretchsuits may appear to fit her still, do check that there is plenty of room in the feet, so that her toes are not cramped. She may now need to go up a size. The number of suits you buy will depend on what else you've bought or acquired since her birth. The most useful rule-of-thumb is still to make sure your baby has at least four sets of clothing in total.

WASHING CLOTHES

● Wherever possible, choose machine-washable garments for your baby. If she has any handknitted clothes, ask whoever knitted them to save a tag from the yarn, as this will give the washing instructions. Many baby yarns are machine washable nowadays.

● Delicate hand-knits in lacy patterns may need special care, however. Hand wash them in warm (not hot) soapy water, then rinse. Blot the garment with a towel to soak up excess water and dry it flat. Spin drying in an automatic dryer can spoil the shape and make the yarn matted.

● Hand-washed garments need to be carefully and thoroughly rinsed to get rid of any traces of detergent or soap, which could irritate your baby's skin.

● When machine washing tiny items, such as socks, mittens or booties, put them into a pillowcase so that they don't get caught up or lost in the workings of the machine.

WHAT YOUR BABY WILL NEED

● *See* Diaper changing, page 106, for how to dress your baby.

Feeding your baby

A newborn baby needs food, warmth and comfort. Being fed in the arms of someone who enjoys caring for him can satisfy all of these basic needs together, which is probably why some babies are happiest feeding little and often, all day long. Although these requirements may seem simple, not all babies are so easily satisfied all of the time. Whether you decide to breastfeed, bottlefeed or combine the two methods, it may take several weeks rather than days for the baby to settle into a predictable pattern of feeding. In the early days feedings can take an hour or more – from the time the baby is picked up for a feeding until he is put back down for a nap. Babies will wake during the night for feedings and as they get older for comfort too. Most babies go through unsettled spells from time to time when they want feeding frequently, and small babies who are developing and changing all the time are generally less predictable than older ones. You will therefore find that much of the time spent with your newborn baby will be feeding him.

In the first year (however early the baby is weaned), breast milk or formula will be the major item of your baby's diet and it is important that you think about which method of feeding will suit both of you best, and for how long.

What is the choice?

There are in fact three choices of feeding method – you can breastfeed, bottlefeed or combine the two. If this is your first child, you will discover that babies have very definite personalities and there is really no method of feeding – nor indeed babycare – which will guarantee you a peaceful baby who sleeps soundly all night and gurgles happily all day. The right choice of how to feed is the one that suits you and your baby best. If you are not satisfied with one method of feeding and want to change to the other, bear in mind that it is easier to change from breast to bottle than from bottle to breast. This is one reason why it is well worth trying breastfeeding first.

Breastfeeding

There is no doubt that breastfeeding is the most natural method of feeding your baby. Throughout pregnancy your breasts will adapt so that lactation (the production of milk) can begin when the baby starts to feed. After the birth they produce milk when it is needed, although they will gradually produce less and less if the baby is not given the breast to suck.

Breast milk contains the perfect balance of nutrients, as well as antibodies to help protect against infection. A breastfed baby is better able to fight off the germs which cause stomach upsets and it is believed that breast milk provides some protection against allergy. In fact, where there is a family history of asthma, eczema or food allergy the mother is often encouraged to breastfeed for at least the first few months to lower the risk of an allergy developing.

Apart from health reasons, the advantage of breastfeeding from the mother's point of view is that it is very convenient and most satisfying – breast milk is readily available for the baby, it is always the right temperature and it is sterile, so requires no preparation by the mother.

The hardest part of breastfeeding is at the beginning when both you and your baby are trying to get the hang of a new skill. However, with the help of an experienced and sympathetic nurse or friend, your confidence will increase and breastfeeding should be well established in a week or two. Once the baby is feeding well and putting on weight, it does get easier and you may even find that breastfeeding is a source of pleasure – just let yourself relax and enjoy being close to your baby.

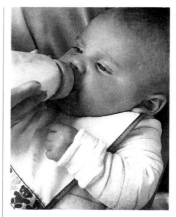

Bottlefeeding

Although most mothers are able to breastfeed (it is rare for a woman to be advised not to breastfeed for medical reasons), not everyone wants to. You may have been put off by someone else's bad experience, but do remember that almost all breastfeeding problems can be prevented or made better with the right professional help. Some women feel embarrassed at the thought of breastfeeding and prefer not to try. Whatever the reason, if you feel tense or frightened it makes it difficult for the baby to feed. Although the milk can still be produced, it is prevented from entering the milk ducts (in the same way that your voice may dry up if you are asked to speak in public).

There is no need to feel guilty if you choose not to breastfeed. After all, it is the care and affection that you give your baby that is important, not just the feed, and these emotional needs can be satisfied just as well while bottlefeeding. Preparing the formula is quite simple and, with practice, not nearly as time-consuming as it might seem at first. Your partner can be involved in feeding the baby too and you will be able to take turns at getting up in the night to give the baby his bottle.

Bottlefed babies can thrive just as well as breastfed babies, but don't expect them to sleep through the night from an early age or to demand any less comforting than breastfed babies. Too often the many normal problems of tiny babies are blamed on the method of feeding and a mother will switch from breast to bottle or from one brand of formula to another quite needlessly.

Breast and bottle

You don't have to choose between breastfeeding and bottlefeeding – you can do both. You may find that the combination suits your lifestyle better, or you may be returning to full- or part-time work before the baby is six months old (when you will have to leave him for several hours during the day) and will probably have to bottlefeed as well as breastfeed anyway. However, don't allow your milk supply to dry up before your baby is weaned onto a bottle; express some breast milk for him instead. Once you start to give your baby bottles of made-up or formula milk regularly, you must be prepared for your supply of breast milk to decrease.

FEEDING YOUR BABY

WHEN TO FEED?

Most babies develop a feeding pattern if they are allowed to, but it won't necessarily be every three or four hours. It is a mistake, therefore, to take routine or demand feeding too seriously. If you let a baby cry for too long between feedings, he may end up too tired to suck properly. On the other hand, if you wait for your baby to ask, you will never get anything done. Feeding times should be times when you can concentrate wholeheartedly on feeding. If this means waking your baby a bit early or leaving him for a little longer while you get something to eat, then do so. If your baby seems to want feeding all the time but is gaining weight well, make a note of his daily feeds – you may not be feeding him as often as you think. Are you letting him have a full feeding each time or are you letting yourself get distracted? A wakeful baby may keep asking for the breast or bottle simply because he likes sucking. A pacifier may be the answer.

See Your baby's health, page 126.

Breastfeeding

From the very beginning of pregnancy your body is preparing to nourish the newborn baby. You will notice several changes in your breasts as they prepare for feeding. This is because the glands in the breast increase in number and size ready for the production of milk. After the birth the firm sucking action of the baby on the nipple stimulates the milk glands to produce milk. The earlier and more frequent the sucking in the first few days, the more easily and successfully breastfeeding will be established.

Preparing for breastfeeding

The best way to prepare for breastfeeding is to watch a baby being breastfed, so make a point of observing friends or relatives feeding their babies whenever you can. Apart from this, keep your breasts clean and comfortable. Avoid using soap on your nipples as this will make them sore and remove the natural lubricating oils which help to keep the nipple clean as well as supple. When you start feeding, you can put a little lanolin or breast cream on the nipples to protect them and keep them soft.

You can also check to see if your nipples stick out when you touch them. If one or both of them fail to respond then speak to your doctor at your next prenatal visit. She may suggest that you wear a special plastic shell inside your bra to help draw out the nipple. Flat or inverted nipples often right themselves after the baby is born.

Nursing bras
You don't have to wear a bra if you don't want to, but you will feel more comfortable if your breasts are supported. Make sure the bra fits properly: cotton is the best material as it allows the skin to breathe, whereas nylon is less absorbent. A front-opening nursing bra is ideal for breastfeeding and the bottom hooks can be left undone during the later weeks of pregnancy when your belly is highest. If you buy a bra with a flap cup, check that there are no constricting seams. After the birth you will need an adjustable bra that can be let out at the back as your breasts will swell and soften during the day. If the bra becomes too tight when the breasts are full, you may risk damaging some of the milk ducts, which can be painful. Breast pads worn inside the bra help control leaking and prevent chafing (*see* problems, page 90).

How breast milk is made

Apart from a little milk which collects in the ducts between feedings, most of the milk a baby takes is made during the feeding itself. The warmth and pressure of the baby's mouth around the nipple stimulates the milk glands to produce milk. Then a reflex response prompted by the brain – the "let-down" reflex – triggers the release of the milk into the ducts. Some women feel the let-down reflex as a warm tingling sensation.

HOW THE BREASTS PRODUCE MILK

At the birth of your baby, hormonal changes take place in your body and the main milk-producing hormone – prolactin – is released into the bloodstream. This affects the "let-down" reflex which controls the flow of milk from the breasts. As the baby sucks at your breast, squeezing the areola (**1**), the dark area around the nipple, a message is sent to the brain which stimulates the milk glands (**2**) to produce milk. This is released into the milk ducts (**3**) and collects in the reservoirs (**4**) behind the nipple, where the baby can obtain it as he feeds.

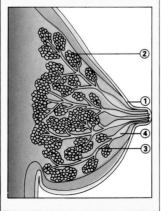

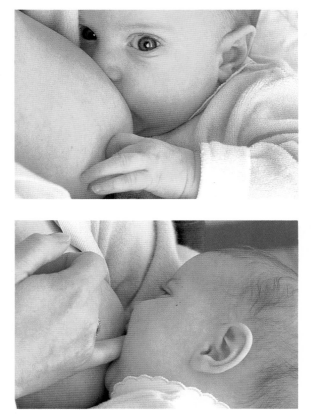

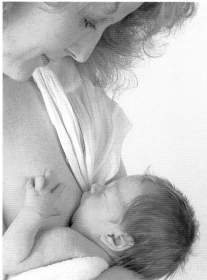

Getting started

The sooner breastfeeding starts the better. The baby's sucking reflex is greatest shortly after birth so make the most of his desire to suck. There are two important requirements for producing milk: the mother must feel comfortable and relaxed, and the baby must have the nipple positioned well inside his mouth so that the let-down reflex is triggered. At first the whole process can feel rather awkward but the more you practice the easier it becomes. Hold the baby in your arms with his head up and cradled in the crook of your elbow, with your hand supporting his bottom. If you are nursing in bed, you can lie the baby facing you, with his head on the crook of your elbow. Direct the nipple at the baby's nose and let it (or your finger) gently brush the baby's cheek. He will then automatically turn his face in the direction of the cheek that was touched and search for the nipple. This is called the "rooting" reflex. If a baby is delayed from sucking (maybe due to illness in you or your baby) for half a day or more, this reflex is weakened and it is sometimes difficult to get the baby to take the breast. In this situation make sure that you have someone (preferably a nurse) with you at each feeding to help the baby to latch onto the breast until he gets the hang of it. When you want to end the feeding, either insert your finger lightly into the baby's mouth between his gums or press on his chin gently to release the vacuum and his hold on your nipple.

Top left *Make sure that your nipple is well inside your baby's mouth so that he can feed properly.*
Above left *To stop the baby sucking, insert your finger between his gums so that the nipple is released gently.*
Above *If a baby is sucking well, you will see her ears move in time with the muscle actions of the jaw and cheeks.*

First feedings

For the first two to three days your baby may not be particularly hungry (he is born with some reserves of fat) so he may not cry to be fed. However, you should still pick him up and let him suck at least every three to four hours for as long as is comfortable. Frequent short feedings of just a few minutes each side are kindest to inexperienced nipples, and the more practice you and your baby get the easier it will be when breastfeeding starts in earnest. At this stage you will also be supplying him with colostrum – a yellowish liquid which is rich in nutrients, contains antibodies for fighting infection and prepares the baby's digestive system for the milk when it "comes in".

When the milk "comes in"

Two to three days after the birth you will probably find that your breasts are uncomfortably hard and swollen (fortunately this engorgement doesn't last more than a day or two). It is the time when the colostrum in your breasts is gradually replaced by milk and the best way to reduce the swelling is to encourage the baby to feed. At about this time your baby will have discovered what it is to feel hungry and he will be impatient for the breast. However, painful breasts, a crying baby, tiredness after the emotion of the birth and constant interruptions from visitors can make you feel that breastfeeding is more trouble than it is worth. Just remember that this is the worst stage – it should get better from now on. If possible find a private place, like the hospital nursery, or simply turn and sit facing a wall so that you can concentrate on letting your baby feed without distraction. You may find it helps if you lean forward and gently stroke the breasts downwards towards the nipples to release a little milk. This will soften the nipple so that your baby can latch on to it more easily. A warm shower or warm washcloths on your breasts will also help. The nurse may suggest that you take a couple of pain-relieving tablets if your breasts are particularly tender.

Supply and demand

Soon your breasts will be producing milk automatically and they will also adjust the composition of the milk itself during the feed. The first flow of milk in any breastfeeding is thin and watery. This is called "foremilk" and it is a thirst quencher. The rest of the milk, known as "hind milk," is richer and more filling, which is why a baby gradually becomes full on one breast but is able to go on to feed happily from the other. The more a baby feeds – whether he sucks for longer at each feeding or simply feeds more frequently – the more milk will be produced. This is known as supply and demand feeding. A baby who is going through a growth spurt may demand more feeds over a day or two in order to step up the supply of milk.

At about this time you will find that the contents of your baby's dirty diapers change from black to dark green and then eventually to yellow. He may also regurgitate some

See Diaper changing, page 107, for bowel movements.

milk after a feeding. These "spit-ups" look worse than they are and they are often caused by the baby sucking in air while he is feeding. This is particularly likely to happen when the breasts are engorged and the nipples less flexible so that the baby cannot get a proper grip, but it may also happen if he takes more milk than he needs. At the end or in the middle of a feeding your baby may want to bring up gas. Hold him upright with his back straight and his head supported, and gently rub his back – after a couple of seconds a burp (if there is one) will come up of its own accord.

As feeding becomes more established

Once the milk has come in and the breasts have started to feel more comfortable, you will find that you are getting the hang of feeding, although it seems to take ages. Feedings can last for up to an hour – from picking up the baby to settling him down again. He may not spend all this time sucking; often food in the stomach triggers off a bowel movement.

Your baby may want to pause during a feeding – perhaps to bring up some gas – or he may even doze off and then wake up a few minutes later to feed again. After the feeding he may need cleaning up (if he has spit up) and a diaper change. Finally he may need a bit of time to settle. Some babies feed so eagerly that they fall asleep right away, while others need a little gentle rocking.

The end of a feeding, and your contented baby drops off to sleep snuggled against your shoulder.

Preparing for a feeding

It is important to start establishing a routine for feeding your baby as early as possible. This means getting yourself in the right mood for feeding as well as feeling comfortable, so that your let-down reflex is encouraged to work and the baby will have a satisfying feeding.

Before the feeding make sure you have a drink – and perhaps something to eat – and place some tissues nearby for mopping up afterwards. If you are ready, but the baby has not yet woken up, then wake him and start the feedings before he begins to cry.

If you have a baby who demands very frequent feeding then set aside a corner of the room which has everything ready and all that you will need for changing his diaper afterwards (*see* page 104). Leave the telephone off the hook so that you will not be disturbed. If you are prepared, you will feel more confident and will be able to "think" milk and so produce it. In a couple of weeks you will not need this ritual so much and eventually you will find that a feeding will actually calm you down and make you feel better if you are tense. In the early days when you are getting breastfeeding established, nurse your baby at least six to eight times a day. Gradually he will settle to a pattern of five or six feedings a day.

A loose top pulled up allows you to nurse your baby comfortably – and rather more discreetly – than a front-opening blouse.

Expressing

There are several reasons why you might want to express breast milk for your baby: if your breasts are very uncomfortable or engorged and the baby has missed a feeding; if you have more milk than the baby needs; or if you want to leave some breast milk for your baby while you are out or at work. Expressed breast milk can be stored in a sterile plastic container in the refrigerator for up to 24 hours or in the freezer for a couple of months.

HAND EXPRESSING

USING A PUMP

1 Open out your thumbs and forefingers and place them well back around the outer edge of your breast with your elbows raised at the side. Using the flat of your hands and thumbs, massage the breast gently but firmly towards the nipple.

2 Push the outer edge of the areola back towards the breastbone and squeeze gently to release the milk. Do not squeeze the nipple itself.
Catch the milk in a sterile container.

Place the horn, which is attached to a bottle, over the breast. Squeeze the bulb while pressing the horn against the breast. To help start the flow of milk, apply gentle pressure to the breast and release the bulb.

Expressing by hand, if done correctly, is very effective for small amounts of milk. However, don't use too much pressure as you could damage the breast tissue. If you find this method too slow or painful, try using a hand-operated pump instead.

Using a breast pump is a more efficient way of expressing milk and is kinder to sore nipples, although some people find the pressure too much. There are three kinds of hand pump available: the syringe type, the bulb type, or you may be able to get a battery-operated one. Remember to sterilize all the component parts of the pump before and after use.

An electric pump is sometimes used if you have to pump large quantities of milk (perhaps for a premature or ill baby). Most maternity hospitals have an electric breast pump for this purpose. As well as enabling you to express a large quantity of milk, an electric pump will also help to stimulate your milk supply.

Combining breast and bottle

If you do decide to combine the two methods of feeding, you will have to work out a careful balance between giving your baby the right number of bottles at an early stage (the first couple of weeks after the birth) so that he gets used to them, but not so many that he ends up rejecting the breast completely or you find that your milk supply diminishes because he does not suck enough. Probably the most sensible course of action is to start giving a bottle of expressed breast milk every few days after the first two weeks (*see* Expressing). Then, as your milk supply builds up and your baby gets used to both methods of feeding, you can gradually give a bottle more frequently – for example, once a day. One bottle a day is usually enough to enable your partner or a relative to take a turn at looking after the baby or giving the occasional night feeding.

> **PREMATURE BABIES**
> A baby born before term (40 weeks) may have difficulty co-ordinating his sucking, swallowing and breathing reflexes which is why he cannot always be fed from the breast or bottle at first. He will probably be in a special care baby unit for the first few days or weeks and will be given nourishment directly into the bloodstream and then through a tube in the stomach. Even though your baby cannot come home with you, you must remember to pump your breast regularly to keep up the milk supply. You can store breast milk in sterilized bottles in the refrigerator. As soon as your baby can take milk feeding, he can be given your breast milk. As your baby gets stronger, you may be able to let him suck at your breast. Just talking to him and caressing him will do much to help you feel closer to your baby.

Problems with breastfeeding

Never be afraid to ask for help if you have any problems with breastfeeding. You can consult your pediatrician or contact your local LaLèche League chapter. The LaLèche League is an organization devoted to promoting breastfeeding. (*See* Useful Addresses, page 298.)

Sore nipples This often happens when the baby starts feeding. If the soreness persists, check that the nipple is well inside the baby's mouth so that he does not have to pull on it. You could try a different feeding position (*see* page 86) and feed him more frequently, starting on the less sore side. Don't let him suck for too long after a feeding if you are sore. Dry your nipples after a feeding and leave your bra off for a while, if possible, to let the air get to your breasts. There are creams available that help to prevent sore nipples by softening the skin, but once they have become sore you may want to ask your doctor about special creams to treat them.

Cracked nipples If your nipples crack or bleed you may need to take the baby off the affected side for a day or two to rest it. Express your milk by hand to prevent engorgement but don't use a breast pump as the action can aggravate a crack. Alternatively, you could ask your doctor about a special cream for sore nipples, or a nipple shield that will protect the nipples and enable you to carry on feeding.

Engorgement It is common for the breasts to swell and become engorged a few days after the birth. They can also become engorged if the baby misses a feeding, or simply if you have been sleeping in a warm bed. If your breasts are too hard for your baby to latch onto, then very gently massage them forward to express a little milk and so soften the nipples. Putting warm washcloths on your breasts between feedings will also help to soften them. This problem usually sorts itself out after a couple of days but avoid expressing too much milk as this will encourage the breasts to produce even more.

Soft breasts Your breasts will probably become softer and smaller about six weeks after the birth. This is simply because the tissue is less swollen – it makes no difference to your milk supply.

Blocked ducts This can occur because the ducts are not being emptied properly or because of pressure – perhaps from a tight-fitting bra. The ducts can also get blocked when the breasts are engorged. The result is a hot, tender lump in the breast which may become very sore and red. To relieve the blockage you can try expressing some milk or start nursing the baby and gently stroke the affected part in the direction of the nipple. Put warm washcloths on the breast first to relieve the pain. Rough handling will just make the problem worse and may cause an abscess. If it does not clear quickly, ask your pediatrician or a Lalèche League leader for advice.

Leaking Full warm breasts can easily leak. Breast pads or a clean handkerchief worn inside the bra will mop up small leaks. You could also try pressing the side of the breast with the heel of your hand to stem the flow.

You can nurse your baby quite safely in bed if you hold him securely.

YOUR HEALTH

If your baby is to thrive on breast milk he will need a healthy mother. Looking after yourself will also give you more energy to enjoy the time you spend with your baby. Try to eat sensibly, drink plenty of water and fruit juice and get some fresh air and exercise regularly. You could join an exercise class, which is a good way of getting back in shape. Never diet if you are breastfeeding, and check with your doctor if you are prescribed any medicines as these could affect the baby. If you find that you need more rest try to take it while your baby is sleeping, and don't ignore your social life – it will give you a break to get out with other people.

Not enough milk This may occur because you are feeling tired or run down (*see* below). It will help if you nurse the baby for longer and more frequently to help build up the supply of milk. If you are advised to supplement the feeding with a bottle then try expressing some milk an hour or so after a feeding and giving this to your baby. This will also help stimulate your milk supply (*see* Expressing, page 89).

Feeling tired Breastfeeding may not be tiring in itself but a small baby can be, and you may feel better after a break from him. Express some breast milk and leave this in a bottle with someone you can trust to look after the baby for a couple of hours while you have some time to yourself. You should also make sure that you eat well and try to make up for the sleep that you have lost during the night (*see* Your Health, right).

Something in your diet disagreeing with him If your baby suffers from a lot of gas, and cries a lot, his digestive system may be reacting to something in your diet, and you should discuss this with your pediatrician (*see* Colic, page 96). Any alteration in your diet – however slight – should be supervised by your pediatrician as you may need substitutes for the things you cut out.

Weak suck This sometimes occurs if your baby was premature or has been ill and his sucking action is not strong enough to build up the milk supply. Use a breast pump between feedings to help stimulate milk production until the baby is stronger (*see* Expressing, page 89).

Thin watery milk Mature breast milk, which usually comes in by the tenth day, is thin, watery and bluish in color compared to the richer early milk which is mixed with colostrum. Don't worry – this is how it should be.

Night feedings In the early days your baby will probably be having at least seven feedings a day. Some babies start to drop a night feeding at around six weeks but many more do not. You can get used to a certain amount of sleep disturbance, but if the problem seems much worse than the experience of other mothers with babies the same age, then speak to your pediatrician about it.

Bottlefeeding

Bottlefed babies need just as much care and attention as breastfed babies and you will appreciate these intimate times with your baby. Once you have developed a routine of sterilizing and making up formula, bottlefeeding is not difficult to manage. Nowadays commercially prepared infant formulas are very convenient to use. Instructions for preparing the formula are clearly printed on the can or container. The expiry date is also always marked clearly.

It is a good idea to buy at least six bottles. This way you can make up all the bottles for the day and store them in the refrigerator. There are two sizes of bottle – the 4-ounce for a very young baby and the 8-ounce for when he is taking more milk.

Choosing a brand of milk

There is a varied range of formula milk available for babies, and all brands have to comply with strict safety regulations. To begin with, look for a brand which states on the label that it is suitable for newborn babies. These milk formulas

WHAT YOU WILL NEED
If you use well water you must sterilize all bottlefeeding equipment to protect your baby's health. You need, from left to right:

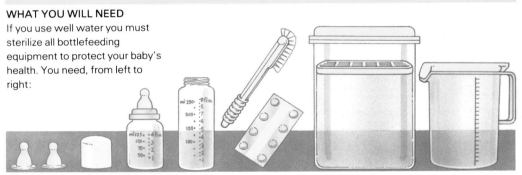

● Nipples ● Caps ● Bottles ● Bottle brush ● Sterilizing tablets ● Sterilizing tank ● Measuring pitcher

are specially treated so that the nutritional composition is much closer to breast milk than the cow's milk from which they are made. All these formulas are available either as iron fortified or without additional iron. Your pediatrician will advise you which kind you should get for your baby. Cow's milk, or formula milk that is prescribed for older babies, is too rich for young ones. The modern formula milks allow bottlefed babies, like breastfed babies, to be fed as often as they need to be, provided the feeding is made up exactly as stated on the label. If the feeding is too concentrated it may make your baby ill or overweight, if it is too diluted he won't be getting enough nourishment.

Once you have chosen a brand of baby milk, try to stick to it as too much changing will not help your baby. But sometimes if there is a history of allergy in your family (such as asthma, eczema or hay fever) or your baby becomes allergic to the milk formula, you may be advised by your pediatrician to try a formula based on another protein, such as soy or chicken. This is because cow's milk is thought to cause an allergic reaction in some babies (*see* Allergies, page 96). Do not confuse the baby milks based on soy protein with soy milks found in supermarkets or health food shops as these are definitely not suitable for giving to babies.

Baby milk comes in liquid or powder form and you will find instructions on the container for mixing the formula. Infant formulas are available in various forms; ready-to-use in 32-ounce cans, ready-to-use in disposable bottles, concentrated (dilute with an equal amount of water) in 13-ounce cans and powdered formulas in 16-ounce cans. If you are on welfare, or have a low income, you may qualify for the Federal funded special supplemental Food Program for Women, Infants and Children (WIC Program). If you enroll for this you will receive food vouchers regularly for your baby's formulas, juice, and cereals. You can get information about the WIC Program from your prenatal clinic or your child health clinic.

Keeping equipment clean

Attention to hygiene is essential with bottlefeeding. Milk is an ideal breeding ground for germs which cause stomach bugs so it is vital that all bottlefeeding equipment (bottles, nipples, caps, measuring spoon, plastic knife, and pitcher) should be washed thoroughly and sterilized after use.

The most commonly used method of sterilization is by boiling in water after thorough washing. This is also the simplest and most effective method. All your bottle-feeding equipment should first of all be rinsed out and then thoroughly washed with soap or detergent and a bottle brush. If you have a dishwasher you can use this, stacking the bottles and nipples on the bottom rack.

For the sterilizing you will need a large container that will hold all the 8-ounce bottles that you need for a full day's feedings, the nipples, caps and rings and, ideally, a couple of smaller (4-ounce) bottles for water. You can buy a large kettle or stove-top sterilizer and these usually come complete with the rack and tongs that you will need. A rack is useful because you can stack the bottles upright in it and then, at the end of the sterilization, lift the whole thing out quite easily. Tongs, which should be sterilized each time with the rest of the equipment, are useful for lifting the bottles out of the rack when they are still hot. You can also use them to place the nipples upside down in the bottles once these have been filled with water. If you don't have tongs, try only to touch the edge of the nipples.

When you are ready to sterilize your equipment, put the bottles upside down in the rack so that the steam can get into them and water run out more easily. You may find it convenient to have a jar with holes punched in the top to hold the nipples, cap and rings, and this should also be placed upside down in the rack.

Pour two or three inches of hot water into the sterilizer, put the top on securely and bring to the boil. Boil hard for five minutes. Allow to cool a little before removing the top.

Keep the nipples on a sterile surface – you could use the inverted lid of the sterilizer – while you fill the bottles.

Making up feedings

It is a good idea to set aside a time of day when you will not be distracted and make up all the milk you will need for the next 24 hours. You can then store it in a sterile container, or bottles that have been sterilized and covered, in the refrigerator until you need it.

Before you start, read the manufacturer's instructions on the label of the package or can of formula you are using. Follow them carefully, making sure that you mix the milk powder and water in the right proportions. Use only the scoop provided for the milk powder, and a sterile knife to level it off. Make up the formula in a pitcher so that you can fill enough bottles for the day's feedings. Invert the nipples in the bottles before putting the caps on.

HOW TO PREPARE FEEDINGS

1 Use cooled (but still warm) freshly boiled water as this will make it easier to mix the formula. Measure the correct amount of water into the pitcher (or bottle).

2 Using the scoop provided, measure out the correct amount of powder. Allow the powder to lie naturally in the scoop – don't try to pack more in. Use the flat edge of a sterilized knife to level the powder in the scoop. Add the powder to the water and stir the milk.

3 Pour the milk formula into the bottle, place the nipple and cap on and shake well. If you are putting extra bottles of the made-up milk into the refrigerator, invert the nipples and put the caps on the bottles.

When it is time for a feeding, take a bottle from the refrigerator and warm the milk by standing the bottle (nipple re-inverted and cap replaced) upright in a pitcher of hot water, or use a bottle warmer. When the milk is the correct temperature, use it at once, because harmful bacteria can grow if it is left for any length of time in a bottle warmer. Never use a microwave oven to heat the milk as it will be scalding while the bottle remains cool.

At night you can put the exact amount of warm boiled water in a sterilized thermos bottle and have the measured powder ready in the bottle. You can then mix up the feeding directly and quickly when your baby wakes up and wants to be fed. Alternatively, you can take a bottle of made-up milk from the refrigerator before you go to bed so that by the time your baby wakes it will be at the right temperature. It can be left out of the refrigerator for a few hours in a cool room as long as the cap is on the bottle.

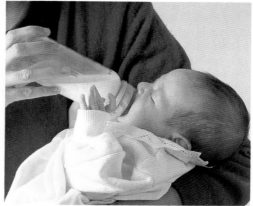

Giving a bottle

You and your baby will benefit if you have some time and space to yourselves so that you can concentrate on an undisturbed and satisfying feeding. Bottle feedings can take just as long as breast feedings so make sure that you are comfortable before you start, with everything you will need beside you. Test the temperature of the milk by shaking a few drops onto the inside of your wrist; make sure that it is warm rather than hot. At the same time check that the milk is dripping in a steady flow from the nipple hole. If it drips slowly then the nipple hole is too small. You can enlarge it with a needle.

There is no recommended amount of milk to give your baby, but you could start with 3 ounces and see how you go. There should be a little milk left over at the end of the feeding; throw this away as it will spoil very quickly once it has been mixed with saliva. Wash and sterilize the bottle and nipple immediately.

Changing over from breast to bottle

This should be done gradually over a period of a week or two. If your baby is used to bottles and your milk supply has already decreased, then the changeover may be quicker. However, don't be surprised if your breasts start to fill up with milk. If tension has been the reason for you giving up breastfeeding, the relief of making a decision may allow the let-down reflex to work properly for the first time.

Start by dropping one feeding (when your breasts feel less full) and substituting a bottle. Dilute the first bottle of milk formula with an extra ounce of water as breastfed babies sometimes spit-up their first full-strength bottle feeding. One or two days later substitute a second bottle for another breastfeeding, and so on, until you are down to one breastfeeding a day. You can continue with this last feeding for as long as you and your baby want to.

A slightly older baby who has already started solids may need persuasion to take a bottle at first. Let him have an empty bottle to play with so that he gets used to it. Babies under 12 months should only be given breast or formula milk, not the milk that you drink.

Above left Let the bottle touch her cheek so that she responds with the sucking reflex.
Above Enjoy a cuddle with your baby while you are feeding her.

BOTTLEFEEDING SAFETY
You may be tempted to leave your baby for a few minutes propped up with the bottle in his mouth. This practice is extremely dangerous as he could choke very easily. Also, if a baby is lying down to suck (and he should never be lying flat), a pool of milk can gather in the back of his mouth and nose and cause infections of the inner ear. If you are called away during a feeding, put the bottle down and resume feeding later. After all, breastfeeding mothers have to stop feeding when another child hurts himself or the vegetables boil over.

Common feeding concerns

Breastfeeding and bottlefeeding mothers find that their babies share many of the same problems. Probably the most common causes for concern are discomfort brought about by colic, an allergic reaction, such as eczema, or your baby putting on weight too fast or too slowly.

Colic

If your baby has periods when he screams and cries continuously, cannot be comforted and draws his knees up in apparent pain, he is probably suffering from a bout of colic. These spells usually start a few weeks after birth and may continue for a few months. Although it is distressing for both the parents and the baby, colic is not dangerous.

The cause of colic is not known although there are several theories. These include the baby's sensitivity to cow's milk in the mother's diet, or air getting trapped in the bowel following a feeding. Some babies are particularly prone to attacks of colic, which are often worse in the late afternoon or evening. This may be due to the last feeding being hurried or the fact that you were at a low ebb at the end of the day and the baby did not have a satisfactory feeding.

There is no point in worrying unduly about causes. All you can do is try not to get too tense (as this will only make the baby worse) and cope as best you can. However, don't always assume that prolonged crying is caused by colic – unexplained crying should be investigated by the doctor.

If the baby is not ill but unhappy, try to calm him (*see* box, left). If all else fails, your doctor may suggest that you cut out milk and dairy products from your diet for a couple of weeks if you are breastfeeding – sometimes cutting down rather than cutting out helps. Always consult your doctor if you are altering your diet as you may need supplements of calcium or extra vitamins to compensate.

Allergies

If there is a history of allergy in the family (such as eczema, asthma, hay fever or food allergy), giving the baby breast milk alone for the first four to six months can help prevent the allergy from developing. Breastfed babies still develop allergies but these are probably not as severe. The extensively treated modern milk formulas are less likely to trigger off allergies than ordinary cow's milk or the baby milks used in the past. There are also formula milks based on soy protein, but these are no more likely to prevent allergies than ordinary formulas, *unless* the baby has a particular sensitivity to cow's milk.

The baby's diet

Research is going on at present to discover ways of helping babies at risk of developing allergies. The best advice seems to be that you feed your baby *only* breast milk for at least four months. If possible, keep it up for six months but remember that an older baby may need more frequent feeding in order to take sufficient milk. If you give vitamin drops, use those that are free from artificial coloring.

When you start your baby on solids, give foods that are least likely to provoke an allergic reaction (*see* page 99). Introduce new foods one at a time over a period of a week so that you can see if there are any adverse effects, such as an itchy rash or runny nose. Use only those commercial baby foods that have single ingredients, or ones you have already tried on your baby. The following ingredients all mean that milk or egg is present – butter, cream, cheese, cheese powder, skimmed milk powder, nonfat milk solids, casein, caseinate, whey, lactalbumin, and egg lecithin.

The mother's diet

In recent years there have been suggestions that mothers of babies at risk of developing allergies should avoid foods such as eggs or milk during pregnancy and while breast-feeding. Although it is known that substances from food can cross into the placenta or get into the breast milk, it is not clear whether this causes the difficulty. Only about a quarter of allergic babies have been helped when their mothers tried cutting out these foods from their own diets. If you are breastfeeding you could try cutting out cow's milk or egg for two weeks. If the baby's health does not improve, then you can start eating these products again. If you have to give up these foods for a longer period, you may need professional guidance to work out a balanced diet. It is vital for you and your baby that you eat a good diet.

Weight gain

In the early days many parents worry that they are not feeding their baby enough, or that he is getting too chubby. Every baby is an individual and, fed the right diet, will grow at the rate that is right for him. A baby who is heavier at birth will stay heavier than the one with a low birth weight. If your baby's weight drops too far below his average, he may not be getting enough to eat – if it is too far above he may be overweight. Speak to your pediatrician if you are concerned.

FEEDING YOUR BABY

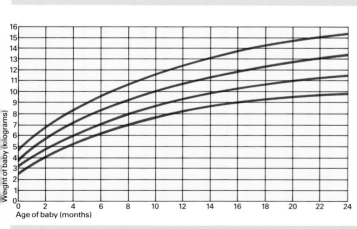

RECORDING WEIGHT

Your baby's weight is checked regularly by your pediatrician and recorded on a weight chart. In the early months his weight gain will probably be very rapid, doubling between four and six months and tripling at about a year. It should follow a steady curve as he grows. The chart on the left shows typical growth lines for four babies of varying birth weights.

See Your baby's health, page 126.

Introducing solids

Weaning your baby from the breast or bottle can be a slow business and you may feel impatient and want to hurry things along. However, babies will not be hurried if they don't want to be and it is better to start introducing new tastes slowly and gradually. At the beginning, solids will merely supplement the baby's milk feedings and it may be some time before they replace these completely. Remember that for most of the first year milk is the main item of your baby's diet.

Many women are eager to start weaning their babies at an early age. This may be because they want to return to work and so stop breastfeeding altogether; because they want "proof" that their baby is growing up; because they hope that he will sleep through the night or feed less often; or simply because everyone else is doing it. Starting solids is sometimes seen as the answer to these problems but very often you are just swapping one set of troubles for another.

When to start?

Your baby may not want, or need, to start solids before he is six months old, but you can certainly introduce him to them from about three or four months if you think that he is ready (*see* left). Once your baby shows signs of being interested in food and is putting objects in his mouth, give him a small amount of pureed food and see how he manages. If he seems to be hungry but is not yet interested in solid food, simply give him extra milk feedings for the time being. Some babies thrive on milk alone for as long as 12 months, others are ready for solid food at three to four months. Sometimes night waking after the early months is caused by hunger, but it is also true that babies will go through spells of waking at night throughout the first year or two of life anyway. Sometimes all that is needed is a little comfort sucking to help them go back to sleep. Even when he is weaned, your child may lose interest in solids sometimes and want the familiar reassurance of the breast or bottle for a short while before he feels ready to start feeding from a spoon again.

An unhurried approach to weaning is important for a number of reasons. Introducing solids before three months is not recommended as it is thought that if the baby's digestive system has not developed sufficiently to cope with solids they can cause food allergy, rashes, diarrhea or tummy upsets. Giving solids too soon can also make your child overweight. In the case of a child whose close relatives suffer from allergies, weaning should be delayed for even longer (*see* page 96).

Exploring and learning

Once you have started your baby on solid food you should keep a close watch on him to see how he reacts so that you can learn to keep to this pace. As in all other aspects of development, babies make advances at different stages and

---

IS HE READY FOR SOLIDS?
Your baby may be ready to be weaned at any time between three months and a year. Signs to look for are:
● when he starts to put objects such as a rattle or teething ring into his mouth
● when he shows an interest in what other people are eating and tries to grab some for himself
● When he is able to take food from the tip of a spoon (you should never have to push food into a baby's mouth as if you were giving medicine)
● when he is able to keep pureed food in his mouth without pushing it out with his tongue.

you should never push your child into doing anything before he is ready – he'll get around to it in his own good time, and you'll only put him off if you insist. In the early weeks of weaning, solids are really for experimenting with rather than for proper nourishment. Regard them as a supplement to milk feedings to begin with and give a little more solid food only as your baby demands it.

First foods

A baby's first foods should be sloppy purees with the consistency of a thick soup. You can either prepare the food yourself or use a commercial brand of baby food. The latter is useful for trying out new flavors or for traveling, but don't get into the habit of relying on foods in cans or jars as the baby gets older. For home-cooked foods you can use a blender or food processor for pureeing. Some fresh foods (vegetables, meat, and cereal) may have to be diluted first because if they are too bulky for a baby to digest, he may retch or refuse to eat it. Some fruit is better stewed first with a little boiled water or milk from a feeding and then pureed to make it easier for him to eat.

Commercial brands of baby food either come in puree form or as dried granules to which you simply add water. Most of these foods are specially formulated to include vitamins and iron, but check the ingredients on the package if you are not sure.

Introduce new foods one at a time over a period of two or three days to begin with. This way you can identify any particular likes or dislikes, as well as giving your baby a variety of tastes to try. You will also be able to identify any problem foods that may cause a rash or tummy upset. Offer the same food on several occasions to see if your baby

Suitable first foods for your baby need to be very sloppy. The chart below gives a variety of foods which can be pureed or mixed to the right consistency. The key tells you which foods need to be cooked only, which need to be pureed, and which should be cooked and pureed or sieved.

SUITABLE FIRST FOODS

Fruits	Vegetables	Cereals and legumes	Other
◪ apple	◪ carrot	■ baby rice	■ egg yolk
☐ pear	◪ cauliflower	◪ peas	◪ chicken
☐ peaches	◪ sweet potato	◪ lentils	◪ turkey
☐ apricots	◪ green beans	◪ Lima beans	◪ lean beef
◪ prunes	◪ rutabaga	(remove skin)	
☐ banana	◪ leeks	From 4 months:	■ cooked
	◪ parsnip	precooked	☐ pureed
	◪ potato, thinned	cereals – wheat,	◪ cooked and
	with milk	oats, barley	sieved/pureed

AVOID: ● **Egg white** – until 6 months because of risk of allergy ● **Pork and lamb** – as these are too fatty ● **Fruit with small seeds** – strawberries, tomatoes, until child is at least 6 months old.

is getting to like it or not. You could start with baby cereal and then move on to vegetables and fruit. Once you know which foods your baby will take quite happily, you can start to combine some of them. A baby often becomes constipated when he first starts solids because his digestive system has not quite adapted to the intake of solid food.

First tries

Give your baby his first taste of food when he is not desperately hungry – if necessary start him half an hour or so before one of his usual feeds. You can serve the food cold, but if you are giving it warm, test a little on the back of your hand first. If it is too hot you will put your baby off trying anymore. Put a soft bib on him and push up his sleeves. He may want to grab at the bowl or to suck his wrist to help him swallow (it is difficult for babies to swallow at first because their natural reaction to something in the mouth is to suck it).

You can either sit him on your lap or put him in a chair facing you. Scoop up a quarter of a teaspoonful of food puree and put the spoon just inside his mouth. His initial reaction may be to push the spoon away with his tongue, but try rubbing the contents of the spoon lightly against his upper lip to allow him to get used to the new taste and texture. Young babies often lose a lot of food from the corner of their mouths but don't worry about this – you are only trying to accustom him to the idea of solid food and you shouldn't expect him to have a meal at this stage. Start off with one or two teaspoonfuls once a day and err on the side of giving him too little rather than too much. If he is obviously enjoying it then let him have a little more, but remember that he may not be interested every time. If you have problems at first, and your baby starts to cry or turn his head away from the food, then stop and just give him milk. If this happens two or three times then try giving him some milk before you give the solid food.

EQUIPMENT
- Soft bibs
- Disposable bibs (useful for traveling)
- Plastic spoon or special weaning spoon – this will be softer on the baby's gums than a metal spoon
- Bowl or dish – plastic delays heat loss, china helps to cool food. Choose one that is not easy to tip over.
- Bottles and nipples should still be sterilized; spoons and bowls need only be washed thoroughly
- Bottle or plastic spoon for drinks
- Blender or food processor

Suggested weaning
Gradually build up the amount of solids you give your baby over a few weeks, until he has a pattern of three "meals" a day as well as milk feedings.

STAGE 1	STAGE 2	STAGE 3
1st feeding Breast or bottle feeding	**1st feeding** Breast or bottle feeding	**1st feeding** Breast or bottle feeding
2nd feeding Give 1-2 teaspoons of fruit or vegetable puree or baby rice plus breast or bottle feeding	**2nd feeding** 1-2 teaspoons of baby cereal plus breast or bottle feeding	**2nd feeding** 1-2 teaspoons of baby cereal plus breast or bottle feeding
3rd feeding Breast or bottle feeding	**3rd feeding** 1-2 teaspoons of pureed vegetable or broth, or commercial baby food plus breast or bottle feeding	**3rd feeding** Pureed vegetable and meat or commercial baby food plus breast or bottle feeding
4th feeding Breast or bottle feeding	**4th feeding** Breast or bottle feeding	**4th feeding** 1-2 teaspoons of fruit puree plus breast or bottle feeding
5th feeding Breast or bottle feeding	**5th feeding** Breast or bottle feeding	**5th feeding** Breast or bottle feeding

● *See* Feeding your baby, page 150, for constipation.

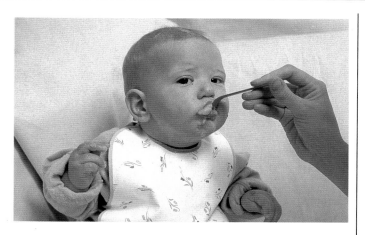

A new taste can be a bit puzzling as he explores the smell, texture and flavor of the food.

In a couple of weeks, if everything goes well, you can try him on solid food twice a day – for example, baby rice in the morning and a pureed fruit or vegetable at midday. In the meantime, start to build up the amounts as and when he seems ready for them. When he becomes more efficient at feeding, you can gradually make the consistency of the feeding a little bit thicker. As he takes more food at one meal so he will gradually begin to take slightly less from the breast or bottle until he is able to drop one of his milk feedings altogether.

Starting drinks

The first foods you give a baby (pureed vegetables and fruits) are often so sloppy that he may not need any extra liquid. However, by the time he is taking a complete meal of solid food he will probably need something to drink too.

Babies cannot usually drink very efficiently from a cup before they are six months old so first drinks can be offered in a bottle or training cup. If your baby sucks too hard on his cup, causing him to splutter, or he is not used to drinking from a bottle, offer him sips from a spoon at first. You could let him have a bottle and nipple to play with for a while so that he can explore its shape and texture on his own. Then try putting some breast milk onto the nipple and let him taste that. If he will happily take milk from a bottle then he probably doesn't need additional fluids.

Some babies like to drink plenty of water, and this should always be boiled (and left to cool) for a baby under six months of age. Some babies take a little milk in the morning and then refuse all drinks until a little more milk before they go to bed. Providing a child is wetting his diapers you can be sure that he is getting enough liquid.

If you want to let him try baby syrups or fruit juice, then make sure they are well diluted. Use one teaspoon of baby syrup to one fluid ounce of water, or dilute one part fruit juice with four or five parts water. A very slight sweetness is all that is needed to encourage a baby to drink. If you make his drinks too sweet, you will find it very difficult to wean him onto less sweet drinks later on, and a child who ends up drinking large quantities because he likes the sweet taste will harm his teeth.

Diaper changing

Although diaper changing is not something that parents-to-be look forward to, it doesn't take long to learn how to do it, and it does provide an opportunity for you to talk to and play with your baby.

Cloth or disposables?

Choosing the right sort of diaper can be a difficult task, simply because there are so many different kinds on the market. However, with a little thought you should be able to pick the kind that suits your lifestyle best.

Cloth diapers

Cloth diapers are large squares of highly absorbent toweling which are folded around the baby and usually secured with a pin (or pins). They're worn with waterproof pants to help protect your baby's clothes and bedding, and a diaper liner (*see* page 105) inside, either a disposable or a reusable one, to prevent moisture seeping back onto the

CLOTH VS DISPOSABLES

Each type of diaper has its pros and cons – it's up to you which kind you want to use.

Advantages of cloth
- They are cheaper in the long run, especially if you have more than one child.
- Ecologically safe.
- Folded to fit and worn with waterproof pants they are reasonably leak-proof.
- More comfortable.

Disadvantages
- They need soaking, rinsing, washing, and drying.

Advantages of disposables
- No diaper buckets in the bathroom.
- No washing and drying.
- They are quick and easy to put on and take off.

Disadvantages
- They are more expensive, and they also create more garbage.

Left to right – *diaper square, shaped cloth, diaper liners, tie-on waterproof pants, pins, all-in-one disposable diaper, waterproof pull-on and snap pants, disposable diaper.*

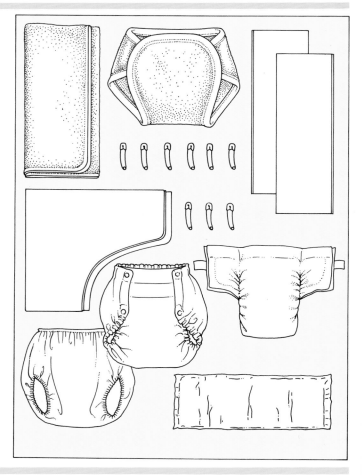

baby's skin. The used diapers, whether soiled or just wet, should be immersed in a bucket of water containing soap or detergent and, after soaking, washed or rinsed to remove all traces of the solution. Some people still prefer to boil diapers – though most find that this is not convenient. You will probably need a washing machine if you are using cloth diapers, and an automatic drier is certainly a help in winter when things don't dry so quickly outside. Never boil waterproof pants or dry them in an automatic drier.

You can buy specially shaped cloth diapers which look neat and are easy to put on, though they do take longer to dry than ordinary squares. Fine muslin diapers can be used for tiny babies or as a diaper liner, but most parents find these more useful as a "dribble cloth" and for general wiping up. Specially thick cloth diapers may be handy if your baby needs extra protection at night, although two diapers worn at once is as effective, if rather bulky.

So long as you have adequate washing and drying facilities in your home, then cloth diapers can be a good choice. They are probably cheaper than disposables in the long run, although you need to count in the cost of liners, pants and pins – plus electricity if you put them in the washing machine. They are also hard-wearing, and will last through at least two children. The more expensive cloth diapers are more absorbent and worth paying extra for, if you can afford it. You will need to buy at least two dozen to keep up with all the washing and drying involved. Alternatively you can use expensive diaper services which

Folding the diaper
There are several effective ways of folding a cloth diaper. You'll soon work out the easiest and favorite way for you, but here are two popular methods.

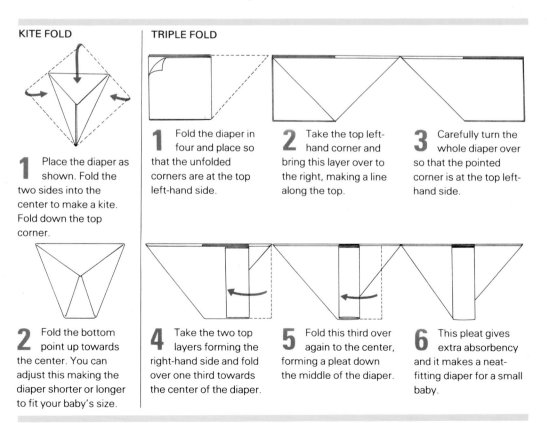

KITE FOLD

1 Place the diaper as shown. Fold the two sides into the center to make a kite. Fold down the top corner.

2 Fold the bottom point up towards the center. You can adjust this making the diaper shorter or longer to fit your baby's size.

TRIPLE FOLD

1 Fold the diaper in four and place so that the unfolded corners are at the top left-hand side.

2 Take the top left-hand corner and bring this layer over to the right, making a line along the top.

3 Carefully turn the whole diaper over so that the pointed corner is at the top left-hand side.

4 Take the two top layers forming the right-hand side and fold over one third towards the center of the diaper.

5 Fold this third over again to the center, forming a pleat down the middle of the diaper.

6 This pleat gives extra absorbency and it makes a neat-fitting diaper for a small baby.

A PLACE TO CHANGE

Anywhere that is warm and free from drafts can be used as a place to change your baby's diaper. You may like to arrange a special corner of a room where everything is at hand. A baby box for equipment may be useful. For safety's sake, never leave your baby alone on a raised surface; she could easily roll off. You could change your baby's diaper on the floor as long as she's on some protective covering, such as a changing mat.

CHANGING YOUR BABY

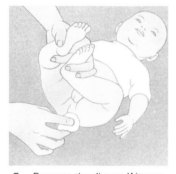

1 Remove the diaper. If it was soiled, use tissues to wipe the baby's bottom. Using cotton balls and warm water or baby lotion (or baby wipes), clean the diaper area carefully.

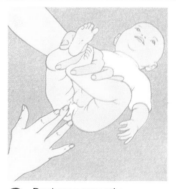

2 Dry her very gently – especially in the creases around the thighs – if you've used water. Apply baby cream generously with your fingers (if you're using it).

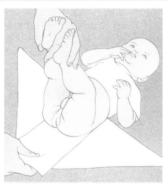

3 Lift your baby carefully by her feet with your finger between her ankles, and place the clean diaper under her bottom.

collect and clean diapers on a weekly basis.

Disposable diapers

Disposable diapers are very convenient as they don't need washing and drying. They are also, now, much more effective at keeping a baby clean and dry.

The most commonly sold disposable is the "all-in-one" which is a plastic-backed diaper that fits round the baby and fastens with sticky tapes. Although they are very absorbent, disposable diapers do have a tendency to leak, even with elasticated legs, because the fit is not as good as a cloth diaper worn with the right plastic pants.

You can save time as well as money by buying disposables through your local drug or discount store. One drawback of disposables is that they cannot be flushed down the toilet, especially if you have a septic tank. This does mean a lot more trash for you and the environment.

Waterproof pants

There are advantages to buying the more expensive waterproof pants made of soft nylon – the material doesn't split so easily and the finish is better than on the cheaper versions, so they do last longer. Snap-fastened pants give a good fit. However, you may prefer to use elasticated pants. Both prevent leakage, but they do tend to keep the baby wetter because dampness that might otherwise evaporate is trapped. Therefore, you need to check the baby's diaper frequently to avoid diaper rash from developing.

Diaper liners

Buy the best disposable diaper liners you can afford, as they are more absorbent and make diaper soaking and rinsing less messy. There's no doubt, too, that they can help to protect the baby to some extent from diaper rash, especially the slightly more expensive "one-way" liners.

> **WHAT YOU NEED**
> ● Ready-folded clean diaper (plus liner and pins, if using a cloth diaper)
> ● Clean waterproof pants, if using a cloth diaper
> ● Tissues
> ● Cotton balls
> ● Warm water or baby lotion or baby wipes
> ● Baby cream (zinc ointment, A and D ointment or other special barrier cream)
> ● Changing mat
> ● Diaper bucket
> ● Can or bag for trash

DIAPER CHANGING

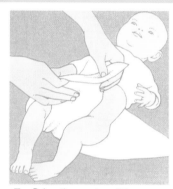

4 Bring the center of the diaper up between her legs and hold it in place while you bring the first side piece over.

5 Bring the second side piece over on top and carefully fasten the three pieces together with a pin. Put on waterproof pants.

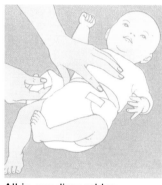

All-in-one disposables
Make sure the end with the sticky tapes goes under the baby's bottom. You can then fasten the tapes at the front of the diaper.

Keeping your baby clean

You should clean your baby's bottom properly at every diaper change, as this will help prevent soreness. If she has passed a more-than-generous bowel movement, washing with water and plenty of absorbent cotton is really the best way of cleaning her, but on other occasions you can use cotton balls, tissues, and baby lotion. Baby wipes – small disposable cloths impregnated with a cleanser – are very convenient, especially when traveling.

Make sure that you wipe a baby girl from "front to back" to prevent germs from the back passage entering the vagina. You may want to put some protective cream, such as zinc ointment, on your baby's bottom before putting on the clean diaper. This acts as a barrier to help protect her skin and stop it from getting sore.

DRESSING YOUR BABY

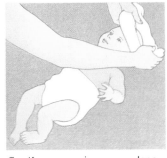

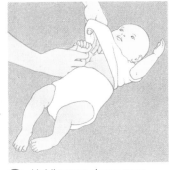

1 If you are using an envelope neck undershirt, stretch the neck of the shirt wide before you put it on. Slip it over your baby's head, supporting the back of her head as you do so.

2 Holding one sleeve open, take your baby's hand and guide it gently through the sleeve. Do the same with the other sleeve and carefully pull the undershirt down.

3 To put on her stretchsuit, first gather up one sleeve in your hand. Slip this over the baby's wrist and unroll the sleeve up her arm. Do the same with the other sleeve. Next guide one of your baby's legs in – then the other – and fasten up the stretchsuit.

STERILIZING AND WASHING DIAPERS

If you find it inconvenient to wash every day, two buckets will be necessary – one for the diaper you've just removed and one for the previous day's sterilized diapers. Use buckets with close-fitting lids and make a fresh mixture of water and soap or detergent each day. Also make sure you rinse all traces of soap or detergent out of the diapers and avoid detergents that can cause diaper rash on a sensitive skin.

Diaper rash

Being in a diaper all day can give your baby a sore bottom. Don't feel guilty if this subsequently becomes a painful diaper rash (inflamed patches of broken or "weeping" skin) because some babies are just more susceptible to it than others. There are, however, some things you can do to make it better and perhaps prevent it from happening again.

The first thing is to make sure that you change your baby's diaper whenever it is wet or dirty. She is likely to get a sore bottom if she is left for too long between changes. Diaper rash can be caused by bacteria reacting with the baby's urine or stools, so frequent changing of the diaper is important. You may need to change it twice as often as usual if she is particularly sore. It is also important to clean your baby's bottom carefully at every change. If you can, leave off her waterproof pants from time to time to allow the urine to evaporate or, even better, leave her on the changing mat without a diaper while she has a little kick, so that the air can get to her bottom. Make sure that you rinse cloth diapers very thoroughly to eliminate all traces of soap or detergent as these can irritate your baby's skin.

Treatment

You can ask your druggist for a special cream for diaper rash, and if the first one you try doesn't improve the condition after a day or so, try another brand to see if it suits your baby better. These creams protect the baby's skin from the wetness of the diaper while soothing and healing sore skin.

If the rash persists, ask your pediatrician for advice. In some cases the rash can be complicated by a fungal infection, such as thrush. Your doctor will be able to prescribe the appropriate medication once the trouble has been diagnosed.

Bowel movements

There may be changes in your baby's bowel movements from time to time. Some baby formulas make the baby pass green stools because of the ingredients in the formula. In fact, all babies pass the occasional green stool and, if it's only once in a while, it's nothing to worry about, but if it is more frequent then it's wise to seek advice from your doctor.

True constipation is very rare in a breastfed baby. It's perfectly normal for some babies to go for a few days between bowel movements, just as others may open their bowels several times a day. Diarrhea can be the result of an infection, and with both breastfed and bottlefed babies their stools become watery and mucusy. You need to consult a doctor if your baby's diarrhea is persistent or if she's also vomiting.

Once she is on even a small amount of solid foods you will notice a difference in your baby's stools. They may become more "formed" and certain foods will pass right through the digestive system without changing. This is particularly true when the baby is taking lumpier foods.

THE CONTENTS OF YOUR BABY'S DIAPER	
You will notice a change in your baby's bowel movements over the first few weeks as she becomes fully breastfed or bottlefed.	
Greenish-black, sticky	This is meconium, the first bowel movements of a newborn baby. It is passed two or three times in the days after birth.
Greenish-yellow, rather looser	Known as "transitional stools," these are passed in the week or so after birth.
Bright yellow, very loose	The stools of a fully breastfed baby.
Pale brown, bulkier and more "formed"	The stools of a bottlefed baby.

DIAPER TIPS
● Always make a habit of fastening the diaper pin to your clothing as you take it out, so that you don't mislay it when you're putting on the clean diaper.
● When fastening a cloth diaper, place your hand between the diaper and the baby's tummy so that you can't stick the pin into her. For safety, always put pins in horizontally so that if they do come undone they will do less harm.
● When putting on a disposable diaper, make sure you have no trace of cream or lotion on your fingers as this can prevent the tapes from sticking.

NAPPY CHANGING

Your baby will enjoy having a good kick, free of the restrictions of a diaper. It can also help diaper rash to expose the skin to the air.

● *See* A-Z of common ailments, page 272, for constipation and page 275, for diarrhea.

Bathing your baby

WHAT YOU NEED
- Baby bath
- Baby soap or baby bath liquid
- Two towels
- Baby nail scissors
- Cotton balls
- Small container, or bowl, for clean water
- Clean diaper plus pants, cream, etc
- Set of clean clothing
- Changing mat (if needed)
- A waterproof apron, if wanted
- A soft hairbrush

If you've never done it before – and most new parents haven't – the idea of bathing a tiny kicking baby can be nerve racking. But there's no need to worry; you'll soon gain confidence and, as you do, you'll find that bathtime becomes a real pleasure for you and your baby.

Opinion varies about when to start bathing a baby. In some hospitals your baby may be bathed shortly after birth; in others the policy may be to wait a few days. A healthy newborn baby won't come to any harm either way, but a slightly smaller, weaker baby may have a problem regulating her body temperature and a bath is best avoided until she's more mature.

You may get the chance to watch a demonstration of how to bath a baby at your prenatal classes or on the maternity ward. You may also be able to bath your baby with a nurse to guide you – this helps if you feel clumsy at first. Whatever happens, the day will come when you're at home and bathing your baby on your own.

HOW TO BATH YOUR BABY

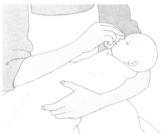

1 Undress your baby, leaving just her diaper on, and wrap her in a towel. Using cotton balls and warm water from a small container, wipe her eyes. Then, wash her face, ears and neck (*see* sponge bathing, page 111). Gently pat her skin dry.

2 Hold your baby's head over the bath, supporting her back on your arm and using your hand to support her head. With your free hand, wash her scalp. Pat her head dry gently with a towel. Remove her diaper and, if it's soiled, clean her bottom.

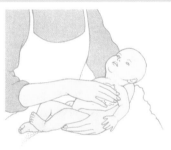

3 If you're not using baby bath liquid, you'll need to soap your baby's body. Open the towel and, using some baby soap, gently rub it over her body and limbs. Turn her over and soap her back. Remember the soap will make her body slippery.

Preparing your baby's bath

A baby's bath needs to be warm, but not as warm as you would make your own. Test the temperature of the water by dipping your elbow in – it should feel pleasantly warm but not hot. Don't use your hand to test the water as it is better used to withstanding hot temperatures and doesn't give such a good indication. If you prefer, you can use a special bath thermometer to check that the temperature is right before you put the baby in.

To avoid making the bath too hot, put the cold water in first. Then, if you put the baby into the water and have forgotten to check the temperature, or you haven't finished

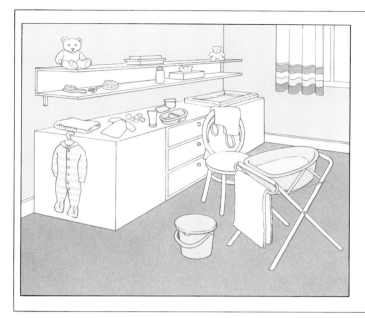

A PLACE FOR BATHING

If you have a separate baby bath, any warm room in your house will be suitable for bathing your baby. In some houses the bathroom is rather cold, and not an ideal place for undressing and bathing a tiny baby. You can use the kitchen, as it is easy to keep warm on cold days, with warm water at hand. Don't fill the bath too full; the water should be deep enough to keep most of your baby's body immersed while you support her head and shoulders out of the water.

BATHING YOUR BABY

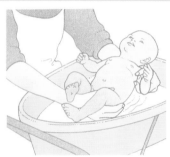

4 Support the baby's shoulders with one arm and hold her firmly with your hand around the top of her arm. Use the other hand to support her bottom and lower her gently into the bath water.

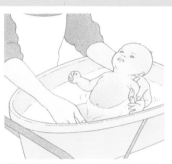

5 Continue to support the baby's shoulders and hold her arm while you swish the water gently around her with your free hand. Rinse off all the soap.

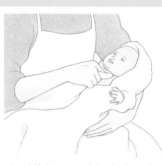

6 Lift her out of the bath and wrap her in a towel. Use another towel to dry her gently, making sure you dry in all her little creases. Apply baby cream, if using, and then put on her undershirt, clean diaper and the rest of her clothes.

mixing the water, there is less chance that she will be harmed. If you put the hot water in before the cold, you also risk heating up the bottom surface of the bath – temporarily but dangerously – and scalding your baby as you lower her into the bath.

Once you're sure the temperature of the water is right, add the baby bath liquid (*see* Toiletries, page 110) if you're using it. If the bath is a new experience for your baby, or she is a little nervous at bathtimes, talk to her (and sing if you like) to make it more fun and to give you both more confidence. By the time she is about three months old, your baby may enjoy splashing about in the bath. If so, allow her more time to play.

SAFETY NOTE

Never leave your baby alone in the bath, even when she can sit up on her own. She could drown in just a few inches of water.

Toiletries

You can either use baby soap or a baby bath liquid for washing your baby. If you are a bit anxious about holding a slippery soapy baby, you may prefer to use the liquid – it can be added to the bath water before you put your baby in and then you won't need to use soap at all. If you do use soap, choose a special baby soap or a mild pure one – perfumed soaps are not suitable.

At first you'll just want absorbent cotton to wash your baby's face. When she is a little older you can use a clean face cloth kept exclusively for her. This is probably more hygienic for a small baby than a sponge, as it's so much easier to rinse through and dry out, although your baby may enjoy water from a sponge squeezed over her head. You won't need baby shampoo for a while, unless your baby has a lot of hair; a little soap, or water with baby bath liquid in it, will do for now. You'll also need two towels – one to wrap her in and the other to dry her. You could buy a special toweling robe to keep her cosy after her bath. An extra towel (or waterproof apron) for your lap is a good idea, too.

It is better not to use baby powder on young babies because it can be easily inhaled. Instead, you can use cornstarch. Shake it into your hand first and then rub it on your baby. Do make sure your baby is quite dry before using the powder, otherwise it could cake and stick in the folds of her skin. Avoid using cotton swabs as it is tempting to poke in the baby's ears and nose and this could hurt her.

When to bath your baby

Choose a bathtime that suits you and your baby best. It needn't be at the same time every day. A young baby's day is unpredictable and it's generally easier at first to take each one as it comes. When she gets a little older, you might find that a regular bathtime fits in better with family life and helps to structure your baby's day. In the early days, a good time for bathing is when she is wakeful, but not hungry. Try to avoid bathing a young baby immediately after a feeding, too, as the extra handling could make her spit up.

Make sure that the room is warm before you wash your baby and, on cooler days, don't keep her undressed for longer than you need to. Make sure your hands are clean before you start and have everything you need beside you.

Bathtime problems

Some babies hate being bathed at first and it is not always clear why this is so. If your baby cries at bathtimes and seems to dislike it, first of all check that there is nothing making her uncomfortable and that the water is not too hot or too cold. You can also try to make bathtimes more fun by talking and playing with her as she gets a little older.

Your baby won't come to any harm if she isn't bathed for a few days, just so long as you keep her clean by sponge bathing (*see* opposite). Often a short break from the bath is all that is needed to help her overcome the problem. She will usually forget whatever it was that upset her, and you can start from square one. If you insist on bathing her, despite her cries, this will only make the situation worse. When you're trying to get her used to the bath again, talk to her all the time, keeping your voice calm and reassuring.

If your baby has very sensitive skin – or perhaps a recognized condition such as eczema – a bath could irritate her or maybe dry her skin too much. You can ask your pediatrician's advice about this – it could be that a simple change of bath products is all that's needed. Just occasionally a baby's skin may be sensitive to soap or to baby bath liquid. You may be able to get soap-free products from the pharmacy or from a health food store.

Sponge baths

Although it's an important part of the routine care of your baby, bathing isn't something you need to do every day if you don't want to. On the days you don't give her a tub bath it's sufficient to "sponge" (that is, wash her face, hands and bottom) to keep her clean.

HOW TO GIVE A SPONGE BATH

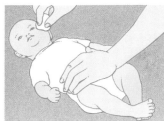

1 Using absorbent cotton and clean warm water from a small container, wipe her eyes first. Remember to use a fresh piece of cotton for each eye and wipe from the inside corner out.

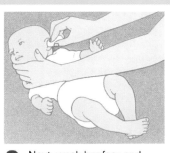

2 Next, wash her face and neck. Use moistened absorbent cotton to gently wipe her ears. Never poke inside her ears or nose – just wipe the surface of them. Wash and dry her hands and check to see if her nails need cutting.

3 Remove her diaper and clean her bottom (*see* page 104). In the early days you'll need to gently clean round her umbilical stump each day with alcohol, until the stump is thoroughly healed and dried. Put on a clean diaper and her clothes.

To the big bath

It's entirely up to you when you start to bath your baby in the family bath. If you have an older child or children, you may find it suits you to combine their bedtime routines by letting them share a bath. Your baby can go in the water first, and if necessary, you can add some more warm water for the older child. He can splash about in the bath while you dry the baby. In the big bath, the rules about the temperature of the water still apply – put cold water in first and then add hot.

You can get your baby used to the change by bathing her in her small bath, placed within the big one. This makes it easier to fill and empty, so you could try it earlier.

Sleep and bedtime

The amount of sleep that you and your baby get will be one of your main concerns for some time to come. It takes time for a baby to establish a pattern of feeding and sleeping and, although he will spend much of his time asleep, he will wake frequently to be fed or to be settled. This may make it difficult for you to catch up on your own sleep.

How much will your baby sleep?

The amount of sleep that babies need does vary. Some sleep most of the time in the first few weeks and may even need waking up for feedings, but there are also babies who never sleep for more than a total of 10 or 12 hours out of 24 from the start. To begin with, sleep is closely related to feeding: your baby wakes because he is hungry and is unlikely ever to fall asleep happily unless he feels full and satisfied. He will probably have one period of the day during which he remains wide awake for some time, often in the afternoon or early evening.

Your baby's sleeping pattern will be changing as he becomes more sociable, and he will be waking up not just for food but to enjoy your company too, ready for stimulation. By the time he is three or four months old he is likely to have two or three wakeful periods each day. Now his daytime sleeps can really be counted as naps and will gradually become shorter as the months pass.

Where should your baby sleep?

At the beginning he will sleep anywhere so long as he is comfortable, whether it is in your arms or in a carriage, infant carrier or crib. He will sleep just as much as he needs to and, fortunately, a very young baby is unlikely to be awakened by any noise you make. Babies adapt to the noise level around them, so you don't have to tiptoe around or blame yourself if he wakes up – it's much more likely to be because he is hungry or uncomfortable.

In the early days some parents like to have the baby in their bedroom at night, so that they can hear him when he wakes and feed him without too much disruption. Within three or four months the noise you make will wake him more easily so, if he doesn't have his own room, when you go to bed move him to the hall or living room if they are warm enough (*see* Settling your baby, right).

From the very beginning it is worth making a distinction between where your baby sleeps at night and during the day. Although it will be some time before he notices the difference, it will help you to try and establish a bedtime routine. Put your baby into his bassinet or crib at night and draw the curtains in his room. Until he is a little older, and can change position himself, put him down to sleep in his crib on his stomach, not his back. Then, if he does bring up any milk after a feeding, it will trickle out of the side of his mouth and not make him choke. He shouldn't have a pillow in his crib until he is about a year old. If you have a carriage, you can put him to sleep in this during the day – either inside or, if it is fine weather, outside where you can keep an eye on him. Don't forget that a screen or mosquito net is essential for the carriage, to protect against animals and insects.

Many mothers, particularly if they are breastfeeding, get into the habit of giving nighttime feedings in bed and then keeping the baby in the bed with them. This practice should be discouraged for the baby's safety, the mother's better rest and because the habit is hard to break later.

Should you leave your baby to cry?

If you have a very wakeful baby you may feel tempted to leave him to cry from time to time. In the early months babies only cry when they need something, and research has shown that babies who are *not* left to cry become confident and secure rather than spoilt. However, many babies cry for a little when they are first put down to sleep. You will eventually come to recognize this "tired cry" and know that if you leave him he will soon stop. Miserable grumbling is very different from frantic and persistent crying which should not be ignored.

Getting a good night's sleep

Few babies sleep through the night in the early months (many still wake at night when they are over a year old), and parents long for a full night's sleep more than anything else. Even if your baby is spending about one six-hour stretch asleep, you will almost certainly have to get up during the night to feed him.

Make things easier for yourself by getting everything you need for the feeding ready before you go to bed. Then nighttime feedings can be dealt with quickly in the semidark, with no playing, so there is little incentive for the baby to stay awake.

SLEEP AND BEDTIME

A very young baby will take all the sleep she needs, even if it is not always when you want her to!

Your day together

With your baby snug in a sling, you can keep an eye on her while preparing the lunch.

During the first weeks with your baby, a "day" is a full 24 hours. Getting to know her is exhausting as well as exciting – no book will be able to tell you exactly what to expect from this unique individual.

Working out your priorities

Your baby will settle into a routine sooner or later, but there is nothing you can do to make it happen any faster. Until a pattern emerges, the best you can do is to take one day at a time. Concentrate on enjoying your baby, tend to her needs and look after yourself too. Tasks that will soon seem like second nature to you, such as feeding and changing diapers, need all your attention while you are learning to carry them out. But to be able to enjoy looking after your baby, you must take every opportunity to rest.

Planning your day

Before long a routine will start being established, and it can then be slowly and gently changed to fit your lifestyle. Any attempt to force a pattern on a newborn baby will be frustrating for you and will make her miserable.

If you have other children, then your day already has a pattern into which the baby must fit, but if this is your first baby you might like to plan a little to break up the day.

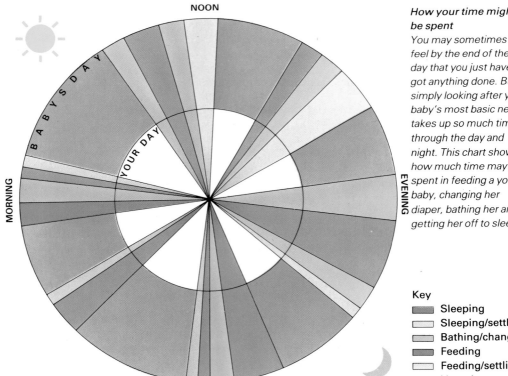

NOON

BABY'S DAY

YOUR DAY

MORNING

EVENING

MIDNIGHT

How your time might be spent

You may sometimes feel by the end of the day that you just haven't got anything done. But simply looking after your baby's most basic needs takes up so much time – through the day and night. This chart shows how much time may be spent in feeding a young baby, changing her diaper, bathing her and getting her off to sleep.

Key

- ▨ Sleeping
- ▢ Sleeping/settling
- ▨ Bathing/changing
- ▨ Feeding
- ▢ Feeding/settling
- ▢ Your time

However, the idea at this stage is to be as adaptable as possible; if you plan too much, you may be frustrated when your baby doesn't co-operate! Aim to have an outing once a day – the change of scene is important for both of you. The fresh air is good for the baby and she will enjoy being outside, even if it is cold and you have to wrap her up warmly. Choose a time that would suit you best – the morning when you have to do some shopping, for instance, or the afternoon if you feel like getting out then.

Evenings and weekends

At this age your baby may have very wakeful periods, often in the evening and through the night. When your partner is at home, he could help by looking after the baby while you rest or get on with something else.

Getting things done

There are a certain number of chores that you have to do, but it may be difficult to fit them in while your baby is awake as that is when she'll need your attention most. There is no right time to do the cleaning or prepare the vegetables for supper, but deciding to do only the essential things frees you to give most of your time to your baby and take the rest you need. When she is very young, your touch and voice give your baby more pleasure than anything, so try carrying her in a sling and chatting to her while you work.

As she gets older you can place her where she can watch you work – for example, in a bouncing cradle – or perhaps lie her on a blanket on the floor for a while, first on her tummy and then on her back. She'll be able to kick to her heart's content. When she has more control of her head you can prop her up on a chair or sofa for a while with lots of cushions, but keep an eye on her to see that she hasn't slumped. Keep a stock of interesting clean playthings for her: a rattle, toys with bells, a wooden spoon, a plastic brick. Once she has become more mobile and can roll over, you really will have to keep an eye on her all the time.

As your baby becomes more wakeful during the day, you will have to do something for and with her every few minutes – this is not spoiling her, it's just what she needs at this age.

Friends and neighbors

The most sympathetic people at this time will be those with a child of the same age. You may find that your social circle changes to include these friends because they have similar interests and concerns. For practical reasons it is good to know near neighbors with a child of about the same age as your own, who may be able to help out when necessary. You will probably meet other mothers who live nearby when you go to your pediatrician, or you could join a new-parents group. You might consider starting a group that meets informally once or twice a week. Some time spent with other mothers and babies will make you feel less isolated and allows you to discuss any worries with people who share them.

YOUR DAY TOGETHER

A DAILY PATTERN

If your baby does not seem to develop any feeding pattern after a while, try and look at the day as a whole. Think about giving her a regular getting-up time when you dress her in day clothes; regular walks in the fresh air to help her sleep soundly; visits to see other babies and young children; times when she can have the full attention of both parents; a bathtime; and a bedtime routine of changing into nightclothes and having a lullaby or nursery rhyme sung to her. You will both get accustomed to the familiarity of events in your day and feeding times will come to fit in around these activities. This is after all what happens with a second baby, when the toddler has her own routine and the new baby has to fit in with this.

Going out in the carriage gives your baby a change of scene and will help to calm her if she is irritable.

115

Growing and learning

Secure and totally relaxed, your newborn baby's body molds snugly against yours.

Right from the start your newborn baby has a personality of his own. He may be restless, sleeping for only short periods, crying and wanting to feed frequently, or he may be quiet and need to be woken to feed. Your child is an individual, different in many ways from other children, and it is this which makes his development unique.

The way he responds to you will vary according to whether he's contented or hungry, tired or uncomfortable. When he's in that half-wakeful, half-sleepy state you can see him starting to communicate with you, listening to your voice and the sounds around him. When he's tiny he will explore your face by looking at it in a quizzical intense way. Later you will see his hand try to reach up to you.

The seeds of the skills that are to emerge over the months and years ahead are there in these early days. His play, his contact with you and other people, and all his other experiences will help him to develop and use these skills. To start with, he's only able to show a little of what is to come but he's taking in much more than he shows.

Getting stronger

Your newborn baby doesn't have the strength or control to move any part of his body in a purposeful way. When he is born, his movements are spontaneous and called reflexes. He cannot at first move his arms deliberately to reach for something nor his legs to kick against something. As his muscles strengthen he will gain more control over his arms and legs. His limbs will lose their early jerkiness and by three months he'll be kicking away vigorously.

The curled-up position he lies in during his first few days, with his arms and legs bent and tucked under his body and his bottom slightly raised up, is very similar to the fetal position he was in before birth. In these early weeks he will mold his body into yours as you carry him close. Gradually he will stretch out his limbs and his body will lie flatter against you.

BECOMING STRONGER AND MORE CONTROLLED

These months see rapid progress in the control your baby has over his head and back. From being curled up when he's first born, his whole body unfolds, he learns to lift his head, then push up on his arms and look around purposefully. As he approaches six months he may be sitting up with some support.

In his first weeks your baby will lie in a curled-up position with his bottom up and his arms and legs tucked under him.

He'll soon learn to lift his head up, at first only for a few seconds but soon he'll hold it up for longer.

You need to support his head when you lift or carry him in these first weeks. His head is the heaviest part of his body and the muscles in his back and neck are too weak as yet to hold it up. It will probably be about a month or two before he can lift his head up and keep it steady without it wobbling or flopping back.

At about six weeks old he'll start, when he's on his tummy, to lift his head up briefly before it comes to rest on one side. Then by three or four months, as the muscles in his shoulders, back and neck strengthen, he'll be able to push up on his forearms, lift his head and chest off the mattress and have a good look around.

When he's lying on his back, his head flops over to one side at first. By the time he is three months old, though, he will be able hold it still while he watches a mobile or his own fingers in front of his face.

Once he's a couple of months old he'll enjoy sitting supported in a chair or bouncing cradle. Over the next few months he'll be getting ready to sit unsupported for a while. His back will be straighter now, but he will need to learn to balance before he can sit without help.

Above Babies love physical contact especially when they can watch your face. This baby is enjoying the feeling of being gently raised up and then let down again.
Left She's learned to push up on her arms and is now pushing on her legs as well as enjoying gazing around her.

When he's three to four months he'll be able to push up on his forearms, raising his chest and holding up his head.

At about five months your baby will be able to support himself on his straightened arms while he turns his head and looks round.

When supported in a sitting position, his back will at first be quite curved and his head will come forward.

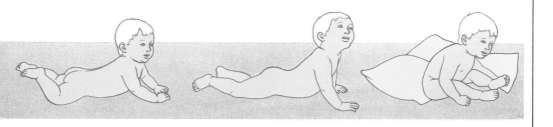

117

HOW TO ENGAGE YOUR BABY IN CONVERSATION

Hold your baby up in front of you with his head cupped in your hands and his back against your forearms. His face is close to yours.
Rock him gently back and forth so he's fully awake. His eyes will search out yours. Talk to him quietly and he will start to copy you – nodding his head, blinking and smiling back at you.

Looking, holding and reaching

Your baby can see even in his first few days. He will gaze intently at your face if he's held upright about 8-10 inches away. He will be attracted by things such as faces, striking patterns, lights and bright colors, particularly red or green. His gaze at you may be quite intense at first and by the time he's six to eight weeks it may be accompanied by a smile.

While you're changing his diaper or when he's lying on his back in his crib, you can see him beginning to follow objects with his eyes. He'll turn his head, watching all the time, then his head will flop back again.

As he gets stronger he can control his head and eye movements more easily. By three months he is moving his heavy head and looking around him. By the time he's six months old he enjoys watching everything, his eyes following people right across the room.

When he's first born he holds his hands closed, but he will gradually open them and begin to move his fingers. He'll soon learn to bring his hands together in front of him and look at them. He'll also start to reach out towards toys, touching them, though he cannot yet open his hands to grasp them. If a toy is put in his hand, he may hold it and bring it to his mouth. By the time he's six months old he may be passing a toy from one hand to the other, or holding one in each hand. He'll be able to reach out to pick up toys and play with them.

Communicating and responding

Babies, even the newest, have a great many ways of telling you things. At first, crying is the most obvious. The rather feeble cat-like cry of the newborn baby soon changes to a stronger, more demanding tone. The urgency of his cry may help you to detect whether he's hungry, uncomfortable, tired or even just bored. He may stop crying when he's picked up or when you speak to him. He's slowly becoming more responsive to people.

She'll gaze with rapt attention at her own fingers as she gently moves them in front of her eyes.

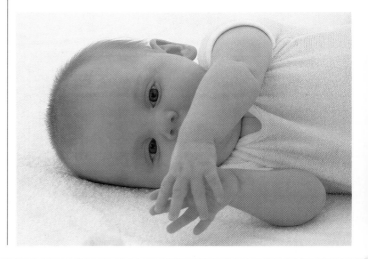

Once she can hold a rattle and bring it towards her it can be studied, shaken, sucked and, quite soon, felt with both her hands.

USING HIS HANDS

During your baby's first weeks he'll hold both his hands tightly closed in a fist.

He'll gradually begin to open his hand out and move his fingers.

By six months he'll grasp a toy and may be passing it from one hand to the other.

Your new baby can also make a number of different facial expressions. These range from a peaceful sleepy look, often interspersed with "grins," to a red screwed-up look when he is cross or has a tummy ache! His contented snuggling on your shoulder will also tell you how he feels, compared to the tenseness of his body when he has gas.

He can hear even before he's born and you may have felt him move in the womb when a loud noise is made near you. When he's first born, sudden loud noises will cause his whole body to start while a quieter, more continuous noise may soothe him. Later, he'll recognize certain noises and show he's listening. At first, he will seem to search for the sound with his eyes, but later he'll be able to turn his head to find the sound. He may stop when he's feeding to look in the direction of a voice.

When he's about six weeks old he'll start to utter little gurgling noises when he's content and may start to "coo" when you talk to him. He'll wave his arms, smile and wriggle his body when he's excited. You will have noticed fleeting smiles when he's younger, but there comes a time when he definitely smiles back at your face. Smiles lead to laughter, and the first "ka" and "goo" sounds are soon followed by others as he enjoys hearing his own voice.

When he's six months old he'll be well aware of what's going on around him. He may become excited at bathtime and wriggle in your arms once he sees his bath is ready.

Safe in your arms, he is beginning to form his own view about the wider world around him.

THE CENTER OF HIS WORLD
As a parent you will be called upon to fulfill many roles in bringing up your child. In the earliest weeks you are the center of his world and provide all he needs to thrive. You
● provide the love and comfort that make him feel secure
● provide the necessities for his survival – food, protection and shelter
● give him variety in his experiences – he hears your voice, looks at your face and smile, touches, smells and clutches at your clothes and face
● give him the opportunity to try new things, for example, as you carry him he gets the feeling of movement
● help him find out about his world as you tell and show him things. His early experiences are very important for his later development.

She'll love touching and exploring your face.

Making himself at home

That tiny helpless newborn baby has an amazing ability to learn and fit in with the new world surrounding him. In the first days and weeks he'll adjust to life outside the womb. He may settle down quickly or he may take time to adjust and get into a pattern. There are so many different things for him to see, feel and hear; even the temperatures are different now. He will have got used to the gradually changing rhythms of life inside the womb, so it is not surprising that his new world comes as a bit of a shock to him. The cuddling and contact that he has with you provide him with the comfort and security that are so necessary for him to thrive and develop.

His behavior gradually changes as he settles down into family life and his personality starts to emerge. You'll begin to find out what soothes him when he's upset and what routines he likes and dislikes. He may be a noisy, restless baby or quite placid by nature. He might like always sleeping in the same position or he may be willing to sleep anywhere. A big feeding every few hours may satisfy him or he may demand more frequent, small feedings. Some of these early ways of behaving will be reflected when he gets older; others will disappear.

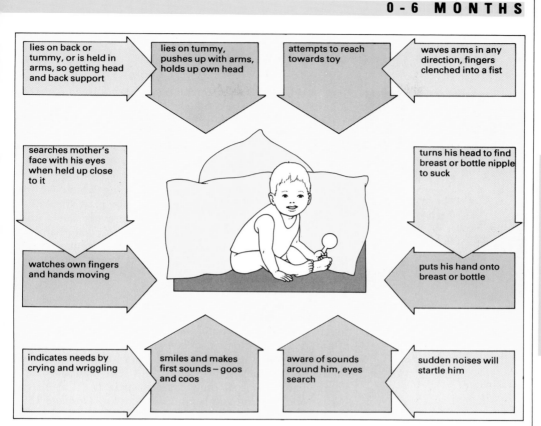

lies on back or tummy, or is held in arms, so getting head and back support

lies on tummy, pushes up with arms, holds up own head

attempts to reach towards toy

waves arms in any direction, fingers clenched into a fist

searches mother's face with his eyes when held up close to it

turns his head to find breast or bottle nipple to suck

watches own fingers and hands moving

puts his hand onto breast or bottle

indicates needs by crying and wriggling

smiles and makes first sounds – goos and coos

aware of sounds around him, eyes search

sudden noises will startle him

Becoming aware of his world

A new baby's world is small. It is limited to what immediately surrounds him and you are very much the center of this world. At first, the way he sinks into your arms when you hold him close makes it feel as if he's still part of you. You are providing not only the essentials for his survival such as food, warmth and comfort but also all he needs to look at, listen to, touch and smell. When you're carrying him around he experiences the feeling of movement while also still being close to you. He also is able to see everything from a completely different viewpoint. As he gets older he'll reach out to grab at things. He'll love tugging your hair or pulling off granny's glasses.

As he develops, so his world expands too. By the time he is three or four months old he'll be spending more time quietly awake and will be becoming aware of the familiar people and routines in his life. He may be learning, for example, that his evening bath followed by a feeding signals the time for a longer sleep than his naps in the day. He won't "know" it's nighttime but he's learning a bedtime routine that may be the beginning of a night's sleep.

Being awake more now, he'll be noticing things outside the immediate surroundings of his carriage or crib. The leaves fluttering on trees in the park, bright pictures on his bedroom wall and people talking may all attract his attention. You're still the center of his world but it has now expanded and he's ready to make his own mark in it.

From newborn to six months
This chart shows the progress you will see your baby making in different areas. These all work together and contribute to his reaching the stage where he is able to sit up with some support and hold a rattle in his hand while he looks up at you and laughs.

Play and toys

The world, which is so familiar to you, is a foreign planet to your baby. Before she can make any use of the learning that schools will one day offer her, she has plenty of learning of her own to do. She has to find out about her own body and how it works, about other people, and about all the objects and experiences which make up her world. Nobody else can teach her these things; she'll discover them for herself through the exploring and experimenting which we call "play." You won't have to make your baby play; she will do it instinctively. But you do need to provide her with a secure, safe and happy environment. For a young baby the most important part of this is people, and for some time you will be her main source of pleasure and interest.

Play and learning

Below A guide to the playthings your baby will enjoy, and what will interest her as her skills develop.

Your baby learns about the world through her five senses – touch, sight, smell, taste and hearing. Just cuddling and talking to her stimulates her senses and is something that is rewarding for you as well as for her. One of her first interests will be her own hands and feet, and even as a young baby she will enjoy games such as "This Little Piggy" and "Round and Round the Garden" (*see* page 125). She will respond to your touch and the sound of your voice, and will love it when you stroke her cheek, tickle her tummy and sing nursery rhymes to her. When she has her first toys she'll enjoy them more if you spend a little time playing with her and showing her what the toy can do. She is more likely to explore the ducks strung across her carriage if you have shown how they jump when patted.

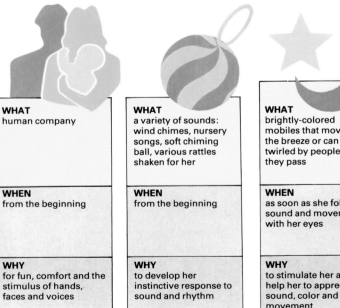

WHAT human company	**WHAT** a variety of sounds: wind chimes, nursery songs, soft chiming ball, various rattles shaken for her	**WHAT** brightly-colored mobiles that move in the breeze or can be twirled by people as they pass	**WHAT** playthings that move when she hits them – a baby gym or a row of toys or beads stretched across her carriage or chair
WHEN from the beginning	**WHEN** from the beginning	**WHEN** as soon as she follows sound and movement with her eyes	**WHEN** she starts to wave her arms about and reach towards things
WHY for fun, comfort and the stimulus of hands, faces and voices	**WHY** to develop her instinctive response to sound and rhythm	**WHY** to stimulate her and help her to appreciate sound, color and movement	**WHY** to help her to entertain herself and to recognize cause and effect

A soft cuddly toy feels nice and is a friendly face she can respond to.

The ideal first playthings for your baby are ones that are colorful and easy to hold. She will particularly like bright colors such as red and green. She will also enjoy playthings which make a noise or move when she touches them. Anything that gives her the chance to control things a little will interest her. A soft toy or woolly ball dangling within reach can be made to swing as she touches it; in time she will learn to reach for it deliberately. A tiny bell, or bright buttons, securely stitched to the mittens she wears out of doors will give her pleasure from the very beginning as she waves her hands about. Some of the more sophisticated toys she is given may not be appreciated until she is a little older, so put them away until she can enjoy them.

WHAT	WHAT	WHAT
toys that are colorful and easy to hold, simple rattles to wave, a small rag doll or teddy to cuddle	teething rings and plastic toys that are clean, unbreakable, nontoxic and with no detachable pieces	pictures in her crib or carriage, and a bright nursery wall hanging for her bedroom
WHEN	**WHEN**	**WHEN**
her hands are no longer clenched all the time and she is able to hold onto things	her hands often go to her mouth and she likes to suck and chew	she can sit up and focus
WHY	**WHY**	**WHY**
to encourage her to use her hands and distinguish different sounds and textures	to encourage her to explore taste, texture and temperature with her mouth	for the pleasure of looking at shapes and colors

CHOOSING SAFE SUITABLE TOYS
● Soft toys should be *soft* with eyes and limbs held securely in place.
● Paint and other materials should be nontoxic.
● Toys should not have components small enough for babies and young children to push into noses, ears or mouths.
● All edges should be thoroughly smooth and rounded – no sharp points or edges.
● The toy should not be so fragile that it might break or split and become dangerous.
● Moving parts, if any, should not be capable of trapping fingers.
● The toy should not be made from a highly flammable material.

PLAY SAFE
A small baby is sometimes at risk from the affectionate attentions of older brothers and sisters who want to share their toys (or even pets) with her. Toys that are perfectly safe and suitable for an older child can be hazardous to a baby. Warn your other children not to give their new brother or sister:
● anything sharp
● anything with long strings or ribbons
● anything small enough to fit into the baby's mouth (such as a bead or a sweet) – even quite large objects can be swallowed if the baby is lying down, and they can easily make her choke or cause an obstruction
● anything heavy – babies are likely to hit their heads with anything which is put into their hands
● any pet, however soft, small and lovable!

Choosing safe playthings

As children get older they are able to choose what they play with, but a baby – while she knows what she likes – has no sense at all of what might be unsuitable or even dangerous. To a child of this age everything is a toy, and you are therefore responsible for deciding what your baby can safely play with and enjoy (*see* left, and "Choosing safe suitable toys" on previous page). All toys made either in the U.S. or imported and sold here must comply with the government safety regulations. Any toy or baby equipment that proves unsafe should be reported to the U.S. Consumer Product Safety Commission which has a toll-free hot-line (1-800-638-2772) during busy toy-buying seasons for information on safe toys and furniture.

Play with your baby

Because a new baby makes a lot of work for you, it is possible to think of her as *just* another chore and want to leave her alone and get on with something else once the bathing, changing and feeding are done. But think how the other members of your family would react if you ignored them, except to prepare their meals and wash their clothes. Your baby is a person in her own right and needs to be treated as one. While coping with all the necessary tasks involved in looking after your baby, leave some time for singing, playing and talking with her. She will enjoy your company and will learn from you and the rest of the family about fun and affection. You, in turn, will find you enjoy her more, as she starts responding to your attention. This is the beginning of your lifelong relationship with her.

DANCE WITH YOUR BABY
You won't be able to do anything very sophisticated at this stage but you can move together in response to rhythm and sound, and that is what dancing is all about. Some babies enjoy the stimulation and exercise enormously. You simply hold your baby securely in your arms, or in a baby carrier or sling, and dance to whatever music you both like.

To do the following exercises, you can put the baby on her back on the floor or your knees, or sit on the floor with your knees bent and rest her back against your thighs.

1 While singing, counting or listening to music, take the baby's hands and gently stretch her arms out horizontally. Bring her hands in to touch her chest. Then, stretch her arms up by her head and down again.

2 Take her feet in your hands and move her legs in a gentle bicycling movement, first in one direction and then the other. If she enjoys this, repeat the exercise several times.

Play and language

Most people instinctively talk to babies quite differently from the way they talk to one another. They put their faces very close to the baby's face and use their mouths and eyes to make funny faces which are often an exaggerated version of the baby's expression. They use a different tone of voice too, using much higher and lower sounds than usual.

You might think that other people look silly having a conversation with their baby, making faces that mirror the baby's own expression, but don't let that stop you. It is exactly what your baby needs. She can focus more easily on a face that is close to her own and she will enjoy seeing your expressions and hearing the sound of your voice. As you play with her like this, she will begin to respond with noises and gestures of her own, and so start your first "conversations." This is one of the most fascinating times with your baby and it is rewarding for you to be with her as she learns to communicate through play.

Advice not to take

There may be someone who tells you that you will spoil your baby if you play with her, rock her, sing to her or merely keep her company. Take no notice. Your child's understanding of the world develops through play and through contact with people. Nobody thinks that you are spoiling her when you give her as much food as she needs, or clothes to keep her warm. Your baby also needs the comfort, affection and understanding of a familiar adult to be able to play happily. To suggest that playing with your baby is spoiling her is an old wives' tale. Don't ignore the baby, ignore the old wives.

Toys are more fun when parents join in with the games.

FIRST GAMES

Round and round the garden goes a teddy bear
  (your forefinger traces circle round baby's open palm)
One step
  (move finger to baby's wrist)
Two steps
  (move finger to baby's elbow)
Tickly under there!
  (under baby's arm)

This little piggy went to market
  (wiggling baby's big toe)
This little piggy stayed at home
  (wiggling second toe)
This little piggy had hot roast beef
  (*or whatever your family likes*)
  (wiggling third toe)
And this little piggy had none
  (wiggling fourth toe)
And THIS little piggy
  (wiggling fifth toe)
cried "Wee, wee, wee" ALL the way home!
  (tickling up baby's leg)

Repeat both rhymes on the other hand or foot.

Your baby's health

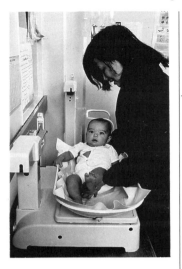

Before your baby was born you probably made contact with your pediatrician or had already made up your mind which child health clinic you were going to take your baby to. At your pediatrician's office or at the child health clinic, you will find in addition to your doctor, physician's assistants and pediatric nurse practitioners who are always available to discuss any problems you may have and give you advice on feeding or other matters. Each time you visit your pediatrician or clinic, your child will have a physical examination, and her weight, height, and head measurement will be recorded. She will be given a developmental screening test (*see* below) including vision and hearing.

Weight gain

Don't go out of your way to weigh your baby. A healthy baby who takes her feedings happily and who moves her bowels regularly usually gains weight steadily. Your doctor keeps a close watch on your baby's weight gain. Carry your baby's health record book with you each time you visit her doctor so you can then refer to this little book and see exactly how much weight your baby is gaining.

Help with feeding

Your pediatrician is well trained in all aspects of baby and childcare, and he is a good source of advice on feeding. However, if you feel you need extra advice on breastfeeding, ask him if he can put you in touch with the local LaLèche League chapter. Your pediatrician will also advise on bottlefeeding and will tell you about giving your baby vitamin supplements, and fluoride drops to help create strong healthy teeth. She can also give you advice on weaning, sleep problems, colic and first illnesses.

Immunization

One of the most important things you can do for your child is to ensure that you have her immunized against serious diseases. Not only are you protecting your own child from illness, but also your next baby and other people's children who have not been immunized.

Most babies have their first vaccinations when they are about two months old. These consist of polio vaccine and the triple vaccine (DTP) for diphtheria, tetanus and whooping cough (pertussis). The repeat vaccinations are given when the child is four months, and six months. These would complete the first three DTPs and polios. It is important that your child has all three sets.

At fifteen months of age, your child will receive a combined measles, mumps and rubella (German measles) vaccine (MMR). At eighteen months of age, she will receive the fourth DTP and fourth polio. Between four to six years of age she will receive the fifth DTP and the fifth

See Feeding your baby, pages 96-97, for colic and weight gain

See A-Z of common ailments, page 266

polio. Between fourteen and sixteen years of age she may receive the combined tetanus and diphtheria vaccine.

The vaccinations your child is given rarely cause any serious side effects. She may have a slightly sore patch on her skin from the injections, or appear a bit off color the evening after, or the following day. Sometimes the measles (MMR) vaccine causes a rise in temperature, or a mild rash or slight diarrhea a few days later. In a very few cases, the whooping cough vaccine can cause a fit or convulsion, leading to brain damage, but this is very rare and it is important to remember that whooping cough itself is a serious disease which can cause brain damage or even death.

Be sure to tell your doctor if your baby has any adverse reaction to the first injection, as she may not be given further immunization. You can also discuss any worries you have about the vaccinations with him beforehand. He may advise postponing them if your child is not well, although a slight cold is not usually considered a reason for delay. (For contraindications, *see* Immunization, page 279.)

RECOMMENDED IMMUNIZATION SCHEDULE	
AGE	VACCINES
2 months	First diphtheria, tetanus and whooping cough (DTP) and first polio
4 months	Second DTP and second polio
6 months	Third DTP and third polio
15 months	Measles (MMR), mumps and rubella
18 months	Fourth DTP and fourth polio
4-6 years	Fifth DTP and fifth polio
14-16 years	Tetanus and diphtheria vaccine

Developmental tests

These checks are done in a simplified form which is called a developmental screening test. They are usually done each time you visit your pediatrician or child health clinic. If the doctor found that a baby was not developing as expected, she would refer the child to a developmental specialist or a developmental pediatrician for a thorough examination.

If you have worries about your child's development do talk them over with your pediatrician. You need not necessarily be concerned if your baby seems in just one or two things to be slower than other children. Comparisons can be misleading and your child will probably catch up.

Some common concerns

Most parents are anxious about the health and well-being of their newborn child and, when everything is new and strange, it is hard to know what is normal and to have confidence that all is well with your baby. It is quite natural to be worried about why he is crying, whether he is getting enough milk and how you will know if he is ill. You will gradually get to know his different cries, but never hesitate to seek advice from your doctor when you are worried or think your baby is really unwell. There are certain signs (*see* page 263) which indicate illness in a baby or young child and these should never be ignored.

Why is he crying?

Babies cry for different reasons, hunger being the most common. They also cry because they are too hot or too cold (feel the back of a baby's neck to see if it feels cold or sweaty) or from lack of physical contact. Picking your baby up is often an instant cure, or carrying him around in a sling may keep him happy. You will find that your baby responds to one treatment, such as rocking, one day and something else, such as a walk, the next. Babies sometimes cry because of pain from gas or colic, but frantic crying that does not respond to any comforting may be caused by illness, especially if the baby is feverish.

Many babies cry because they are tired. A baby will not always drift off to sleep when he needs to. Some babies become more and more tired and tense, and work themselves up into such a state that they fight sleep. Many such babies respond to being held in your arms while you walk up and down. Small babies often scream before and after their bath and when their diaper is being changed. If bathtime is too distressing, bath him only every two or three days. Babies are also very sensitive to the atmosphere around them, and if you are angry or tense he will sense it and cry even harder.

As the baby becomes more settled – between six weeks and three months – you will probably begin to recognize the different kinds of crying. Once this happens, and you gain confidence in handling your baby, you will find that diaper changing and bathtimes become much easier and more fun for both of you.

Colic

Many young babies have a regular spell of crying at about the same time every day, often in the evening. If this is quite different from his usual hungry cry and is like a scream, and if he draws up both legs to his stomach, then your baby may be suffering from colic. It does not need medication, but can last two to three months. You can try extra burping, putting him face down over your lap, gently rubbing his back or applying a warm pad to his stomach. Unfortunately, these often do not work.

See Feeding your baby, page 96, for colic

Night waking

Many mothers find that they hardly sleep at all in the first few months because the baby wakes two or three times during the night. This is probably the most difficult thing you will ever have to cope with as a parent. Each feeding and diaper change will take at least an hour and the baby may take some time to settle back to sleep.

Some babies are naturally more wakeful than others, but most are having their long sleep at night by the time they are three or four months old. You can help your baby to learn the difference between day and night by encouraging sociable times during the day, and by talking to him as little as possible and keeping the lighting low at night.

Skin rashes

It is quite common for small babies to suffer from minor skin blemishes and rashes. Birthmarks often disappear within the first few months or by the time your child is about five years old. Some babies develop a characteristic skin rash in the early weeks, which is often most noticeable when the baby is too hot. This is known as milk rash – its medical name is neonatal urticaria – and no treatment is needed; it usually vanishes after two to three weeks.

Diaper rash is another common worry and almost every baby suffers from it, at some time. It can help to change your baby's diaper as soon as it is wet or dirty, and to use a barrier cream to protect his skin.

Teething

Your baby will probably cut his first teeth at around six months, but the teeth will be moving in the gums before he cuts them and this may cause discomfort. You may notice your baby biting furiously on everything, dribbling and appearing unusually fretful. However, there is no evidence that teething causes a baby to be unwell – a runny nose and temperature are more likely to be symptoms of a cold.

Crib death

There can hardly be a new parent who has not at some time crept into his or her sleeping baby's room to check that he is still breathing. Crib death, or sudden infant death syndrome, as it is also termed, has been given a lot of publicity and can be a real concern for some parents, especially if they know someone to whom this tragedy has happened. The cause of crib death – when a baby is put to bed in apparently good health and is found dead – is unknown, but research does seem to show that it is more common among bottlefed babies than breastfed babies, that more crib deaths occur in winter than in summer, and that it tends to run in families (and therefore may be caused by an inherited condition). Prevention is difficult as no one knows why crib death happens, but do watch out for your baby getting either too hot or too cold, and don't use a pillow in his crib until he is at least one year old.

USING A PACIFIER
You can try using a pacifier, or soother, to stop your baby crying if he isn't hungry – the sucking may soothe him and send him to sleep. But some babies become dependent on the pacifier to go to sleep and others will wake more often in the night because it has fallen out and they need you to put it back in. If your baby does use a pacifier, make sure that it is sterilized regularly and kept absolutely clean.

SOME COMMON WORRIES

See A-Z of common ailments, page 268 for birthmarks, page 271 for colic, page 273 for crib death, page 284 for rashes

Your family life

The arrival of a new baby, particularly your first, means a tremendous change in your life and the lives of everyone close to you. Adjusting to the idea of yourself as a parent, and the responsibility and maturity which that implies, takes getting used to and is different from the equally complex issues of learning to look after and getting to know and love your baby. Your relationship with your partner is bound to alter. The early hectic weeks take it out of both of you and you will have to adjust to being a small family unit, no longer just a couple.

The extended family – your parents, brothers, sisters and others – are all affected. Your position within your own family changes now that you are a parent and you often find that you want and need more contact with family members than you did before. If your relationship with your family is good, you will find that they all want to be involved now that there is a new baby. Help and support at this time is tremendously important and, while you will value it, you'll also find yourself bombarded with advice that is not always welcome. First-time grandparents may provide invaluable support but they also have some adjusting to do – not least learning the lesson that they can't always interfere and that you are now parents in your own right as well as their children.

The big change

As the new mother you have the most adjusting to do, quite simply because you have been through a tremendous physical experience as traumatic as an operation. After any similar experience you would expect to be prescribed plenty of rest, but in this case you are immediately plunged into the very demanding business of looking after your tiny helpless baby.

For the first few days you'll feel shaky and beset by physical problems such as sore stitches, difficulty going to the bathroom and perhaps discomfort when you move about. You'll wonder if you will ever be able to match the quiet competence with which the nurses handle your baby, possibly fearing that you may not be a good mother, or that you are not able to love your baby enough. This is a normal reaction which soon passes.

Going home from the hospital is exciting and often a great relief, but once you're at home you will have a lot to cope with. For much of the time you are likely to be looking after the baby on your own or juggling the needs of your new baby with those of your other children, who may be particularly clinging because you have been away. You are likely to be more tired than ever before, yet you've got your chores to fit in and possibly streams of curious friends and relations to entertain. To begin with, everybody gives a great deal of attention to the baby and very little to you. This can be slightly depressing, especially as you are working so hard.

Taking time to get to know your baby is very rewarding.

Coping with tiredness and depression

Tiredness is a fact of life for the first few weeks. Newborn babies sleep a lot but they wake every few hours, so it can be weeks before you're able to sleep for a long stretch. Somehow, catching up with sleep during the day is not the same but you will have to do so if you are going to manage. So long as you remember that your relationship with the baby and the rest of the family is more important than keeping a perfect house, you may find it easier to accept any help that is offered to you by friends and relatives.

Baby blues

Baby blues is the name given to the depression that many mothers suffer, usually three or four days after the birth. Sometimes there is an obvious reason, such as tiredness, soreness, or problems with feeding or handling the baby. But often there is no reason in particular. Many mothers, thinking that they should be delighted, feel guilty and worried about depression. Fortunately, it usually passes quite quickly, but if you continue to feel low, talk to someone sympathetic – your partner, your mother or someone you know who has been through it. Don't cut yourself off; continue to see people, especially female friends with young babies. Ask your doctor, childbirth instructor, or at the hospital where you delivered if there are groups in your area for young mothers. Try to have some time off during the day, or in the evening with your partner or a friend, leaving your baby with someone you can trust.

Postpartum depression

If you continue to feel miserable then you may be suffering from postpartum depression, which can go on for months after the baby's birth. This is something that you should not tackle on your own. Seek help soon. In the first place you should go to your doctor and explain how you feel; he may be able to help. The social services department of the hospital where you delivered or your family doctor have lists of postpartum support groups. They can also put you in touch with women who have felt like you.

POSTPARTUM CHECK-UP

You should have a check-up about four to six weeks after your baby's birth. You should go to your GP or your obstetrician for it. This is what the check-up covers:

● **Weighing**
You will be checked to see how much weight you have lost – after six weeks you should be near normal.

● **Urine testing**
A sample will be analysed to check that your kidneys are working properly.

● **Blood pressure check**
This is to make sure that it is back to normal.

● **Physical examination**
Your stitches will be checked to make sure that they have healed; your womb will be felt to see if it has returned to its normal size; also your pelvic muscles which should have regained their elasticity.

● **Rubella vaccine**
This is given if you are not immune to German measles, to protect future babies.

● **A talk with your doctor**
Write down any questions you want to ask before the visit.

YOUR FAMILY LIFE

Your relationship with your partner

Inevitably, your lifestyle and relationship with your partner undergo a change after the baby is born. The romantic notion is that a baby cements the bond between you, but that's not necessarily so at first. Moments of tension can arise from the fact that you and your partner may feel more tied together by the arrival of the baby than even the emotional or legal commitment between you. It can take several months just to get used to having another person around, and either partner can feel jealous of the other's attention to the baby. You may be disturbed because your partner, who was considerate during your pregnancy, expects you to return to normal soon afterwards. He may be battling with feelings of jealousy, fear of responsibility or he may feel superfluous because you seem to have taken control of caring for the baby.

It is important to talk about any mixed feelings that either of you have, even if you think they are silly, irrational or bad. The fact that you are both tired from broken nights can make you snappy so you'll have to make allowances for each other. But it is an exciting time and the new baby will

give you both tremendous pleasure and reward. The more both of you share in looking after your baby, the closer it will bring all three of you.

Your partner and the baby

Many men are more interested these days in involving themselves with the practical side of bringing up a child, and the tendency for fathers to be present at the birth helps to foster this involvement. You should encourage your partner to help you with the baby, particularly if he is at home on paternity leave or for other reasons. He will appreciate the joys and problems of being a parent better, and understand what you have to cope with if he has shared

Above Managing those wriggly arms and legs is a good way for a new father to get over any nervousness he may feel.
Above right Make the most of your time together when the baby is asleep – staying friends will help you cope with the shared responsibility of a new baby.

in the day to day care of the baby. But don't dazzle him with your expertise; it can be very off-putting if you keep butting in to show him how things are done and he may then decide that it is less trouble to leave everything to you.

Sex life

Medically, it is safe to make love again as soon after the birth as you want to, so long as the discharge from your vagina has stopped and your stiches have healed – which usually takes about two weeks. However, you can become pregnant again as soon as the baby is born so you should take precautions (see Family Planning, right).

Many couples, however, simply don't want to have intercourse for several weeks after the birth and so find other ways of being loving and coping with their sexual feelings. Usually it is the new mother who does not feel like making love again just yet, and it is quite normal for this feeling to last for several months. Sex difficulties arising from the birth of the first child are among the most common problems that marriage guidance counselors are asked to deal with and there can be real physical reasons for this. Tiredness, hormonal changes, or painful scar tissue can all cause such problems.

Some women find that they "turn off" to their partners sexually for months and don't know the reason for this themselves. Understandably, partners can feel hurt, angry and rejected, though it sometimes helps to hear how common a problem it is and that it usually sorts itself out. Sometimes the reason for loss of desire is traced to the level of prolactin in the body. This hormone, necessary to the production of milk, is linked to lack of sexual desire. If the hormone level remains high after breastfeeding has ceased, drugs may be prescribed to bring it back down to the normal level.

Sometimes the birth itself is the reason for you or your partner not having sex for a while. The father may find it difficult to make love again after having watched the birth. Similarly, some mothers are temporarily unable to have orgasms because of association with the pain of giving birth. If you are reluctant to have intercourse, discuss with your partner how you both feel rather than making excuses or picking fights. You can usually work through this difficult time together by talking about it and gradually resume your sex life as you both feel ready. Sometimes, however, these problems are not easy to deal with on your own and if you and your partner feel that you need professional advice, talk to your doctor. He may suggest that you seek advice from a marriage guidance counselor if things don't get better.

Time together

It is easy to lose sight of the fact that you are a couple as well as parents. Try to pick up some of your old habits of doing things together – just the two of you, even if it's just relaxing together in the evening, and chatting about your day. As soon as it is feasible, find a friend or relative who can babysit so that you can go out together again. It can be hard to talk really constructively and openly if you constantly have an ear out for the baby.

FAMILY PLANNING

Think about this immediately, as you can become pregnant very soon after your baby is born – even if you are breastfeeding – and you could be fertile even if your periods haven't yet started again. You can discuss family planning at your postnatal check-up.

● **The Pill**
If you are not breastfeeding you can continue to take your usual contraceptive pill. If you are breastfeeding, take it only if it is a low-dose mini pill, which does not reduce your milk supply. Remember that it is not reliable for the first 14 days, so you will need extra protection.

● **The sheath or condom**
Used by the man, who slips it over his erect penis to catch the sperm. Almost as effective as the pill, particularly if used with spermicidal cream or jelly.

● **The cap or diaphragm**
Placed over the cervix and used with spermicidal cream, it is an effective barrier, but don't be tempted to use one that was fitted before you had the baby. Your cervix will have changed shape so the diaphragm may not fit properly after the birth. You can have a new one fitted at your postnatal check-up.

● **Natural methods**
Precautions, such as the rhythm method, need to be carried out with a high degree of accuracy. Always follow your doctor's instruction to the letter.

Your older child will soon find her own ways of getting to know her new baby.

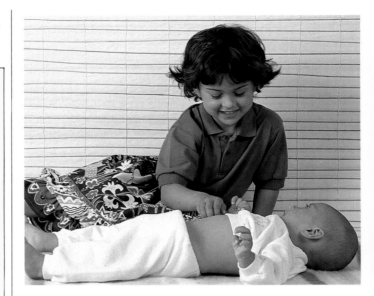

REGAINING YOUR FIGURE

After your baby is born your stomach may be rather flabby, but it will soon return to its former shape with exercise. While you are in hospital you will probably be taught some postnatal exercises. Walking is also good exercise and tones up the whole of your body in the most natural way, so taking the baby out in the carriage is beneficial for you too.

You will still be heavier than you were before your pregnancy. Don't try to lose weight. You need a healthy diet with a variety of foods to keep you going in the first tiring weeks. Cut down on fatty and sugary foods, but step up fiber-rich foods, such as fresh fruit, vegetables and wholewheat bread, to help prevent constipation.

EXERCISES

Lie on your back with a cushion under your head. Keep your knees bent and your feet flat on the ground. Repeat each exercise three times.

1. Pull your tummy in and tighten the muscles in your bottom until you feel your lower back pressing into the floor. Hold for a count of three. This strengthens your stomach and back muscles.

2. Stretch out your legs, cross them at the ankles and point your toes strongly while "holding yourself in." Hold this position for a count of three, then cross your legs the other way and repeat. This is good for your pelvic floor muscles.

Other children

If you have other young children, the first few months will be even more hectic, although you do have the advantage of knowing how tiring a small baby can be. You will have the additional problem of coping with the reactions of your other children. Try to make some time during the day when you give your attention exclusively to each child.

Returning to work

If you are going back to work you should make your practical plans well in advance. You must feel happy with the child care arrangement you make, and finding the right option for you and your baby may take some time. Check with the department of social services or your local community zoning board to see what facilities are available in your neighborhood. These agencies are often responsible for licensing day care. Also check the bulletin boards in your local supermarkets, libraries, Ys and churches. You can put advertisements up at the same time.

Choices in child care

The choice for most mothers is either a family day care or a day care center. Family day care refers to someone who takes care of your baby in his or her home. Only a few homes – between 5 and 10 per cent – are supervised by a social service agency, church group, school or day care center. These are usually licensed by the state department of social services, which makes periodic inspections to see if everything is satisfactory. Even so, regulations and standards vary greatly from state to state. As a rule, home day care providers have no formal training and they vary tremendously in their approach. Ideally, you would like someone who feels the same as you about child-rearing and who has a home similar to yours. Ask friends about their sitters and visit the homes of any that you like the sound of

● *See* Your family life, page 222, for coping with jealousy.

to get an idea of how they operate.

Good infant day care centers which accept children under one year old are exceedingly hard to find. The best are usually run by nonprofit agencies with the children being looked after by trained day care-takers. Most of them have long waiting lists and even those that have licensing and funding are expensive.

It is hard to find – and to afford – a full-time housekeeper, though sometimes it is possible to share the cost of one with other mothers. A competent babysitter who has had experience with babies is another alternative, or a relative or friend may be able to look after your baby.

You may be lucky enough to have a daycare center at work or, if you work for a large organization, you might want to look into the possibility of starting one.

Vacations and excursions

Going on vacation, or even just out for the day, with a young baby requires a certain amount of foresight. Make sure that you are equipped with everything you might need, such as disposable diapers, plastic pants, at least one change of clothing, a sweater, some baby wipes and, for a bottlefed baby, sterilized bottles and formula.

If you are going abroad, check with your doctor to see if your baby needs any vaccination, and with your travel agent that you can buy essentials such as disposable diapers at your destination. It is worth, however, packing the formula that your baby is used to because a change might cause problems. Remember to add your baby to your passport.

If you are traveling by car, your baby should be in an approved baby seat, or in an infant carrier with a restraint (*see* page 78). If you are traveling by air, allowing your baby to suck on the breast or bottle helps her adapt to the change in pressure while the aircraft is taking off or landing.

ANIMAL SAFETY

If you already own a pet, you should be aware that it can cause problems.

● Make sure your pet can't get to the baby's crib or carriage when he is sleeping. A dog could knock it over; a cat could settle on his face and smother him.

● Ask a friend to take your dog for walks in the first few weeks after the baby comes home.

● Take your pet to the vet before the baby is born to see that he has no disease that could be passed on to the baby. Check for fleas and worm him regularly.

● Never let your pet lick the baby's face.

● Wash pets' feeding bowls separately and keep them out of reach once your baby is crawling.

A shared day out provides a refreshing change of routine.

See **You and your sick child**, page 265, for vacation checklist.

THE OLDER BABY

Now your baby is taking a more and more active part in life and has become an established member of the family. Increasingly aware of everything going on around him, he will soon be on the move, making sure he doesn't get left out of anything. Gurgling, waving, playing with his toys and yelling for attention, he's a little person who loves life and is learning how to make the most of it.

You and your older baby

He'll become totally absorbed in his play and exploration.

Tickle her tummy or her toes and she'll bury her head against you in sheer delight.

In this second six months your baby really takes off. No sooner has she learned to sit steadily than it seems that all she really wants to do is be on the move. You may notice her "see-sawing" on the floor – head and shoulders up one minute, bottom in the air the next. In the end she'll find her own method of moving and, whichever she goes for – crawling forwards, backwards, or shuffling on her bottom – you can be sure that within weeks she will have perfected it and become the fastest creature in the house.

She can now follow you from room to room and find her own entertainment, but your previously safe home is fraught with potential dangers for the mobile child. She knows what she wants now and goes all out to get it. She's fast, and she can reach and grab with great skill. Electric sockets, thumb tacks, brightly colored bottles of bleach – all attract her like magnets. It really seems as though the more dangerous it is, the more she wants it. She learns by feeling as well as by listening and looking, and everything she finds goes into her mouth. No nasty taste will put her off, because she has yet to understand that mouths are used for eating – she is still exploring with hers.

Keeping her out of trouble

Suddenly you look at your house from your child's viewpoint, and the result is a succession of safety measures to protect her, and your more valuable possessions. Sometimes you may feel so exasperated that you could scream. It doesn't matter how many times you tell her "no," she continues to put herself in danger. You really have to be one step ahead all the time, and keep yourself sane by remembering that she will learn – eventually!

She's happier now to make her own entertainment and let you get on with things, but her devotion to you has reached fever pitch. It is now clear to everyone that you are the person she is most attached to. Cries and misery may accompany your every departure, even if you have just stepped into the bathroom for a second. The most sociable baby also starts to regard strangers and occasional visitors with deep suspicion.

Fun and games

In many ways your baby is becoming much more fun to be with, and she is much more interesting to other children too. She is likely now to wake up in the morning in a wonderfully good mood. Instead of the cries you used to hear, you'll be woken by gurgling laughter and chattering, as she greets teddy and plays with her crib toys. She's learned other uses for her voice too – she'll shout and scold. It doesn't matter that the words aren't there because *you* know what she means.

Now when you play with her she plays too. As she learns to imitate your gestures and tone, games like Pat-a-cake become fun. She'll invent her own games: pushing her toys in front of her as she crawls around the room, getting faster and faster; banging a block on the table to make you jump, and then roaring with laughter as you both repeat it over and over again. And if you are both in a silly mood, there's nothing like making funny faces or blowing raspberries at each other until you are red in the face.

Gradually her mealtimes coincide with yours and she becomes easier to feed. She'll soon be eating the same foods as you – but mashed or sieved. Before long she'll have four front teeth to gnaw with. She'll be quite an expert with finger foods now, although her attempts to wield a spoon may mean that she misses her mouth completely and makes a lot of mess. She'll also play her favorite game: dropping things out of her highchair and letting you know she wants them picked up. She can't understand your exasperation when it happens for the umpteenth time – it's endlessly fascinating to her.

She'll gradually change her sleeping pattern and may soon be taking just two short naps a day. Even if she

Left From quite an early age, babies will enjoy the company of other children.
Below She delights in her ability to attract and hold your attention.

doesn't sleep through them she's likely to be a bit happier in her crib, particularly if she has things to play with.

Making strides

As her first birthday approaches you'll find you can communicate with each other a lot better. She can now understand more of what you are saying to her and she can respond with a greater range of sounds and gestures.

Before her first birthday she will be able to pull herself up to a standing position – and then cry miserably because she doesn't know how to sit down again. Later she'll love cruising around the furniture, and when she's more confident there will be the first shaky steps. Meanwhile you'll be having to dish out a lot of comfort as her stubborn attempts result in bumps and falls.

What your baby will need

Life gets more complicated once your baby is on the move. Many babies at six months old are able to roll around the floor, and a few are beginning to crawl. By the end of the first year, your baby may be walking, if somewhat unsteadily and only with your help. He will also be able to reach out for things and he may be quite determined in his efforts to do this. Despite this growing independence, he is still not able to anticipate danger, or to remember you said "no" the last time he tried to reach something you didn't want him to have. He's not being naughty when he goes "out of bounds," just naturally curious, but his perfectly normal desire to explore and understand his surroundings can lead him into trouble nevertheless.

It is your responsibility to keep your baby from harm and this means thinking ahead. You should develop good safety habits early on even for 6-12 month old babies. Look carefully around your home to see what things, even at floor level, are within your baby's reach and could be harmful. Bear in mind that some babies in this age group are able to climb onto sofas and armchairs and so reach even further. The answer to your baby's increased mobility and vulnerability doesn't have to be to put him in the playpen all day, when he may get bored and frustrated, but being aware of what he might be able to do helps you to prevent accidents.

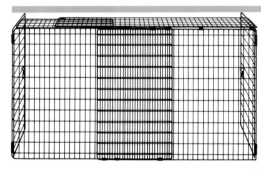

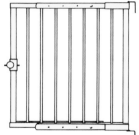

Fireguard
Fix a guard around every fire in the house, whether it is open, gas or electric. A fireguard that can be fixed to the wall is much safer than the old-fashioned fold-out kind, which could be knocked over. Never put anything on top of a fireguard or let your child slip things through the bars.

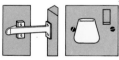

Safety catches
These should be fixed onto doors, cupboards and drawers as soon as your child is mobile.

Socket covers
All electrical sockets should have safety covers to curb your child's prying fingers.

Safety gate
This prevents your child from going up or down the stairs on his own. It can also be used to block off doorways, if you need to keep your child out of, or inside, a room. A removable steel or plastic mesh safety gate is useful for this purpose as it can be moved around easily and placed wherever you need it. However, a wall-mounted wooden gate is probably the safest because it is fixed. Use it in the places where you need a gate all the time (such as the stairs). Check when buying a safety gate that it can be operated by an adult, but not by a child, and make sure that your child cannot climb over it.

Stove safety
Remember always to turn pot handles inwards so that your child can't reach up to them and pull over the pot. You can get covers for electric burners that may help to prevent accidents. Some gas stoves come with an electronic ignition switch which prevents children from turning burners on accidently.

Safety in the home

As a general rule, make sure that all poisonous substances are kept well out of your child's reach. For a young child, poisonous substances also include alcoholic drinks, cigarettes, perfumes and cosmetics, cleaning materials, matches and, of course, medicines. Check the bathroom. Your usual place for storing items on the danger list may be low shelving or perhaps the floor. Choose a safer place now, such as a child-proof cupboard or cabinet (*see* page 290). In the kitchen, too, make sure that any potentially dangerous items are put away (this includes sharp knives) and that the garbage can is not accessible to the baby. As you do not smoke, discourage visitors from smoking in your house by putting away matches, lighters and ashtrays.

To prevent small hands from opening cupboards or drawers, you need to fix safety catches to them. However, it may be a good policy to allow your child access to one floor-level cupboard, filled with safe playthings (such as plastic containers and unbreakable crockery) so that he doesn't feel too frustrated. Opening doors and emptying cupboards is such fun for a baby who is enjoying his newly acquired physical skills, but do beware of him trapping his fingers in the cupboard door.

You should also consider buying a child-proof catch for the refrigerator. Refrigerators have a special fascination for small children – they love to see the light as the door is opened – but this is one more place they should certainly not be allowed.

Safety in the car

Your child will need a properly fitted convertible safety seat, to replace the infant seat (*see* page 78) once he is over 20 pounds in weight. It is advised that children under 40 pounds always be in a car seat during car travel. The most convenient seats to use are those with a harness/partial shield. Do make sure that your baby is big enough to be safely restrained in the seat. There should only be enough space between the strap and shoulder to slip two of your fingers. Retractable harness models work best. Your baby will be happiest in a seat with built-up "wings" at the side to give extra protection and support for his head. A seat which reclines is comfortable and allows your baby to sleep during journeys.

The more mobile baby

As your baby grows and becomes more active, no amount of special equipment can take the place of vigilance, and you may feel that you need eyes in the back of your head too. If you have to leave your baby for a second, put him in a safe place on the floor, where he cannot roll over onto anything. A crawling baby can move very quickly, too, and should never be left alone unless you're sure he's safe. Getting your baby used to a playpen (*see* page 73) can help, although if you keep him in it for longer than he's happy you'll have difficulty getting him to tolerate it at all.

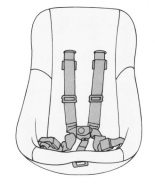

Toddler safety seat
This safety seat, which attaches to the anchorage kit, can be used upright, semireclined, or fully reclined for the sleeping baby. One of the advantages of this safety seat is that the baby can see out the window and enjoy the scenery. You can buy a plastic play and food tray accessory which clips onto the seat allowing him to play with his favorite toys, or eat some finger foods, on a long journey.

● *See* Safety around the house, page 290.

Clothes

For indoors, your baby's needs are not very different from before. Stretchsuits are still tremendously practical for a growing baby; they're great to crawl in as they can't ride up, and are easy to wash and dry. However, you may want to make some changes with your baby's everyday outfits. Garments with elasticated waists don't work very well for this age group; tights, pull-on trousers and jogging pants are soon lost as your baby crawls across the floor! Dresses can be a problem, too, for little girls who are determined to

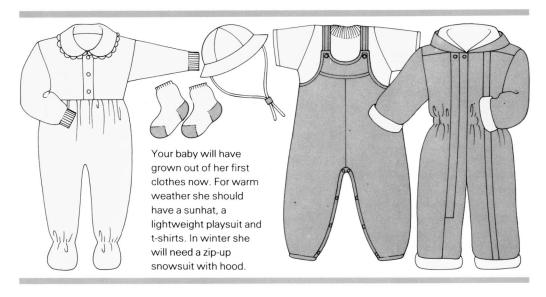

Your baby will have grown out of her first clothes now. For warm weather she should have a sunhat, a lightweight playsuit and t-shirts. In winter she will need a zip-up snowsuit with hood.

crawl. Overalls, or stretchy trousers with a bib and shoulder straps, stay in place much better, but try and find some with snaps down the inside of each leg – on the stretchsuit principle – as it is a great help for diaper changing.

Clothing for your older baby will certainly include outdoor garments, if you haven't bought these already. A sunhat is an important item for the summer – choose one which ties under the chin if your baby is inclined to pull his hat off. You'll find some guidance on choosing outdoor clothes for your growing child on page 185.

Highchairs

By the age of about six months, many babies have started taking solids. Up until now you may have been giving your baby his food on your lap, or perhaps in his baby chair, but once he starts making more of mealtimes, you'll find that he's much easier to manage in a highchair. It means that you can confine the mess to your baby's face, hands and bib, and spare your own clothing. He is also at a better height for you to spoonfeed him comfortably, while you are sitting at the table, and he'll feel he's taking part in a family meal if he has his own chair at the table.

There is a fairly large selection of highchairs on the

● *See* Feeding your baby, page 100, for feeding equipment.

market and this can make it difficult to choose. Highchair design, just like most other nursery items these days, can be attractive as well as practical, so it is really a matter of taste and budget in the end. Your baby is likely to use his highchair at least three times a day for the next couple of years, so it's important that you choose a model that is safe and will stand up to wear and tear.

When you consider the safety factors, look in particular for attachment points for a safety harness (*see* Safety, right). Be careful if there are any casters or wheels on the legs of the highchair; they should have a brake (or two wheels, not four) so that the baby can't move the chair himself. Check carefully for stability – even lightweight models should feel sturdy and stable on a flat surface – and look for a smooth simple framework that won't trap fingers (or food) and can be cleaned easily. The tray should be raised or contoured at the edge to prevent plates of food sliding off and onto the floor. A removable tray is a helpful feature, and it means that the chair can be used without the tray if your child wants to sit at the table. Some highchairs convert to a low chair and table for the older child.

Think carefully about the size of the highchair too: if the room where you intend using it is fairly small, then widely splayed legs – although these give extra stability – could take up valuable floor space, and you may decide to select a folding highchair instead. If the highchair you choose doesn't have a padded seat, you can buy a cushion that fits inside the seat and back of most kinds of highchair. This gives extra comfort and will help if your baby is a bit too small for the chair at first.

SAFETY
● Always make sure your baby is properly fastened into a safety harness when he is in his highchair.
● Never leave a baby alone with food or drink – he could easily choke.

WHAT YOUR BABY WILL NEED

Supersitter
This highchair is a raised version of the low chair (page 73). By adding a stand that folds flat for storage, the low reclining chair converts easily to an upright highchair. The chair has wipe-clean surfaces and a detachable play and feeding tray.

Folding chair
This highchair may be the answer if space is short, as it folds as flat as an ironing board when not in use. The tray swings back overhead when not needed.

Baby walker
Your baby may enjoy being in a baby walker from about six months old. It's an extra and won't help him to walk any earlier, but some babies enjoy being able to "cruise" around the room. You can get a circular or a square model, and if space is short, look for a folding design. Always supervise your baby, and watch out for steps and uneven floors.

Feeding your baby

By the time your baby is six months old she is beginning to show signs of independence – she is growing up and wants to start doing things for herself. At this age she can hold a spoon (although she won't do much with it), turn her head away to indicate she has had enough food, grasp pieces of food (and may or may not put them into her mouth), and is ready to learn to drink from a cup. From now on you may notice her excitement when she recognizes foods that she likes, and she may sometimes tell you what food she doesn't like. She will become more competent at eating sloppy food from a spoon and she will begin to chew the food round and round in her mouth. When she gets her first teeth she will practice using them – on food, toys and sometimes you! Eventually she will want to try and feed herself, at first with her hands. Feeding herself may include putting any small objects she comes across into her mouth, so keep a close eye on her at this stage.

Early weaning

Babies vary greatly as to when they develop certain skills so they are not necessarily ready to start weaning at the same stage. Some babies will already be on three meals a day at six or seven months; others will be on milk feedings only. If you are about to start your baby on solids, then follow the advice given for the younger baby initially (*see* page 98). An older baby may take to solids a bit more quickly – providing she is ready and willing to be weaned. A six-month-old can be safely introduced to a wider range of foods than a four-month-old baby can manage. Solids need not be quite as liquid because she can cope with a slightly thicker consistency now, although foods should still be pureed.

Gradually, as your baby is introduced to a wider range of foods, there is no reason why she should not eat some of the foods that you eat, provided you adapt them to suit her ability and taste.

Establishing three meals a day

When your baby has become used to her first tastes of solids and has got the idea of taking food from a spoon (albeit rather messily), you will be able to build up the quantity she eats at the same time as cutting down on the amount of milk she drinks at that particular feeding. By the time she is having solids three times a day she will probably be taking only two milk feedings. You can offer her a drink from a training cup with a spout, or a small cup or spoon if she finds this easier. If she has had pureed fruit or vegetables as part of her meal she may not be particularly thirsty.

The chart on page 146 gives some suggestions for meals at this stage and although there is quite a wide choice, babies who have just started on solids probably won't mind eating the same breakfast each day or the same lunch or supper three days in a row.

YOUR BABY'S SKILLS

At about 6 months
May hold bottle. Can begin to drink from a cup. Likes brightly colored food (such as carrots, peas). Able to show likes and dislikes. Can grasp and drop food. May like to play with it. Begins to chew. May want to start feeding herself.

At about 7-8 months
Takes food off spoon easily. Can take sips of drinks. Likes more variety of texture. Can begin to have mashed food or soft foods, such as rice or pasta. Appetite problems may begin.

At about 9-12 months
Chews with her gums. Feeds herself more competently – mostly with her fingers, rather than spoon. Uses spoon clumsily.

Phasing out "comfort" feedings

If your baby enjoys solids but is one of those babies who want frequent breastfeedings or bottles of juice, you will now have to start teaching her that any comfort sucking she wants should be restricted to particular times of the day – such as the times *you* might expect to have something to drink. You will also have to learn to look on breast or bottle milk as food and to help your baby to find other ways of taking comfort, such as giving her a cuddle instead. Many babies will go on needing a comfort object for some time, but problems can arise if it happens to be the breast or bottle. If it's the breast it won't always be convenient for you to comfort her with more than a cuddle as she gets older. However, you don't have to give up breastfeeding if you are still enjoying it, but you can begin to think about keeping it to specific times of the day. If the comfort object is a bottle, the baby runs the risk of damaging her teeth if she has a small amount of juice – however diluted – always in her mouth.

Night waking

Needing the breast or bottle to fall asleep is also a common cause of disturbed nights. The baby wakes up in the middle of the night and is then unable to go back to sleep unless she can settle herself by sucking. She will have to be encouraged to go to sleep after the last feeding, rather than during it. The less she has to be picked up and handled – thus thoroughly waking her up – the sooner she will learn to go back to sleep with a little caressing, or perhaps her favorite toy or comforter. Once she is eating three good meals a day as well as some milk, you can feel confident it is not food but reassurance she is asking for in the middle of the night.

Offer your baby a little pureed food at a time and let him take it from the spoon himself. He'll enjoy exploring new tastes.

145

Commercial baby foods

It is a sensible precaution to keep some jars or packages of baby foods in the cupboard. These can be particularly useful when visiting or traveling – or when you haven't got time to cook, or defrost and cook, something homemade. The varieties that provide only one ingredient, such as fruit, vegetable or plain rice, are particularly good at the beginning of weaning, when you are introducing new foods gradually.

However, it is not a good idea to rely on commercial foods all the time for a number of reasons. They usually work out to be more expensive than home-prepared foods and, as they tend to be the same consistency, there is no variety of texture for the older baby. You are also putting off the time when your child will be able to eat the kind of food you eat.

Below Five different menus to give you ideas for meals. You don't have to give a baby something different at every meal, but if you encourage her to enjoy a variety she will be easier to feed now, and later on.

BREAKFAST	LUNCH	SUPPER
baby cereal mashed or sliced banana milk or juice	finger foods, chopped liver; potato and cauliflower stewed apple and custard drink*	pasta with cheese seedless grapes drink*
BREAKFAST	**LUNCH**	**SUPPER**
oatmeal mashed or chopped pear bread and spread milk or juice	finger foods; fish, white sauce, pasta and carrots chopped fresh fruit salad (grated apple, not lumps) drink*	mashed vegetables plain sponge cake, yogurt drink*
BREAKFAST	**LUNCH**	**SUPPER**
cream of wheat chopped or mashed peach milk or juice	finger foods; chicken, leek and rice in white sauce yogurt and prunes drink*	scrambled egg with toast or bread finely grated carrot and apple in a little yogurt drink*
BREAKFAST	**LUNCH**	**SUPPER**
soft boiled egg orange puree or canned mandarin oranges toast and spread milk or juice	finger foods; lean meat, potato, peas and gravy rice pudding and stewed apricots drink*	sandwiches of chopped chicken or liver banana drink*
BREAKFAST	**LUNCH**	**SUPPER**
baby cereal grated apple milk or juice	finger foods; lentils, rutabaga, parsnip and greens with onion sauce junket drink*	broiled fish fingers, bread and spread ripe melon pieces drink*

SUITABLE FOODS: fresh milk • cheese • yogurt • strawberries • tomatoes • whole egg • fish • beans • polyunsaturated margarine

UNSUITABLE FOODS: salt and salty foods (stock cubes, yeast or yeast extracts) • sweets • fried foods • fatty meat • too much butter or margarine • too much sugar • whole shelled nuts • cookies between meals

DRINKS* Dilute one part fruit juice with 4-6 parts water. If using freshly squeezed juices, strain them first. If using fruit syrups, dilute very well so that there is only the merest flavor added to the water.

FEEDING YOUR BABY

Healthy eating

While milk is still forming a large part of your baby's diet you don't need to worry too much about whether she is getting the right nutritional balance from the other foods she is eating. On the whole they will just provide her with more of what she is already getting from milk (vitamins, iron and protein).

However, as your baby gradually drops milk from her diet, it is more important that the foods which replace it provide all the nutrients she needs. As long as a child is offered a selection of nourishing foods she will usually be getting the right amount of calories, protein, vitamins, minerals and fiber; and she will eat what she needs of them. If she does not seem to eat very much but is otherwise healthy and well, there is no need to worry. The same goes for a baby or child with a large appetite, provided that she is not overweight and you are not tempting her with fatty or sugary foods. A healthy baby may be slim or plump – a chubby baby often loses some weight once she starts crawling and becoming more active.

A word about milk

A baby in this age group who still drinks a lot of milk should have breast milk or formula until she is taking a good proportion of solids and preferably until she is one year old. Skimmed milk should not be given to children until they are about five because they need the fat and calcium contained in whole milk. If your baby is overweight or underweight, you will need to discuss her milk consumption, and the rest of her diet, in more detail with your doctor.

VITAMIN SUPPLEMENTS
Vitamin drops, which provide vitamins A, D and C, are available for all children under five years of age. They are there as an insurance policy during the winter months and for poor and fussy eaters. If you are satisfied that your child is eating a varied diet that includes some fresh fruit and vegetables most days, then she should be getting enough of vitamins A and C. A natural source of vitamin D is sunlight, so when your child is covered up in winter, she is particularly likely to need a supplement.

EQUIPMENT

● Highchair – a molded plastic tray is easier to keep clean than a wooden one.
● Safety harness for chair.
● Bib – plastic overall or pelican type.
● Baby spoon and fork.
● 1 or 2 small-bowled spoons.
● 2 bowls – straight-sided plastic bowls are the easiest kind for self feeding, and they're unbreakable.
● Training cup with a spout.
● Apron for you to wear, just in case your baby gives you a sticky offering.

Preparing your own baby food

The ideal diet for a baby is one that is nourishing, wholesome and balanced. Try to include at each meal: some whole-wheat bread, cereal or potato; some milk, lentils, beans, meat, chicken or fish; and some fresh fruit or vegetables. If you give your baby something from each of these three groups she should be getting all the fiber, protein, vitamins and minerals she needs in order to grow and thrive. By the time she is ready for chopped-up versions of family meals, you will have discovered how to encourage her to eat a healthy diet.

Preparing meals for the baby gives you the opportunity to think about your own diet and how healthy it is. Food for the baby (and for you) should be cooked without salt and with very little fat. Fresh vegetables are best steamed or lightly cooked in a small amount of water to preserve the vitamins. Root vegetables, such as carrots, parsnips and rutabaga, can be cooked more quickly if cut into small pieces first, but don't cut greens too finely before cooking as much of the vitamin C content will be lost. Try using naturally sweet foods, such as ripe bananas, eating apples or pears, to sweeten puddings.

PREPARING FOOD FOR THE FREEZER

1 Blend baby food to a smooth consistency using a hand-held or electric blender. Chewier pieces – meat, chicken or beans – may need a little liquid added before blending.

2 Measure out the amount needed for one meal and store in individual containers in the refrigerator or freezer.

3 Remove the lid from the container and reheat the food gently in simmering water.

Cooking

If you have a freezer you can cook bulk quantities of vegetables and fruits, and whole casseroles or stews. Larger quantities will be easier to puree and are less time-consuming to prepare than small portions. By doing this, you can make and freeze a number of meals in advance. The equivalent of an adult's portion of a meal will probably be about three to six baby portions (depending on the age and appetite of your baby). You can also store cooked food in the refrigerator so long as you use it within 48 hours.

When cooking, don't use salt, stock cubes or yeast extracts (which are usually high in salt), because a young baby's kidneys cannot cope with the extra salt. Fresh meat or chicken casseroled in water with some vegetables will make its own flavored stock. Young babies also find too much fat indigestible, so choose lean cuts of meat. Remove the skin from chicken, cut the fat off meat and use margarine, butter or cooking oils sparingly. When reheating food, put it into a heat-resistant cup and place in gently boiling water to heat through. You can do the same with a jar of baby-food (*see* page 148).

Blending

After cooking, mix everything (later on just the meat part) in a blender or by hand. Add sufficient liquid to make it the consistency of a thick soup or puree. If the meat does not blend properly you will need to add some extra liquid. A baby of six or seven months can manage mashed vegetables, rather than puree, and you can also introduce small pieces of food such as cooked rice at this stage. From the age of nine months, give foods that are well chopped.

Freezing

Freeze the combined foods as ready meals in small jars or containers, or individually in large-cubed ice trays. Once frozen, you can empty the food cubes into a freezer bag and then take out as many as you want a few hours before you need them. Potatoes don't freeze well so freeze them in combination with the meat part of the meal, or with other vegetables.

Cooking for two
Save some time by cooking the same food for yourself and the baby and blending her portion. Gradually build up the amount of food you give her, following stages 1, 2 and 3 below.

RECIPES: BUILDING UP FROM BASICS

STAGE 1
Pureed carrots
Cut a couple of carrots into small pieces and cook in unsalted water – just enough to cover the vegetables – until they are tender. Puree in a blender with some of the cooking water until smooth and soft. The more liquid you add, the smoother it becomes.

STAGE 2
Pureed potato
Peel or scrub potatoes (removing any blemishes or green parts) and bring to the boil in unsalted water. Simmer until cooked, then beat with a little milk until smooth.
*If combined with carrots, this makes a filling meal for the time when your baby is beginning to rely on solids for nourishment.

STAGE 3
Fish with vegetables
3 medium potatoes
cauliflower or broccoli florets,
leek, parsnip, green beans
2 cod steaks
milk
water
a little chopped onion

Boil the potatoes and steam the other vegetables until tender. Steaming conserves more of the nutrients and flavor than boiling. Puree or mash the vegetables separately or together, leaving some aside for yourself.

While the vegetables are cooking you can poach the fish in a mixture of milk and water, with the onion. Simmer for 10-15 minutes (turn over halfway through if cooking on the burner) until the flesh is white all the way through.

Thicken the cooking liquid slightly with a little cornstarch mixed with cold water and cook for 3 minutes. When it has thickened, add some chopped fresh parsley and lemon juice to taste. Put your own portion to one side and mash the baby's portion with the vegetables and potatoes. You can thin it with a little milk if necessary.

STAGE 3
Chicken casserole
2 chicken breasts
1 tspn unsalted tomato
puree, mixed with
a little water
or ½ water, ½ grape juice
a little chopped onion
or leek

Remove the skin from the chicken pieces. Place them in the liquid and sprinkle one of the vegetables on top. Place in a moderate oven for 30-40 minutes or until clear juices run out when the meat is pierced. Keep one piece for your own lunch and blend the other with the cooking liquid until soft. Combine the blended portion with pureed carrots and potato to make a nourishing meal for your baby.

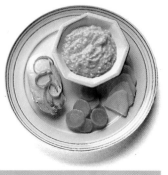

FINGER FOODS

Even if your baby does not insist on feeding herself, it is a good idea to get her started on some finger foods. She can eat these while hot food is cooling, or during the meal. They can also be eaten between meals if she has to go for a longer period than usual, but don't encourage between-meal nibbles regularly as she may get to prefer these to proper meals and they can harm teeth as well as cause problems with eating at mealtimes.

Some good examples are: bread, zwieback, breadstick, cooked vegetables (pieces of carrot, cauliflower sprigs, cubes of potato, green beans), cooked pasta shapes, large pieces of apple (not small lumps), segments of ripe pear or peach, orange quarters, slices of banana.

Self-feeding

Some time between the ages of six and twelve months, your baby may want to start feeding herself. She will attempt to explore her food in the same way that she explores her toys and will feel frustrated if she is not allowed to do so. Mealtimes can then become miserable events with your baby crying and even refusing her food.

One reason why between-meal snacks can so easily become the main diet of some children is because foods such as cookies and zwieback are the sort that a child is allowed to hold herself and to eat as slowly as she likes. Allowing her independence between meals while trying to control her behavior at mealtimes is one of the most common reasons for eating problems developing. It is as natural for a child to want to feed herself as to want to learn to walk, but do try to provide her with sensible and manageable foods.

Some babies will be content just to hold the spoon but the more determined will insist on feeding themselves. The least messy course of action is to provide finger foods that she can pick up in her hands and nibble while you spoon in the rest. If, however, it is the bowl and spoon she really wants to play with, you will need two bowls and several spoons. One bowl should be the sort that your baby cannot easily tip over (such as one with a firm base and straight sides) and in which you put a small amount of her food. Be prepared for a certain amount ending up behind her ears, in her hair and on her knees, as well as on you. A plastic tablecloth or newspaper under the highchair will spare the floor and a good sized apron will protect your clothes if her hands and spoon start to wander. With time and practice your baby will get better at feeding herself, but for the time being taking these precautions will help you to feel more relaxed about the whole business of feeding.

Weaning problems

Gagging A young baby may gag because the food is too thick; an older baby gags if too much is put in her mouth. If you find that you become anxious at mealtimes you may trigger this response from your baby. She may have had enough to eat so persuading her to take more will probably just make her vomit.

Constipation Some constipation occurs when a baby first starts solids. The baby's movements also begin to smell more but this is quite normal. Fruit purees – particularly prunes – can help prevent constipation during this stage.

Loose bowels An older baby can produce frequent very soft movements – rather like a very young baby. This is not necessarily a sign that her digestion is upset. A diet which has a good amount of fiber in it – from beans, fruit and whole-wheat bread – should produce easy-to-pass movements.

Won't drink If she is still producing wet diapers she is not dehydrated, but simply does not want or need more fluid than she is getting from her milk and sloppy food.

Won't take beaker or cup Try a small quantity of liquid in a tiny mug so that she does not gulp down too much at once. Too much fluid can cause her to cough and splutter which may frighten her. If she simply loves sucking, as she may for the first year, then forget about using the training cups for drinks and just let her play with it.

Small appetite Don't expect your child to eat increasing amounts at this stage – a child's appetite often decreases in the second half of the first year, and you may be overestimating how much she needs. Some babies have large appetites, others don't. Coughs and colds can also lessen her interest in food or she may be drinking too much milk which is dulling her appetite. If she doesn't eat much, try to make mealtimes more fun, and remember that if you are anxious you may depress her appetite still further.

Overweight Encourage your baby to feed herself – this may slow her down at meals. Cut out cereals and highly sweetened foods and give plenty of low-calorie vegetables to fill her up if she has a large appetite. Encourage her to get as much exercise as possible.

Underweight If you have been advised by a doctor to feed

Your baby will soon develop his own ideas about when he has had enough.

your baby more, then extra milk and cereal foods are the easiest ways of giving her the necessary calories. Sometimes intolerance to a particular food can cause a baby to eat less.

Doesn't like solids A few babies are simply not ready to be weaned until about eight months or so. Trying to make them take solids earlier can further delay matters. If your baby is afraid you are trying to take away her beloved breast or bottle she may resist even more. It is not uncommon for a baby who had been taking solids to suddenly go through a spell of wanting milk feedings again. This is particularly likely to happen if you are trying to wean the baby off the breast at the same time. Let her have more milk feedings again for a few days to reassure her. If you are going back to work and you know your baby will take milk from a bottle, then you can rest assured that she won't starve.

CARE OF TEETH

As soon as your baby gets her first teeth you can introduce the habit of brushing teeth – at this age she will probably find it an interesting tickle! Don't let her eat sweet foods between meals and if you give her fruit juice to drink, make sure that it is well diluted and that she drinks it quickly. Slow sips or repeated sucking on the bottle are the easiest ways to harm baby teeth.

Diaper changing and bathing

Bathing your baby and changing his diapers is likely to fall into a pattern in these later months, as your life becomes more organized and manageable.

Diaper changing

In the second half of the first year your baby will have learned to control his bladder better, and his bowel movements may be more regular once he is on three solid meals a day as well as milk. This may mean that you're changing his diapers less often than before. However, if your baby has frequent dirty diapers you needn't be anxious, unless you suspect that he is ill. Consult your pediatrician if you're not sure.

At night your baby will need extra protection because he's likely to have dropped his late-night feeding and may be sleeping right through. Even if your child is wakeful in the evenings and through the night, it's not a good idea to change his diapers unless you have to. Your aim should be to keep everything calm and quiet to encourage him to go back to sleep. A diaper change may disturb him even more.

If your baby is in disposable diapers, you can now put him in a larger, more absorbent kind (possibly one designed for an older baby or especially for nighttime). Alternatively, your baby could wear his usual diaper with a disposable pad tucked in. Some parents use two cloth diapers at night, or an especially thick cloth diaper designed for nighttime use, or even a cloth diaper with a disposable pad inside. Make sure that his waterproof pants are not too tight, or there will be no chance for urine to evaporate and this could make his bottom sore.

Bathing

With you to supervise him, your growing baby can splash about and play with toys in the bath now. However, he is much more active and you will still need to keep a steadying arm around him so that he doesn't slip. You can also use a slip-resistant mat in the bath if you are worried about the big bath being too slippery. Although bathing doesn't have to be strictly a daily routine, as long as both you and your child enjoy it, it's a very useful way to help structure the day, to wind things down for the evening and to signal to your baby that bedtime is somewhere on the not-too-distant horizon. It may suit you better to give him his bath shortly after supper now that he is a little older. If you bath him before supper, it may end up all over his clean sleep suit.

Hair washing

Babies of this age may not have much hair but some do need a proper hair wash at some time during this stage. Use a mild baby shampoo or a pure soap lathered up, although

TEETH
Your baby's first teeth need special care. Give them a daily wipe with a clean cloth, kept specially for the purpose, or with a moistened cotton swab. You could also start brushing them with a soft baby toothbrush, but toothpaste isn't necessary yet.

See Diaper changing, page 107, for changes in bowel movements.

WASHING YOUR BABY'S HAIR

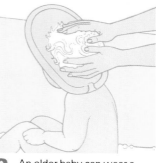

1 Avoid wetting his face by scooping water over his head as he lies in the bath, his shoulders supported on your arm.

2 A shower gives a gentle spray, but remember to check the temperature of the water first.

3 An older baby can wear a shampoo shield to keep the soap and water off his face.

the latter is not so suitable for a baby with a lot of hair as it doesn't rinse out very easily. A shower attachment is useful as it gives a gentle controlled spray for wetting and rinsing.

A younger baby can still be held over the bath or sink to have his hair washed, or you can lie him back in the bath, supporting him securely while you wash his hair with your free hand. An older, more active baby who can sit up (and who can resist your attempts to make him lie back!) may be better off sitting on your lap at the sink to have his hair washed.

Washing hands and face

You'll need to wipe your baby's face and hands after every meal – eating is a messy business for him at this age! You will find baby wipes very useful for cleaning up; most babies of this age hate having their faces wiped and these do the job quickly and efficiently. If you use a wash cloth instead, make sure it's kept clean or you'll encourage even more resistance to the regular clean-up. Check that your baby's hands are clean before meals (this is a good habit which should start early) as he'll soon be dunking them in his food and then into his mouth.

Bathtime fears

Try to deal calmly with any fears of bathing that your baby develops. You may know what has caused him to become frightened in the first place and will have to take care not to splash his face, for instance, or perhaps the temperature of the water needs to be slightly warmer or cooler.

Putting a few toys in the bath may help to make bathtime fun for your baby and distract him, although there is no point in persisting with a regular bath, night after night, if your baby continues to get upset. If nothing you do seems to help, then the best solution could be to skip bathtime for a couple of weeks and to keep your baby clean with an all-over wash instead. The chances are that after a short break your baby will have forgotten what it was that frightened him.

> **BRUSHES AND COMBS**
> A plastic brush and comb are the easiest to keep clean. A baby with short hair (which doesn't tangle) will only need a soft baby brush.

DIAPER CHANGING AND BATHING

● *See* Diaper changing and bathing, page 195, for bath toys.
● *See* Diaper changing, page 106, for diaper rash.

Sleep and bedtime

Once your baby is six months old, she'll be spending less time asleep and her daily pattern of feeding, sleeping and playing will be more flexible. Until she is about nine months old nothing will keep your baby awake if she needs to sleep, and you can't force her to sleep for longer if she is wakeful. From about nine months most of her sleeping time will be at night and she may be asleep for as long as 12 hours at a stretch, giving you much of the evening and night undisturbed. Daytime naps may last only a few minutes or could still be hours long. Trouble may start when your child develops the ability to keep herself awake even if she needs to sleep.

Making naps pleasant

Though your child is now sleeping less, she is more active during the day and therefore still needs to rest. Make sure that she enjoys her naps by giving her a few toys so that she can play quietly until she nods off, or when she wakes. But don't leave her miserable or bored for too long after she's woken or she may get to dislike her rests.

As the months pass, she will tend to grumble more when you put her down to rest. She may cry a little, but after a few minutes she will usually settle down.

Going to bed without problems

Almost all children make some fuss about going to bed. But when your baby is about nine months old, she hates being parted from you and you will probably have some problems. This is the time to develop a regular and pleasant bedtime routine. Give her a bath with toys to play with in it, followed by a cuddle on your knee with songs and nursery rhymes. You can then tuck her in with a favorite toy and her night-light on and the door ajar. Some fathers like to spend this time with their child when they get home, and this could further mark the division between day and night for your baby. If the same things happen at the same time each evening, your baby will get to know that her bedtime is near. A calm pleasant routine helps her to go to bed feeling happy, rather than tense and over-excited, and this makes falling asleep much easier. If she has become attached to a comforter – whether it is her own thumb, a toy or a piece of fabric – this can help her to settle.

Sleep problems often start when there is a major change in your child's life. This may be something that is outside your control, such as if she has to go into hospital, but even going on vacation (where the routine is very different) can be disruptive at this stage.

Reluctance to sleep

At this stage your child is very likely to call or cry out for you after you have put her to bed for the night. You will

---

AVOIDING SLEEP PROBLEMS
- Don't ever shut her in the bedroom, or even put her to bed as a punishment, as she won't want to go there at bedtime.
- Try to avoid disrupting her bedtime routine for any length of time – on vacation, for instance, try to keep her routine as near normal as possible.
- Keep early evenings calm: too much noise, argument or even excitement can make bedtime difficult.
- Make sure that either you or your partner goes to her when she calls or cries. Resettle her, but don't get her up again or she'll come to expect it.
- Put her comforter – pacifier, blanket or soft toy – where she can find it when she wakes up.

Your baby will sleep when she needs to – her daytime naps may now be quite brief.

have to go to her if she persists or she might work herself up into a very miserable state. But try to keep your visits brief – settle her in, cover her up and say good night again, but don't take her out of her crib or she will begin to expect and demand it. If she doesn't settle at once, call to her so that she knows that you are still around and haven't vanished.

The early waker

Many babies wake early in the morning – hours before you are ready to consider the day has begun. Aim to stretch the time she is willing to spend alone by a few minutes every day. Have a few toys and books in her crib so that she is immediately able to occupy herself, and a night-light so that she can see what she is doing. If necessary, change her diaper or give her a drink, but encourage her to understand that it's not yet time to get up.

Some fathers who have to get up early to go to work enjoy taking over the task of getting the baby up. They can breakfast together and allow you a bit of extra rest from time to time.

The night waker

Some babies continue to wake up at night, even when they no longer need to be fed. The policy of letting them "cry it out" rarely works – you won't be able to sleep and your baby doesn't learn not to do it. Go to her as you would in the early evening, pacify and resettle her, but don't get her up again. It's hard not to get angry and irritated when this happens, but it's not her fault – babies don't wake up on purpose. You and your partner could take turns at getting up and settling your baby when she wakes. Some fathers find that they are more tolerant of the disruption as they may not have seen the baby all day.

Do what you can to see that the baby's room is cosy and that she is not disturbed. If possible, choose the quietest room for her and, if she is at the front of the house, put heavy curtains at the window to keep out the lights of passing traffic. Again, a night-light will ensure that her room looks familiar and friendly when she does wake.

Your day together

Going out – even if it is only to the local shops – gives you both a change of scene.

During this time your baby will be sleeping less and will be very much more active. To make sure that you are not constantly saving him from danger – or precious belongings from damage – you should make everything as baby-proof as possible. Making things safe for him doesn't mean you can leave him unattended but it does mean that you don't have to keep a close eye on him every minute.

Out and about

Try to take your baby out every day; he'll get even more pleasure from it now than he did before. As he nears his first birthday he'll be more aware of other children and interested in any he sees. A walk in the park or along the street gives him the opportunity to look around. When he can sit steadily or crawl, the park is a good play area for him. He can try the baby swings with you holding him, and he will find the sandbox great fun with plenty of space for crawling around.

Establishing a routine

You will now find that your day gradually falls into a routine. Babies of this age like it when they can expect the same sort of things to happen each day: it means they are better able to cope with the new and unexpected events.

You may find that your baby always needs a nap at around ten in the morning but wakes full of bounce an hour later, ready for an outing. The period after his afternoon nap could become a special time for play and songs. Another playtime might coincide with when your partner comes home, so that he can join in the ritual of bath, supper and bedtime. In between times, you will probably be getting on with other things so that you are not concentrating solely on the baby.

Your more dependent baby

As he begins to crawl around after you, it will be harder to get on with chores at your normal speed. He won't like letting you out of his sight, so the best solution is to involve him. Let him help by holding things or handing them to you, or give him some safe household objects to play with beside you. This very dependent phase passes before long, but meanwhile don't be tempted to dump him in his crib as he may come to associate it with being miserable, and develop sleeping problems. Resign yourself to doing some things one-handed, with your baby on your hip.

Even a wakeful baby will be happy to rest in his crib or carriage sometimes, especially if he has some toys to keep him occupied. These are the times to carry out the chores for which his presence is a hindrance. You'll keep your temper if you do them when he is resting, or in the evening when you have settled him down. He may be less reluctant

See **What your baby will need, page 141, for safety in the house**

Your baby will be quite happy playing beside you while you work – and you can give her attention when she needs it.

to stay alone in his crib if he has developed a comfort habit, or has become attached to a toy. He's more likely to relinquish you without protest when you are not the sole source of comfort in his life.

While he is going through this very clinging stage your child will need reassurance, so even when you have to leave the room for a moment, call and chat to him so that he knows you are close by. There will be times when you have to go out and leave him with someone else. Make sure that he knows, and is fond of, the person you leave him with, and let him know when you are going rather than sneaking away.

Playing and learning

As your baby becomes more dexterous and mobile he'll be able to amuse himself for longer periods. However, he will be much happier to play if you are within chatting and watching distance.

His struggles for control of his body – learning to sit steadily, crawl, stand, and later walk – will be helped considerably if you are there to avert falls, or kiss a bump better. Bathtimes and mealtimes are good opportunities to chat with him. He is able to understand more now and will start to recognize certain words. Name the different parts of his body while you're changing or bathing him ("That's your hand . . . here's your knee"). Eat your lunch with him and let him have a go at feeding himself, however much mess he makes. He wants to be like you, and that includes eating the same food, so let him try bits from your plate if he wants to – your meal often looks more tasty to him!

Coping with frustration

With the best will in the world, you will not be able to avoid extra-busy days and extra-irritable days when your child will just seem exasperatingly clinging. If he insists on doing something that is either dangerous or just inconvenient, try a complete change of scene. His memory is still very short and he is easily distracted once you offer him something else.

How your time might be spent
As your baby gets older you will spend more time playing with him and keeping him occupied during the day.

Key

	Sleeping
	Sleeping/settling
	Bathing/changing
	Feeding
	Feeding/settling
	Playing
	Your time

NOON

BABY'S DAY

YOUR DAY

MORNING

EVENING

MIDNIGHT

Growing and learning

Sitting up is an adventure, giving a whole new perspective on the world.

That tiny helpless newborn baby has now developed a very definite character of her own. Over these next few months she'll also be changing a lot physically. She will be making great progress in sitting, moving and standing up.

Her particular likes and dislikes will also be more apparent now. Her behavior will vary according to where she is and she will probably act quite differently in an unfamiliar place. You may also find that she is quite shy and wary of people she doesn't know. She may cling to you or put up her arms to be picked up. At home, though, she'll be much more confident, joining in with whatever is going on and beginning to do things for herself.

Your baby will be well established in the family by now and really making her presence felt. She recognizes the people she knows well and also familiar places and routines. She's also starting to sort out who she is now, and will be turning and responding when her name is called. But she'll still be unsure of who that baby is who smiles back at her when she looks in the mirror. Toys and other objects are now becoming more important to her as she begins to get interested in what different things do. But even though her interests are broadening she still needs time with you.

Sitting and moving

Your baby's body has gradually become stronger and more controlled. During her second six months she'll be sitting up on her own, starting to move around and finding her feet ready to take her first steps.

She'll start to sit unsupported when she's somewhere between five and eight months old. She is already used to sitting propped up and supported, and this will have helped her learn to balance. Before she can sit on her own, though, she will also need to be more confident and to have better control over her head and back.

At first she will only be able to sit without support for a moment or so before flopping over to one side. If you place

---

HOW TO GAIN YOUR BABY'S ATTENTION

If you want to show your baby something new, gain her complete attention first of all by:

● making sure there is not too much background noise, for example, from the radio
● calling her name
● making sure she looks towards you
● directing her gaze towards the object while naming it or talking about it.

Colds can affect clarity of hearing at times so it is important to get her to use both what she sees and what she hears.

LEARNING TO SIT AND GETTING MOVING

Your baby will get more confident when sitting and will soon be reaching out for a toy and straightening back up again. She may stretch out and find herself on her hands and knees. She'll also be ready to pull herself up to feel her feet.

At first she'll still bend forward, using her hands to help her balance when she's sitting without support.

She'll soon be sitting with a straight back although she'll occasionally topple over.

Left Sorting out arms and legs, hands and knees can be quite a difficult business.
Below Your baby may, by now, be pulling herself up to stand, sometimes on her tiptoes.

GROWING AND LEARNING

cushions behind and on either side of her, this will help her and increase her confidence. Soon she'll no longer need to use her arms and hands to steady herself but will be able to use them for other things. She'll be able to reach forward, then to the side and then, as her confidence grows, she'll turn to reach behind her. In time she may swivel round and grab a toy or wriggle to stretch for one out of reach – she's starting to move! But she may, of course, have started to move around even before she could sit on her own.

Rolling over is often the first means a baby will use to move. She'll roll from her side or tummy onto her back first, then a little later she'll roll over from her back.

By the time she's nine or ten months old she may be using a combination of methods to get around. As well as rolling and wriggling, she may now be crawling or using her legs to propel herself along on her bottom. It may take her a little while to get her movements right, and her initial

Now she can sit quite steadily, able to turn and reach behind her and also to lean forward and straighten up again.

From sitting she'll be finding a means of getting around, and this may be on her hands and knees.

As she reaches a chair or table she may crouch and reach to pull herself up to stand.

frustration as her struggles to move forward often only result in a backwards shuffle quickly turns to pleasure as she masters her new-found skill. She may also like to stand up and walk around, holding onto the furniture.

Throughout these months she'll be gaining more and more control over all parts of her body. When she's about six months old she'll be lifting her legs off the mattress, when she's lying on her back, and grasping them in her hand. Soon her feet will go into her mouth to be sucked, just like any other object. She's got more power in her legs, too, and will enjoy drumming them on the changing mat. Later, when she's held on her feet, she will bounce up and down with excitement. Once she's ready, she'll pull herself up onto her feet by grabbing hold of the furniture. This will lead her on to stepping around the furniture but it may still be a few weeks before she's quite confident enough to take her first unaided steps.

Picking up and playing

Your baby will now be sitting or lying on her tummy, picking up toys, feeling them, looking at them and trying to see if one fits inside another. Her movements are no longer hesitant and uncoordinated. Soon she'll be able to pick up and examine anything she chooses.

By now she can stretch out, reach and pick up a toy. She may then bring it to her mouth or pass it from one hand to the other, turning it over and looking at every side. If she has a set of stacking cups, she may take them apart, throwing them to one side. Later she may bang them together, holding one in each hand, and she'll discover how a smaller one fits into a larger one.

She's learning to pick up smaller and smaller objects. At first she uses her whole hand, cupping it around the toy to pick it up. Gradually she will learn to use just her thumb and first finger. She's developing what is known as a "pincer grasp." You can watch her sitting on the carpet picking up small pieces of tissue or thread. Now that she's able to hold a spoon or a cup for herself, she's learning to be more independent at mealtimes.

She's gaining more control of her arms as well as her fingers. She can knock down a pile of blocks or cups. She can pull a string to draw a toy towards her or crumple up a

She'll devote all her attention to examining an object and exploring it minutely with her fingers.

USING HER HANDS

At first your baby will use her whole hand to pick something up, cupping it round what she wants.

She'll gradually learn to pick up quite small things with just her thumb and first finger – this is called a pincer grip.

She'll learn to control her fingers separately so that she can just use her index finger to poke and to point at things.

Left Toes are good toys too and she'll soon get her foot to her mouth to be sucked.
Below You will be able to encourage her to let go by holding out your hand and asking for the toy.

GROWING AND LEARNING

piece of paper. She can wave good-bye now, and point at quite distant objects, showing you what she's noticing.

She'll begin to learn how to let go voluntarily. At first she'll just cast a toy away out of her hand or she may seem to press it down on a firm surface: she's not quite sure how to let go. She has to learn to open her hand and move her arm so that the toy goes where she wants it to. Life becomes more fun as she learns how to drop toys and then look for them. By the time it's her first birthday she'll be picking up a toy and letting it go on purpose, watching it drop onto the floor. She will quickly discover that she can also drop things from her highchair! This will soon make mealtimes much more work!

Shouting and babbling

As well as finding her feet during these months, she'll be finding and using her voice too. She can make a wider range of sounds now, and she'll also be listening and copying what she hears with increasing accuracy. At about six months she'll be turning immediately towards your voice, even before she can see you.

She will enjoy practicing her new vocal skills and will start to join sounds together to make rather tuneful noises, such as "ah-muh," "adah" and "er-leh." Talking back to her and repeating some of her noises may extend these little chats. She will have learned to distinguish when you're cross or pleased from the tone of your voice. Similarly she makes different noises which tell you how she's feeling. She can laugh and chuckle with pleasure, squeal with excitement and shout with annoyance. She will have learned, too, which of her toys make noises and will shout with glee at the jangling of a chime ball rolling around.

After nine months or so she will be starting to babble. These long repetitive strings of noises sound very much like our own talk. The only difference is that they don't use real words yet. For example, you may hear "da-da-aga-erba-ada-ba." These babbles are like our own conversations and she really wants to tell you things now. Her first real words may emerge amongst a lot of babble. "Dada" and "mama" are two of the first words that she'll say. Her knowledge of everyday words and commands is quickly expanding. She'll probably understand "no," "bye-bye" and "clap your hands," and she may have the right actions to go with them, too!

Now that he's really found his voice he'll yell with pleasure when he's excited.

She'll enjoy playing peek-a-boo and will learn to hide her own face and chuckle with glee when you "find" her.

Joining in

Once your baby can reach out to grab what she wants, she'll start to take a more definite part in things that involve her. When she's being fed she'll probably cup her hands around the bottle or breast. She can now hold a cracker or crust for herself. Soon she'll be trying to grab the spoon as you're feeding her. As her first birthday approaches she may be trying to feed herself – using her fingers mainly, although she'll be starting to use a spoon as well.

She will also want to join in when she's having her diaper changed and being dressed. Her arms and legs will no longer be rather limp and awkward to get into clothes; now she can push into sleeves and trousers. However, dressing may be more difficult as she can also struggle away from you and crawl right off the changing mat!

Looking and noticing

Your baby is now active and exploring. She's exploring her toys, her food and your things. By her first birthday she will know her favorite things, what's new and who is familiar.

At first she will have been taking all her toys to her mouth, and you have to be very careful that she doesn't get hold of anything that she could choke on or swallow. This mouthing now begins to happen less as she learns what her toys do rather than just how they feel. She can also copy and will watch how you ring a bell, wave or clap, and then do it herself. "Peek-a-boo!" becomes a favorite game. Later on she won't just copy you but will start a game herself. She may hide behind a curtain waiting for you to find her, peeping out all the time, or she may clap her hands when she does something new. She can now remember how to make something happen, or what will make you laugh, and she can repeat this again and again.

She's finding out all the different things that her toys can do. She may make a ball roll accidentally, then she may try to make it happen again by pushing it, and later on she will pick it out of her toy box and roll it. She's doing things intentionally as well as learning how things happen.

Now that she's remembering more, she can follow an object when it rolls out of sight and remember that it is there. She may even find it if it has rolled under a cushion. She also knows what she likes best. Earlier, at about six months, you could easily have substituted one toy for another. This is not so easy now as she doesn't want her favorite toy to be taken away from her.

Her understanding of situations is developing all the time. She's finding out how to let you know what she wants and also that she can give you something. She may hold out a toy for you to take, but as yet she can't always release it, or she may decide to take it back. Later on, if asked, she may give you a toy or her cup, if she wants a drink.

Taking control

Your baby's personality and her experience since birth influence how she will respond to every situation. She may be an outgoing child who waves continuously at people while you are out shopping, or she may be more cautious. Despite these individual differences, there are certain common patterns of behavior that you may notice at this age. Your child may become quite clinging when you first visit a new friend and may reach up to be held. She no longer smiles at everyone but will cry for you and be more difficult if you leave her in a new place.

When she wants to be picked up you may find her at your feet, arms raised up high to show you what she wants. She's

"She's taking my toy!" The baby who is on the move may score for a while but these differences soon even out.

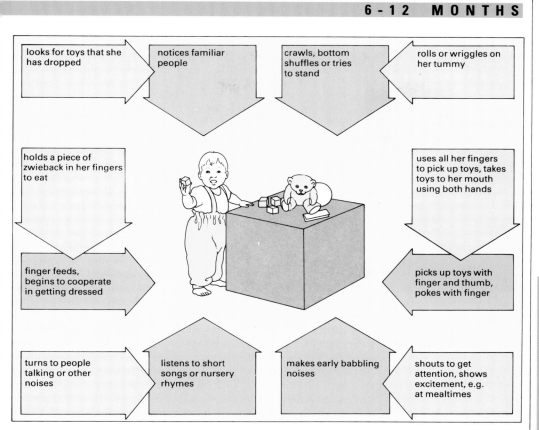

looks for toys that she has dropped

notices familiar people

crawls, bottom shuffles or tries to stand

rolls or wriggles on her tummy

holds a piece of zwieback in her fingers to eat

uses all her fingers to pick up toys, takes toys to her mouth using both hands

finger feeds, begins to cooperate in getting dressed

picks up toys with finger and thumb, pokes with finger

turns to people talking or other noises

listens to short songs or nursery rhymes

makes early babbling noises

shouts to get attention, shows excitement, e.g. at mealtimes

having more of an impact now on your daily routines as she learns how to control things by her own actions.

Individual differences are becoming more noticeable too. Some nine-month-olds seem very active, racing around on hands and knees, handling everything. Others just sit and watch. It is so easy to compare children that such differences can sometimes cause unnecessary worry. Each child usually gets there in her own way and in her own time and there isn't necessarily a "right" way.

Becoming aware of her world

Your baby has learned how to chuckle now and how to get attention by reaching out, waving bye-bye or clapping.

Not only is she getting to know people but she's also playing with everything around her. Although she enjoys exploring, she has also become shy and a little cautious with people and places that she doesn't know.

She's finding out more about the world outside her home now. While she's in her stroller she'll enjoy looking at all that's going on. She'll be fascinated by such sights as children playing or animals running around. You may notice her sitting upright, watching something intently.

This is also the time when some children become attached to a blanket. It becomes a treasured possession that helps her to cope with new things and to settle when she's tired. The blanket habit may soon be dropped by the child, or it may be continued for some years.

From six months to one year
Your baby is building further on her different skills now and becoming more able to take part in things. By the time she's about one year old, she will be able to start holding onto something for support while she hands you a toy and babbles away.

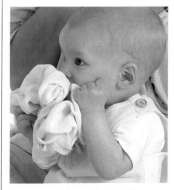

Instant comfort – the familiar smell and feel of his chosen object will reassure him.

165

Play and toys

A child of this age is busy growing up. He wants to try everything – to sit, crawl, stand and later walk. His interest now shifts from people to things and as he becomes more dexterous he can grasp them, pick them up and suck them. Despite this developing curiosity, he still needs a secure base from which he can explore and this can only be provided with your continuing support, affection and time.

Exploring his toys

Your baby will tend to concentrate on one new skill at a time. When you are deciding what playthings he needs, it may help to think about both what he is able to do at the moment and what he will want to do next. The best toys can be played with in different ways as your child develops.

If he shows no interest as yet in becoming mobile but likes sitting supported in a chair, he'll enjoy a variety of smaller objects to handle and explore, perhaps on a tray in front of him. Suction-based toys are fun as he can make them rock and they won't roll away; wobbly toys with a weighted base are also good. Some babies enjoy playing with small objects, such as rattles, measuring cups, spoons, or a wooden car, perhaps with a figure inside which can be lifted out. At this stage he will probably put everything to his mouth first, so a set of teething rings is also ideal.

As he gets better at reaching for and grasping objects he will need safe things to play with and practice on. He will enjoy different textures and colors, and he may like toys that squeak or play a tune because he can make these work by himself. An activity center is good value because it offers a range of pushing, sliding and twisting activities. Rattles

Below A guide to the playthings your baby will enjoy, and what will interest him as his skills develop.

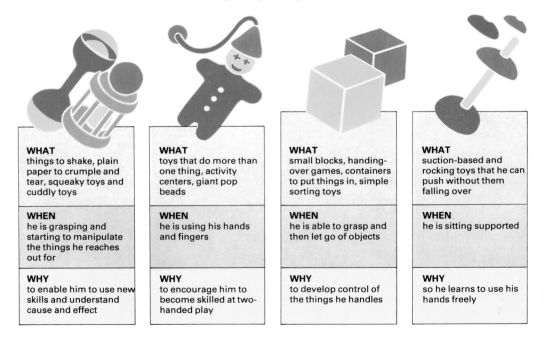

WHAT things to shake, plain paper to crumple and tear, squeaky toys and cuddly toys	WHAT toys that do more than one thing, activity centers, giant pop beads	WHAT small blocks, handing-over games, containers to put things in, simple sorting toys	WHAT suction-based and rocking toys that he can push without them falling over
WHEN he is grasping and starting to manipulate the things he reaches out for	WHEN he is using his hands and fingers	WHEN he is able to grasp and then let go of objects	WHEN he is sitting supported
WHY to enable him to use new skills and understand cause and effect	WHY to encourage him to become skilled at two-handed play	WHY to develop control of the things he handles	WHY so he learns to use his hands freely

A toy with moving parts is a fascinating mystery for your inquisitive baby.

> **PLAY SAFE**
> ● Empty spools of thread are popular for piling up and threading together, but some of the plastic ones have a clip-on end which should be removed before the baby plays with them.
> ● Plastic bags and transparent wrap can easily suffocate a small child. Keep all such materials out of his reach.
> ● Don't ever offer expanded polystyrene (used as packaging and to make egg cartons) to a baby. Once swallowed, inhaled or pushed into ears or noses, it clings in position, cannot be broken down by the digestive juices and is invisible on X-rays.
> ● Don't let your baby have glossy colored brochures or magazines to tear up and suck. The bright colors often contain lead which would be harmful to him.

with bells or knobs at either end will encourage him to use and strengthen both hands.

If your baby is determined to sit unsupported on the floor he probably still needs both hands to balance, and he will get more enjoyment from larger toys that he can turn towards and reach out for, such as a soft toy or a few fabric blocks. If you have the time and energy, you can make and stuff a toy very easily from a kit or pattern, or create your own.

Toys to handle and drop

Your baby will get a great deal of pleasure from his ability to handle and control the things around him. Young babies can grasp things but may not be ready to let go yet. You will know when your child has discovered the fascinating new trick of grasping and releasing things because he will start to

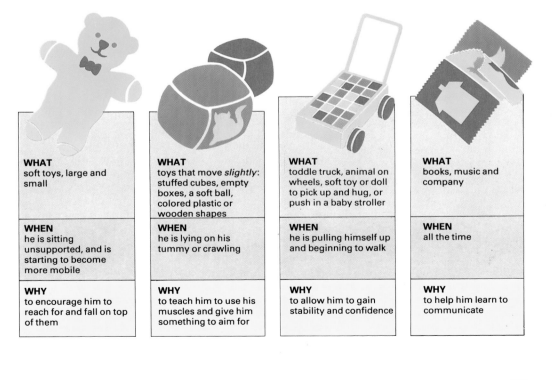

WHAT soft toys, large and small	**WHAT** toys that move *slightly*: stuffed cubes, empty boxes, a soft ball, colored plastic or wooden shapes	**WHAT** toddle truck, animal on wheels, soft toy or doll to pick up and hug, or push in a baby stroller	**WHAT** books, music and company
WHEN he is sitting unsupported, and is starting to become more mobile	**WHEN** he is lying on his tummy or crawling	**WHEN** he is pulling himself up and beginning to walk	**WHEN** all the time
WHY to encourage him to reach for and fall on top of them	**WHY** to teach him to use his muscles and give him something to aim for	**WHY** to allow him to gain stability and confidence	**WHY** to help him learn to communicate

drop them on the floor. You need to give him something to practice on, other than his dinner or the groceries you left too near him in the carriage! Simple sorting toys that involve dropping shapes into holes in a container are good for this and also help him to recognize different shapes and colors. For his first sorting toy, cut a round hole in the lid of a shoe box and provide him with a few small objects (such as a wooden clothespin or spool and plastic cup) to pop through. Show him how to retrieve them by removing the lid and starting all over again. When he is good at this, make a square hole in the box; this is more difficult as he has to fit the object to the shape before it will go through.

A good game to play with your baby as he gets a little older is to let him hand his playthings to you, thank him and hand them back, first to one hand and then to the other. Or you could hide the toy behind your back and make it reappear. As he plays like this with a friendly adult, he is learning the social skills of sharing a game.

Building is a good game to share, and an opportunity for your baby to learn a little patience

. . . but she'll find demolition more fun!

Toys to build with

When he is able to grasp and release small objects he will be able to play with stacking rings and building blocks. At first he may just push them around, bang them together and line them up, but gradually he will start to place the hoops on the stick and balance one block on top of the other. At this stage he needs only a few small blocks to play with, but later on he will get great pleasure from building, so buy plenty or get a well-known brand so that you can add more of the same kind as time goes on. Colorful stacking cups in graduated sizes are easy to grasp and can be used for water play too. You can have a lot of fun with your baby if you explore together the possibilities of all these interesting new toys. He will enjoy knocking down your neatly stacked blocks and think this is a great game to be repeated again and again. He is not being destructive in doing this; he needs to learn how things work and what he is able to do to make them work.

Right Reaching a toy under your own steam is quite an achievement . . . and it's easy to get hold of once you get there! *Below* A little extra help with the first faltering steps can build up confidence, and it's so exciting to be on the move at last.

PLAY AND TOYS

NEVER UNDERESTIMATE A CARDBOARD BOX

They can be filled and emptied, banged with a wooden spoon, peeped round, hidden in and crawled through. And they're free. Only remember to check that they are not held together with heavy metal staples; replace these if necessary with strong sticky tape.

Boxes are also very good for crawling round, although it may take a little time for your baby to realize that the toy you have put behind the box can be reached by moving round to it. If you remove the top and bottom of the box, the crawling baby may enjoy going through the "tunnel" and meeting you or a toy at the other end.

On the move

Learning to crawl can be a very frustrating business and your baby may be encouraged if he has something to aim for. Balls tend to roll right away before the baby can reach them, so he may prefer soft fabric cubes or a large soft toy which provides a cushion if he topples over. Hold up a favorite toy and encourage him to crawl towards you, or place a selection of objects – ordinary household utensils, some brightly colored plastic cups and saucers, or a shopping basket filled with a variety of safe playthings – on the floor so that he can reach for them. As he gets better at crawling he may enjoy having something to push and chase, such as a large inflatable ball, a small toy on wheels or simply a big empty box.

When your baby is no longer content with life at floor level and he wants to pull himself up and try to walk, he will appreciate a sturdy truck that he can push in front of him. But don't give it to him before he can get to his feet unaided. A well-made riding truck is good value as he can carry on playing with it long after he has learned to walk.

Your baby will be fascinated by pictures long before she can talk, and will love sharing books.

First books

Choose books for your baby that have large simple pictures in bold colors and very little writing. As far as possible the books need to be babyproof: cloth books can be clutched, dribbled over, chewed and washed, and strongly bound board books – especially those with shiny wipe-clean surfaces – are useful and the pages can be turned by the child himself.

Your baby will get a lot of enjoyment from his first books, particularly if you share them with him as he sits on your lap. In time he'll learn to recognize, in books and pictures, the people and everyday objects that he sees around him in the real world.

Messy play

"If there's a mess to be made, he'll make it!" is many a mother's cry and it's true. However, it is quite natural for your child to want to explore different textures and substances and to find out what can and cannot be done with them.

There are plenty of messy things in the world – clay, water, sand, mud and vegetation – but water is probably the first experience of messy play that your baby will have. Many children find playing with and in water very soothing and satisfying, and by this age many of them love bathtime. You can buy toys to float in the bath or provide ordinary household objects for your baby to play with: corks and ping-pong balls will float or pop to the surface when submerged, sponges absorb the water and can be squeezed, and sieves allow the water to flow through the holes.

Water play can be offered at other times too. If your baby can sit unsupported, he can have a small shallow bowl of water beside him on the floor, together with one or two small containers – plastic cups and measuring spoons – to fill, pour from one to another and splash about with. The floor can be protected with a bath mat or newspaper to soak up splashes if the child is playing indoors. If yours is a real "water baby," you might be able to provide a shallow paddling pool out of doors in the summer. But do remember that whenever your baby is playing with or in water he must *not* be left alone, even for a minute. It is easy for a baby to topple over and, while an adult who suddenly gets his face in water holds his breath, a baby will inhale it and can drown very quickly in only an inch or two of water.

Music and songs

As well as exploring what things feel like, your baby will enjoy discovering the different sounds they make. At first he will be more interested in rhythm than in tunes and probably won't appreciate formal musical instruments at this stage, although he will enjoy banging on something and making a noise. A wooden spoon to bang on an empty box is cheaper than a toy drum and more bearable to listen to. As he gets older and more skillful you can offer him a smaller object, such as a plastic container or an empty tin. A tin with rounded edges and a plastic lid, as used for dried milk or ground coffee, makes an ideal first drum – it is small and light, and offers a different sound at each end and another noise when it is filled with a few small objects (attach the lid with sticky tape).

Your baby will start to make noises of his own as he prepares to talk, and he will enjoy music on the radio or a toy music box that lulls him to sleep at night. Some young children are attracted by toys that play a tune for them when a string is pulled or a knob turned, and these can usually be managed by the child himself. More elaborate music boxes are best left for later on and brought out in the care of an adult.

But at this age your child will get the most enjoyment from songs and nursery rhymes. In order to appreciate them fully, he needs to have them sung to him by someone whose face he can watch. Sing to him whenever you feel inclined (or sing along with a record) and once he is fairly steady on his feet, you can hold his hands and both sway gently to the music.

Above A leisurely bath, with Mom or Dad to join in the play, can be great fun for both, as well as a good way to calm down before going to bed.
Right If you can bear the noise, a homemade drum gives a lot of satisfaction and is a safe way to indulge her urge to bash.

DISCOVERY GAMES

By the time your baby is about nine months old he is beginning to realize that he is a person in his own right, with a name and an identity. At this stage he will appreciate a baby mirror in which he can see himself and other people.

The older baby is reassured by games which help him get used to the idea of things – and people – going away and coming back again. Variations on "Peek-a-boo," in which a person or small object is covered up and revealed again, are very popular. So, too, are rhymes such as "Two Little Dicky-birds."

Two little dicky-birds sitting on a wall
    (both fists up, forefingers raised)
One named Peter
    (wiggle right forefinger)
One named Paul
    (wiggle left forefinger)
Fly away, Peter
    ("fly" right hand backwards over right shoulder, lower finger and bring fist back)
Fly away, Paul
    (same procedure for left hand)
Come back, Peter
    (right fist back over shoulder, bring it back with forefinger raised)
Come back, Paul
    (same procedure for left hand)

If you are very clever (and are prepared to do the trick over and over again) you can put a "bird" on each forefinger – use a piece of paper or small feather scotch-taped to the finger or draw a smiling face on the finger. You then tuck that finger out of sight while your hands are behind your shoulders, putting an undecorated finger up instead. In this way your hands can reappear the first time without, and then with, the "bird."

Some common concerns

By the second half of your baby's first year you should have enough confidence in your ability as a parent and in your understanding of your child to make you less anxious about her in general. However, each new stage of her development brings new problems: How do you protect your mobile baby from accidents and injury, when do you start to introduce a healthy diet of solid food, and how do you establish a routine that keeps you both happy?

Safety is one of the biggest worries at this stage. The young, active baby seems to know no fear and has no idea of what is dangerous, so you will need to make sure that fires are guarded, breakables like glass and china are out of reach, and medicines, boxes of detergent, bleach and other poisons are safely put away. There is a lot of safety equipment that you can buy for the home (*see* page 140), but sensible precautions, like turning all saucepan handles on the stove inwards, locking cupboards containing dangerous articles and keeping hot liquids – mugs of coffee, teapots – out of reach, are even more important.

Most babies of this age will put everything they pick up into their mouths. This is a natural stage in your baby's development, as she uses her mouth to explore, and she may be very frustrated if things are constantly taken away. However, do be careful not to leave sharp objects like pins lying around, and don't give a baby anything small, or with ties or ribbons, on which she could choke.

Disturbed nights

Most parents expect that their six-month-old baby will be sleeping through the night, but many are not. To encourage your child gradually to drop night-time feedings, try going in, comforting her, perhaps offering a little water or diluted fruit juice and then putting her back to bed again. You may be tempted to take a constantly waking baby into bed with you. Some parents even favor this, but most find that this merely aggravates sleep problems for the whole family and that persuading the child to go back to her own bed can become a terrible struggle as she gets older.

Many babies make a fuss about going to bed as well, screaming when you leave them as if their hearts would break. It's best to be firm but kind; go back to let her know that you are there but don't get her up again – it's time for her to go to sleep.

Learning to behave

It is too early to talk of discipline with a six-month-old baby, but as she becomes mobile she will have to learn that there are some things she cannot touch or do. Restrict the number of forbidden things to the minimum and remove her from them with a firm "no." At this stage, she is very easy to distract; give her something else to do and she will soon forget what went before. She is beginning to explore

● *See* Safety around the house, page 290.

the world and if you start to lay down a few rules and can be consistent in applying them, you might find that you manage to escape some of the worst battles of the toddler period.

For a start, don't keep feeding her bits and pieces, such as cookies, to keep her quiet, as later on she will expect it. Don't let her do something one day and the next get angry when she starts doing the same thing. Don't keep her up for the whole of one evening, entertaining your friends, and then expect her to go to bed without a fuss at six o'clock the following day.

Your baby will now be beginning to attempt to do things which are just beyond her capability. She will watch you building a tower out of blocks, but when she tries to copy you the block falls off. In frustration she may scream and knock them all away. She watches you taking the milk out of the refrigerator, but when she wants to do it, you pull her away with an angry reprimand. She then screams with rage and heads straight back to the refrigerator. If you once give in and let her take things out, just for a few minutes' peace and quiet, you are sure to regret it for the next week. It is better to let her know that one thing is forbidden and to offer her an alternative, such as giving her a special kitchen drawer which she can fill and empty to her heart's content.

The dependent phase

At around eight or nine months many babies are very clinging. Until this stage your baby will probably not mind when you go out and leave her with a relative or sitter, but now she suddenly becomes aware that you are going. She may cry and make a terrible fuss as you go, and will probably cry the minute you come back as well. This is particularly difficult for a working mother, who may just be settling back into work after her maternity leave. When you have to leave your baby, don't prolong the farewell scene as it won't make it any easier for either of you. If you are at home with her, you may find that she cries every time you leave the room and constantly insists on being picked up. This is a trying time for many parents, but just accept that she will become more independent in time and try to give her plenty of attention when you are with her.

Comfort habits

Many babies of this age start to have definite comfort habits, such as sucking their thumb, pulling their hair, or becoming very attached to a "cuddly," such as a blanket or teddy bear. Comfort habits are not a bad thing, so long as your baby doesn't come to rely on them so much that she cuts herself off from other sources of comfort. If cuddling up with a teddy helps her to go to sleep, that's fine. But if she constantly prefers a cuddle with one of her favorite toys to joining in with you or meeting other people, then it may be a sign that she is insecure. Parents often find their child's comfort habit quite appealing until she reaches a certain age, when they suddenly feel that she is too old for it. Try not to interfere; the secure child will eventually grow out of it in her own time.

> **YOUR BABY'S HEARING**
> Your baby's hearing will be tested by your pediatrician, but if you suspect that she is not hearing properly, try a few simple tests yourself. Using her ability to turn her head towards the direction of sound, see if she responds to:
> ● a rattle being shaken, or a whispering voice
> ● a spoon stirring in a cup, or your voice calling her name.
> Tell the doctor if you think your baby has a hearing difficulty.

SOME COMMON WORRIES

Your family life

By the time your baby enters the second half of his first year your life will have settled down properly into a new routine. You will now know your baby, his likes and dislikes, his habits and patterns. During these months he is at his most dependent, most clinging and most wary of strangers – which means that the burden on you is sometimes great. The more people around for him to get to know, the better it is for both of you. Otherwise there may be times when you will feel irritable or emotionally drained by the demands of your child.

Babysitters and helpers

To make time for yourself, and to be alone with your partner, you will have to have a good network of babysitters and helpers. Anyone you leave with your child should be fully competent – at this age a teenager is probably not the best choice. Other parents with children of the same age are a possible source of help and the way to find them is to join a babysitting cooperative or pool in your area. The usual system is that you babysit for each other for no money, but earn credits for reciprocal sitting instead. On a quiet evening, you or your partner can babysit for a neighbor while the other one stays at home with your own children. This way you can build up credits for when you need them.

Anyone who looks after your child, day or night, should be told all his habits and rituals so that they know how to manage him with the minimum of disruption. For instance, you may be trying to get your baby to settle at night by pursuing a policy of visiting him whenever he calls after he has gone to bed, seeing to him but never getting him up. All your good work may be spoiled if the babysitter leaves him to cry or takes him to sit with her while she watches television. Similarly, you should tell your stand-in if you are allowing your baby to feed himself no matter what mess he might make. It is also useful for the babysitter to be told how long his naps are during the day, and if he has a fussy time when he needs cuddling. Some parents make notes about a typical day, writing down any particular things they want the helpers to remember, updating this record regularly. Obviously the more your helper is around while you are caring for the baby, the more he or she will know how to do things your way. Make sure also that the babysitter has the telephone number of the place you are going to, and your doctor's number.

Going back to work

If you are fortunate enough to have the choice of taking a long maternity leave, you may plan to go back to work some time after the baby is six months old. This gives you some time together and the chance to breastfeed (if that is your choice) without too many problems. The disadvantage of starting work again at this point is that it may be your baby's

Grandparents will take great delight in the newest member of their family.

most dependent phase. By the time he is eight or nine months old he will notice and mind very much whenever you leave him, however briefly. For this reason it might be wise to return to work a little earlier, possibly part-time, as at three to five months he will settle better without you.

Try to get him used to occasional separation, before you have to leave him every day. Ideally he should already know and be attached to whoever you leave him with. It helps if he has also spent quite a lot of time alone with that person (it may be a grandparent) and therefore feels secure. If he is going to a day care center or a sitter, ask if you can start taking him there well in advance so that you can spend the morning or afternoon with him at first. Then you can occasionally make an arrangement to leave him for the day and so gradually get him used to the parting.

Facing the tears

However carefully you prepare your baby for the separation he may still cry when you leave him. As it is distressing for you when he cries, you may get into the habit of just slipping away when you see that he is occupied, thinking that he won't notice. This is a bad policy as he could become more upset when he finds you gone and feel reluctant to let you out of his sight. Bear in mind that he won't go on crying all day and will soon be distracted.

Always let him know that you are about to leave, and tell him that you are coming back and will see him later. At first this will mean little to him, but time and time again you will be proving that you mean what you say and he will become more secure and relaxed about you going.

Inevitably, you will find working and having a young baby at home tiring. At the end of the day you can no longer just flop, or unwind with your friends after work. You have to rush to pick up your baby if he is not being looked after at home. However, you are likely to find his company a real pleasure, having been deprived of it all day, and you will value the time you spend with him before he goes to bed. Of course, you will still have things of your own to do, and possibly other children to talk to, but you may be able to share this with your partner.

THE SINGLE PARENT

A growing proportion of parents are bringing up children without the help of a partner, either by choice or through circumstances. Many well-balanced and happy children are brought up in this way and their parents are content to do so. However, there are things to bear in mind.

● **Widen the circle**

At this clinging stage your baby won't have a second parent to attach himself to, so he will become more dependent on you. There should be other adults (family or friends) whom he can become attached to so that you can take a break, or they can look after him if you are ill.

● **Working arrangements**

Single parents are more likely to return to work — check to see if there is a day care center where you work.

● **Babysitting**

You can join a babysitting cooperative even if you are a single parent. You can build up babysitting credits by taking your baby with you when he is young enough. Later on, you can have other babies to stay the night and then make reciprocal plans.

The mother at home

A day at home with your baby at this stage is particularly demanding. He will probably hang around you and want your attention all the time, and sometimes you may feel that you need to make some time for yourself. If you have other children as well, you still need to create some special time for them too.

Just as the working mother does, you should make efforts at this stage to attach your baby to other people whom you trust – so that you have a little more freedom when you need it. This could be a close friend, neighbor or member of your family, and, if your child grows fond of them, he will be reasonably happy to be left without you for a few hours, or occasionally a whole day.

It is sensible to make this slight break even if you have no particular need or desire to make time for yourself: accidents or illness can mean that you are forced to be away, so the more people your baby can relate to, the better all round. Your parents or parents-in-law may live nearby and enjoy spending a day with their grandchild.

Social occasions and get-togethers brighten up the day for you and your baby. He will love the company and will benefit from getting to know other adults and children. You can also use these times with friends to share any worries you may have.

Older children and the mobile baby

Once the baby starts moving around, your older child or children may find him a bit of a pest. He will want to get into everything they are doing or playing with, and can be extremely annoying. Your baby may be quite happy in his chair or playpen for a short time if he has a few toys to play with. However, he also needs as much space as possible to crawl so, if you foresee difficulties, suggest that your older child plays somewhere she cannot be disturbed – in another room or at a table too high for the baby to reach. She won't resent the restriction in the way the baby would because she knows she can go somewhere else whenever she wants. Try to encourage older children to play with the baby – they might find real pleasure as well as to think themselves as a big helper to you.

Danger from older children's toys

Your baby will be attracted to toys that the older children play with. He may spoil them (crumple a book or suck cardboard puzzle pieces until they lose their shape), so let the older child know that she must keep such things away from the baby. Explain to her that the baby cannot concentrate on two things at once, so if he has got hold of a prize toy the trick is to offer him another rather than to try and wrench it away.

However, some toys are dangerous for the baby. Anything small enough to be swallowed should be kept out of reach, as should construction sets with paint or glue, sharp scissors and knives. Take time to assess your older children's toys and think what the baby might do with them. Then make sure that the dangerous ones are always put away after use, so that the baby cannot get at them.

Vacations and trips

During this half year it is worth remembering that any major change, such as a vacation, will disrupt your baby's sleeping pattern. Although he is very adaptable at this stage and will be easier to take around than a toddler, you will probably find it hard to get him back into his sleeping routine when you return home. If this is important to you, you may decide to skip your vacation or take it at home this year. However, if you feel that going away is an essential break for the family, you might consider making it as similar to home as possible – by booking accommodation with housekeeping facilities – so that you can keep to the same routine.

Disposable diapers are a good idea to take on vacation. For the older baby at night, you might like to use the ultra-absorbent "overnight" disposable diapers. It is worth getting an older baby used to bathing in the big bath before you go as you won't want to pack a baby bath.

Take some of your baby's favorite toys – these are useful both for the journey and when you arrive. He may be upset if you don't pack any he is particularly attached to; and leave a spare comforter at home in case it gets mislaid.

First birthday

The fact that it is his birthday won't mean very much to your one-year-old, though he will enjoy any treats you prepare for him and you will probably want to celebrate yourselves. He's too young to appreciate a proper party – the best kind of celebration for this age is a family one.

You can let him open all his presents – he will particularly love tearing off all the wrapping paper – but once he has seen them you might like to put them away and introduce them again one by one, over the weeks, so that he can get the maximum pleasure and learning from each. If they are left around he may tire of them more quickly.

If you have other children you may decide that all of them get a small gift on each other's birthdays. Older children often enjoy being given a little money and going with you to choose a present for the baby.

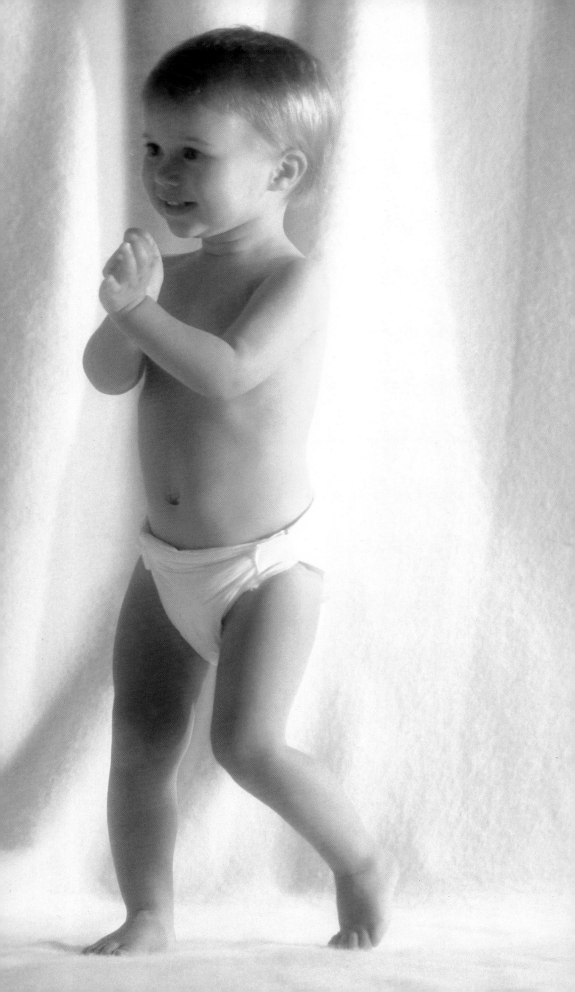

THE TODDLER

Once your child takes her first steps there's no looking back. She's on the go all the time and into everything. Inquisitive and energetic, her zest for life is infectious. Exploring, trying out new things, constantly testing herself – and you – she may still seem quite a baby sometimes while at other times she's a small child – willful, lovable and totally absorbing.

You and your toddler

The energetic toddler confronts each new day with a great sense of adventure.

A toddler in the house is a challenge and a joy. From a baby dependent on you for everything he develops into a child with his own personality. Sometimes referred to as "the terrible twos," this is a time of whirlwind activity. He'll be into everything. His drive to learn all he can about the world means that he can create chaos in an orderly room in just a few minutes. His inventiveness will make you exasperated one minute and surprised with pride the next.

First steps towards independence

The first steps that made you feel excited and proud of him now turn into a breakneck toddling that can have you fearing for his safety. His ability to accelerate often outstrips his talent for stopping. The delight on the face of a toddler who has got up enormous speed will soon change to tears when he falls. But "if at first you don't succeed, try, try, try again" could be the motto of this stage of life. In the face of disappointment, including your displeasure, a toddler will persevere to get what he wants.

It is an in-between stage that can be difficult at times. He doesn't want to be treated like a baby anymore, but he's not yet mature or competent enough to be treated like a child. As he works towards independence, he likes to know you are there for the times when he cannot cope. He doesn't understand about danger and needs to be diverted from hurting himself, and he needs to be comforted when he cries tears of frustration.

In an independent mood he will be furious when someone tries to help him with something he thinks he can handle himself – like putting on his boots. But there will still be times when he is tired and weepy and he'll be glad then to have some assistance.

During this time he will be delighting you and everyone with his attempts to talk. From his first words, which are likely to be the names of his family and familiar objects, to his first sentences, formed like telegrams, his new-found means of communicating makes life even more fun for him.

You will find that you adopt his words into your family vocabulary, and that things he says make you look at everyday life in a different way. Two toddlers sitting quietly together will chat happily – pausing while the other speaks, but not listening to a word.

Learning to be more grown-up often involves making a lot of mess, and it is sometimes hard to stand by and let your toddler fumble at something you could so easily do for him yourself. His attempts to feed himself with a spoon will result in a lot more food on his face and on the floor than in his mouth, but he will be upset and disappointed if you insist on taking over from him. Only by practicing can he learn how to feed himself, and the pride he feels when he succeeds is a joy to you too.

He will feel particularly proud when he finally outgrows the need for diapers, and during this time you will be helping him toward that end. It is a slow process, but each stage is rewarding. Without the bulky diaper, in his new slimline clothes, he really does look like a little child now – no longer a baby.

Toddlers are often thought to be naughty, but they don't mean to be. Insatiable curiosity and a short memory mean that they simply forget what they have been told in the overwhelming desire to find out all they can.

You can't stop him exploring, touching, opening and emptying, but if it is not going to drive you crazy, then you may have to make some temporary adjustments to your house. Put away or out of reach everything that is likely to be dangerous to him, or that is precious to you.

Understanding his world

He's too young yet to understand what you think is important, so he will be perplexed if you let him play with the saucepans on the kitchen floor in the morning while you are washing up, but then get angry when he wants to do the same in the evening when you are preparing for guests. Neither can he understand what it is like to be someone else. When he pushes or hits another toddler he may be amazed at the tears, and surprised when he is punished.

The "naughtiness" that most parents dread is a tantrum. An expression of extreme frustration, it can be disturbing and upsetting to watch, and if it happens in public, very embarrassing. A toddler in a supermarket confronted by a temptingly low shelf of candies, for instance, is likely to be outraged if his mother says he can't have any. Toddlers can't control their emotions or understand what "later" means, and sometimes they explode in a way that shocks them as much as their parents. If tantrums are met with anger and punished as misbehavior, the result is an upset and worried child. A child who is comforted and reassured – though never allowed to believe that a tantrum will get him what he wants – will quickly grow out of this stage.

This can be one of the most rewarding times to be a parent. A zest for life is catching, and showing even ordinary things to a child who finds everything new and fascinating is a pleasure. Participating in his delight shows him that you approve, which makes his journey into the next stage of childhood a step he's happy to take.

Below Plotting further mischief? – or just swapping notes!
Bottom left Family life can be very rewarding as baby and child interact and enjoy each other's company.
Bottom A major milestone, as your baby takes his first steps.

YOU AND YOUR TODDLER

What your child will need

All the safety points you've considered already will continue to apply as your child gets older, and her increasing curiosity and mobility will mean that you'll also have to be aware of new hazards. You should now check that all switches for electrical appliances are safe. They may have been well out of reach of a smaller child, but a toddler on a chair could reach them more easily. Now is the time to make sure that all windows are fitted with safety locks too – your child may be tempted to climb onto something and lean out of the window.

Everything in your child's room should be nontoxic, so make sure that surfaces, fixtures and fittings are safe. If you buy second-hand furniture and are not sure if the paint is lead-free, strip it and repaint it. Store your child's toys at a low level so that she can reach them easily and don't leave electrical cords trailing where they could trip her up.

From crib to bed

Sometime around your child's second birthday you'll probably think about moving her from her crib to a bed. If she is agile and starts to try and climb out of her crib sooner than this, you may feel it's safer to make the move earlier. All cribs eventually become too small and, added to this, a toddler who's going without diapers at night needs to be able to get to the potty or bathroom quickly. You may want to wait until she's dry at night before you move her from the crib, as full-size sheets are so much more cumbersome to change and wash than crib sheets. If she does move to a bed, remember to protect the mattress with a waterproof sheet.

Making the move from crib to bed seldom causes problems, but if you are worried that your child might fall out, place a bed guard on one or both sides (*see* Bed safety, page 184). Even a chair placed by the bed for the first few nights will be enough to remind her to roll back to the center.

From nursery to child's room

Take the opportunity now to think about adapting your child's room. The idea is to increase the floor space in the room as much as possible and begin to make it a bright attractive place that she will eventually see as a playroom as well as a place to sleep. Remove the rocking chair, baby bath and other nursery equipment and push the bed against the wall to give her more space to run around in.

You may have bought a crib and changing unit for your baby which now convert to a bed and desk, or play table. However, the most important need now is storage space for your child's growing collection of toys. At this stage a child's toys are all sizes and need boxes and open shelves as well as space for trucks, tricycles and dolls' strollers. Although some drawers are useful for clothes and things that you tidy up, open shelves, where a child can not only reach things but see them from the bed and later display

---

STORAGE IDEAS

● A bright tin tray for a tea-set; a toy garage to park the cars in; a carriage or lined box as a "bed" for all the soft toys – all these will make the tidying up fun.

● Brightly-colored plastic stacking boxes are inexpensive and ideal for large toys and dressing-up clothes. When empty, they can be played with too.

● Small toys, such as dolls' shoes or farm animals, tend to get lost in large toy boxes, so need to be in shallow drawers, small boxes or on shelves.

● Boxes and shelves can be labeled – cars, blocks, dolls, teddies – to help your child begin to recognize words and encourage her to put some things away.

● A shoe bag with a number of pockets can be hung on the back of the door and used for shoes or toys.

● *See* Sleep and bedtime, page 200.

precious objects, are more useful. Low open-plan shelving that is divided into compartments helps a child learn to sort toys so they don't become one big jumble. Although you can't expect your child to be tidy at this age, if you provide a space for everything she will be able to find her toys and will eventually learn to put things back in their place.

A good investment for your child's room is furniture that is practical and adaptable. A unit with boxes for storing toys and a small table and chair are all useful. Your toddler can sit at the table to do jigsaw puzzles and drawings, or the space can be used as a shop counter or picnic table when she is playing imaginative games. Alternatively, buy a small chest of drawers or cupboard for clothes and toys, and cover it with a wipe-clean surface.

If you are planning to have two children sharing a room eventually, you will have to consider their changing needs as they grow. Your toddler, as she nears school age, will need her own play and storage space away from a meddling little brother or sister, and this is when a bunk bed with drawers is very useful, even if she doesn't make full use of it now. Whatever limitations you are working with when it comes to space or the cost of new furniture you can always brighten up a toddler's room with colorful posters, wall hangings and fabrics.

Make good use of a light corner with adjustable box shelves for displaying books and toys, and fitted cupboards for storing them.

Wardrobe (1) with plenty of hanging space and some adjustable shelving

A few low hooks (2), which your child can reach, for robe, scarves and bags

A good-sized bed (3), placed against one wall

A bed guard (4) may be needed for added security when your child first moves from crib to bed

Pictures, drawings and posters (5) to brighten up the room

WHAT YOUR CHILD WILL NEED

Easily accessible
shelves for books and toys (6)

Chest of drawers (7) for small
items of clothing

Low-level table and chair (8) for
drawing, tea parties and games

Right A small child's room should have as much floor space as possible for playing. Choose a storage system that is both simple and practical – with drawers, cupboards and shelves – so that the room can be tidied quickly and easily. Favorite books can be kept on a small bedside table with a lamp.

See What your child will need, page 228, for the older child's room.

Now that she is more aware of her surroundings, you can have fun adding other details to her room. A lamp shade in the shape of a hot air balloon will delight her, and a plain window can be enlivened by a blind decorated with a bright picture or design. A colorful border, attached to the wall at your child's height and covered with clear adhesive film to help survive sticky fingers, creates another interesting focal point for her.

Choosing a bed

Exactly what bed you decide to buy for your toddler will depend on how much space you have and whether you plan to have more children. A child's bed is grown out of very quickly and, unless you have another baby who will inherit it, it makes more sense to buy a full-size single bed. Many stores sell single beds with removable safety bars which offer a safe and reassuring transition from crib to "grown-up" bed. Beds with drawers underneath, for clothes or toys, not only provide storage space but avoid that space under the bed where dust collects and toys get lost. Make sure the

Day bed
A day bed will last for years if you take the trouble to buy a good quality one. If your child eventually moves on to another type of bed it will always be useful as a spare or as a sofa with a throw-over cover and scatter cushions.

Bed with drawers
The extra storage space is the main advantage of this bed especially if your space is limited. The drawers are easily accessible to the child, which can help encourage tidiness as she gets older. The presence of a headboard makes sitting up to read in bed more comfortable.

Trundle beds
If you decide to buy trundle – or stacking – beds, check the folding mechanism. Make sure it is neither so easy to operate that the child can do it unsupervised nor so complicated that it becomes a chore for you. Check also for any dangerous places where the child's fingers could get trapped.

Bunk beds
Bunk beds are space-saving as well as great fun. However, for safety's sake you must prevent very young children gaining access to the top bunk and the beds should be pushed firmly against the wall as there is a safety rail only on one side.

mattress is firm – and don't be tempted to buy second-hand. A child's mattress takes a lot of battering (even if you do forbid bouncing!) and needs to be of good quality if it is to last.

A trundle, or stacking, bed – where one bed slides under the other – saves space as well as providing a spare bed. Bunk beds also have these advantages, although your toddler is too young at this stage to sleep in the top one. For the time being, remove the ladder and use the top bunk as storage space. The extra bed will be useful not only for a second child but for friends coming to stay the night as your child gets older. If you want a spare bed that is easy to pack and store, a junior travel bed is a good buy.

Highchair alternatives

Two to two-and-a-half is a slightly awkward, in-between age. Your child may find that her highchair is becoming uncomfortable, even when the tray is removed to allow the chair to be drawn up to the table. Yet when she's seated on an ordinary chair her chin is barely level with the edge of the table. You could give her a large cushion or cushions to sit on, but she may not feel very steady seated like this.

Some highchairs convert to a chair for the toddler (*see* page 143), but the alternative is to buy a child's booster seat once she has outgrown her highchair. When attached to a stable chair, this rigid seat brings your child to the right height for the table. You have a choice of two heights, depending on which way up the seat is used.

Another kind of table seat, which is useful for traveling because it folds down and is portable, can be used by a child who is still in a highchair. Make sure that your child wears a safety harness in one of these seats and never leave her unattended as she might try to climb out or fidget too much and upset the seat.

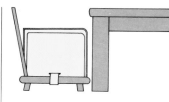

Two-height booster seat
This adaptable seat can be strapped securely onto the back or base of most chairs.

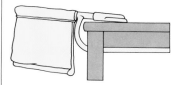

Folding table seat
This attaches easily to any suitable stable surface.

Clothes for the toddler

For this especially active and energetic stage of your child's life, buy her clothes that are hard-wearing, that look good after repeated washing, and need little or no ironing.

Trousers are highly practical for both boys and girls, but don't forget to check when you buy them that they'll fit over a diaper if your child still wears one. You may find that you have to buy a larger size to get the necessary width around the hips. Remember that toddlers don't have waistlines, so trousers without an elasticated waist don't fit comfortably. Overalls are very popular for toddlers because the straps keep them up and the fastenings can be moved to give extra length on the legs as your child grows. They're not ideal when you're potty training, however, as they don't come off very quickly!

As little girls of this age don't have a "waist" they can't wear skirts very easily, unless you choose those with elasticated waists or over-the-shoulder straps. Jumpers and dresses are generally better. Sweaters that button up to the neck can be worn fully buttoned under overalls or jumpers, as well as over blouses and shirts.

A jogging suit is a smart and practical outfit for toddlers of all ages and shapes. As it's suitable for a boy or a girl, it can be passed down the family to a child of a different sex. Toddlers seem to enjoy wearing jogging suits, probably because they're comfortable.

Outdoor clothes

For outdoor wear, it's more practical to get a zip-up snowsuit or perhaps a hooded parka (with matching leggings) instead of a winter coat, which is more expensive and can be bought when your child has grown a bit. Most snowsuits and parkas are machine washable, whereas winter coats need to be dry cleaned. Hats and mittens are needed when it's chilly outside: Attach some elastic to the mittens and thread it through the sleeves of the snowsuit or jacket so they don't get lost.

Underwear and nightwear

Your toddler will need three or four undershirts and the same number of socks or tights. If she is just out of diapers, she will need at least six pairs of underpants. Boys need extra pairs of trousers at this stage, but you could keep the washing down by letting your son go without trousers in the house when it's warm enough.

At night, pajamas and nighties can take the place of stretchsuits. For use after the bath and early in the morning, your child will need a cosy bathrobe – for the winter months at least. If she is a restless sleeper and inclined to toss the covers off, you could put her in a zip-up sleeper that is warm enough to use as a nightgown. A terry bathrobe can double as a changing robe at the swimming pool or at the beach.

LEARNING TO DRESS

Most toddlers like a bit of independence, but your child will still need help with dressing and undressing. You can make things easier for her by laying her clothes out the right way round so that she can step into them or pull them over her head the right way.

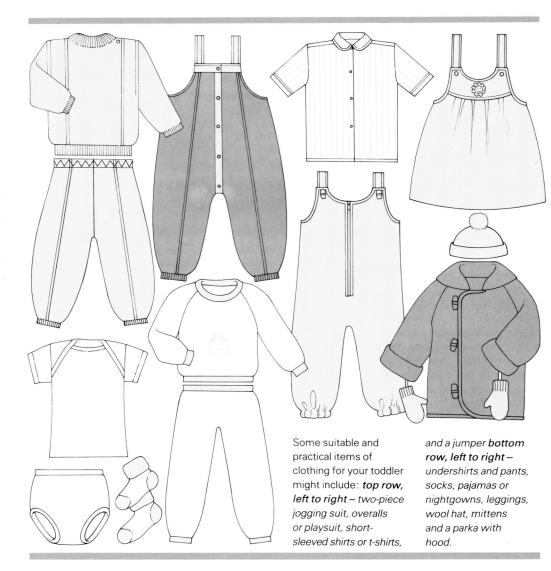

Some suitable and practical items of clothing for your toddler might include: *top row, left to right* – two-piece jogging suit, overalls or playsuit, short-sleeved shirts or t-shirts, *and a jumper bottom row, left to right* – undershirts and pants, socks, pajamas or nightgowns, leggings, wool hat, mittens and a parka with hood.

Footwear

The most important thing to remember when buying children's shoes, socks or tights is that they must fit properly. For shoes, choose a shop where the staff are trained to measure children's feet correctly. The length as well as the width of each of your child's feet will be measured, but there are other factors to consider too. For example, your child's instep may be particularly high or low, and this could mean the shoe you have chosen will not fit correctly. Make sure your child tries the shoes properly in the shop, by walking a little way across the floor. Ask her if they are comfortable – the sales person will check that the feet are not restricted in any way and that the shoes fit properly at the heel. He may suggest another style of shoe if he thinks that it will give a better fit. First shoes should either be completely flat or have a very low heel – children should never wear high heels while their feet are growing.

CHOOSING SHOES FOR YOUR CHILD

Heel should be low, and hold the foot snugly.
Fastening should be adjustable and hold the foot firmly in place.
Upper should have no seams which might rub.
Toe should allow room for the child's toes to wiggle freely without touching the end.
Sole should be flexible, light and non-slip.

Leather bar shoe

Leather sandal

Canvas play shoe

Leather walking shoe

Rubber boot

Choosing shoes and socks

You should have your child's feet measured every three or four months to check that her size is still the same – no shop with a reputation to maintain will mind doing this for you, whether or not you decide to buy some shoes.

Leather uppers are best for children's shoes, as leather soon molds to the shape of the owner's feet (which is why you shouldn't pass shoes down the family). Plastic or canvas shoes are fine for occasional use as playwear, however. Your child will also need some rubber boots once she is walking outside in all weathers, and possibly slippers too (unless she still wears a sleeping suit with feet).

The size of your child's socks and tights is as important as the size of her shoes. Socks and tights can restrict toes in just the same way as shoes if they're too small. Tights and socks that are too big in the feet are just as bad – the unused part may bunch up inside the shoe, causing discomfort. Check your child's socks and tights regularly, to make sure that they fit well.

Feeding your child

By the time your baby is a year old he will have tripled his birth weight, but from now on his growth rate will slow down considerably. He should now be able to chew his food, feed himself quite efficiently with his fingers and manage a cup or mug on his own. He is also able to sit with everyone else at table, in a highchair, and can usually eat the same food as the rest of the family, although it will have to be chopped up well for him.

Looking back over his first year you can appreciate just how much your baby has developed and the amount of progress that has been made in a relatively short space of time. He has successfully completed the first stage of growing up and is entering a new phase of increasing confidence and independence.

What lies ahead

Over the next few months he will stop trying to put his spoon sideways into his mouth and you will both get pleasure from his new skills such as drinking through a straw, picking up a cup and replacing it without spilling the contents, and the delicate art of licking an ice-cream cone.

But he will also discover – to his delight if not yours – that he has the ability to throw food onto the floor and to spit it out of his mouth. He will also learn that he can "ask" for a paticular food by pointing to it, and he will get to know when you are eating something you don't want him to see and where the cookie jar is hidden! He will start to imitate you saying "no" and he will come to realize that just as he has the ability to eat food, he also has the power to refuse it – so beginning the process of making decisions for himself.

Now that he can walk there is a whole new world for him to explore and often this urge to discover things will be stronger than his desire for food. Because his growth rate is slowing down and likewise his appetite, he may well dawdle more and more over his food, even being able to refuse whole meals without showing signs of hunger before the next. You may now find that while your toddler still needs your attention at mealtimes, he may start to resent your interference.

Final weaning from breast or bottle

If your baby has not relinquished the breast or bottle by the time he is a year old, you may find that it is hard to make the break in the second year. This doesn't mean that all babies should be fully weaned by the time they reach their first birthday, but it will help your child to grow up if you encourage him to give up the breast or bottle as a comfort object by this stage.

Many small children have, and need, some kind of comfort object – whether it is their thumb, a piece of cloth, pacifier, baby cup or toy. It can be a good idea to try and encourage your child to have a variety of comfort objects so that he doesn't become too dependent on one. If the breast or bottle is your child's comfort object you will have to think carefully about when it is needed – does it help him to go to sleep, for example? Very often a break in routine is all that is needed for your child to drop his comfort habit. He may go to stay on his own with his grandparents for a few days or you may decide to move him from his crib into a bed – in fact anything that will help your child feel "rewarded" because you have acknowledged that he is growing up will help him relinquish his old habits. However, if he is not ready and thinks you are simply trying to deny him a beloved object he may cling to it all the more, so that he is hanging onto it out of habit, even though he no longer really needs it.

Sometimes it is *you* that really needs the comfort object, rather than your child. You may be convinced that a feeding last thing at night will help him to go to sleep quickly and so you are unwilling to let him give it up when he is in fact ready to do so.

DIFFICULT EATER

If your child is a difficult eater, first of all make sure that he is perfectly well. Continual bouts of ill health, such as ear infections, colds and sniffles, can turn a child off to eating for a time. If your child is in good health and is not losing weight, you can rest assured that he will not make himself ill by not eating. He may become miserable if he sees that you are anxious. Stop worrying – he will relax, too, and you will have fewer battles.

FEEDING YOUR CHILD

Food as a weapon

The toddler's fierce independence at mealtimes can be bewildering for a parent who has become accustomed to a baby who eats his food well. If you are feeling confused by your toddler's behavior, you may view his normal fads and lulls in appetite out of all proportion. Food can easily become a weapon between parent and child, particularly if you are continually telling your child off or, conversely, if you allow him to run around during meals and give him a monotonous diet of toast and fruit juice, all for the sake of peace and quiet and the reassurance that at least *some* food is being eaten. The best policy is to try to relax and avoid making a fuss. Only offer your child food at mealtimes (not in between), try to avoid distractions during meals, and if he only wants to eat one ingredient, then let him. He will eat more if he is hungry.

If you let meals become a battle you may often find yourself the loser! Let her get used to new foods by seeing them on the table, but serve only small portions in her bowl. Respect your toddler's independence by letting her decide whether she wants more or not.

Shared mealtimes are an important part of family life and can be a very pleasant way to start the day.

Meals with the family

Managing mealtimes with a toddler requires a certain amount of tact as well as firmness on your part. In the first place you need to recognize that your toddler is becoming independent and that he will want and need to practice this independence as much as possible. You can help him feel grown up by giving him his own set of utensils (knife, fork and spoon), even if he doesn't use it yet.

You can also serve the food for the meal in a large dish on the table and offer him a choice. However, don't expect him to estimate accurately how much he can eat. The eyes of small children are usually far bigger than their stomachs! If he does not want the meat or potatoes the first time around, he may eat them separately as a second helping. If necessary, serve him last when he has seen everyone else choose their food. This gives him the chance to understand what is going on and gives hot food an opportunity to cool. You could also have some brown bread on the table which he can eat with his fingers if it is one of those days when he does not fancy anything put in front of him.

Serve a poor eater with tiny helpings to start with; he will then feel less daunted by the business of eating and having the pleasure of asking for a second helping. A fussy eater will also become used to the sight of other foods so that they lose their strangeness and gradually become familiar. Your child will feel braver about trying any new foods if he can start with the tiniest taste of something that he has chosen himself.

If you allow him to exercise his independence you can then feel more confident about deciding on a few rules and making him – and yourself – stick to them. What rules you make and how many will depend on your general approach to discipline as far as the rest of his behavior is concerned. The kind of rules you might consider are: allowing him to eat only when he is sitting down – if he gets down, then the food is taken away until he sits down again – and establishing a time limit for eating – if he dawdles over his food then you could make it a rule to remove his dish after about 20 minutes. If he refuses to eat, or only eats a small part of his meal, then you should be firm about not letting him eat anything else until the next meal. However, don't fuss if he refuses to eat an ingredient that he doesn't like.

Finally if all else fails, it may be more realistic to accept that your toddler is not yet ready to eat with the rest of the family. In this case you could give him his meal before – or even after – everyone else so that you are able to give him your full and undivided attention. When he can cope better with his food he can join everyone else again.

Meal suggestions

Now that your toddler is able to eat the same foods as the rest of the family, the meals you prepare for him will depend on the other factors. Will he be eating on his own, with an older brother or sister, with another toddler or with the family as a whole? What he eats at one meal will also depend on what he has eaten at other meals during the day and whether for example, he was allowed to fill himself with cookies or crackers while out visiting.

If your child frequently eats on his own, then it can be easy for a mother – quite unintentionally – to end up giving the child a lot of processed convenience foods such as baked beans, fish sticks and fruit yogurts. It is all right to give these occasionally, but not a good idea to allow them too often as they contain additives and are of limited nutritional value. Children can easily get used to this sort of diet – so much so that, when they are given a meal of boiled potatoes, fresh vegetables and fresh fruit, it seems dull.

You can give your child simple wholesome meals (*see* right), which will provide him with a healthy diet based on fresh foods. As with the younger child, try to see that every meal contains some bread, cereal or potato; some fruit and/or vegetables; and some milk, meat, fish or legumes. Between them, these foods will give him all that he needs for a balanced diet.

Breakfast

Breakfast provides an excellent opportunity to give your child some fiber-rich cereal. Encourage him to eat breakfast cereals that are wheat-based or unsweetened dry cereal (but don't give children under five whole nuts as they can be inhaled or cause choking). This can be followed by whole-wheat bread or toast and a scraping of butter or, better still, polyunsaturated margarine. Some fruit or fruit juice will round off a nourishing meal. If your child has a big appetite at breakfast time, you could also add an egg, grilled bacon or baked beans.

Meals for two

If you are planning to cook an evening meal and don't want to prepare another in the middle of the day, then you could make a larger quantity and freeze or keep a portion for yourself and your child to eat the next day.

SIMPLE MEALS
- pasta, cheese sauce and a salad of grated apple and carrot
- baked potatoes topped with baked beans or diced ham and grated cheese, followed by fresh fruit
- savory whole-wheat sandwiches followed by stewed or mashed fresh fruit with yogurt or custard
- cod steaks in a sauce with fresh vegetables
- chopped meat and beans with brown rice
- flaked tuna or chopped chicken with chopped potato or rice, corn, pieces of orange, apple, grapes and red pepper with orange and lemon juice and fresh herbs. Serve separately so that your child can choose his own combination.

LIGHT MEALS FOR ONE
- vegetable soup and bread
- scrambled egg and tomato on toast
- banana sandwiches and a cup of milk
- pancake with stewed fruit
- an individual pizza of cheese and tomato, or tomato sauce broiled on bread, followed by fruit
- fishcakes (mix up left-over fish and vegetables, sprinkle with flour and fry in a little oil)

FEEDING YOUR CHILD

Snacks

By the time your child is mixing with other toddlers it is difficult to avoid between-meal snacks. The trouble with eating between meals is not so much the frequency of eating as the kind of foods that are generally made available. Cookies, ice pops and candies eaten between meals are not only bad for a child's teeth but they can spoil his appetite for the more nourishing foods. Unfortunately, however good your intentions, you will find that other people – whether they are friends at home or in toddler play-groups – will offer children a drink and a cookie and often visitors will bring gifts of sweets or chocolates for your child.

The way you cope with this problem will depend on the circumstances. It may be embarrassing for you to refuse these gifts, and impossible for a very young child to understand why he can't have one, but with a positive attitude you can explain that your child does not eat many sweet things and that you try to restrict them to one day at the weekend. At this age you can very often get away with letting your child have just one candy if he is given a packet. You can then throw the rest away or keep them for a special treat. You could suggest that friends and relatives give small toys, puzzles or books instead of candies.

If you are visiting or at playgroup and don't feel you know the other people well enough to suggest providing an alternative to sweet cookies, you could take along some food – a breadstick, some melba toast or fruit, or a piece of bread cut into a gingerbread man – for your child to eat instead. At least you will know that he is filling himself up with something that is wholesome.

Helping out

As your toddler gets older he will be eager to help around the house and he may want to help you choose and prepare the meals. This is not only an important stage in his development (after all, every child should be able to plan, shop for and cook some simple food by the time he leaves school), but it is also a good way of encouraging interest in food so that he will enjoy his meals. It may also be a good time to suggest that he tries small pieces of new foods. Playing with a doll's kitchen, pouring water from a pitcher, using scissors and shaping play pastry are all important at this stage and soon he will want to use the real ingredients.

To begin with he can help you choose the food at the supermarket, or select a saucepan for you at home, put a tea bag in a cup and so on. His contribution will give him pleasure at the same time as giving him the opportunity to practice skills such as gripping and coordination. He may particularly enjoy carrying things for you, so let him take an unbreakable plate of cakes or cookies through to the living room, but don't let him have anything hot at this stage.

The overweight toddler

Most toddlers have pot bellies and round faces without necessarily being overweight. However, if you cannot see your child's ribs, then he may be a little too plump. Ask a friend, or your pediatrician, to look at your child without his clothes on, and see what they think.

If your child is overweight, your goal is not to make him lose weight but to stop him from gaining much more weight before he grows taller. If you have a weight problem as well, it may be that the whole family's diet needs rethinking. Are you using a lot of fat in cooking? Do you often have sweet puddings, or cookies between meals? Are you expecting the family to eat several large meals a day whether they feel hungry or not? You may be encouraging your child to eat more than he really needs. If he says he has had enough, don't try to persuade him to take more – he may do this just to please you.

If it is just your toddler who has a large appetite, try to encourage him to be more active. Most children like running, jumping and climbing, but your child may enjoy swimming or going to dancing classes too. Look, also, at the kind of food he eats and try to cut out fatty and sugary things. Give him low-calorie foods and skim milk instead. If he is hungry, fill him up with extra vegetables. Don't always put butter on his bread and toast – he will probably eat it quite happily without. You can also encourage him to feed himself as this tends to slow down a fast eater.

Above She'll find it fun brushing her own teeth – a fluoride toothpaste helps protect her teeth and gums. *Below* Foods in the right-hand column are salty, fatty or syrupy, so avoid these whenever possible. Provide a balanced diet from the foods in the other two columns.

ENCOURAGE

green beans
breadsticks
breakfast cereals such as
   cream of wheat or oatmeal
brown and whole-wheat bread
chicken
fresh fish
lean meat
liver, kidney
lentils
fruit and vegetables – fresh
   and lightly cooked
pasta
baked, boiled or mashed
   potatoes
rice
plain or low-sugar yogurt

ALLOW

baked beans
breakfast cereals such as
   cornflakes or rice krispies
white bread
cheese
french fries
dried fruit
eggs
fruit juice
fish sticks
fruit yogurt
ham
lean ground meat
low-fat cheese and low-fat
   sausages
plain cookies and cakes
polyunsaturated margarines
nut butters
canned fruit in fruit juice
canned vegetables without
   salt
zwieback

AVOID WHERE POSSIBLE

butter, other margarines
crackers
chips – thin, crinkly or
   deep-fried
fatty meats, such as
   sausages or processed
   meat
honey
jam
jelly
tomato ketchup
instant puddings
salt
sugar
sweet cookies and cakes
puddings
ready-sweetened breakfast
   cereal
soda pop and fruit-flavored
   drinks
canned fruits in syrup

FEEDING YOUR CHILD

Diaper changing and bathing

You will have to accept that your toddler is bound to get dirty – she is busy exploring and trying things out. Encourage her to wash her hands from an early age and teach her, by example, about hygiene. Sometime during the next year or so, she will no longer need to wear a diaper during the day as she gradually becomes accustomed to using her potty. This is an important step but it doesn't have to be difficult for either of you.

Changing diapers

As a rule, toddlers simply hate having their diapers changed. It means that their activities are brought to an abrupt halt when Mom or Dad says it's time to lie down and stay still for a minute or two, and they may resist strongly, wriggling and kicking in protest every time. Whether yours is a child who objects at every change, or only occasionally, it's a good idea to think of ways of distracting her; it will help you to keep your patience too. Keep a store of three or four small objects which your child can play with and examine while her diaper is being changed. You could also try singing her a special song each time or keep a musical box handy, to be played with only at diaper-changing times. You'll probably find that your child becomes more cooperative once she realizes that you aren't going to be deterred from changing her diaper. It really does help to accept that the problem will pass; getting angry and frustrated only makes the situation worse. You may even find that your toddler learns to ask you to change her diaper because she feels uncomfortable, and this may be a cue for you to think about taking her out of diapers altogether (*see* Potty training, page 196).

Bathing and daily care

Most families have a regular evening routine by the time their child has reached her first birthday and this usually includes a bath. As well as enjoying being in the water, your toddler will soon start to make moves towards washing and bathing herself, although most of the work at this stage will still be done by you. You can encourage her by giving her a sponge of her own – she can play with this in the bath, as well as using it to wash herself.

She can hold a toothbrush herself now and as she gets older will be able to brush her own teeth, although you must be prepared to supervise her to make sure she does it properly. Many dentists in fact recommend that parents brush their children's teeth until they reach the age of seven or eight. You can start using toothpaste for your toddler but you will need only a small amount. Toddlers are not able to spit out very much and most of them end up swallowing all the toothpaste you put on the brush. This isn't necessarily harmful, of course, but most toothpastes contain some chemicals, so you'll probably want to prevent your child from swallowing too much of it.

By the time your child is about two-and-a-half years old, she will be able to wash her hands and face, put on and take off at least some of her clothes, and help you dry her after the bath. This is a significant progression considering that your one-year-old's cooperation probably extended as far as holding out her foot for you to put on her sock and shoe!

Hair washing

This shouldn't present any particular problems at this age. However, if your child particularly dislikes having her hair washed, she could wear a shampoo shield (*see* page 153), or you could give her a small towel or dry washcloth to hold over her eyes so that they don't sting.

Long fine hair may be difficult to comb and brush after washing, as it tends to get tangled, but a small amount of hair conditioner (your own is probably suitable) will help to keep it free of tangles.

Making bathtime fun

Your child is now at an age when she can fully appreciate bathtimes. She will be used to the water by now and may actually enjoy splashing about and getting wet. Make her bathtime a time to play as well as to wash – you can add some children's bubble bath to the water and give her a selection of things to play with. She will enjoy containers for pouring water, objects that sink or float, and sponges she can squeeze. You can buy interesting toys for the bath too – from simple plastic ducks to wind-up toys that move across the water. Bubbles are great fun, and have the added advantage that they keep the tub clean, by preventing a ring from forming on the inside. You can keep all your child's bath toys tidy in a waterproof string bag which you can hang up between the bath taps.

BATH TOYS
Children are fascinated by water and any toy that floats or pours will give them hours of fun. Make sure the toys have no places to trap dirty water or metal parts that could rust.

DIAPER CHANGING AND BATHING

● *See* Play and toys, page 170, for bath play.

Potty training

There's no guaranteed method of potty training – and no rigid rules that apply to all situations and all children. Staying calm and patient yourself is a great help!

In the past, many mothers used to start what they called "training" more or less from birth. The infant was held at frequent intervals over the potty – sometimes before, after and even during a feeding – and occasionally something was caught. It must have saved the odd wet or dirty diaper, which may have been helpful in the days before washing machines, but beyond that there is nothing to say in favor of this approach. These days, parents are far more likely to delay introducing the potty until they feel it's reasonable to expect the right response from their child. There is very little point in starting before the child is ready.

When should you start?

You can gauge your child's state of readiness by considering a few things. Can she understand and carry out simple requests? Is her diaper dry occasionally when you come to change it? As your baby gets older, her bladder stores increasing amounts of urine at a time without releasing it. It's a gradual process and, just as with other features of growth and development, children don't necessarily progress at the same rate. As a general rule, if your child seems to pass urine more often than once every hour-and-a-half to two hours, you'll find it easier to delay training until she is slightly older. Watch for other signs too. If your child is left without a diaper on (in the back yard, perhaps, or at bathtime) does she ever show she understands the link between her body and the puddle she occasionally makes? Has she shown curiosity about other people – perhaps you or older children – using the toilet? Does she care about having a wet or dirty diaper – or even notice the difference between that and a clean one?

It's not always easy to be completely certain about these questions, but there is nothing to stop you trying your child on the potty, even if you're not sure that you'll make any real progress. If she doesn't seem ready for it, do be prepared to give in gracefully and abandon the whole idea before either of you gets too fed up. Remember that very few children are ready to start potty training before the age of 18 months, and the majority get on better when they are nearly two years old; on the whole, boys tend to be a little slower than girls.

Choosing a potty

The advantage of starting with a potty is that it is portable. You can bring it to your child very quickly, or your child can get it herself, and this can save valuable seconds with a younger child who cannot hold on for very long. Make sure that you choose a potty that is suitable: it could tip over when your toddler gets up suddenly, unless it has a wide base.

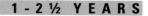

POTTIES AND ACCESSORIES
Potties come in all shapes, colors and sizes. You can get a potty that is like a little seat and your child may find this more comfortable. Little boys need a potty with a splash guard.

For an older child who is using the toilet, a "grow tall" step is useful to help her get up to the seat, or it can be used for a boy to stand at the toilet. A special child's toilet seat can help your child gain confidence when using the toilet. It fits over the big seat and allows a toddler to sit comfortably without having to be held.

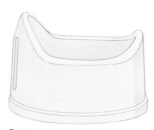

Potty

Toilet seat and step

Introducing the potty

You could begin by introducing the potty at bathtime, with a casual explanation about what it's for. Suggest your child sits on it to see what it's like. If on any occasion your child succeeds in using the potty give her some praise, but don't overdo it or she will think that failure is naughty. You could perhaps give her a cup of her favorite drink as a reward, once you're sure that she is progressing well. Increase the frequency of sessions on the pot as long as your child is happy about it. If she is not, slow down the pace a little.

A very active toddler will resent spending more than a few seconds on the potty at a time, but you could make her more relaxed by looking at a book together while she is sitting on it. It's really counter-productive to get irritated or to try and force your child to sit or stay on the potty – it won't take much to turn her off to the whole idea.

The time will come when you can leave your child's diaper off in the house, but ask her regularly and casually if she wants the potty. Leave it in an easily accessible place where you can grab it quickly; and have two potties – one upstairs and one down – if this helps. When you have to go out of the house, try and encourage your child to sit on the potty just before you go. You could then put her in a diaper (or pants with a diaper tucked in), although a child of this age may find it rather confusing to have one on sometimes but not others. It is better to take a potty with you when you go out, or simply risk the odd "accident." Extra thick terry cloth training pants or disposable pull-on diaper pants can be useful for children who are "halfway trained" like this.

Coping with "accidents"

Once you are leaving your child in pants all day – at home and outside – you should accept that you're bound to have the odd accident in the house, in other people's houses and possibly when you are out shopping. This is an unavoidable feature of potty training and of childhood in general. Even kindergarten teachers, dealing with much older children, accept that there will be occasional accidents. Of course, there will be times when you wonder just how accidental it really is, but don't forget that it is hard when you're two years old or less to have the sort of control that makes you ask for the potty when you're in the middle of an interesting game. Many of these accidents are of the "left it too late" variety. At other times, your child simply may not notice she wants to go. For your part, don't let her think that clean dry pants are vitally important, or that wet dirty ones are horrors to be avoided. They may be uncomfortable and inconvenient, but that's all. If your child gets the feeling that potty training is a constant battle, your life together could be very difficult for a while.

Problems with potty training

It may happen that you start potty training your child, but you don't seem to be making any real progress. She occasionally has good days, and then she regresses for a few days and you find that you're either mopping up or looking at an empty potty. If this happens, take a break: either your child is not quite ready or she's going through an awkward phase. Putting her back in diapers for a few weeks should help; it will ease the pressure on both of you.

Another fairly common situation is when your child is "bladder trained" before she is "bowel trained." It usually happens the other way round, but this is by no means always the case. Some children are quite capable of waiting until they have a diaper on (perhaps for the daytime nap or when they are ready for bed) before opening their bowels. Try not to get irritated or anxious if this happens – if you remain tolerant it will sort itself out in the end. However, do check that constipation is not the cause of the problem – maybe your child needs more fiber or extra fluid in her diet.

Avoiding dependence on her own potty

It does help if you get your child to use different potties and toilets from the start. Unfamiliar ones can be rather upsetting for a small child, and if she is dependent on her own, you may have to cart her potty around with you for months. Once she is ready to sit on the toilet, you could give her a child seat (*see* page 197), but when you are away from home, let her see that she's quite safe on the toilet because you are holding her steady. When you visit a new place, make a special point of seeking out the toilet. Exploit your child's natural curiosity by saying something like "Let's see what color Aunt Pat's bathroom is . . . ," or "I wonder if you'll be able to flush the toilet here all by yourself."

Out and about

When you are out shopping or away from home for the day, it's a good idea to plan your stops so that you can take your child to a convenient public toilet. If you can't find one nearby, don't be shy about asking a shop assistant if there's a staff toilet you could use. When you're traveling some distance by car and expecting your child to sleep on the way, you may have to compromise a little. Thick terry cloth training pants could be the answer, so that you don't undermine your child's confidence by putting her in a diaper again.

Staying dry all night

Few children manage to remain dry at night at the same time as becoming dry during the day, and a more absorbent diaper is often needed at night-time for some months at least. You could try encouraging her to use the potty before she goes to bed, but it's unlikely that she'll have enough control at this age to last through the night.

Leaving it till later

Some parents prefer to leave potty training until the child is a little older, say two and a half years, or even later. Choose a period when your child is generally cooperative (and not the stage when "no" is her favorite word). If you have left the potty around, she may have seen it used by other children and will be quite happy to try it herself. You could even miss out on the potty stage altogether and put her straight onto the toilet. Simply explain what you want her to do – perhaps asking an older child to demonstrate – and because your child is old enough to understand she may take to it quite quickly and without much fuss. The main disadvantage with this approach is that your child will be in diapers for longer.

Your child may be quite happy to sit on her potty if she has a favorite book to look at.

See Bathing and everyday care, page 232, for night dryness.

Sleep and bedtime

Although uncertain of her reception, a toddler may come downstairs again and again rather than accept that it's bedtime.

Your toddler still needs plenty of sleep, but more of it will now be taken at night. As he becomes more assertive, going to bed and staying there often becomes an area of disagreement between you.

Lack of sleep won't hurt your child, but you are likely to feel that you and your partner deserve the evenings and the night to yourselves after an active day. If this becomes a time for battles with your toddler instead, it can make your relationship with him difficult during the day as well.

Daytime rests

Your child will still benefit from a rest during the day, even if he doesn't want to sleep. He will probably be ready to drop one nap, and this is often followed by an awkward period when he is a bit miserable due to over-tiredness. As in all dealings with a toddler some tact is needed at this time in order to find ways of getting him to rest. Doing something quiet together, such as reading or listening to music, is one way. You can also continue to put him down for a rest with a few toys, so that he can play quietly and fall asleep if he needs to. Another ploy is to take him out in the stroller for a long walk. When he does fall asleep at nap times, it will be deeply and he won't like being woken up, so allow him plenty of time to adjust to being awake.

From crib to bed

You may move your child to a bed when he is about two years old. Sometimes this can help with sleep problems, as he will have more room for his toys in the bed. But, like any change, it can also lead to an unsettled period. If your child is inclined to play up at bedtime, being in a bed will make it easier for him to get up and come in search of you. With time and patient firmness, he will settle down.

The flexible bedtime

Keeping to a bedtime routine is important, but bear in mind that your child is likely to try to make this time last as long as possible. After you have finally said good night he will probably cry and grumble a bit, but if he continues to get worked up you should keep looking in on him, as you did when he was younger. Settle him down, say good night again, but don't show him that it is worth his while making a fuss, by reading another story, singing a song or staying to chat or play a game.

If your partner arrives home lateish in the evening, your child may try to stay awake to see him. In this case you could put your child to bed in the usual way, but leave the story reading and final goodnight to your partner when he gets in. You may find that it suits all of you if your child goes to bed a bit later in the evening and continues to have a nap during the day.

A rest in the afternoon, when your child may be tired and a bit irritable, will help him to wind down.

Waking at night

If your toddler wakes in the night, it is better to go to him when he calls out; if you leave him to cry he will start to associate being in bed with loneliness and misery. Once he can get out of his crib or bed, he may start coming to look for you if you don't go to him. If he wants to come into bed with you, you will need to decide if you are going to allow this. Bear in mind that you must start as you mean to go on; it will be much harder for you to insist that he stays in his crib or bed if he has once been allowed to get in with you.

Early mornings

Your child is likely to continue to wake early if he has got into the habit of doing so. Try to get him used to staying in his bed or playing in his room for a while. It may help if you put a drink within his reach, and make sure he has toys to play with. If he is quite happy with this arrangement, you won't have to get up as soon as he wakes.

Nightmares

Nightmares are usually related to things that happen during the day. A toddler is coping with many new experiences, learning by leaps and bounds, and often clashing with you over things. A frightening meeting with a dog can result in nightmares for a short time, and anger felt during the day can spill over into disturbed dreams. If your toddler is having a lot of nightmares, try making life as calm as possible for a while. Be attentive to him during the day and make the evenings relaxed and happy times.

Deal with all night fears immediately. Go to him if he screams suddenly or cries loudly – the sight of your familiar friendly face will usually calm him, but if he is left to cry he will only become more frightened. You can talk to him gently until he is calmer and able to fall asleep again. Put a night-light in his room; it makes the room look familiar, and unthreatening, or leave the door ajar.

THE BEDTIME ROUTINE
An enjoyable and familiar routine is one way of preventing problems at bedtime. Here are some ideas:

● **Start early**
Try giving him his bath before supper so that he can wind down gently.

● **Make supper enjoyable**
Give him food that is easy to eat and that he likes. Try to avoid battles over food.

● **Take your time**
Tell him a story, sing songs or nursery rhymes, and have a cuddle and a chat – either while he is in bed or in his room so that not all the "nice" things happen downstairs.

● **Include his toys**
Say good night to them too – and tuck in his favorite.

● **Make the room friendly**
Have a night-light on and leave the door ajar if he likes some light.

● **Don't disappear**
Let him know that you are close at hand if he wants you.

● **Don't let him get up**
The day is over, he can't make it last forever.

Your day together

Your toddler loves to be helpful and may find sorting the washing an absorbing task.

The toddler is a powerhouse of energy, and having one around the house can be exhausting. You have to be on the alert all day, for she is still too young to understand what she should or shouldn't do and increasingly able to do what she wants. She is also becoming aware of herself as a separate person with her own needs: she's more demanding and will clash with you head-on if you try to thwart her. It can be a difficult time for both of you, or it can be delightful (and only occasionally frustrating), depending to a large extent on how you handle her.

Going out and about

Now that she is more likely to make mischief, the task of keeping your toddler amused is very important. Going out is always a good idea; she'll enjoy the park and playground or you could take her swimming at the local pool. Parks that have a separate section for under-fives are fun and provide an excellent opportunity for your toddler to meet other children. But do remember that she's not ready to understand about being fair, or even gentle. You must steer her away from conflicts and be ready to offer comfort all round when there are scraps. Mother and toddler groups are good for her and provide company for you. You can also arrange visits to other parents with toddlers, but when you return the invitation, be prepared for some hostility as well as fun. Your child may be disinclined to let anyone else play with her toys, or another child may boss her. Sort problems out in a matter-of-fact way, and don't worry: it won't always be like this, and your child will at least be learning important lessons about cooperation.

Avoiding confrontation

Getting through your day without major upsets is an exercise in diplomacy. Your child will fight orders or attempts to baby her, but may respond if you issue exciting challenges – "I bet you can't put all those things back in the drawer before I finish making the bed!" – rather than giving commands.

By now she will know your routine and understand that she can't have your undivided attention while chores are being done. However, you will have fewer grumbles if you let her join in as much as possible. She can help with the dish washing, use the dustpan and brush, or tidy the saucepans. She'll be more of a hindrance than a help, but she'll be in a good mood.

It will make life less frustrating for both of you if you try saying "no" to her less often. Her memory is still short and you have more chance of gaining cooperation and avoiding confrontation if you are less strict. Objects you never want touched should be hidden away as she can now climb to get the things she has set her heart on.

You should decide your policy on discipline with your

How your time might be spent
Once your child has settled into a pattern of three meals a day your time together will have more of a routine.

Key

▰	Sleeping
▰	Sleeping/resting
▰	Bathing/changing
▰	Eating/drinking
▱	Playing
▱	Your time

NOON

BABY'S DAY

YOUR DAY

MORNING

EVENING

MIDNIGHT

partner. It can be confusing to a child when one parent reacts strongly to certain behavior, while the other is more lax. Ultimately this can lead to your child playing you off against each other, or behaving in a way that neither of you like because the messages have not come across clearly enough. Resist the temptation to threaten a naughty child with the absent parent: "Just wait till your father gets home" can turn him into a feared figure, or backfire when you forget to tell him of the misdeed or he reacts leniently. Anyway, punishment which is given hours later teaches your child nothing useful about good behavior.

Getting some exercise

A toddler is much more likely to be happy and content if she has plenty of outlets for her physical energy. Going out is important as she needs plenty of room to practice walking and running. If she chooses to walk rather than go in her stroller, you'll have to wait for her because she'll probably want to wander away, stop and examine a shiny stone, or stop and talk to a cat. If you are taking her shopping, give yourself plenty of time otherwise her delaying tactics may make you impatient.

Time for play

Always try to play with your child for a while each day, and talk and listen to her so that communicating begins to mean more than simply shouting for attention. She may have given up one of her naps and is likely to go through a slightly clinging phase. This is a good opportunity to introduce quiet play, such as looking at books together.

Make bathtime enjoyable by giving her toys to fill, pour and float, but don't be tempted to leave her alone as she can drown in *very little* water. At a stage when going to bed may be causing trouble, bathtime is a pleasant way to introduce a nighttime routine and you and your partner can take turns in putting her to bed and reading her a story.

INVOLVING YOUR TODDLER

Six foolproof but messy ways to keep your toddler happily occupied.

● **Washing up**
Surround the sink with newspaper or a bath mat, fill it with soapy water and give her a sponge and lots of plastic things to wash.

● **Shopping**
Arrange a "supermarket shelf" with lots of unbreakables and give your toddler a large handbag or two to fill to capacity.

● **Painting**
Sit her (in clothes that don't matter) on a washable floor with lots of newspaper and some finger paints.

● **Delivering**
Fix a piece of string to a large cardboard box so that it can be pulled along, and give your toddler plenty of things to fill it with.

● **Tidying**
Let her take all the pots and pans out of a low cupboard, clatter around with them and put them back (check first that there is nothing dangerous there).

● **Cooking**
Sit her at a table with a ball of dough, a floured pastry board, a rolling pin and pastry cutters (you can get animals shapes). She can make her own tarts to bake in the oven (*see* page 231).

The local playground provides an outlet for your child's exuberant energy, but she needs you to help her use the equipment safely.

YOUR DAY TOGETHER

Growing and learning

Moving freely and confidently, toddlers get enormous pleasure from their new physical skills.

Now she can squat very steadily and reach out for a toy.

Now he's a toddler he seems so much more aware of everything and everyone. He's into all your cupboards and your bag, he's climbing up armchairs and maybe onto tables, and he's running around after other children. He's taking an active part in things and his own personality is so much more obvious.

This is the time when his imagination starts to develop. At first he copies you, pushing his toy buggy along just as you do or using his toy drill. He loves playing with bags and hats. With time he is able to act out little stories, such as taking his cars to the garage for gas.

In these months your child is learning to use language. To begin with, this will be just to tell you what he wants – he'll empty his cup and let you know it by saying "Gone!" – but later he will chat to himself about what he's doing while he's playing with his toys.

Your child is changing a lot and you will need to get to know him as a toddler. He's more impulsive and he's trying you out. He soon learns what you don't want him to do but he'll watch you, waiting for your reaction as he pulls off the heads of your flowers or tips his drink over. He's learning the limits of his behavior and how you react when he's naughty. Remember, to him it's all a game.

He's changing physically too. His legs and arms appear to be longer and he's moving about easily. He's able to examine all his toys and find out which ones fit together, which ones move and which ones make a noise. He's no longer mouthing everything but is beginning to learn how things work. To him everything is a toy and although he's fun he'll keep you on your toes, watching him all the time.

LEARNING TO WALK FREELY

He's getting ready to walk by himself and learning to stand, to balance and finally to move forwards without support. At first his hands and feet will be widespread for balance and his gait will be awkward. He'll topple and not be able to get up by himself. From these first staggering steps he'll soon learn to walk quite steadily, starting and stopping when he wants to and getting up by himself.

Getting around

Many toddlers take their first steps before they are a year old, others seem to move so efficiently on all fours that there is little incentive for them to start walking. Whenever your child starts to walk he will go through a series of stages which are common to all children. First of all he will cruise around holding onto the furniture, then, as he becomes more confident, he may stand or try reaching out and stepping between two pieces of furniture. Finally he will turn toward you and take his first steps. He'll seem to stumble to you, feet apart, arms outstretched and with a broad grin on his face. He'll have some tumbles and you'll have to take care that he doesn't fall on a hard surface.

By the time he's about 18 months old he'll be moving about quite freely, carrying a doll or pushing a toy as he walks. He may be able to run a little, every part of his body seeming to help him along and his eyes fixed on the ground in front. When he's two he'll be squatting down quite steadily to reach a toy, climbing up onto the furniture and sitting on a trike, trying to ride along.

Before he learns to walk he is still a bit unsteady standing so he may like to play sitting down. When he tries to sit he'll seem to collapse by bumping down on his bottom, or he may fall forward onto his hands and then sit back. As yet he hasn't enough control to sit down slowly.

Climbing becomes an achievement for him now. He can climb up and down stairs, he can climb up and look out of the window to see daddy coming home and he can climb up the steps of a low slide.

Gradually his movements are becoming more controlled. By the time he's two and a half he'll enjoy showing you how he jumps, stands on tiptoe and throws a ball. He really is enjoying his new-found independence and skill.

Top Once he's taken his first steps, he will rapidly learn to walk quite confidently.
Above Climbing adds a new dimension to life and enables him to explore further.

GROWING AND LEARNING

Once he can pull himself up he'll begin to step sideways around the furniture holding on with both hands. Occasionally he'll stand holding on with just one hand.

With time, he'll be confident enough to turn and step out towards another piece of furniture, bridging the gap with his outspread hands.

Once he's taking one, then two steps on his own to bridge the gap between supports he'll soon be walking forwards a few paces towards you.

Building and scribbling

By his first birthday your child can move his arms, hands and fingers with precision. He can pick up the smallest toy with care and put it down where he wants it to go. He can now concentrate on the game he wants to play and forget about getting the actions right in order to play it. His movements start to become more deliberate. He'll be building towers out of boxes, turning the pages over in his books, placing rings over a central stacking pole and collecting small toys together in a box. Then he'll move on to new games such as putting his toy men into their car and moving it around as if it is on a road or driving down a slope.

He'll also be interested in how things work. Does this toy roll? What happens if I throw it or pull this string? These are

Below At first she just clutches a crayon holding it in the palm of her hand with all her fingers and making random marks with it. *Below right* He's interested in how things work and has developed more precise control over his movements.

Now she's learned to control her crayon and make more purposeful marks on the paper.

the kinds of things he'll be trying to find out. Much of his exploring will be helping to strengthen and expand some of his finer movements. Turning knobs and taps, for example, and filling up and pouring out water or sand from containers are games which the toddler enjoys and these activities also help to strengthen his wrist movements and teach him to control his actions more precisely.

Once he is two years old he'll be showing a preference for either his right or left hand. However, it may not be until he's at school that he shows a total right or left handedness. By his second birthday he'll also be making reasonable attempts at unscrewing tops or lids, threading large beads and holding the paper steady while he scribbles or paints. For all these activities he has to use both his hands and be able to coordinate them working together.

The way he plays with a crayon or pencil shows how his skills with his hands develop during this second year. At about 15 months old he can mark the paper with a crayon but in a haphazard way, clutching it with all his fingers and holding it in the palm of his hand. By one-and-a-half to two years old he can make more controlled pencil lines, first straight ones, but soon circular ones as well. He may start holding the crayon in a more adult fashion, with his thumb and first two fingers on the shaft. This will mean that he can control it better and so he'll be able to make more purposeful strokes. Soon he'll be mastering a circle, knowing where to start and stop his crayon to complete it.

Now that he has greater control over his movements the two-year-old will be showing more elaborate building skills as well as purposeful drawing. He may build walls or tall towers with his blocks. He may be lining his cars up in neat rows or sitting his teddies carefully on toy chairs to give them tea. A creative element is now present in his play.

Using words and knowing what to do

By the time he's two-and-a-half years old your toddler will be using some words to communicate. This is quite a change from when, at a year old, he pointed or pulled you along to show you something. He may use his first words before he's about 15 months old, or he may not speak much until nearer his second birthday. Whenever he starts to speak you'll find that he already understands a great deal. When he hears "Let's go for a walk" he'll fetch his coat, or he'll rush upstairs when you say "It's bathtime."

Before he starts talking he communicates with you by babbling and pointing. He'll let you know what he wants and doesn't want! He may copy your mannerisms – you may find him holding the phone over his shoulder, jabbering expressively and nodding all the time. This is the real beginning of talking and it's every bit as important as his first proper words.

At first he may seem to use parts of words or shortened words. "N, n, n" may mean no and "der," there. His ability to say some sounds develops later than others. Quite early on he can use p, d, g or m, much later on he can use s, f, th, ch or v. Inevitably he'll make mistakes and that's normal. It will help him if you repeat words for him to hear, but try not to correct him when he gets things wrong. You're his model and he will learn just from hearing you say a word correctly.

Speech and understanding develop in the same way, following the same stages, in all children. Your child's use of mainly single words to name things will change into two-word phrases. Sometimes you will find that these have several meanings. "Daddy car" can mean "Here's Daddy's car" or "Daddy's got a car." You can only understand what he's really saying by watching to see what he means. When he begins to use three- or four-word phrases you can really follow what he's saying. His sentence structure may not be quite right yet but he's communicating more easily. With time he'll begin to use more verbs, adjectives and pronouns, and the development of his language will become more subtle. It may only be by looking back and comparing that you'll realize how very much better he's become at communicating.

As his language develops he'll enjoy listening to nursery rhymes, stories at bedtime or some children's television. While he's listening he's learning new words and new ways of expressing himself. Learning songs and rhymes also helps him to use his memory. You, the people he meets and the things around him are all helping him to talk and understand.

She'll enjoy copying you and as she chats away she may adopt quite adult gestures.

GROWING AND LEARNING

HELPING HIM TO TALK

● Make sure you always look at him when you use a new word.

● Point to the toy or object you're naming.

● Don't bombard him with too much information all at the same time.

● Instructions need to be short and simple.

● Avoid long sentences.

● Don't speak too quickly.

● Listen to him.

● Don't correct him too much, just be a model for him to copy.

Above When she's looking through a book she'll begin to recognize things like cars and toys that she's seen around her.
Right He'll learn about different shapes and be able to fit the simplest ones into a sorting box.

SOME THINGS THAT THE 2½-YEAR-OLD WILL KNOW

● He'll know his own name.
● He can choose the biggest and smallest toy.
● He'll know whether he is a boy or a girl.
● He can find all the toys with wheels and pick them out from his toy box.
● He's beginning to understand "same" and "different." For example, he can sort out the socks in your washing pile if you start him off, and he can sort out all the round buttons from a mixture of different shapes.

Matching and linking

As your toddler's play becomes more deliberate he'll be beginning to work things out for himself. When he's about a year old he can find a toy when it rolls out of sight behind a chair, or if you hide it under a box while he's watching. He'll be able to match new things he sees and hears with ones he already knows. For example, he might point at and later name the picture of a car in his book, remembering how you pointed out some cars to him when you were out shopping. Soon he may be finding one of his own toys which is the same as the one shown in his book. By the time he's two he'll be able to link his memory of a familiar

person with that person's picture. He'll recognize close relatives or friends in a photograph, but he's still unsure when shown a picture of himself.

By matching and linking together things that he sees and hears your toddler will be building up ideas about how things are organized around him. His improving memory and language helps with this. At first his ideas about things are very vague. For example, he may use the word "doggy" to include all four-legged things. When he's between two and three years old, he'll be applying the word just to dogs.

In his second year he'll also be interested in shapes, and his growing skills at matching and linking will help him to master sorting boxes and simple puzzles. At first he may just try to see what different shapes can do. He'll discover that square ones are easiest to build with, but round ones roll and are easiest to fit into a sorting box. By the time he's two he may be fitting the square and triangular shapes into his box as well. He'll be more interested now in the shape of puzzle pieces rather than just the picture on the piece. He may try to force the correct piece into its space, but it will be upside down or the wrong way round. Soon he'll be remembering not only where the piece goes but also which way round it goes. He'll be stopping and thinking more before he takes action.

Taking control

The toddler is well known for his liveliness, curiosity and impulsiveness. He shows his feelings immediately, and often in an exaggerated way. He'll be growing more confident and independent and taking control over many of the things that affect his daily life, such as feeding, washing and dressing. But at the same time he is still emotionally dependent on you. His feelings and behavior are very changeable as he tries to cope with so many new skills and demands. There may be times when he returns to the clinging behavior he showed in his first year, when he wanted help with everything. The next minute he may get cross or refuse to cooperate because he really wants to do the thing for himself. Sometimes he will seem quite fearless, then at other times he may feel less sure of himself, perhaps because he's tired, unhappy or upset. At these moments he may clutch a favorite teddy, or suck his fingers or piece of blanket. If he doesn't have a comfort object he may cling tightly to you or clutch at your dress. His need for comfort is stronger than ever.

His personality will influence the way he shows his feelings. He may have long noisy tantrums when he's cross, or he may sulk in a corner. However, like most children at this age, he probably shows his feelings in a very immediate and uninhibited way. This is true not only when he's cross but also when he's pleased or happy. He'll give you big hugs or chuckle loudly without any embarrassment.

Although he's taking more control over his actions he'll still want you to be involved in his play. He'll probably not give up easily in his demands now, and will know your weak spots and how to annoy you. Everything has to be done *now* and he does not yet understand about waiting or "later." If he has tantrums when things go wrong, these will probably reach a peak when he's between two and two-and-a-half years old, and then they'll gradually start to disappear. This can be a trying time but it's also fun. He has so much energy and enjoys the simplest games.

A favorite and familiar toy is always a friend.

He'll still feel unsure of himself sometimes and need your reassurance to help him cope with new things.

She's beginning to learn to do some things for herself.

It takes times – and a lot of patience – before they will learn to share toys and really play together.

Looking after himself

This is the stage when your child is increasingly independent. He wants to do things for himself however long it takes! You may notice his first attempts to look after himself when he rubs his own hair as you wash it or tries to undress himself. At first he may just lift his leg up to help you take his shorts off, then he may try to pull them off himself. He'll find loose-fitting clothes easier to manage.

Feeding himself with a spoon is another skill which he will be trying to master after his first birthday. He will want to use a spoon for everything and some things (for example, chopped meat and peas) he'll manage, others (like jello) he won't. By the time he's 18 months old he'll have fewer accidents when he's eating as he is becoming more competent.

As your child's second birthday approaches he'll be talking and understanding a lot more. Now he can tell you when he's hungry, tired, thirsty or if he needs to "pee." He'll be enjoying his new-found independence.

By the time he's two-and-a-half he may be ready to play his own part in the outside world. You may already have taken him to a toddler group or left him to play at a friend's house. He needs to be able to cope on his own and it is at this point that he can show all the skills he's learned. He can pull down his pants and cope with going to the toilet. He can use a spoon and fork to eat and can say if he wants a drink or if he's too hot.

Children vary a great deal as to when they attain these skills, and often girls seem competent earlier than boys. If there is a new baby in the family, or if he's ill, he will be more dependent and need more of your attention. He will settle again with time but you may need to be patient.

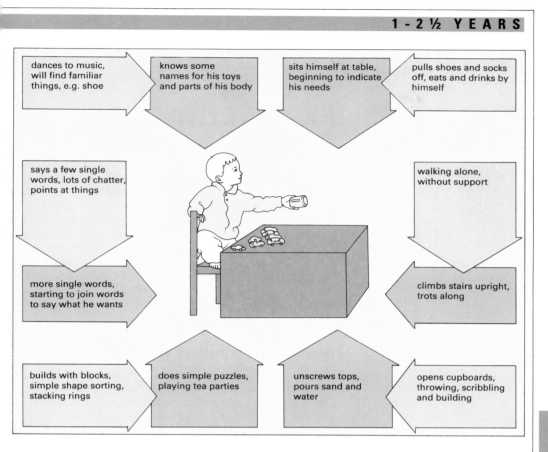

dances to music, will find familiar things, e.g. shoe

knows some names for his toys and parts of his body

sits himself at table, beginning to indicate his needs

pulls shoes and socks off, eats and drinks by himself

says a few single words, lots of chatter, points at things

walking alone, without support

more single words, starting to join words to say what he wants

climbs stairs upright, trots along

builds with blocks, simple shape sorting, stacking rings

does simple puzzles, playing tea parties

unscrews tops, pours sand and water

opens cupboards, throwing, scribbling and building

Making sense of his world

Your toddler is more able to get around and look after himself now. Most toddlers have an intense curiosity about their surroundings and, as he becomes more sure of himself at walking, he will want to go off alone to see what he can find. He'll soon want to be with you again though.

As his language develops and his play becomes more constructive and creative, he'll enjoy being with other young children. At first he may just make friendly advances, perhaps waving or smiling at them. Then he'll enjoy playing with his toy near another child, but he's not old enough yet to join in and play a group game. He'll probably not be very willing to share you or his toys with anyone yet. He may get very possessive if he thinks another child wants what he sees as his belongings. Other adults too can be seen as taking up time with you which he wants for himself. A regular outing to a toddler club or park, where he can have contact with other parents and children on neutral territory (that is, not his own house and toys), can be a welcome break. These are places, too, where he can have a go at climbing, riding on big toys or kicking a ball.

Your toddler's world is expanding all the time. Now shopping trips, rides on buses, short visits to friends and so on are all adding to his knowledge and understanding. At home too you can see him taking more interest in whatever is going on. By helping you with sorting the washing or tidying up, he's learning what different objects do.

From one to
two-and-a-half years
During this period your toddler's skills are expanding and he is increasingly able to let you know what he wants. By the time he's about two-and-a-half he'll be acting out little stories with his toys, chatting away as he plays, and using language to get what he wants – such as another drink.

HELPING HIM BECOME INDEPENDENT
● Break things down into small steps so that he can do some things for himself.
● Try not to get angry if he makes mistakes or regresses a little in his behavior.
● Look for the signs that he wants to be independent. Does he look uncomfortable when he needs to pee? Is he trying to get his own clothes on by himself?

GROWING AND LEARNING

Play and toys

This is the time when children are into everything and it can be very hard work for whoever has the job of keeping them safe and happy. Sometimes it is easy to forget that what makes your toddler so exhausting – her energy, her curiosity, her eagerness, her desire for new experiences and her determination to do things for herself – are the very qualities that make her fun to be with and that you should be encouraging; they will be important assets throughout her schooldays and in adult life. As she plays, your toddler is learning to handle and control the things around her, and each success gives her confidence to go on to the next stage. If you can provide your child with playthings which will allow her to make discoveries and experience new things as she needs to, you will make your life together easier and more rewarding and you might find yourself saying "no" a little less often.

Toys to push, pull or ride

To a child who has just learned to walk, the feeling of mobility is a great delight. Once she no longer needs a toddle truck – or the furniture – to give her stability, your child will enjoy having something to push along as she walks. A toy on wheels that can be pushed, or even pulled on a string – especially if it wobbles and clatters as it moves – is a great success at this stage. You will find that there is a good range of this kind of toy in toy shops, or you can make an improvised pull-along toy by sealing a few small objects (dried beans or buttons) inside an empty plastic container and attaching a string to the neck or handle.

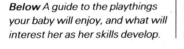

Below A guide to the playthings your baby will enjoy, and what will interest her as her skills develop.

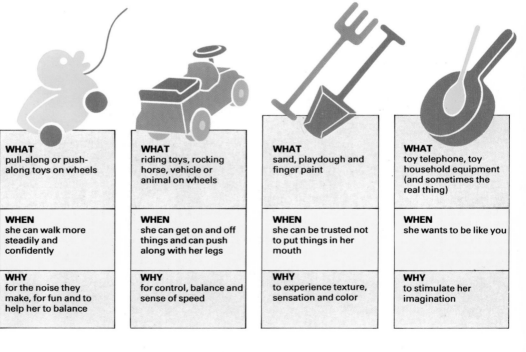

WHAT pull-along or push-along toys on wheels	**WHAT** riding toys, rocking horse, vehicle or animal on wheels	**WHAT** sand, playdough and finger paint	**WHAT** toy telephone, toy household equipment (and sometimes the real thing)
WHEN she can walk more steadily and confidently	**WHEN** she can get on and off things and can push along with her legs	**WHEN** she can be trusted not to put things in her mouth	**WHEN** she wants to be like you
WHY for the noise they make, for fun and to help her to balance	**WHY** for control, balance and sense of speed	**WHY** to experience texture, sensation and color	**WHY** to stimulate her imagination

As the child's legs get stronger she will enjoy a toy that she can ride. Most of these are vehicles (such as toy tricycles or tractors) or animals on rockers, wheels or castors. Toys with wheels or castors have no pedals – the child simply propels herself along with her feet. Castors restrict the speed at which the toy moves, but they do have the advantage of allowing her to move sideways without tipping the toy over. If you don't have much space in your house or wish to spare your furniture from possible damage, you might prefer to keep these as outdoor toys.

Above left and right Racing around on a truck or pulling along a wiggly toy can get rid of a lot of energy at that active time of day!

WHAT
pegboard, crayons, buttons, construction toys, puzzles and sorting toys

WHAT
small cars, dolls and carriage, farm animals, play house or tent

WHAT
plenty of picture books, stories and rhymes

WHEN
she can handle small things

WHEN
she wants to create a world of her own

WHEN
she enjoys books, looking at pictures, singing and dancing

WHY
to develop manipulative and co-ordinating skills

WHY
to express her understanding of the world

WHY
so that she can learn about the world she lives in

SAFE PLAY
Outside
● Tell your child firmly never to throw sand – if it gets into eyes it can scratch or irritate.
● Make sure the sandbox is covered when not in use, or dogs and cats may use it as a litter.
● Keep a watchful eye on her when she plays in the wading pool.
● If you have a swing or climbing equipment in the yard, check it regularly for wear.
Inside
● Don't let your toddler run around carrying sharp pencils or scissors. She could fall and hurt herself.
● When choosing a riding toy, check that it won't tip over too easily.

PLAY AND TOYS

Outdoor play

Your child may love climbing and it is far better to provide a way for her to do it safely, rather than to forbid it altogether. If you are lucky enough to have a yard and can afford to buy a climbing frame, now is the time to get one. Some frames offer more than one activity, with attachments such as a slide, balancing bar or rings to swing from. Equipment like this is expensive, so make sure that your child likes this kind of activity before you go out and buy one.

Outdoor toys do not have to be elaborate to provide a challenge; children enjoy playing outside purely for the fun of it and because it allows them to "let off steam." A stout plank in the yard, supported at each end by a stable brick, box or cinder-block, can be balanced along, stepped onto, jumped off and jumped over. Your toddler may also enjoy kicking a large ball around outside, or practicing throwing and catching with an adult or another child.

Messy play

Toddlers love to explore different materials, so if you can provide some sand, indoors or out, it will give them many hours of satisfying play. Sand has the added advantages that it is inexpensive and makes little mess if you have an outdoor sand-box for the children to sit and play in. The best sand to buy is "washed" or "playpen" sand, as builders' sand is far too coarse and will stain everything yellow.

Dry sand has similar qualities to water – it can be poured or trickled through holes – and you can use the same tools as for water: cups and jugs, containers with holes in (old colanders or a four-holed plastic flowerpot), tubes and funnels. You can also combine sand and water, as damp sand can be molded, packed into buckets or plastic glasses and turned out to make sandcastles or pies. With your help, your child may enjoy constructing a basic road system with bridges so that she can play with her plastic cars. Very wet sand is delightfully sloppy and can be played with using only hands, or perhaps a scoop. Indoors, it is better to stick

Your toddler is always on the go, and kicking a ball around outside with Dad provides her with some exercise, and fresh air too.

Don't expect her to make sculptures with playdough at first. Show her how to make simple shapes, such as balls and sausages, and encourage her to enjoy the feel of the dough.

to dry or slightly damp sand, perhaps in a large dish pan or baby bath. You can put the container on a large towel so that the floor doesn't get too messy.

Finger paints

Although painting is not "art" at this age, your child may enjoy handling and experimenting with paints, and it is a good way for her to learn about color and texture. There is a saying, "Fingers were made before forks" – they were also made before paintbrushes. There is no point at this stage in giving your child neat little boxes containing a fine-haired brush and small blocks of color; get some finger paints instead. You can buy pots of nontoxic finger paint or you can make your own by mixing a little flour or cornflour with cold water, bringing it to the boil and cooking it until it thickens – the ideal texture is like creamy salad dressing. Color it with food dye or nontoxic powder paint, or with a squirt from a bottle of ready-mixed nontoxic poster paint.

Finger painting is no fun on a small surface. Give your child large sheets of paper, a sheet of heavy-duty plastic or a large tin tray. If she likes the idea of finger painting, but is timid about putting her hands into a bright color, try her with the homemade uncolored paint first, adding small quantities of color gradually as she gets used to it. She will enjoy watching the colors mix together.

Finger painting is a good pastime out of doors but it can also be done in the house and cheers up many a wet afternoon. Make sure you give your child a bowl of clean water to wash her hands in, as messy fingers can touch an amazing number of surfaces on the way to the bathroom!

Playdough

Playdough is just as satisfying for your toddler, although it is less messy than finger painting. Again, you can buy some or make it yourself (*see* right). Young children enjoy the texture of the dough, which can be squeezed, poked, stretched, patted and modeled.

PLAYDOUGH RECIPE

The basic mixture is flour and water. If you add a little oil to the water and salt to plain flour you will have a mixture which can be rolled and kneaded. If you use self-raising flour and water only, and knead it well, you will have a wonderfully stretchy dough. Either of these mixtures will keep for a month in the refrigerator and are cheap enough to throw away when they get really dirty. If you want a mixture that will keep for even longer follow this recipe: combine in a saucepan 1 cup of salt, 2 cups of plain flour, 2 cups of water, 2 tablespoons of oil and 4 teaspoons of cream of tartar. Cook till it leaves the sides of the pan and be sure it has cooled before the child handles it. Any of these dough mixtures can be colored with food coloring before mixing. If you mix it plain and then add the coloring afterward, you will get a pretty marbled effect.

PLAY AND TOYS

215

Playing at being grown-ups is fun and you don't need much equipment to create a new personality!

RHYMES FOR ACTION

Your child will want to join in with the rhymes and songs you sing to her and will enjoy sharing the actions (such as clapping her hands and dancing) with you too. Sit facing her and encourage her to clap her hands against yours in time to the rhythm of the verse.

Pat-a-cake pat-a-cake baker's
    man
Bake me a cake as fast as
    you can
Prick it and pat it and mark it
    with 'B'
And pop it in the oven for Baby
    and me

When she is good at it, introduce variations – clap your right hand against her right, then your left against her left.

Put the thumbs and forefingers of your hands together and twist them across one another to make the movement of:

Incy wincy spider climbing up the
    spout
Down came the rain and washed
    the spider out
Out came the sun and dried up all
    the rain
Incy wincy spider climbed the
    spout again.

Imitating and imaginative play

Children learn to take their place in the world by imitating the adults around them and they can be encouraged in this by having some "grown-up" things to play with. Provide playthings that allow her to copy what she sees you doing in and around the house, such as a shopping bag to fill and empty. She will be starting to invent her own games now and is good at using whatever props are at hand, so avoid buying too many toys for her.

Dressing up

Toddlers are not fully into pretend play yet – they love dressing up for its own sake rather than as part of a group activity. Adult clothes and hats are popular with them, and you can buy or make outfits for doctors, firemen and others. Often, though, a colorful hat or head-dress will give more pleasure at this age than a smart uniform.

Although at some stage of their development children do tend to identify with an adult of the same sex, don't expect that girls will always want to play female roles and that boys will only want to imitate male heroes. At this stage they may like to experiment and try out all the options – and the clothes that go with them. This is perfectly natural, so don't try to push them one way or the other.

While they are experimenting at "being someone else," children like to have somewhere private to go. A sheet draped over a table makes a good den or hide-out. Alternatively you might consider buying a wigwam or play house as a birthday present, but look for one that can be put up indoors as well as outside.

A pretend world

As well as acting out for themselves the adult roles they see around them, children like to organize small worlds of their own. For this purpose they want miniature versions of the real world – cars, dolls, farm animals, and the garage, crib or farmyard that goes with them. A large number of assorted blocks is useful at this stage: they can be used to make stables, fences, forts, road layouts and houses, as well as being fun to play with on their own.

This is the time when you will appreciate having bought a really sturdy riding truck earlier on. It can now become a doll's carriage, an ambulance for carrying sick toys or a transporter for small cars or farm animals. All you have to do is supply the "trimmings" – bedding for the carriage and cars for the transporter.

Scribbling and drawing

Although most children are a long way from writing and drawing, they do have the urge to scribble. Look for chubby wax crayons at first, or the very thick soft black pencils sold in art shops and by educational suppliers. Don't waste money on good paper – it is size and quantity, not quality, that is important. This might be a good time to get a small blackboard and some chalks so that the child can scribble a picture and then rub it off and start again.

Matching and fitting

Some toddlers get great satisfaction from their new skill in handling small objects and will spend a long time negotiating pegs in pegboards or threading large beads onto a lace. As soon as your child has passed the stage of exploring small things with her mouth, she will learn a lot from handling, comparing and matching the contents of your button box.

Sorting toys continue to provide her with a challenge, and she will be learning to manage more complex ones now, with several pieces of different shapes and sizes. Jigsaws also use similar skills – to begin with, look for a board jigsaw puzzle with colorful inset shapes which can be lifted out by means of a knob on top. The best of these have another picture underneath – for instance, you lift up the ambulance and find the patient on a stretcher inside. Tray puzzles and huge interlocking floor puzzles with at least a dozen large pieces are also good.

You may now think of buying a simple construction toy which can be assembled by the child according to her own skill and imagination. Choose one that you can add to later, not just in quantity but in range and complexity. These toys are expensive, but if you pick well they will give your child a lot of pleasure for up to ten years, which makes them very good value.

Below left Toys which were cuddled in infancy and crawled over in babyhood are now given a role in a make-believe world. *Below right* Although toddlers tend to play independently at first, sharing a sorting game can mark the beginning of cooperation.

Books

The range of picture books for under-fives is excellent so make the most of them. Join the local library and take advantage of their selection. Look for simple repetitive stories and clear pictures in which your child can recognize her own surroundings and interests. Fantasies about witches and goblins have no place in her life yet; it is the magic of the real world which fascinates a child of this age.

The time you spend reading to her now is one of the best investments that you can make. A child's early experience of stories, pictures and writing, and the sharing of these with her parents and other members of the family, will make language and other aspects of learning easier and more enjoyable in later years.

Some common concerns

Some of the most significant progress your child makes – such as learning to walk, to speak and to use the potty – will be during this time, and it can be worrying for parents if they feel their child isn't progressing fast enough, especially if they constantly compare him with other people's children. Often a child develops one skill at the expense of others, which he catches up on later, so don't worry and try to push your child – it's best for him to develop at his own pace.

Potty training – how to go about it and when to start – is a very common worry, and it often seems as if mothers are competing to see whose baby is trained first. A child cannot be made to be clean and dry until he is ready, and has both the physical control and an understanding of what is required of him. With most children this doesn't happen until they are about one-and-a-half or two years old. Wait until your child shows that he is aware of being wet or dirty and then suggest that he uses a potty. Think of it as helping your child to keep clean rather than as "training" him.

Safety is still a worry, as many toddlers are very active and also want to copy everything they see you doing. Basic safety precautions still apply, but your child can now begin to learn that stairs are steep and that sharp knives cut. If you keep everything dangerous out of sight and reach, then he will not know why it's unsafe to have them if he comes across them elsewhere.

Avoiding conflict

A large part of your toddler's behavior is attention seeking. For example, he may decide that he doesn't want to go in his stroller, but wants to walk; fifteen minutes later he starts to whine and demand to be carried. At this age he needs firm handling and he needs you to make the big decisions for him. Let him make small choices instead, such as which trousers he wants to wear.

It helps if you can see a conflict coming and try to avoid it: if you see him heading for the refrigerator (which you have forbidden him to open), don't wait until he's reached it and then say "no." Instead, distract him before he gets there. Similarly, a command of "Tidy up those blocks!" will get you nowhere, while "Let's see who can get the most blocks into this box" may well enlist his cooperation.

Temper tantrums

The toddler cannot think ahead and wants everything instantly. Telling him to "wait for five minutes" does no good, as being told to wait is the same as being told "no." Often, at the end of a long day, your toddler's frustration erupts into a full-blown tantrum. The best thing to do is to take no notice. Don't make things worse by shouting at him, but wait patiently until he is a little calmer and then you can try to give him a cuddle. Some children of this age

● *See* Potty training, page 196
● *See* A-Z of common ailments, page 269, for breath-holding

react to frustration in an extreme way, by holding their breath, sometimes for so long that they go red and then blue in the face. This is very worrying for parents, but often a light slap or shake will make the child take another breath. Treat these attacks matter-of-factly and, if you see that your child is getting angry, try to distract him.

Aggressive behavior and shyness

Some toddlers act aggressively because they are naturally extrovert and full of mischief. Often they try it on to get your attention and will pull another child's hair or push him over, looking round to watch your reaction. If your child behaves in this way, don't resort to smacks; you are just teaching him to deal these out in return. Tell him firmly, but gently, that neither you nor anyone else will accept this kind of behavior.

The shy child, on the other hand, does not want to interact with other childen at all and seems to be afraid of every encounter. You cannot force anyone to be sociable, but you can get your child used to being with other adults and children gradually, and from the safety of your lap.

Introducing discipline

Parents of toddlers often worry about discipline, and how firm or lenient they should be. Some feel that their child has got to learn how to behave; others that he's only young and won't understand. Neither of these attitudes is appropriate. Children need a certain amount of discipline to show them the boundaries of their behavior. Since your child loves and wants to please you, being firm will encourage him to act in a way that will earn your approval and eventually allow him to make decisions for himself.

Disciplining your child does not mean punishing him only when you are fed up and want some peace; it means telling the child calmly and consistently when he has done something unacceptable. A quick smack in the heat of the moment will do your child no harm – it is quickly forgotten, and is far better than giving a cold-blooded punishment later (such as going without his pudding or being sent to bed early) when he has forgotten all about his misdemeanor. On the other hand, don't overdo the physical punishments; a slap will be more effective if used rarely.

Your child will be exploring everything at this stage – if there is a cupboard he will open it, or a knob he will twiddle it. Try not to stop him all the time as this will drive you both mad. Instead, find things he *can* explore and fiddle with, such as an old battered telephone or a radio that no longer works. When you say "no" to him, you should really mean it. Always try to give an explanation; he will understand in time.

Sometimes you have to let him make mistakes so that he finds out that something does hurt. You can tell him a hundred times that the chair will tip over and he'll fall, but he'll only learn when he does it himself. Life can be very trying for a toddler; he needs your love and support to help him through this difficult phase.

PREPARING FOR A NEW SISTER OR BROTHER

Many children between the ages of 18 months and three years are faced with the prospect of a new baby in the family. Some of the possible feelings of resentment and jealousy can be prevented if you get your child used to the event and involve him in the preparations (getting the baby's room and clothes ready, for example).

Coping with the first weeks

● Be watchful – don't tempt your toddler by leaving him alone with the baby for too long – he won't understand how helpless a baby is.

● Meals or visitors calling can be difficult times – try and involve your toddler, or have some activity to occupy him (*see* page 221, How father can help).

● He may behave in a babyish way – for example, he may start sucking from a bottle again – but don't make a fuss, it will pass.

● He will enjoy some time on his own with you, such as sharing a story when the baby is asleep. (See Your family life, page 222, for coping with jealousy.)

SOME COMMON WORRIES

Your family life

Life with a toddler leaves you little time to catch your breath, yet it is around this time that you may be thinking about having another baby, or you may be pregnant already. Even if having another baby hadn't occurred to you yet, other people will probably ask you what your plans are and this may prompt you to think about it.

Planning another baby

Before you think about when you are going to have another baby, you should decide *if* you are going to have one at all. There are pros and cons on both sides. Only children are not necessarily spoilt or lonely – many positively thrive in a small family unit and are charming and well-balanced. Some only children, though, ache for company or find themselves at a disadvantage when school starts and they meet bullying or unfairness for the first time. Alternatively, some children from larger families never get over the jealousy or resentment they feel towards a sibling, while others find their relationships with brothers and sisters loving and rewarding during childhood and later on. There is no way of knowing in advance how your children will react – family relationships depend very much on individual personalities and – to a certain extent – your own handling of them. Whatever others say, it is not necessarily wrong to have only one child or irresponsible to have six, just so long as you as parents can cope with your family.

What is the best age gap?
This is another question that has no right answer. Children close in age may get on very well and become best friends or they may suffer terrible jealousy and envy of each other and fight all the time. A large age gap can equally well result in your children becoming good friends or it could make them feel remote and emotionally detached. Again, much depends on how they harmonize.

The practical considerations
The other major factor to consider when planning a baby is, of course, a practical one. The timing must suit you and your partner. Some mothers prefer to have their babies close together so that they can get all the diapers over with as quickly as possible. This is sensible if, for instance, you want to return to full-time employment after a few years and not have to break off again to have another baby. Other parents prefer the idea of one child being fairly grown-up and settled before going back to the broken nights and sheer physical work involved in caring for a little one.

Introducing the idea of the new baby
If you have decided that a two-year age gap is right, then your first child will be a toddler at about the time the baby is born. You should start preparing your older child for the birth in advance, both directly and indirectly.

Conversations can begin when you are a few months pregnant. Talk to your child about babies generally – point them out, mention families she knows that have a new baby and read her stories that involve families with babies. She will start to draw the conclusion that a baby coming along is a normal event in family life.

When you think she is ready, you can tell your child that you are going to have a baby. It is best not to leave it for too long as she may absorb the idea from other people's talk, or notice that your tummy is getting bigger. Tell her where the baby is growing – your bulge should be big enough now to make this seem a reality – and let her feel the baby moving. Your conversations now can include descriptions of what life is like with a baby – some funny times, some irritating times – using her own babyhood as an example. Don't build up her expectations of a new playmate as she'll feel very let down when she is then introduced to a helpless baby. You can make her feel important and involved by asking her if the baby can have her old baby clothes. Let her know casually that babies mean a lot of work; with the result that you may have a little less time to play with her. Reassure her that it doesn't mean you will love her any less, and that you will need her help in caring for the baby.

Adapting to the new arrival

The baby is going to cause some disruption in your child's life, but what she will notice and mind most is so much of your attention being focused elsewhere. It helps if there are things she likes to do and people she enjoys seeing, with or without you, well before the baby is born. If there is a network of family and friends for her to visit happily, she won't feel that she is being pushed aside if you occasionally drop her off with them after the baby comes home. If no network exists you should think about creating one while you are still pregnant.

If your child is about three years old, think about starting her at play school a few months before the baby is born. Otherwise she may associate the baby's arrival with her "banishment" from the home.

Close to the time of the birth tell your child that you will have to go into the hospital to have the baby and tell her who will be looking after her while you are away. It makes the transition smoother if her father, or someone else close, has been involved with caring for her well before you have to go into the hospital.

After the birth

It is a good idea for your older child to come to visit you in the hospital, unless you are ill after the birth. She can look at the new baby and spend some time with you. Give some thought to the moment when you return home. It would probably be better for someone else to be holding the baby when you are first reunited with your older child, who will be longing for a cuddle and some attention from you. Try to arrange for someone to be around for the first few weeks – your partner would be ideal. You'll appreciate the help, and your older child can be distracted or played with when you have to give all your attention to the baby.

HOW FATHER CAN HELP
The arrival of a second baby gives a father the opportunity to cement his relationship with his older child and to help her to cope with feelings of jealousy.
- **Before the birth**
He can involve himself more in her day-to-day care, and learn her likes and dislikes so that when you go into the hospital things will continue to run smoothly.
- **Coming out of hospital**
He can hold the baby while you are reunited with the older child, but once you need to care for the baby he can give the other child his full attention.
- **The first weeks**
He can be around to involve your older child in other activities at times when you must devote yourself to the baby. He can plan outings for himself and the older child.
- **Father and new baby**
He can also help by taking charge of the new baby while you give time to the older child. This gives him the chance to develop a special relationship with the baby as well.

You will get great pleasure from seeing your children play happily together but always keep a careful watch to see that things stay happy.

Coping with jealousy

All parents want their children to love each other and some see jealousy as a sign that they have failed in their duty. But jealousy is a natural and normal reaction. There is no way that you can bring a new person into the family without some jealousy being felt so you should be prepared for it. What you have to do is help your child to cope with her strong feelings so that she learns to control them and remain reasonably happy. Don't assume that she will love the baby in the way that you do and don't force her to be affectionate. If she wants to kiss the baby, well and good; if not, it doesn't matter. Some parents believe that their child is not jealous. This may be because the child has understood that she must not express jealous feelings, and indeed feels guilty about them. Jealousy often takes the form of bad behavior from your older child and this may be directed at the new baby. After all, in your child's eyes the baby is behaving badly (frequently crying and screaming), yet you are showering him with love and attention. For a while your toddler may regress (with toilet training, for instance), partly through anxiety and partly because it seems to her that being babyish is the way to your heart.

Young children express negative feelings quite simply, maybe by saying something like "Bad baby!" or "Take him back to the hospital!" Don't be shocked; this is quite healthy, and it allows you to talk about what she is feeling and show that you sympathize. Older children, on the other hand, are more likely to try to hide what they feel. Let your child know that you understand her feelings and that they are not bad, although actions can be: she should never hurt the baby. Instead, try to encourage your older child to help you with the baby in small ways and to adopt a more protective attitude toward her brother or sister.

Growing up together

If you are lucky your children will grow up to love each other and be good friends, but you can't insist that they do so. So long as they respect and tolerate each other they are behaving well. You can help by showing them that you love them as individuals and that they are not lumped together as "my children." In addition you should avoid creating rivalry between them by comparing one with the other. Try to be fair to them all and respect their individual – and often different – needs. Stop the baby from disrupting the older child's games, and don't let the older one do the same, or bully the younger one in subtle ways. As they grow up, continue to make special time for each of your children and occasionally arrange for them to have time away from each other to stay with relatives and friends.

Vacations are a wonderful opportunity for the whole family to enjoy a change of scenery.

Vacations and trips

A toddler can be very demanding on a vacation, so choose a place that won't be too frustrating for her – somewhere she can do much of what she wants without too many restrictions. Insisting that she is good or quiet too much of the time can result in a tense vacation for you all. This also means choosing somewhere that is relatively safe, although you should be aware that a toddler's adventuring can uncover dangers you had never even thought of. Watch out for her becoming over-tired too – left to herself she'll continue playing to the point of exhaustion and then be too strung out to sleep.

On car journeys, toddlers are particularly difficult. They are no longer lulled to sleep by movement and their attention span is very short, so you may have to think of endless ways of amusing them. A good standby is a bag containing toys, which can be passed one by one to your toddler. Don't use all the toys, games and stories up in the early part of the journey because you'll need them for the end when tempers have worn thin. Pack easy-to-eat, non-messy food such as fruit and cubes of cheese and give your thirsty child a small quantity to drink each time she asks so that it is not slopped everywhere. Keep some baby wipes and tissues for any spills, and a potty is handy for the times when it is impossible to leave the car.

Getting out and about at all times is important. Take advantage of whatever facilities your local parks have to offer, particularly play areas that are specially set aside for your child's age group. Large playgrounds can be frustrating and dangerous for a very young child.

Second birthday

A roomful of toddlers at a party is often hard to control. Ideally a maximum of two or three friends is best at this age. Even so, they may fall out and probably won't get the pleasure from party games that they will the following year. If you feel you should invite more children, ask some parents to stay for the party – you will appreciate the extra help and adult company.

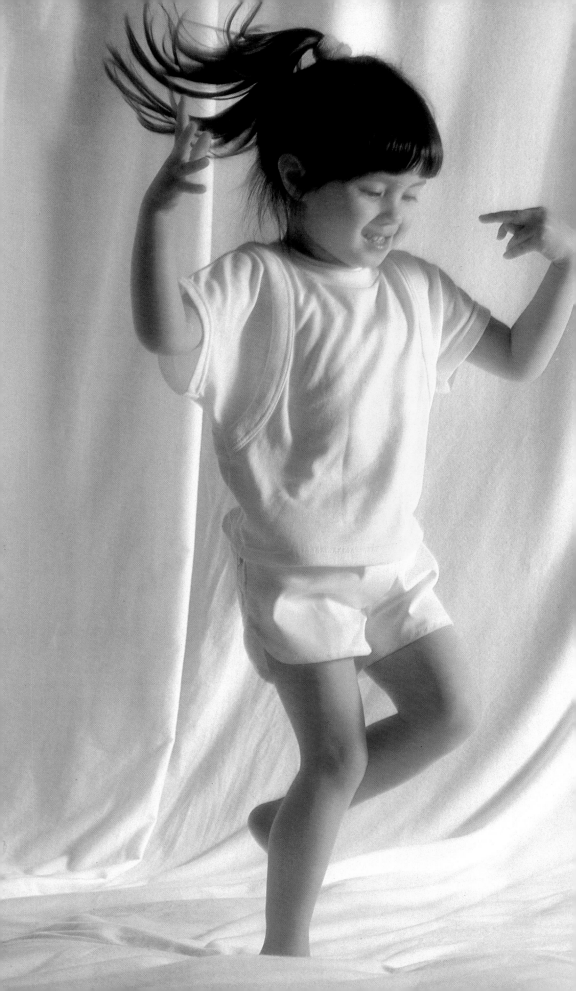

THE OLDER CHILD

Increasingly confident and competent, your child is now on the threshold of a wider world. She's learning to share and to get on with others. She's enjoying running and climbing while also getting great pleasure out of her imaginative play. She's able to do more for herself, understanding a lot but also constantly questioning – sometimes to the limits of your patience! She's inventive, rewarding, full of fun and a great companion.

You and your older child

She'll take great pride in being able to do more complicated things now, and will give her undivided attention to the task at hand.

Gradually you'll start to notice a change in your child. "Watch that step!" you might hear her admonish herself in the tone you've used to her so often, or "I wasn't naughty, was I?" as she sees another child being told off for misbehavior. The signs are that she is emerging from the whirlwind willful stage of being a toddler and all your patient care and teaching is paying off.

From being a baby you have to control and watch constantly, she moves towards school age as a child who becomes increasingly independent and easy to deal with. Because she starts to identify so closely with you – not so much with children of her own age yet – for a while she is very like a miniature adult. You will hear her repeating your very words, phrases and tone of voice. Sometimes it is touching and funny, as she puts teddy firmly to bed with your familiar nighttime routine or attempts to "kiss better" a playmate's bruise. Other times it is quite a shock to hear an irritable remark that you realize sounds just like you. And sometimes you will feel quite surprised, "You didn't say thank you!" she will accuse self-righteously.

It becomes hard to remember a time when she couldn't talk, now that every waking hour seems filled with her continuous chattering. Words stop being mere labels for interesting things and begin to mean a lot to her as she starts to understand abstract concepts. Some days you'll think you are going mad when every sentence begins with "why?" and no amount of explanation stops the endless flow of questions.

Understanding words and ideas better makes everything easier. Now when you explain that you are going out for the day and coming back at dinner-time, she is able to accept and understand it. She might not want you to go, but she believes it when you say you will return, and she knows that every day the hours pass and dinner-time always comes around.

But the fact that she is talking more doesn't mean that she is less active. As she grows taller, slimmer, confident that she can make her body do as she wants, she is constantly on the move, developing her physical skills to a high degree. She literally can't sit still – even watching her favorite television program. Once she can do anything she wants to on her own two feet (boasting all the while, "Look how far I can jump!"), she'll want to graduate to a bike or set herself harder gymnastic tasks. You'll find that Band-Aids are regularly on your shopping list, and that bathtime reveals new scratches and bruises.

A wider world

Out and about together, as you watch her getting to know other children and slowly learning the business of co-operative play, you will be aware of the horizons of her life expanding. You are still the most important person in her life, but there is so much else she wants to do and other

She knows all her favorite stories and enjoys reading to you – and teddy.

people she wants to do it with. It is around this time that you will be making the decision whether to send her to a pre-school or nursery school. It can be exciting and a little strange too, now that she starts to have a life separate from yours, making her own relationship with the teacher and other children, and having new and interesting experiences without you. Pick her up from a morning at a pre-school and, although she's pleased to see you, it is clear that she's also had a wonderful time.

So fascinating are other people that in her increasingly imaginative play you will see her try out what it must be like to be them. Both boys and girls will play at being mommy, and will get equal pleasure from props that help their make-believe games, such as dolls, miniature cooking sets or a toy tool kit. One day your child concentrates on being the garbage man; for a week she is the carpenter down the road – and sometimes she'll invent a friend to keep her company and take the blame for wrongdoings. A dressing-up box is a constant source of delight that will keep her happily occupied for hours.

Becoming friends

Quiet play starts to involve her more than ever before; she'll enjoy looking through books, cutting and sticking and all kinds of drawing and painting. When she shows you a drawing and says "That's you," you can recognize features and limbs, rather than just a colorful scribble.

Now, if she wants a rough-and-tumble and you explain that you are too tired, she is increasingly able to understand. The fact that she is subconsciously modeling herself on you and identifying so closely with you means that she is able to understand your feelings too. She'll give you a hug if you look sad, and utter those magical words "I love you" and mean them. Such closeness means that she takes on your moods – if you are frantic or irritable, she is likely to be so too. But if you are on top of the world she will be right there with you – and will be one of the most enjoyable and rewarding companions you could possibly have.

A playground provides great space for bike riding and larger-scale games.

What your child will need

Your child's room should be a special place – somewhere he will enjoy playing and can keep all his belongings.

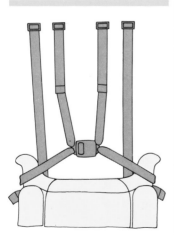

Booster seat
A booster seat, which should always be used with a car safety harness, is ideal for the time when your child has grown out of the car safety seat (page 141) but is not quite big enough to see out of the window of the car.

As your child gets older, and perhaps starts going to a pre-school, his room will become a more important place. Although you must keep safety in mind when buying furniture or organizing his room, he is now old enough to have simple safety rules explained to him, such as the danger of jumping off furniture or leaning out of the window.

Encouraging tidiness

As he can now begin to learn tidiness, it is important that the room is organized to make this easy for him. Drawers should have handles that are easy to grasp. Clothes, well organized and tidy in drawers and on shelves, should be accessible now that he is learning to dress himself. A mirror hung at the right height for him – either in his room or in the bathroom – means he can brush his own hair. Make sure book shelves are big enough to accommodate large picture books – and perhaps put one near his bed as he may like to read before he goes to sleep.

This is the age when a desk really comes in handy – for drawing and puzzles, and for unfinished projects that your child can leave and go back to. Give him a large jar or buy a plastic office desk-organizer for his pens and crayons – this may prevent them being scattered about with the tops off! Small drawers are now useful for those little toys that need to be kept out of the reach of a baby brother or sister.

A room for two

If you are organizing the room for two children, you need to find ways to make clear demarcation lines, as you will find the older child needs some privacy and peace and quiet. Bunk beds can really be made use of now, although your older child will still need a safety rail if he is to sleep in the top one. A gooseneck lamp which can be directed away from a baby's bassinet or crib is also a good idea. Don't see sharing a room as a disadvantage – children often like the company of a brother or sister until they are a bit older.

The playroom

As his confidence increases, your child will spend more time out of your sight as he starts to use his room to play in, on his own or with friends. There are many things you can do to make it fun for him: put a bulletin board on the wall for the drawings and paintings he brings home from play school; stand a blackboard and easel in the corner of the room, or even set into the wall, for when inspiration strikes; and stick a height chart on the wall so he can see how he is growing. A play house is a perennial favorite, even if it is improvised with a screen in the corner of the room. It can be a place for private games and can also be used for tea parties when you have visitors and want the children out from under your feet. Whatever toys you provide, your child will probably derive most enjoyment from his own fantasy games where a toy box is emptied and becomes a boat, or his bedcover is draped over a chair to become a tent. If his room is attractive and welcoming, these games will occur naturally, especially when he has friends to play.

Fun furniture

There is a good selection of practical furniture for children that is also fun – brightly-colored chairs, with drawers underneath, little teddy bear seats, patterned bean bags or floor cushions, baskets for dirty clothes in the shape of animals. You don't have to buy custom-built furniture, however – a small second-hand table with the legs cut down to size, or an old school chair cleaned up, painted a bright color and decorated with a stencil will be appreciated just as much by your child.

GETTING DRESSED
Give your child plenty of encouragement and practice at dressing, and think about what he can do when you are buying new clothes. Pull-on trousers (with elasticated waists) are easier than overalls or trousers with more rigid waistbands. Pull-on sweaters and dresses and zip-up parkas and coats can be managed by most three-year-olds and upwards, and socks are easier than tights.

Above A large room with plenty of floor space is marvelous for a growing child – he can play in it, entertain friends, pursue his hobbies, and later he will be able to do his homework there. A low platform bed, with drawers underneath for storing clothes or toys, is practical as well as fun for the older child.

Right Furniture that can be adapted as your child grows is very good value. A coordinating unit which comprises an adjustable table top, seat and toy box fits neatly into a corner.

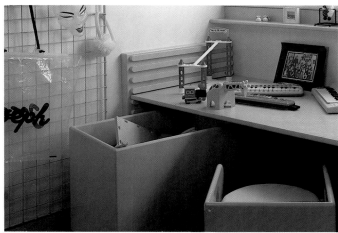

Feeding your child

By the time a child is two-and-a-half years old she is usually talking and should be expected to say "please" and "thank you" when she is offered food. Good manners can, of course, be drilled into a child but it is so much nicer if she expresses her appreciation because she means it. By this time most feeding problems have been sorted out, although some children continue to have difficulties for a while longer. Once your child is ready to start school she is usually able to understand that mealtimes and playtimes are two separate things. Until then, however, she still has much to learn about food and eating – how to cut and spread with a knife, use utensils and try unfamiliar foods, particularly when she is invited out. Mealtimes are not always the best times to teach these skills because your child is hungry; try involving her in the preparation of a meal instead.

Helping out

Babies show interest in their food by playing with it – they pull it to pieces, pat it and prod it. The toddler wants to pour her own drink, to stir her own oatmeal and to roll out pastry. A child of this age will be just as keen to do things for herself and there is now no reason why she should not prepare the occasional dish, or even a whole meal. Start her off with a salad – this is an easy item for a young child to prepare. She can choose and arrange cold meats on a plate, wash lettuce, cut tomatoes safely (if rather messily) with a pair of blunt-ended scissors and practice using a blunt knife to cut soft foods, such as cold potatoes, cucumber, banana or mushrooms. Of course, your child's salad or sandwich may be a rather strange concoction (for instance, you may have to be appreciative of a dish of lettuce leaves, mashed banana and carrots!), but at least it's her own effort. Once she has done this she can set the table and help you to serve the meal. At the end of this activity she will have a sense of achievement and will discover that it is nice for the cook to be thanked and appreciated.

HELPING IN THE KITCHEN

When you're cooking, let your child lend a hand
- mixing and stirring
- sifting flour
- fetching and passing ingredients
- pouring
- undoing lids
- weighing
- spreading and icing

Helping in the kitchen is a favourite pastime for a four- or five-year-old and can be a positive way of avoiding food problems.

Porcupines
1 bridge roll
can of pineapple chunks
toothpicks
cubes of cheese
2 raisins
1 black grape
1 custard cup filled with
fruit juice

Spear one cube of cheese and a piece of pineapple together and push the other end into the bridge roll. Repeat until the roll is covered with toothpicks. Use the grape as a nose and the raisins for eyes. Point the porcupine's nose toward the fruit juice and your child has made a complete meal, with drink!

Pizza tarts
frozen shortcrust pastry
(or homemade)
chunks of tomato (can be cut up
with scissors)
a little grated cheese
chopped mushroom and red
pepper (can be cut with a table
knife)

Roll out the pastry and cut it into circles with a pastry cutter. Place these in a muffin tin. Fill the pastry tarts with the tomato, mushroom and pepper. Sprinkle each one with grated cheese. Bake for 10-15 minutes in a hot oven.

Flower pudding
1 banana
1 carton of natural yogurt
1 small can of peaches or
mandarin oranges in fruit juice
1 raisin or seedless grape

Either mash the banana and mix it with the yogurt, or whizz up both in a blender (children love pressing the buttons). Pour the mixture into a dish. Decorate the top with peaches or mandarins for the petals, using the grape or raisins as the center of the flower. Crushed nuts could be added to the decoration to make a stalk for the flower.

Packed lunches

When your child starts school you may have to provide her with packed lunches. These should really be cold versions of main meals and it helps if you do a little planning at the beginning of term. If you have a freezer you could, for example, bake a quiche, cut it into portions and freeze them. You could also roast a dozen chicken pieces and some low-fat sausages for freezing. You can then take one or two items out of the freezer the night before school, put them in a plastic box with a lid and add some chopped cold potato or bread and some sticks of carrot and cucumber or other salad ingredients. On another occasion you could include a little jar of cold baked beans or some corn or some chopped tomato with pasta shapes. For dessert you could provide a banana or an orange, cut into quarters, a jar of stewed fruit and yogurt or a wedge of melon. Children also like small sandwiches with their favorite fillings – egg, tuna fish or peanut butter – followed by cheese and pineapple cubes on sticks. There is no need to add sweets, chocolate cookies or crackers to a lunch box. All too often the child eats these instead of the more nourishing foods. Some advance preparation will enable you to put her lunch box together in a matter of minutes and also allow you time to make it look attractive.

Above A few simple recipes which your child can enjoy making, with a little help from you.

FEEDING YOUR CHILD

Bathing and everyday care

Your child will now be showing signs of his growing independence and will be starting to cope with dressing and washing himself – although he will probably still need some assistance from you. He may or may not be fully toilet trained by the age of two-and-a-half, but sometime before he goes to school he almost certainly will be, at least during the day.

Using the toilet

Most children are more confident and reliable at using the toilet by the time they are three or four years old. Your child will eventually learn to manage himself, but to help him reach this stage, get into the habit of leaving the toilet and bathroom doors open so that he can get in there when he needs to. Unless the flush mechanism on your toilet is particularly difficult, encourage him to use it after each visit. Some children even consider "flushing" as fun.

Younger children may need accompanying to the toilet in other people's houses and possibly at pre-school or nursery school. Before your child is due to start kindergarten though, it's wise to encourage him to do everything for himself. This includes teaching your child to wipe his bottom (a girl should be taught to wipe front to back). This will help the teachers as well as making sure that your child is not "different" from the other children.

Most little boys will be tall enough to stand at the toilet by the age of three or four. There may be urinals at school, but they will probably be at an easy-to-reach height. If you get the chance to visit your child's school before the start of term, together with your son or daughter, then use the opportunity to check out the toilets and to show your child anything that is slightly different from at home.

Night-time dryness

You may want to use a diaper or pull-on diaper pants at night, even after he has learned to stay dry during the day, as night-time control is something that comes later for most children. When he reaches the stage where his diaper is often dry in the morning, tell your child that he has made good progress and can do without a diaper at night from now on. Some children are able to make the final step toward regular night-time dryness only when they know for certain that they no longer have the "fail safe" device of wearing a diaper.

Some parents try to reduce the chances of a wet bed by taking the child to use the potty or toilet at about the time they go to bed themselves. It's not a good idea to do this without first giving your child a chance to achieve night-time dryness. A few children find it difficult to go back to sleep once they have been disturbed, and this could mean wakeful nights for everyone. The other disadvantage of "lifting" your child to go to the toilet is that you don't want him to empty his bladder while he is barely conscious of what he is doing. You are, after all, hoping to encourage him not to need to empty his bladder during the night or, if he has a full bladder, to wake and be able to get out of bed and go to the bathroom himself. Lifting may save you the trouble of washing a sheet every day, but it may not help your child to make any progress.

Most children are dry at night before the age of four, although as many as 10 per cent are still wetting the bed regularly at five, so a delay is really quite common and not in any way abnormal. It may also help to discreetly cut down on the amount of fluid he takes at suppertime and last thing before bed (though he should, of course, be allowed to have a drink if he is thirsty). Take him to the toilet before he goes to bed and put a waterproof covering between the mattress and the bottom sheet if he is inclined to wet the bed.

Set-backs

Your child may regress with toilet training because of some upset in life, such as starting nursery school, or the arrival of a new baby in the family. He will probably settle down again if you are patient and understanding, but if he doesn't, don't hesitate to seek advice on this or any other related problem. Your pediatrician is a good source of sympathetic and practical support, and she'll let you know whether you are justified in worrying or not. Another reason for a child to start wetting again after he has become dry is if he is suffering from a urinary infection, and you can ask your doctor to check for this.

Bathing and keeping clean

It is impossible to keep an active child clean all day, but you can make sure that he has a bath regularly (daily, if possible) and wash his hair two or three times a week – this should be less of a struggle now that he is older. If he is going through an uncooperative phase, offer to read him a story after the bath or while you are drying his hair.

Your child's nails should be cut short as they will be easier to keep clean. Encourage him to wash his hands after using the toilet and before eating – you'll probably have to remind him many times before he does it automatically. By the time he is five, he should be able to wash his face and hands and brush his teeth quite well, although he will probably still need help with these things.

Brushing teeth

It's a good idea to start your child brushing his own teeth as early as possible, although you will have to supervise him until he is competent. You can encourage him by giving him his own small toothbrush, or allowing him to choose one when you go shopping.

You may have started taking him to the dentist when he was about two years old, and by now he should be used to having his teeth checked. Ask your dentist to explain to your child how he should brush his teeth and gums.

MAKING BATHTIME FUN
Bathtime can still be enjoyable for your pre-school child, although he may begin to make a fuss at this stage. It will make your life easier, therefore, if you provide him with lots of toys and try and vary them so that he doesn't get bored. You can add to his baby toys: wind-up creatures such as frogs, penguins and deep-sea divers, empty liquid detergent bottles to fill up and squirt, and boats that can ferry the soap and washcloth.

Your child may also enjoy washing himself now and you can encourage him by making a game of it, seeing if he can remember the awkward places like behind the ears and between the toes!

BATHING AND EVERYDAY CARE

See A-Z of common ailments, page 268, for bed wetting.

Sleep and bedtime

When small children, however tired, are reluctant to go to bed it can help to be carried upstairs for an extra bedtime story.

By now your child may have overcome any sleeping problems she had, and go to bed quite happily. However, there are many children who continue to have trouble getting to sleep or staying in their own beds. Most children will be dropping their daytime nap around now, although those who go to pre-school may continue to need a rest.

Your child may be one of those who takes a long time to go to bed or to fall asleep, prolonging the bedtime routine for hours, insisting on long cuddles, and repeatedly coming into the living room where she falls asleep through sheer exhaustion; and she may wake in the night and take time to go back to sleep again, often ending up in your bed. If you are very worried about sleep problems, it may be worth discussing the situation with your doctor.

Going to bed

The bedtime routine may have to be modified slightly now that your child is a little older. Sometimes she may be watching a television program that continues after her normal bedtime and you will have less trouble if you don't whisk her away in the middle of it. Always let her know in plenty of time when it is nearing her bedtime, so that she doesn't become deeply involved in a new game or activity.

Problems with settling down

If your child makes a fuss at bedtime and seems to find it hard to fall asleep, this may now seem a problem that looms large in your life. It is something that both parents should tackle together and, however you decide to cope, try to stick to it. Most importantly, be firm about not letting her get up again. This is hard when there is something that you want to get on with or a program you want to watch on television, but she is much more likely to give up trying if you are consistent in your behavior. It means that one of you must be prepared to look in on her regularly when she calls, and perhaps get her a drink of water or stay with her while she uses the potty. It also means that whenever she appears at the door of the living room you should lead her back to bed, not angrily but firmly.

The living room seems much more attractive to a wakeful child lying in a darkened room, having difficulty dropping off, so try to make her feel that she is not missing out. Let her have her bedside lamp on to continue looking through the book you were reading her, or allow her to listen to a story tape. If she is forced to lie in the semi-dark, feeling a bit miserable, her mind is likely to turn to gloomy things. Young children may find that they are kept awake by unpleasant thoughts, and if this happens to your child you should comfort her as you would if she were having a nightmare. The difference at this age is that you can also reason with her, and look under the bed together to reassure her that nothing scary is lurking there!

See What your child will need, page 228, for storage space and bedroom ideas

A wakeful child will fall asleep more happily if he is allowed a little time to look at books or play quietly.

The happier she is in her room, the more inclined she will be to stay there. Don't ever shut her in it as a punishment, otherwise she will grow to hate it – and don't nag her too much about keeping it tidy or she might be put off playing there. When you tidy her room, don't get rid of all her mess. If there was a game she was hoping to get back to, or something she was making into a collection, she will be upset to find them cleared away.

Disturbed nights

Children who continue to wake at night regularly are harder to deal with rationally, so it is no wonder that some parents give in and let their children get into bed with them. It is wise not to encourage such a habit. Besides, this disturbs you and your partner's sleep too. Lead your child back into her own bed as often as it takes to convince her that this is where she must stay. If she can't get back to sleep, don't insist that she lies there with the lights off. She can have a small light on by her bed to look at books or she can play quietly on her own. She will probably fall asleep very quickly.

Bad dreams

Even children who don't wake regularly in the night will be woken up from time to time by bad dreams. Your child will cry or scream suddenly and you should go to her as quickly as you can. If you are there, comforting and soothing her before she wakes fully, she is likely to fall asleep again quite quickly. If she is left for any length of time, she will wake fully and feel very frightened.

Now that she is more articulate, she is likely to be able to explain the content of her nightmares to you and you might find clues as to what is causing them. Worrying about something is an obvious cause, or perhaps jealous feelings at the arrival of a new baby. If you have an idea what is causing the bad dreams, you can help by talking to your child about it during the day. Sometimes being able to express her feelings, or knowing that they are understood by you, is enough to stop them looming up in her dreams.

SLEEP AND BEDTIME

Your day together

As your child becomes more sociable, he'll enjoy having his friends over to play.

DO-IT-YOURSELF PLAYGROUP

Try some of these ideas for keeping your child and his friends occupied at home.

● **Play house**
Improvise one with a clothes rack or table and blankets. Cut holes in an old sheet for windows and door.

● **Dressing up**
Fill a cardboard box with old shoes, hats, dresses, ties.

● **Water play**
If the weather's fine put buckets, a dish pan or wading pool filled with water outside and provide things to float in it.

● **Music time**
Put on a record, sing songs or provide homemade "instruments."

● **Storytime**
Have a quiet time, reading a story out loud.

In practical ways your child is much easier to deal with now. But he is much more demanding in other ways and planning a satisfying day needs more imagination than ever before. You'll need to encourage him to become more independent, and doing this is far more time-consuming and difficult than simply continuing to treat him like a baby and doing everything for him.

You'll be considering whether or not to send him to a pre-school now. Some children are ready to join in at this age, others are not. Whatever you decide is right for your child, you will have to be thinking about your day a little differently now.

Home and pre-school

If your child does go to a pre-school or nursery school he will find all the new and interesting experiences enormously stimulating. You will have the chance to get on with other things while he is out, but when he is back home again he will need much more of your concentrated attention than he might otherwise. After being one of many children competing for the teacher's attention (possibly involved in scraps and having shed a few tears) and with many different exciting activities to think about, he needs your calm familiar presence and to know that you are prepared to devote time to him. His morning out may tire him too, and after lunch you may find he needs a rest.

Keeping busy

Your child will enjoy having the opportunity to develop his skills, even if he doesn't yet go to a pre-school. If he does, he'll still like to have things to do at weekends and during vacations.

He needs other people – adults and children – in a way that he didn't before, so now is the time, if you haven't done so already, to help your child find friends of his own age. Invite children over from time to time; sometimes just one, at other times in a small group. Getting to know other adults is just as important. If he is only used to the way his own family speaks and behaves, later experiences with teachers at school, for instance, can be bewildering.

Use your ingenuity to think of a variety of things to do. Going out to the park will continue to be popular with him although the weather does not always cooperate. The local library may have an afternoon club for children, or a "storytime" session. Other activities will depend very much on his age: a three-year-old has a shorter attention span than a five-year-old. As he begins to develop his own interests, ideas will suggest themselves to you. If he loves trains, for example, you might be able to find a museum that specializes in transportation, or simply visit a railroad station.

The zoo is interesting to all age groups and makes a good day out. Even a short trip to a museum, with exhibits for

Children of this age love to be helpful and will enjoy playing a part in what you have to do.

WATCHING TELEVISION
There are many interesting, entertaining and instructive programs that your child may enjoy – so long as you control and participate in his viewing.
● Familiarize yourself with the programs you select. Watch together so that you can talk about the program afterwards.
● Don't let the television "babysit." Keep an eye on him while you do something else nearby to ensure that he does not switch to another program which may be unsuitable or frightening.
● Don't let television provide all his entertainment. Continue to read stories and sing songs.
● Ration his viewing. As he gets older, let him watch one or two programs a day without interruption. Such concentration is good experience for him.

young children, can be fascinating to those over four, and swimming continues to be fun for two to five-year-olds. He might enjoy a visit to a large department store, with its elevators and escalators, and a ride on the top of a bus or on a train can be a great adventure. He will have plenty to look at and it gives you much to talk about together.

Children of this age benefit from company, so you could arrange a rotation with other parents and take it in turns to organize a playgroup for your children. One week they could all come to you, the next time to someone else's house (*see* Do-it-yourself playgroup, left).

Fostering independence

Learning to do simple things for himself, such as going to the toilet, washing his hands and dressing himself will help to reinforce your child's independence. Any adjustment that will make it easier for him to become independent, such as hanging up his own coat on a specially low coat hook, will help. Get into the habit of making him think for himself at every opportunity. Offering him simple choices is one way of doing this. Does he want orange juice or milk with his lunch? Would he like to choose a book at the library? He has opinions which are often different from yours, so when it is feasible you can consult him about what he wants. He'll appreciate it if you no longer treat him like a baby, to be bundled up and taken along without question.

Toys and play at home

Watch what your child plays with when you're out visiting or at a pre-school. This can help you to know what he'll find stimulating when he's at home. Help him with difficult toys, such as puzzles, to begin with. Quiet playtime can also include watching television, but it is best if you do this together and then talk about what you see.

Your day will be punctuated by a million questions. Try not to become exasperated with your child – he really does want to know what his parents think, and he can learn so much from you.

How your time might be spent
Your child will be more independent now, perhaps playing on his own or with a friend.

Key
- Sleeping
- Sleeping/resting
- Bathing/washing
- Eating/drinking
- Playing
- Your time

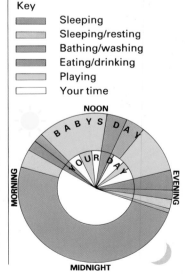

YOUR DAY TOGETHER

Growing and learning

Busy in her own world she uses her imagination to create her make-believe games.

These are very much the "growing" years for your young child. She grows in height, competence and confidence. She can concentrate now on what she enjoys most – playing and using her imagination.

She'll also be learning to control her feelings. The demanding two-year-old will gradually learn how to explain what she wants and how she feels. There may be times when she'll revert to more babyish behavior. Events such as a new baby in the family or starting nursery school may make her feel vulnerable. Reassurance and spending time on activities "only big children can do" can be more helpful than telling her not to act like a baby.

This is the time for "I can do it myself," but she'll still enjoy being watched and helped. She may try to attempt things which seem beyond her, and frustrations will occur.

Her personality is unfolding now and her skills and interests are expanding. Her conversation is more interesting and she enjoys simple jokes and pretend games. She is much more of a companion in your daily life.

Climbing, running and hopping

Your child is now discovering new ways of moving: she's climbing, rolling and riding her trike. There is a lot for her to learn when she tries something new so she may be hesitant at first. When she's on a climbing frame she's got to think about her balance, the position of her hands and feet, and how to push up or swing down.

Some children love trying out new skills while others seem always to be tripping over and falling. They all differ in how long they take to master certain things but if she's absolutely determined to do something like pedal her bike, she'll manage it soon with some help from you.

All her movements are becoming more controlled now.

He'll enjoy the challenge of a climbing frame to try out his new skills.

DIFFERENT WAYS OF MOVING
Now that her movements are so much more controlled she'll get real pleasure from mastering new skills. She'll enjoy climbing, running, hopping, jumping, rolling down banks and doing somersaults.

Soon she'll be able to run in different directions, hop a little and may even try to skip. At first she can only gallop along but with time she learns to skip properly. She will try a somersault and may need your help to put her head and feet in the right place.

Now you can play a game of ball with her. She can just chuck it around at first and kick it if it is still. She's having to coordinate her hands, feet and eyes. Later you can try rolling a ball to her and she may kick it back. By the time she starts school she'll be able to kick a ball when she's running and throw it in the right direction.

A climbing frame in a playground or a bike at a mother and toddler group will give her the opportunity to try out new skills. Swimming is another way in which she learns to use her body and move her arms and legs as she wants. Games also help her become more aware of herself. Ask her to follow you along the pavement; you put one arm out, then she does; you jump, she jumps. She's finding out how to do several things at once.

Your child might need help while he masters the art of turning a tidy somersault.

She'll be able to kick a ball as she's running along.

She can balance just on one leg and hop.

She will learn to jump with both feet.

Above Her coordination is very good now and she can manage quite fiddly things.
Right She'll enjoy the freedom of painting, experimenting with colors and patterns.

STAGES IN DRAWING A PERSON

- circular scribble
- closed circles
- circles with marks in them (these marks represent facial features, usually eyes)
- face is central feature onto which arms and legs are directly added
- fingers, hair and parts of the face added next – a proper body may also emerge onto which legs and arms are drawn but these do not have proper width yet

Making and doing

The hesitant, rather clumsy actions of the two-year-old begin to give way now to very careful handling, so she can concentrate more on what she's doing. This means that her play with blocks, play dough and other materials becomes much more complicated and imaginative. At first she tends to make props for her other toys: for example, fields for her farm animals or garages for her toy cars. Then she moves on to detailed constructions complete in themselves, such as spaceships or castles. These may be big or small.

Her hands work well together now. By the time she's three, she'll be threading beads and undoing big buttons and zips. When she's five she'll be able to complete some simple sewing cards, do up some coat fastenings and attempt to tie her shoe laces.

She enjoys making things now, and drawing, painting, cutting and sticking all help improve her hand skills. Gradually she'll learn how to make pictures or models of things rather than just scribbles or colorful patterns. The lines and circles in her first drawings will start to become pictures of people and houses.

It's probably becoming clear now if she's a right or left-handed child. Some children take quite a long time to settle on one hand and a very few continue to use both throughout life. Up to 10 per cent of children are left handed and certain things, for example, doing up buttons, cutting with scissors, copying shapes and letters can be more difficult for them. There are now quite a few specially designed items, such as left-handed scissors, which can make things a little easier.

Talking and questioning

From the time she's two, your child's language is developing all the time. Her vocabulary expands and she enjoys trying out new long words. By three years old she may know a thousand words or more and may be using short sentences. Suddenly she's able to use words to say what she wants and to comment on what's happening.

When you listen to your two-and-a-half-year-old talking she'll still be making some mistakes and you may still find that you are having to interpret for her. Your explanations act as a model for her to copy and soon she'll get it right. By the time she's four she'll be able to discuss ideas.

She no longer just asks for a toy or book but tells you why she wants it. Later on she'll be able to tell you what happened yesterday and ask you about things. She may experiment with her voice, whispering or yelling. Through looking at books she learns how to tell a story and understand new words. You may find her sitting quietly with a friend or playing with her toys, while she tells them one of her favorite stories.

Questions now begin coming at you fast and furiously. Sometimes you may find yourself endlessly repeating the same answer but your answers are very important to your child. Too long an answer or just saying "That's the way it is" will only make her ask again!

Questioning helps her learn. "Can I do . . .?" tells her what you'll allow; "Is there a monster in the garden?" teaches her what is real and what is not. Gradually she'll begin to give her own answers to questions.

Above Very noisy at times, he'll also be able to whisper in your ear.
Left She'll enjoy telling one of her stories to a friend, just as you have read it to her.

GROWING AND LEARNING

Understanding and remembering

She's beginning now to understand more about what things are the same and what things are different. For example, she's learned that a dog is a dog whether it's a picture of one, a toy model of one or a real large black friendly one.

Objects can be sorted out in many different ways and your child will gradually learn more of these ways. If she's given a pile of buttons, when she's about two years old she may be able to sort the round ones into a pile and the square ones into another. At around three years old she may sort them into piles of different colors. By four years old she'll be using both shape and color, putting all the round red ones together. Later still she'll be able to sort using three ideas at once: for example, putting together all the round blue buttons that have two holes.

DOING PUZZLES
As your child learns how to match shapes, colors and patterns, she will enjoy mastering puzzles of increasing complexity. Start her with
● inset puzzles of different shapes, then let her try
● floor jigsaw puzzles with 6-12 large pieces, then she might be ready for
● small piece puzzles where she follows a picture or pattern.

When she's doing a jigsaw puzzle she's learning to remember what shapes, patterns and colors fit together.

She'll also be sorting things out in terms of what they do. She'll know that a train, a horse, a bike and an elephant are all similar – they move and you can ride on them.

She'll be making comparisons between things too. The two-year-old will be pointing out the largest, the shortest or the heaviest. She'll be gaining an understanding of order: for example, that how tall you are is usually an indication of how old you are.

This is the time too when she's starting to get an idea of numbers. At first she may count "1-2-3-4-5" as part of a rhyming game. She won't yet be matching the number she's saying with the actual number of things present, but she'll learn to do this by the time she starts school. It will be some time though before she can add up in her head. Her understanding of time won't be very advanced yet. She'll know "day" and "night," "morning" and "afternoon," and eventually "yesterday" and "tomorrow" but longer time spans will mean little to her.

Her play will gradually become more prolonged and elaborate now that she's able to concentrate and remember more. As she gets older she'll be taking longer to tackle problems and consider what to do.

Behaving and feeling

As your child's personality unfolds you'll see strengths and weaknesses emerging in her character, just as physically she's good at some things and not so good at others.

The kind of child she is will influence how she behaves and needs to be handled in different situations. The shy quiet child will act differently at nursery school from the more boisterous one, although even the most confident three-year-old will at times be shy or apprehensive.

Your child will gradually be losing the tendency to act out her feelings immediately. She can now *tell* you how she feels and will accept simple explanations more readily. There will still be times when she may revert to younger behavior such as tantrums, clinging, or wetting her pants. Sometimes there doesn't appear to be a reason for this. It could be that her awareness of growing up is too much for her to cope with. She may be testing you out to make sure that she still has her special place within the family.

Feelings of excitement and fear are very evident and these can quickly change from one to the other. Playing a game of chase with a three-year-old may start off with her shrieking with laughter but it can easily end in tears and upset. Fears and worries may also become more obvious now and are sometimes linked with a vivid imagination. Fears of the dark, of big animals, doctors or hospitals are all common at this age but simple explanations will sometimes help to overcome some of the anxiety. Various habits, such as thumb sucking, babyish talking or rocking gently to and fro, can also emerge in these years. They may start when she feels tired or upset and needs comfort, and can last a long time. It may help to distract her by playing a quiet game or chatting about something new.

Your child has many rules to learn – how to behave in different places, what to touch and what to avoid. There will be times when even the most well-behaved child will get exasperated and be naughty or cross. She'll also be learning how to cope with being told off as well as being praised. Most children have times when they lose their temper and some lash out at others. It's often you, whom she loves and trusts, who receives most of her angry feelings.

GETTING READY TO READ
- Children differ in when they can read – getting them *ready* to read is more important than teaching reading.
- Follow your child's interests and never push her beyond what she herself wants to do.
- Encourage an interest in books – these can teach "front" and "back," "beginning" and "end" and the sequence of things.
- Encourage recognition of shapes and letters, for example, matching (alphabet tray), tracing and coloring letters – *not* by reciting the alphabet.
- Never be afraid of reading her the same story – reading comes from listening, understanding and enjoying the anticipation of what comes next.

She may feel shy at times and not want to join in.

GROWING AND LEARNING

She can do more for herself now and will want to show how independent she can be.

LEARNING RULES

● Start with a few rules that really matter, for example, holding hands to cross the road. These should always be adhered to.

● Introduce the idea that certain rules apply in different situations, for example, she doesn't carry her drink around at granny's house though she can at home. Explain why and prepare her for these variations.

● Try to be as consistent as possible in the way you react if she breaks an important rule. Don't threaten to do something you're not prepared to carry out.

● She'll be able to understand simple explanations. Try to make them quite short and not too detailed, for example, "The stove is hot and will hurt you so don't touch it."

Theirs is a wider world now, playing with friends, gaining new experiences and building on the skills developed so far.

Doing things herself

She's learned to do more for herself now and will want to try things out each day. It's important that she learns so that she is able to cope without you when she's at pre-school or out at a friend's house.

Children vary a lot in when they learn to be independent. A second child may learn more quickly, as she's determined to do things at the same time as her brother or sister. Your child may be fascinated by doing up the clothes on a doll or teddy and this will help her cope with her own clothes.

When she's dressing she's got to be able to match a button to a hole, see the difference between very similar things (left and right) and be able to judge that the largest hole in a jumper is for her head. No wonder she can be uncooperative sometimes.

She has to learn to manage things like washing her hands, wiping her nose and pulling her pants down. It may help her to feel a bit more confident if you let her concentrate on just one thing at a time.

At mealtimes she can watch to see how you use a knife and fork. It can help to give her a child's cutlery set and a bowl rather than a flat plate. She'll probably eat messily for a while but her movements will become more precise.

By the time she's five she may seem very independent and competent. She'll enjoy this independence but may sometimes need extra attention from you.

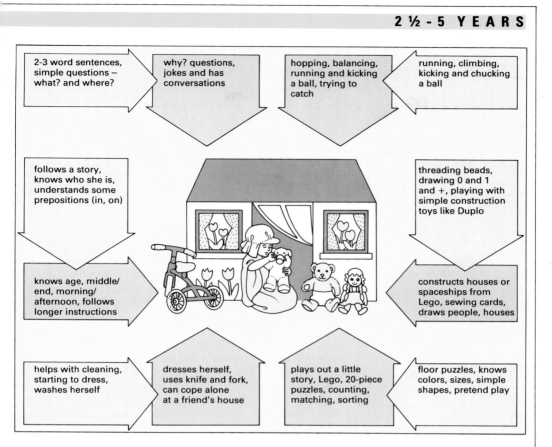

2-3 word sentences, simple questions – what? and where?

why? questions, jokes and has conversations

hopping, balancing, running and kicking a ball, trying to catch

running, climbing, kicking and chucking a ball

follows a story, knows who she is, understands some prepositions (in, on)

threading beads, drawing 0 and 1 and +, playing with simple construction toys like Duplo

knows age, middle/ end, morning/ afternoon, follows longer instructions

constructs houses or spaceships from Lego, sewing cards, draws people, houses

helps with cleaning, starting to dress, washes herself

dresses herself, uses knife and fork, can cope alone at a friend's house

plays out a little story, Lego, 20-piece puzzles, counting, matching, sorting

floor puzzles, knows colors, sizes, simple shapes, pretend play

Making sense of her world

Your child's world is expanding rapidly now. She may join a pre-school or start nursery school and be going out to play with friends. The imaginary world she creates with her toys is also important as she is trying out new ideas.

She's having to learn to share her toys and also her parents if there's a baby in the family. It's important to let her have a time or play area which is just hers. It may help her learn to share if you put very special toys away before friends come to play with her other things.

She's beginning now to enjoy more cooperative play. She and her friends may all play "cowboys and indians" or "mommies and daddies." They will give each other roles to play and enjoy telling imaginary tales.

Being one of a group may be a new experience for her. A new adult may not quite understand her or she may be shy. She'll need to be able to follow instructions now as she may be asked to tidy up or sit at a table.

Your child may enjoy expressing herself in different ways. She may laugh, sing or shout. Sometimes she may get over-excited and "go crazy"; other times she'll love being the center of attention. When she's naughty it can be better to take her out of the room and let her calm down.

A four- to five-year-old's world can be very busy. It may include dancing or music as well as nursery school or pre-school. She's had a lot to learn but will be enjoying her new independence and the variety of her life.

From two-and-a-half to five years

In these years your child becomes increasingly confident and competent as she learns to build further on her basic skills. She'll become quite skilled with her hands, enjoying dawing and making things. She'll be questioning everything and understanding and talking a lot. Her play will reflect her everyday life as she acts out her experiences of a wider world.

GROWING AND LEARNING

Play and toys

Your child has spent his first years acquiring many different skills; he can now delight in using them and in showing them off. He can use language well enough to enjoy playing with other children and adults, and he can handle objects well enough to help his parents with simple tasks, such as setting the table or putting his clothes on. He is still new to these things, however, and needs a lot of adult attention, encouragement and approval.

Physical play

Your child will be seeking new physical challenges all the time, but while he is becoming more independent he still needs you to help him find safe ones. Left to his own devices he might "dare" himself to do something dangerous. A rope ladder or swing, if you can find somewhere safe to fix one, is much more demanding than it looks and will last for years. This is the age for a first pedal tricycle or car, or a scooter with training wheels. Make sure you find a flat area for him to ride it in though – these vehicles can be difficult to handle at first over steps and on slopes.

Below A guide to the playthings your child will enjoy, and what will interest him as his skills develop.

Even if you only have limited space outside, you can practice throwing and catching games together using a soft ball or a homemade bean bag, and children of this age still enjoy jumping and climbing games in the park or yard. Indoors, just keeping a balloon from touching the ground can be fun. However, not all physical activities need equipment: see who can hop on his right foot, hop on his left foot, jump in the air, walk backwards, or even stop moving and stay absolutely still during a game of "Statues" or count up to 5 standing on one foot without support.

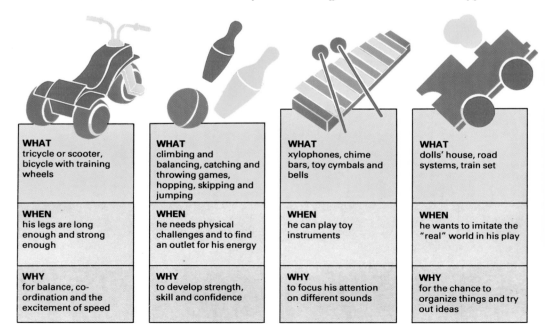

WHAT tricycle or scooter, bicycle with training wheels	WHAT climbing and balancing, catching and throwing games, hopping, skipping and jumping	WHAT xylophones, chime bars, toy cymbals and bells	WHAT dolls' house, road systems, train set
WHEN his legs are long enough and strong enough	WHEN he needs physical challenges and to find an outlet for his energy	WHEN he can play toy instruments	WHEN he wants to imitate the "real" world in his play
WHY for balance, co-ordination and the excitement of speed	WHY to develop strength, skill and confidence	WHY to focus his attention on different sounds	WHY for the chance to organize things and try out ideas

Construction toys

Many boys and girls are fascinated by mechanical toys, but the elaborate electric or clockwork ones force children to be spectators at a time when they prefer doing things for themselves. If you are going to buy a train set, for example, get one with wooden or plastic interlocking lines – putting these together is often the best part of the game at this stage. A good construction set for a three-year-old is one made of large wooden or plastic pieces that can be assembled easily. If your child already has a basic construction set, now is the time to buy more parts for it. A four- or five-year-old will appreciate being able to add more complicated working parts – wheels, hinges, and perhaps gears – to his invention.

PLAYGROUND SAFETY
Keep a close watch on children playing in the local park or playground, and look for:
● slides built over grass or sand so a child cannot fall onto concrete below the chute
● climbing equipment that is not set over concrete
● merry-go-rounds designed so a child's foot cannot be trapped between the moving platform and the ground
● seesaws with completely contained moving parts so there is no risk of a child trapping his fingers
● swings with a restraining device to prevent the child from being flipped over the bar – teach your child not to stand or run behind swings, as he could easily be hit and injured by one
● Remember: make sure your child knows what to do and whom to approach (or not to approach) if he thinks he has lost you in a crowded place.

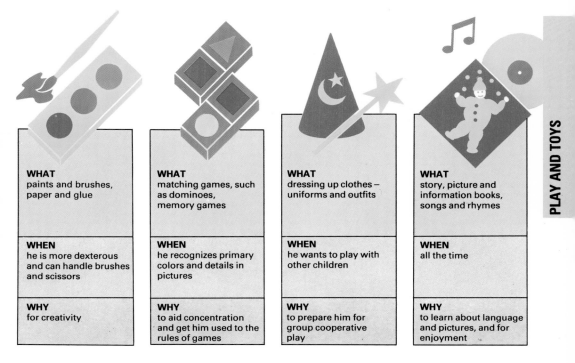

WHAT	WHAT	WHAT	WHAT
paints and brushes, paper and glue	matching games, such as dominoes, memory games	dressing up clothes – uniforms and outfits	story, picture and information books, songs and rhymes
WHEN	**WHEN**	**WHEN**	**WHEN**
he is more dexterous and can handle brushes and scissors	he recognizes primary colors and details in pictures	he wants to play with other children	all the time
WHY	**WHY**	**WHY**	**WHY**
for creativity	to aid concentration and get him used to the rules of games	to prepare him for group cooperative play	to learn about language and pictures, and for enjoyment

PLAY AND TOYS

Imaginative games

Improved physical skills, combined with your child's ability to concentrate better, give scope for more complicated games now. Whereas when he was younger he tended to play mostly on his own, he is now ready to play the sort of games that require the cooperation of other children. This is an age when children love to collect and store, so buy accessories for dolls and dolls' houses, add animals and vehicles to the farmyard or fort, or pieces to the train set. Your child will spend many happy hours playing out his view of the world with his friends, or brothers and sisters. A plastic picnic set and an inverted box with a cloth over it provides a perfect setting for tea-parties, and the same box can be made into an improvised garage or dolls' house; if it's turned over and furnished with a cushion and some old baby blankets it becomes a doll's crib or hospital bed for a sick toy.

As your child grows up you may begin to notice distinct differences in behavior between the sexes: your little girl may prefer her dolls to her cars, or your son may enjoy building and construction games more. Nevertheless, boys and girls are growing up into the same world and they should be encouraged to learn about and get to grips with all aspects of it. Boys as well as girls need a chance to imagine themselves in the domestic world of homes, cooking and babies, so don't discourage your little boy from playing with dolls or household utensils if he wants to. Similarly, if girls are to have an equal chance in today's society they should not be discouraged from taking an interest in more mechanical toys.

Painting and drawing

Paint and brushes come into their own now. You can buy nontoxic water-based poster paints in good toy shops or stores, either as a powder or in ready-mixed liquid form. If you are using the powdered sort, mix it to a thick consistency so that it doesn't run or trickle when used. You don't need many colors at first: your child will be quite happy with black and white, and the primary colors (red, blue and yellow), so that he can mix up any color he needs.

For his first attempts at painting your child needs a thick brush with a short handle. He will not be doing fine and delicate work yet, but will want to make a bold impression on a large piece of paper (the younger the child, the bigger the paper and the thicker the brush). Paper shopping bags, unwanted wallpaper and computer print-out sheets all make good painting surfaces. Don't expect his first paintings to look like anything in particular, and don't be tempted to correct them if they don't; they are your child's early impressions of the world he lives in. If you want to be involved, keep him company while he paints; sit him at the kitchen table with some paper and paints while you get on with the chores. Some children provide a "commentary" as they are painting and this can be very interesting, if you are lucky enough to overhear it.

Right A child's desire to "make it better" can lead to hours of fun bandaging dolls and teddies . . . and each other!

Below left Cutting and pasting can be tricky so your help may be needed at first.

Below right Children of both sexes like to imitate what they see you doing.

Continue to provide plenty of pencils and crayons for drawing as well. You can help your child to hold his pencils with a "tripod grasp" (thumb and first two fingers) which will prepare him for learning to write.

Cutting and pasting

Your child will enjoy cutting and pasting to make pictures. As with painting, don't expect an artistic result at first. For the child, the fun of doing it is much more important than the end product. Provide him with a small pair of scissors, with rounded ends, and teach him how to use them safely; to hold them by the handle only, to carry them with the ends pointed downwards, and *never* to run with them. He will also need some thin card – old greetings cards or small cartons, such as cereal boxes – and a suitable glue. You can buy or make a cold water paste, or you can buy a slightly more powerful glue which is thick and white in the bottle but dries clear. This will wash out of clothes so long as you use cold water first, but try to remove it before it dries completely.

PLAY AND TOYS

249

Music

Your child is beginning to focus more closely on the sounds he hears and can make with musical instruments or toys. If he likes to dance about in time to music, hand-held instruments – maracas, castanets, a tambourine, chime bells or homemade "shakers" – add to the fun. You can make a shaker by putting a few beans inside a shampoo bottle, sealing it and decorating it with self-adhesive paper shapes. A coat of clear varnish will make it last for some time.

An important aspect of music is learning to listen. Help your child to do this by just standing still together sometimes, indoors or out, and listening to the sounds you hear. You can identify bird songs together, or the voices or instruments in your favorite music.

Children's first attempts at making music are more to do with noise and rhythm than melodies, so playing along to nursery rhymes occupies them happily.

Books

Your child's enjoyment of picture books and stories continues throughout this age group and on into school-days. Even when he starts to read to himself, and knows many stories "by heart," he will still want to be read to and will need you to help him appreciate the more difficult ones. At some point, your child will begin to use books to find out things. He will probably have been asking you questions ever since he could talk and the time soon comes when you don't know all the answers. It is useful to be able to show him how he can look for information. There are now some excellent hardback and paperback books for children that give simple, accurate information about the things which interest them – animals and insects, cars and planes, dinosaurs, magnets, or space travel – and these can be found in bookstores and libraries. There are also books designed to prepare children for special events in their lives or to help them cope with situations which they might find upsetting. These cover a variety of subjects, such as visiting the dentist, being adopted, traveling by plane and going into the hospital, and they are well worth looking for.

Joining in with your child's first games can be fun for all the family. A younger child learns from the others how to follow the rules, how to take turns and, sometimes with difficulty, how to cope with losing.

Games to play with other people

His early experience with books and paint will have given your child practice in recognizing shapes and colors, and he is now ready to join in games that give him practice in sorting and recognizing shapes or words. Picture dominoes, in which pictures or patterns replace the dots of the adult version, are fun and introduce the child to the rules of a game, teaching him how to take turns – a difficult step for a young child. At this stage of his development he is eager to be doing things and may find it hard to wait for other people, especially if they are other children who are slow and hesitant.

It is better at first to restrict the number of players to two or three, with one adult to organize the game and make sure it is played fairly. Children have much to learn about taking turns, sharing, and accepting rules, and none of these things come easily. Your help and tact are needed to make things run smoothly, and your task could be made easier by the use of a kitchen timer to regulate turn-taking and ensure that the game is played fairly.

A game such as picture lotto makes fewer demands on a child's patience because all the players look at their cards every turn. Some versions of picture lotto have a picture printed on one side of the card and the word on the other, so that a child can start to associate one with the other. Another game which helps children of four or five to think about words and spelling is "I Spy." It is a useful game on long journeys too, but if you play it with children who are younger, it is better to give clues based on the first sound of the word rather than the name of the first letter. A child of three won't necessarily associate the word "double-you" with "window."

PLAY AND TOYS

Pre-school play and learning

If you decide that your child needs some pre-school experience outside the home before starting kindergarten, find out what facilities there are in your neighborhood. The state human services department can supply you with a list of licensed pre-schools and nursery schools in your area. If you are moving to a new community and must find a nursery school immediately, you can get the names of the schools in your new neighborhood by writing to the National Association for the Education of Young Children (NAEYC). (**See** Useful addresses, p. 298-9.)

Pre-schools

There are several types of pre-schools (schools for children under kindergarten age) to choose from – privately-run facilities, schools run by parents on a cooperative basis, church-affiliated nursery schools, and in a few areas, nursery classes run by the local public school system.

Before you make any decision you need to see the various facilities for yourself. Phone the school or group you are considering and ask if you can visit, with your child, to have a look around and talk to the staff.

What are the facilities?

Don't attach too much importance to the building itself: modern purpose-built premises can be very attractive, but the public halls and old-fashioned school buildings used by some pre-schools and nursery schools can house excellent facilities. Anyway, this is not important to most small children; it's the quality of the play that counts for them.

There is no such thing as a perfect nursery school or pre-school, what you want is one that meets the requirements of your own children. If you know that your child needs greater physical challenges than you can give him at home, look for a place with plenty of climbing, balancing and scrambling equipment, preferably outdoors as well as inside. If you have a child who is very quiet and unused to large boisterous groups, let him build up confidence somewhere more gentle.

Ask at what age your child would be admitted if you decide to send him there. Although most nursery schools and pre-schools admit children from the age of three, pressure for places might mean waiting until he is four.

Your own involvement

One of the most important factors in a child's success at school is his parents' interest in his education. When looking at pre-school facilities, consider what your role will be. Most good pre-school groups try to involve parents as much as possible – co-operative nursery schools are actually managed by parents – so try to make the most of whatever kind of participation is offered. Spend some time in the playroom if you possibly can; you will learn a lot about children – your own and other people's – and you will

---

LOOKING AT A NURSERY OR PRE-SCHOOL

● Is the atmosphere warm and welcoming?

● Is there a good range of equipment? Look for messy play (paint, water, sand, playdough); books and puzzles; scope for adventurous play – indoors and out; things to build with; and opportunities for imaginative play.

● Language and conversation are important at this age. Are there enough adults to ensure that each child gets some attention and a chance to talk?

● Are there physical activities for the bolder children, and can they enjoy them without disturbing the quieter ones?

● Are they free to pursue their own activities, and is support available if they get into difficulties?

● Ask how the staff cope with children who are unhappy or who misbehave.

● Finally, watch your own child's reactions – these will tell you a lot.

A good playgroup will provide lots of opportunity for really creative expression.

Sitting still, concentrating and being in a group of children are all skills that pre-school groups can help your child develop in readiness for school.

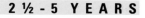

probably enjoy it. If you cannot be involved during the day, consider joining the parents' committee or offering to make or maintain equipment, or perhaps help with fund raising.

Early to school

Experts differ about the best age for children to start kindergarten. Traditionally, five was seen as the appropriate age. In recent years, however, some learning experts have voiced the opinion that a significant number of children would benefit from spending an extra year in prekindergarten class. If you are unsure about whether your child is ready for kindergarten, make an appointment with the principal of your local elementary school. He or she may recommend one of several diagnostic tests.

Every state requires that children beyond kindergarten age receive a full-time education – in a public or private school. Until that time the choice is yours.

GETTING READY FOR SCHOOL
You can help your child make the transition to school more easily by seeing that:
● he is able to manage without you for some part of the day
● adult help at home with games and puzzles has helped him to concentrate
● he can give and take with other children
● he enjoys books
● he can manage going to the bathroom.

PRE-SCHOOL PLAY & LEARNING

253

Some common concerns

From the age of two and a half, many children begin to take their first steps away from the home to become more independent. Parents often worry about how their child will adapt to nursery school and to being with other adults and children, how she will be affected by new influences and how to deal with problems caused by other people's different handling of her.

The key to all these new worries is your child's increasing ability to understand and to make herself understood. Gone are the tantrums and wordless frustrations of the toddler: your child's behavior is now characterized by her positive and expanding grasp of language.

Children of this age become increasingly aware of any family problems and it will be difficult to conceal unhappiness in a marriage, or a grandparent's illness or death. The child will ask questions which need to be honestly answered if her fears are to be allayed. If your child has to go into the hospital, you can help prepare her and explain what will happen in the same way that you can prepare for and explain a happier event like the birth of a new baby.

Becoming sociable

As your child starts to spend more time away from home – at a pre-school or at friends' houses – shyness or aggressive behavior are not uncommon. Her way of coping without your familiar presence may be to withdraw and stand on the sidelines, or she may disrupt the group with noisy or attention-seeking behavior. The pressure on your child to conform to a standard of behavior which may be quite different from that at home can be unsettling for her. Some parents try to over-protect their child and spare her some of the knocks that come her way; others try to push too much independence on their child too soon, not realizing that when she is facing new things every day she needs the familiar comforts of home to cushion her.

Your child's social encounters may also be set back by illnesses. Frequent contact with other children increases her chances of catching infections. Many children of this age seem to have one cough, cold and tummy upset after another, as well as catching other common childhood illnesses, such as chickenpox. You will naturally worry when you find yourself repeatedly at the doctor's office but this is fairly normal at this stage of your child's life.

Learning by her mistakes

As your child begins to try out the lessons she has learned at home, naturally she is going to make mistakes. This is how we all learn, but your child's discomfort can be softened if you find ways to boost her confidence. If she has a difficult afternoon at pre-school, get her to do something when she gets home that she is particularly good at, like a puzzle or a drawing, so that you can praise her for it. If she doesn't

See Your family life, page 257, for family problems, and Pre-school play and learning, page 252 understand something and gets frustrated and unhappy, find out what's worrying her and talk it over with her so that she is not left feeling uncertain and confused. Her limitations are often a source of anger and frustration to her. Your child's vulnerability may cause you pain when you have to stand back and let her find her own way.

Protecting your child

Once your child starts to spend any time out of your care, you may worry about the possibility of her being approached or abducted by a stranger, especially when so much publicity is given to child assault cases. In fact, the awful truth is that the majority of sexual assaults on children are by people they know already, so warning your child negatively about "strangers" is not enough. Parents can, to some extent, protect their children by talking to them about potential risks. Don't just terrify your child with the idea that people might try to take her away; explain that some people might want to hurt her, so it is important that you always know where she is and who are the adults responsible for her safety.

A number of books, videotapes, and films are available to help deal with the widespread problem of sexual abuse of children. The Girls Inc. of Omaha (3706 Lake Street, Omaha, Nebraska 68111, (402) 457-4676) has developed a program called "Kid-Ability" that is being disseminated nationwide. In addition, the Clearinghouse on Child Abuse and Neglect (c/o U.S. Department of Health and Human Services, 400 Sixth Street, S.W., Washington, D.C. 20013, (202) 755-0590) reviews publications and can supply resource lists on request.

Answering questions

A growing command of language can make a child far more demanding: she wants more time, more attention, more explanations. It is the age of "why?" and you may find yourself exhausted by a stream of questions. Your child may now have reached the stage where she wants to know such things as where babies come from. Answer her questions as simply and directly as possible, and remember that you need only give her an explanation that means something to her – she is still too young to understand anything complicated.

Your child will also start to express her opinion about everything, sometimes from morning till night. She may now take a dislike to certain clothes or food, and people come in for criticism too. Even you may not be spared! Give her as much attention as you can, but explain that there are times when you have to do other things. Sometimes a child's constant questioning is simply an attempt to get you to talk to her. If you try to see what she's after you may find your conversations more interesting.

Many parents at this time experience a mixture of feelings: pride in the child and her new abilities, and uncertainty as she becomes more independent. Nevertheless, there will be a certain reward in seeing your child take her place in the world in her own right, for the first time.

TEACHING SELF-PROTECTION

Teach your child these basic safety rules:

● To never get too close to a stranger who approaches her, and not to be afraid to scream and shout to draw attention to herself.

● Encourage your child to tell you about anything that has made her uneasy and not to keep secrets.

● Explain that there are "good" secrets (like hiding a birthday present till the actual day) and "bad" secrets which make her feel guilty.

● Explain about bribes and how to resist them.

● Explain about "good" touches that a child feels happy about and "bad" touches that she doesn't like. It is important that she can say "no" if she feels uncomfortable.

● To illustrate these points, play "what if" games, like what would you do if you saw the next-door house was on fire? (Call the fire department); what would you do if a man said he wanted to show you some puppies? (Say no, and run straight home to tell Mommy and Daddy.)

Your family life

Now that she's older, you can talk to your child about things and explain anything that she may find puzzling or upsetting.

This is the age when your child begins to make sense of the world, seeing himself in context. He is not just your child but a member of a family in some ways different from – and in other ways similar to – the families he sees around him. He knows about growing up to become like the same-sex parent and part of the process of growing up involves trying out what it feels like to be all manner of different people. As the horizons of his life expand you will have the new experience of seeing him attach himself to people you hardly know, such as the teacher at his pre-school or other children in his class.

Sex roles within the family

From as early as his second year your child begins to distinguish between male and female. By the time he is four he has divided up the world into male and female people and is aware of the difference between boys and girls. As he learns more of the world around him his view widens and the conclusions he draws are not simply based on your own family.

Children like to play at being men and women equally, and while parents don't bat an eyelid when little girls dress up as boys or pretend to be cowboys, they may worry if a boy wants a toy vacuum cleaner or likes to dress up as a princess (although this does not mean he will grow up a cissy or homosexual). Some mothers are equally disturbed when their pre-school daughters show a tendency to be ultra-feminine and only want to wear pretty dresses and play with dolls. Remember that these "try-outs" are an important and natural part of your child's development, and think of them as a normal phase which passes.

Identifying with same-sex parent

Eventually your child will come to identify more closely with the parent of the same sex. At this most imitative stage he will tend to closely model himself on this parent, showing physical and verbal mannerisms that are identical. But a deeper identification is going on which survives the years of adolescent rejection and rebellion to emerge in a modified form in adulthood. This process is quite unconscious and many people are surprised to find themselves growing very much more like their mother or father, with whom they believed they largely disagreed.

Coping with a "different" family

Once your child sees what other families are like he may begin to notice how his own family differs. It's easy to feel defensive if your child wants to know why his daddy doesn't live at home or the reason he has a sister with a different mommy, or why he has only one grandparent when other friends have four. His questions don't imply criticism, they just show that he is trying to make sense of the relationships he sees around him and that he wants to know where he fits in. Answer his questions as frankly as you can, in a way that he can best understand at his age.

Single parent

At this stage, when identification with an adult of the same sex is important, problems can arise for a single parent whose child is of a different sex. A single parent from a close family shouldn't have to worry: uncles, aunts and grandparents who are constantly around and are important in the child's life can provide the necessary models. A more isolated single parent doesn't have this back-up and many make a particular effort to meet up regularly with people of both sexes in the same situation, or to live communally.

Divorce and separation

If your relationship with your partner is breaking up it is traumatic for all of you. It is hard enough to cope with your own feelings, never mind what your child is going through. Some people feel that in order to protect young children it is best to pretend that there is nothing very much the matter, but this fails to set young minds at rest. Children are aware that something is wrong because of the atmosphere, and fights or misery can never be entirely hidden. Telling your children about the situation in words that they can understand is very much better; otherwise they might invent their own reasons for the sadness. Their fears and fantasies can build up into something much more frightening than the real truth and, if you don't talk about what is going on, they may come to think that divorce or separation is something shameful. Without an explanation they may even feel guilty – young children do see themselves as the center of the universe so unless they are told otherwise they can believe that all this misery is because of them.

Once your child understands what is happening in the family, explain that he is still loved, for although people can stop being married they never stop being a mother and a father. Try not to let the bitter feelings that you might feel for your partner show too much. Remember that your child feels intensely that he is half mommy and half daddy, and by rejecting the other parent you may make him feel bad about himself. It is tempting to try to get your child on your side, but he will suffer from this more than the one you thought you were hurting – your ex-partner.

After the split you don't have to pretend you are happy when you are not because your child will know it is not true and will be confused. You can say "I am feeling sad because daddy (or mommy) has gone away" – this is the truth and your child will understand it, but it does not involve blame. Bear in mind that after the initial blow and misery, young children come to terms with divorce and separation more quickly than older children or teenagers do.

Bereavement

Some time while he is young your child is likely to encounter death. It could be the death of a beloved pet at home, a rabbit that has been run over, or a relative, such as an ailing grandparent. Death is hard to understand,

---

THE ONLY CHILD

Being an only child does have advantages – one of which is the undivided love and attention of his parents. But sometimes this can make starting school rather bewildering and upsetting, unless you take certain steps at the pre-school stage.

● Make sure your child has plenty of contact with other children – if there are none living nearby, take him to the park regularly or to a playgroup.

● Invite friends and young relatives to stay often – and let him stay with them.

● Don't indulge him too much – if you always let him win at games or have his own way, he will find the demands of other children hard to understand and difficult to fit in with.

YOUR FAMILY LIFE

Your child is now at the right age to derive real pleasure from a pet, but there are some things to think about before you choose one.

● Your child may promise to look after the animal but he is too young to keep his promise – you must be prepared to do it yourself.

● Choose the right pet for your family and house: small puppies grow and need to be taken for walks.

● Pets have to be looked after when you go on vacation – will you be able to make suitable arrangements for them?

● Do you want your pet to breed, and will you be able to find homes for the young?

● Buy from a reputable dealer to ensure the animal has no illnesses that it could pass on.

Good choices

● Gerbils are active during the day (unlike hamsters and mice which are active at night). They like and need to be handled gently.

● Cats are clean and fastidious, and can remove themselves quickly if your child becomes too rough.

● Rabbits like being stroked and cuddled, but do be sure you have room for a hutch and run outside. Choose a small breed which your child can handle easily.

particularly when you are very young, and the fact that it disturbs us as adults means that we are often reluctant to talk about it to our children. However, studies have shown that of children who have suffered the death of a parent, those who are told the truth about death are best able to cope with it.

The facts that children need to know when they ask about death are that it is final and that it happens to every living thing. Euphemisms or stories that soften the experience, such as "grandpa has gone to sleep," do not help a child come to terms with it. Explaining death in religious terms is only a good idea if it is what you really believe – otherwise your answers to your child's questions will eventually show him that he is not being told the truth as you see it. Children can also be told that when a person or animal they love dies, it is perfectly natural to feel very sad and to wish they would come back to life again, even though this is impossible.

If a loved member of the family dies you will have your own grief to live with and you may long to shield your child from similar powerful emotions. But children should be told at the same time as adults when a death has occurred; they are likely to suffer longer if the truth is withheld from them. They need to know that the loved one is gone for good and they will not see him again. You may feel that it is better for a young child to be allowed to attend a funeral so that he understands what the occasion marks. Don't be afraid of letting your grief show in front of your children – it will make it easier for them to express their own sad feelings in a healthy way.

Your child's life outside the home

Even before school starts, your child will begin to have a life outside the home and this can feel strange when the two of you have been inseparable for so long. Sometimes the hardest thing to adjust to is the knowledge that his happiness does not lie solely in your hands anymore, that he can meet and cope with problems when you are not there to put everything right again.

Attachment to teacher

Sometimes mothers find themselves becoming quite jealous when their child becomes attached to a teacher at the pre-school or to whoever looks after him during the day. It is common to become irritated when you are constantly subjected to "Miss Jones says, Miss Jones does, and Miss Jones wears" conversations, but you should be pleased. It shows that you have done your job well and that your child is confident enough to make new relationships without letting the fact that he misses you get in the way. If your child disliked the teacher and longed only to be reunited with you, it would be flattering, but at the expense of your child's happiness when he is not with you.

Fights with other children

Something that is more disturbing for a parent is to hear that the child is having trouble getting on with other children. It is upsetting for you (as it is for him) to hear that he is being bullied, has no friends, or is himself a bully. First of all you should retain a sense of proportion about the problem and remember that learning social graces and how to get along with others is a slow and complicated process – and your child is bound to have his ups and downs for years. Most of the other children will be having similar problems at different times.

If you are seriously worried about the situation, talk to the teacher. You will be told if the problem is more severe in your child's case or if it is fairly normal and something that will settle down in time. If your child's happiness seems to be affected seriously and he displays nervous habits at home or has nightmares or trouble sleeping, tell the teacher and ask her to keep an eye on things.

Vacations and trips

During this time your child becomes so competent at dealing with his life at home that it is easy to forget that he does not yet have much experience of the world at large. On vacation he may get himself into silly scrapes simply because he was unaware of the dangers of a new environment. You will have to supervise him – although not too closely. Sometimes it is a great help to go on vacation or out for the day with other parents who have children of a similar age. The children have each other for company and the adults can take it in turns to see that they come to no harm. At this stage your child will enjoy and appreciate family outings – perhaps a picnic in the country, a day at the zoo, or a trip to the seaside.

Birthdays

From now on birthday parties will be great fun for your child and his friends. They will almost always continue to be exhausting for you, though! When it is possible, try to have one extra adult for every five children you invite. Games and prizes make everyone over-excited so there has to be an adult to mop up the tears, take children to the toilet, or start another game with those who are out of the one being played.

PARTIES

● Don't invite too many children – they can become over-excited at this age.

● If your child is at his best in the morning, and gets irritable towards dinner-time, why not consider a lunch-time party?

● Don't expect a group of excited children to play orderly party games *all* the time. They will enjoy "Pin the Tail on the Donkey," and, if there is room, "Musical Chairs," but they will want to play with your child's toys too. Put out of sight any he doesn't want to share.

● A magician is often successful with the over-threes, but check that he is used to this age group.

● Have food which looks special without being too rich or unfamiliar. Most children like snacks, such as sausages and cheese on sticks; sandwiches tend to get left.

The focus of any birthday tea is inevitably the cake and the great feat of blowing out all the candles.

A-Z OF COMMON AILMENTS

*All parents worry about whether their
small child really is unwell, what might be wrong, how
serious it could be, and what they can do to help.
You will learn to trust your own instincts about whether
your child is ill and to seek advice when you
are concerned about him. It is important to know how
to look after him when he's unwell and helpful
to understand the causes, symptoms and typical
course of the more common ailments.*

You and your sick child

Your child's behavior is usually a good guide to how he's feeling.

It is often quite difficult for a parent to know when a small child is unwell. Babies and young children are unable to tell you when there is something wrong so you will have to learn to look out for warning signs. Sometimes the only indication of illness is a change in behavior – a baby who is reluctant to feed or sleep, or a child who loses her appetite and becomes listless and irritable. At other times the symptoms are more obvious; the child may have a fever or a body rash or she may vomit. Your own instincts will often tell you when something is wrong and when you need to consult a doctor. Learn to trust your own judgment and don't hesitate to seek help for fear of being thought a fussy parent. It is best to seek advice too freely rather than miss something important.

Visiting the doctor

Unless the child is too ill to move, or you think she may be infectious, take her to the doctor's office where he can do a more thorough examination and perform simple tests for which he has the necessary equipment. It is important that the doctor is someone you can trust and your child likes as he may be your family doctor for years to come. You may be able to help your doctor by noting anything wrong with your child and when it occurred. Never be afraid to ask him questions: the more you understand about the symptoms of an illness, the better equipped you are to deal with it.

Treating the illness

Once the illness has been diagnosed by the doctor he will tell you what to do for the child. Treatment with medicines is not always necessary: sometimes the illness will get better on its own, although you may want to relieve a fever or pain by giving something simple like acetaminophen. Make sure you follow the dosage stated on the bottle or recommended by your doctor.

The treatment of many common childhood illnesses depends on whether the infection is caused by a virus or bacteria. Viruses are tiny germs which can be transmitted through water vapor (coughing or sneezing) and they are responsible for most minor childhood infections such as colds and sore throats. Most viral infections do not have specific treatment and they usually clear up on their own.

Bacteria are microscopically visible organisms which are present in all organic matter. Many bacteria are harmless but others can cause infectious diseases. Bacterial infections (such as pneumonia or tonsillitis) are treated with antibiotics (drugs that kill bacteria). Although antibiotics have no effect against viruses they are sometimes prescribed to treat or prevent a bacterial complication of a virus, such as an ear infection.

Another group of drugs are antihistamines, which are sometimes used to treat hay fever and other allergies. They can also help to prevent travel or motion sickness. Antihistamines block the action of histamine, a substance released by the body following an allergic reaction, which can cause irritation and redness.

Whatever medication is prescribed for your child's illness, remember to keep it in a safe place, out of reach.

Coping at home

Now that you know what is wrong with your child you can think about how to make her comfortable at home. At the beginning of an illness the child will probably seek the comfort of her own bed and will either sleep or sit quietly, propped up against some pillows. For the older child it is a good idea to put a drink within reach in case she is thirsty. She may also find listening to music on the radio comforting when you are out of the room, but do pop in and see her regularly to make sure she is all right. A baby or toddler will need to be watched carefully and should be given plenty of fluids. Air the child's room and bed at least once a day and before you put her to bed at night.

As the child starts to recover she will want to play quietly or have a story read to her. At this stage she may feel well enough to sit downstairs in the living room with a drawing book, puzzle or game. This can be an advantage for both of you because she can see what you are doing while you keep an eye on her. There is never any reason to keep a child in bed if she feels well enough to get up; she will only get restless and upset if you confine her to her bedroom.

Going into the hospital

Your child may have to go into the hospital for observation, special tests or an operation. This can be frightening for a child of any age but small children in particular sometimes think that it is a punishment for being naughty. This inevitably leads to feelings of insecurity and you should do all you can to reassure the child and allay her fears. Consult your doctor about how best to prepare the child for going into the hospital and talk to any friends who have had a similar experience with a young child. There are a few good illustrated books for children which you can buy or take out of the library to read to your child. This may also help her to understand the situation better. You can also contact Children in Hospitals (*see* Useful Addresses, page 298). Most hospitals now provide facilities for parents to stay with young children in the hospital. You have every right to insist on staying in the hospital with your child if you think it will help your child. Check with your doctor or the hospital to make sure that they have beds for parents.

When your child returns home after a stay in the hospital you may find that she is more clinging and demanding, or she may be very quiet and subdued for a while. Whatever form her change of behavior takes, it is usually a normal reaction to being away from home and she will settle again in a few days.

It can be a welcome distraction if teddy shares in the bumps, bruises and bandaging.

If your child develops any of the following symptoms consult your doctor urgently.
- Loss of consciousness
- Convulsion
- Breathing difficulties
- Severe or prolonged pain
- Persistent vomiting and diarrhea (which can lead to dehydration)
- A rash that looks like bleeding under the skin
- Blueness of lips or face

Nursing your child

A child who is ill requires special care and attention. Although most children are resilient and get better quickly, you will need to provide essential nursing and comfort throughout the illness.

Taking temperature

The normal body temperature for a child can fluctuate between 36°C and 37°C (97°F-98.6°F). If your child's temperature is higher than this, it is because the body is reacting to an infection.

To take the child's temperature use either a clinical thermometer or a fever strip or disk. Before using the thermometer rinse it under *cold* tap water and then shake it with a flick of the wrist to get the mercury into the bulb. Make sure it has a low reading before you start. The safest way to take a small child's temperature is to place the thermometer under her arm with the mercury bulb in the armpit. Hold the child's arm still for at least two minutes (time this carefully) before taking the thermometer out and reading it.

A fever strip or disk is not as accurate as a thermometer but it is useful for a quick assessment and will tell you whether the child's temperature is normal or raised. All you have to do is place the strip or disk on the child's forehead for a few seconds to get a reading.

Lowering temperature

A child who is hot and feverish should be kept cool and given plenty of fluids to drink. Acetaminophen elixir (given according to instructions on the bottle or from your doctor) will help to bring the temperature down, as will sponging with tepid water. Do not put extra clothes or blankets on a child who is too hot – instead, take a layer off until she has cooled down. Consult your doctor at any time if you are worried (*see* Fever, page 276).

ACETAMINOPHEN

Children under the age of five often find it hard to swallow tablets, so medicine can be given to them as a syrup (elixir), drops or chewable tablets. The appropriate dose will bring down a high temperature. Read the instructions on the bottle carefully. Aspirin should only be given to children if prescribed.

TAKING TEMPERATURE

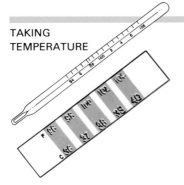

Obtain an accurate reading with a thermometer, or a quick indication with a fever strip.

Thermometer Lift the child's arm and tuck the thermometer under it. Hold for 2-3 minutes.

Fever strip Place the strip on the child's forehead for 15-20 seconds to get a reading.

Giving medicine

Medicine for young children is usually made up in the form of syrup or elixir. As it is sweetened, children will usually take the dose readily from a spoon. For a baby you can get specially designed spoons or a dropper. Your doctor may give you a syringe to measure and administer the dose.

When the doctor prescribes medicine for your child make sure you know what it is and what effect it is supposed to have. Read the instructions carefully, and keep the bottle out of the child's reach. Any medicine that is left after the illness should be flushed down the toilet.

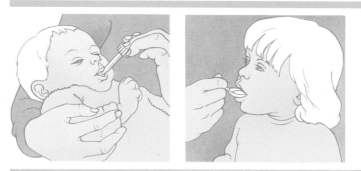

HOW TO GIVE MEDICINE
It is not always easy to give medicine to a young baby. A dropper is useful for this – simply place it in the corner of the baby's mouth and gently squeeze the nipple (far left). An older child will be able to manage medicine from a spoon (left).

Eating and drinking

Loss of appetite is a common and normal symptom of illness so never force your child to eat if she doesn't feel like it. You may find that she will take milky drinks or glucose more readily than food and these will provide some nourishment. As the child gets better her appetite will return and you can start to give her light meals.

Fluids are vitally important when a child is ill so make sure she has plenty to drink. Loss of fluid through vomiting or diarrhea can rapidly lead to dehydration and this is a particularly serious condition in babies and small children. One way of telling if your baby is getting enough to drink is to check her diaper. If the urine is the normal color and the diaper is wet she is not dehydrated, but if the diaper is quite dry or the urine is a dark color give the baby fluids and consult your doctor immediately.

Illness on vacation

Although you cannot guarantee that your child will not be ill on your vacation you can take certain precautions. Pack a basic first aid kit, and ask your travel agent what medical facilities there are in the place you are visiting in case of a more serious illness or accident. You could also inquire about medical insurance to cover treatment abroad.

In some parts of the world you require vaccination against certain diseases (such as typhoid and cholera). Ask your doctor about this as the vaccine is usually given a couple of weeks before departure. You should also make sure that your child's immunization program is up-to-date.

VACATION CHECKLIST
● Your first aid kit could include: sunblock cream, elastic bandages and Band-Aids, antiseptic cream, calamine lotion, absorbent cotton.
● Be aware of the dangers of sunburn and heatstroke with a young child. Protect her from too much direct sunlight and move her into the shade if she gets too hot.
● Pay particular attention to hygiene abroad: buy bottled water as tap water may not be safe to drink, avoid eating undercooked meat and fish, and unpeeled fruit and raw vegetables. If your child does get an upset stomach, give her plenty of fluids. Seek medical advice if it persists.
● Rabies is a serious hazard: if your child is bitten or scratched by an animal, get medical attention for the wound immediately.

YOU AND YOUR SICK CHILD

A-Z of common ailments

The entries on these pages cover the most usual upsets and illnesses for the first five years. Many of them are not serious and most small children, however healthy, will have their share of coughs, colds and rashes. You should always contact your doctor if you are worried about your child's health or behavior; most parents know when something is wrong.

A

Abdominal pain

Abdominal pain or tummy ache is a very common childhood complaint that has many causes, most of which are not serious. However, if pain is persistent the child should be examined by a doctor.

Children can have a tummy ache with something as simple as a sore throat or cold. This is because the glands in the abdomen become enlarged as part of the body's reaction to the infection, causing irritation to the bowel and thus pain. This type of pain disappears without treatment. Sometimes children complain of tummy aches when they are anxious or worried. These pains are similar to the tension headaches which some adults develop. In between the pain the child is well and no treatment is required, but it may be helpful to try and work out what is upsetting him. Pain of this kind tends to occur more frequently in schoolchildren than toddlers.

Abdominal pain may occur with other symptoms. Pain which is accompanied by frequent vomiting or a change in the bowel movements (diarrhea or constipation) could be caused by an infection of the bowel, such as gastroenteritis, by appendicitis or by an obstruction in the bowel. Blood in the stools with a tummy ache may also be caused by a bowel infection or obstruction. If the child is urinating very frequently, the pain may be due to a urinary infection. A child who has any one of these complaints will appear unwell, lose his appetite and energy and may be feverish. The pain will probably come and go, but even when it is not acute the child will not be his usual self.

Any child who experiences severe or prolonged abdominal pain, particularly if associated with any of the above symptoms, should be seen by a doctor who will identify the cause and prescribe treatment. (*See also* **Appendicitis, Colic, Encopresis, Gastroenteritis, Urinary tract infections**)

Abscess

An abscess is a pocket of pus which can occur anywhere in the body. The formation of an abscess is one of the body's defense mechanisms against infection. By separating the infected pus from the surrounding healthy tissue the spread of infection is prevented. A child with an abscess is usually unwell and feverish, but other symptoms depend on where the infection is. For example, with a cervical abscess (in a neck gland) the child will have a tender red lump on the side of his neck, whereas an abscess in the lung, which cannot be seen, may cause the child to breathe faster than normal and to cough. An abscess deep in the body, such as a lung abscess, is more serious than one that lies on or near the surface of the skin.

Sometimes an abscess will "point" to an area where it can burst. If this occurs internally it results in further spread of the infection, but when it occurs on the skin the pus is released and the condition spontaneously cured. To speed up the cure of an abscess a doctor will sometimes open up the infected area and allow the pus to drain out of the body. In a few cases he will prescribe antibiotics to prevent the abscess from getting worse.

Accidents
(*See* Emergencies, page 294)

Adenoids
The adenoids are pieces of lymphoid tissue which lie in the air passages behind the nose and throat. Their main function is to prevent infection of the upper airways and in most children they do this effectively. However, they can become enlarged and this can have two effects.

Firstly, they may block the nose so that the child has to breathe through the mouth constantly. Secondly, they may obstruct the Eustachian tube which connects the nasal passages to the inner ear. If this occurs, fluid from the ear cannot drain into the throat and this results in poor hearing and

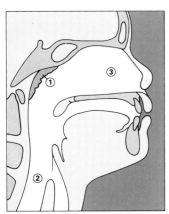

1. Adenoids **2.** Throat
3. Nasal cavity

*The **adenoids**, which are small at birth, begin to grow when the child is about 3 years old. Enlarged adenoids can block the nose, or the Eustachian tube which leads to the ear.*

frequent ear infections. In such cases the doctor may recommend an operation to remove the adenoids so that hearing and breathing are improved. This minor operation is known as an adenoidectomy and is sometimes performed at the same time as surgical removal of the tonsils.
(*See also* Deafness, Glue ear)

Allergic rhinitis
Allergic rhinitis is an allergic reaction of the lining of the nasal passages. It causes a blocked or runny nose and sometimes watery eyes and sneezing. It may be caused by pollens in the air, when it is called hay fever and occurs in the pollen season (April-July), or it may occur as a reaction to other substances, such as house dust, when the symptoms are present throughout the year – this is called perennial rhinitis.

If your child has any symptoms of allergic rhinitis ask your doctor for advice on treatment. Nose drops, sprays and antihistamines can often be used to relieve nasal congestion caused by allergic rhinitis.

Allergies
Allergies are due to an excessive reaction of the body to substances with which it comes into contact. The body can react in many different ways – a rash, bowel disturbance, runny nose and sneezing, or breathing difficulties. Many things can cause allergies in susceptible children, including certain foods, pollens, dust, animal hair, feathers and insect bites. The tendency to develop allergies often runs in families.
(*See also* Allergic rhinitis, Asthma, Eczema, Food allergy, Urticaria)

Ammonia dermatitis
(*See* Diaper rash)

Anemia
Blood is red because of the presence of red pigment (hemoglobin) in the blood cells. Anemia occurs when the

hemoglobin concentration falls below normal. This may be because the hemoglobin content of all the red blood cells is low or because the number of red cells is significantly reduced. Whatever the cause of anemia, the child will look pale, be tired and listless and may become breathless after exertion. If you think your child may be anemic, take him to the doctor. Diagnosis is made with a blood test and treatment depends on the cause of the condition.

The most common cause of anemia in children is insufficient iron in the diet. Iron is needed to manufacture hemoglobin and it is present in meat, fish, eggs and green vegetables. Anemia may also result from blood loss or certain rare diseases.
(*See also* Sickle cell disease, Thalassemia)

Animal bites
(*See* First aid, page 296)

Appendicitis
Appendicitis is inflammation of the appendix, a small sac which is attached to the bowel and has no useful function. If the

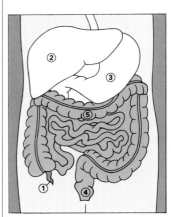

1. Appendix **2.** Liver
3. Stomach **4.** Rectum
5. Intestines (bowel)

*The **appendix** lies at the junction of the large and small intestine. With appendicitis the pain spreads throughout the abdomen, intensifying over the appendix.*

appendix becomes inflamed it causes abdominal pain which starts in the center of the tummy and moves to the lower right-hand side. The child may have a fever, vomit and lose his appetite. The pain tends to get worse the longer it goes on. If your child has these symptoms, call the doctor. Treatment for appendicitis is a fairly simple operation to remove the inflamed appendix.

Very occasionally the inflamed appendix will burst, causing the infection to spread throughout the abdomen. This is called peritonitis and, if it occurs, the child becomes very sick and the pain worsens. In such circumstances call a doctor immediately or take the child to the hospital.

Asthma
Asthma, or repeated episodes of wheezing, is quite common in childhood. It is caused by the narrowing of the small breathing tubes (bronchioles) in the lung which transport air in and out of the body. This narrowing may occur as part of an allergic reaction and is sometimes triggered by a viral lung infection. Wheezing and asthma often run in families and you frequently find that another member of the family suffers from asthma, eczema or hay fever.

The child who has an asthmatic attack will wheeze, breathe faster than normal and he may struggle to get air. He may also cough and even vomit. He should be seen by a doctor who will prescribe treatment. There are a number of drugs which may be used during an asthmatic attack. Some of these are referred to as bronchodilators and they aim to relieve the narrowing or spasm in the airways and so make breathing easier. They can be given as tablets or they are inhaled from an aerosol. A child who is wheezing often has little interest in eating or drinking. It does not matter if he will not eat for a few days but make sure he takes plenty of fluids. It is best to offer fluids

frequently, in small amounts, as the child may vomit if given a large amount at a time. A child who wheezes frequently may benefit from drugs which aim to prevent the allergic reaction from occurring in the first place. These drugs have to be taken regularly, even when the child is well.

It may be worth trying to identify what substances produce the allergic reaction and wheezing. The house dust mite (which lives in house dust), pollen, animal feathers or fur can produce wheezing in susceptible children. It helps to keep the asthmatic child's bedroom as free from dust as possible and to make sure the pillow and bedding are not made from feathers as this can cause irritation. In some children wheezing can be caused by exertion or merely a change in the weather.

Wheezing may start in the first year of life. At this stage it is impossible to say whether or not the child is going to develop asthma. It is only when he has had a few episodes of wheezing that you can assume so. The majority of children with asthma grow out of it during childhood and are left with normal lungs.
(*See* diagram, page 269)

Athlete's foot
(*See* Ringworm)

Bed-wetting
Becoming dry at night is one of the stages of a child's development. Some children reach this stage later than others: in fact 10-15 per cent of otherwise healthy five-year-olds still wet the bed while asleep but will become dry at night within the next few years if they are handled sympathetically. After the age of five, bed wetting (enuresis) is slightly more common in boys than girls and the tendency may run in families.

As the child wets the bed

unconsciously it is a mistake to blame him for doing it. He is more likely to grow out of it if he is treated kindly and praised when he does have a dry night. It may be helpful to reduce the amount of fluid he drinks during the evening and to take him to empty his bladder when you go to bed. Some children who have previously been dry at night suddenly begin wetting again. This may be due to some upset in the child's life. It can also be caused by a urinary infection or a medical condition such as diabetes.

If the wetting is due to an infection, the child will experience discomfort when he urinates or he may pass small amounts frequently. A child with diabetes will pass a lot of urine during the day as well as at night and will be drinking more than usual. If the child has any of these symptoms, consult your doctor.
(*See also* Diabetes, Urinary tract infections)

Bee sting
(*See* First aid, page 297)

Birthmarks
There are several different kinds of birthmark, most of which disappear during childhood without treatment. These include the stork mark – a pink patch on the neck, forehead or eyelids – and the Mongolian blue spot – a bluish mark across the back which is common in black and Asian babies. A less common form of birthmark is the strawberry mark. This dark-red mark is raised and feels a little uneven, but it is not painful. Strawberry marks can occur anywhere on the body and there may be several. They are not usually present at birth but more commonly appear during the first two months of life and gradually fade over a period of months. Most have disappeared by the time the child is five years old.

Bites and stings
(*See* First aid, page 296)

Bleeding
(*See* Emergencies, page 295)

Blisters
(*See* First aid, page 296)

Blood in urine or stools
If you notice blood in your child's urine or stools, you should consult your doctor. The cause is probably a minor one, but it could indicate a more serious condition. (*See also* Constipation, Urinary tract infection)

Blue attacks
(*See* Cyanosis)

Boils
A boil is a small abscess (collection of pus) on the skin, caused by a bacterial infection. The boil may throb, but the child is not generally unwell. Try to keep the child's skin and nails clean to prevent the spread of infection. Sometimes the doctor will treat the boil with antibiotics.

Bow legs
Bow legs are common in toddlers and can be considered as normal in this age group. Provided the bowing is symmetrical (that is, the same degree on each side) it is highly likely to resolve itself by the time the child is three or four. If the leg bowing is severe, asymmetrical or persistent, ask your doctor to examine him. (*See also* Rickets)

Breath-holding attacks
Breath holding is usually caused by frustration and in this respect it is similar to a temper tantrum. Attacks sometimes start towards the end of the first year but they are more common in the second or third year. They rarely occur in children over five. During an attack the child cries, breathes in and fails to take another breath.

The symptoms which develop depend on the interval between breaths. Initially the child goes blue and stiffens, and he may become momentarily unconscious.

THE LUNGS

The lungs are the center of the respiratory system. Each lung contains large breathing tubes (bronchi) which branch out into smaller breathing tubes (bronchioles). At the tip of each bronchiole is an air sac (alveolus) where the exchange of oxygen and carbon dioxide takes place.

1. Trachea (windpipe)
2. Left lung **3.** Bronchi
4. Bronchioles

See Asthma, Bronchiolitis, Bronchitis, Pneumonia

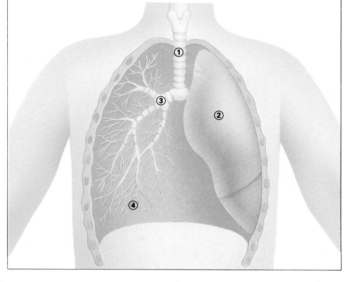

Normal breathing usually starts again spontaneously – the child takes another breath and his color gradually returns. If it does not, call a doctor at once.

Breath-holding attacks are frightening for parents, particularly as there is little that can be done once an attack has started. However, some parents find that giving the child a shake or light slap makes him take another breath more quickly. Try to prevent an attack by avoiding situations which are likely to be frustrating for your child and distract him when he looks as if he is about to start screaming. It is also important for the child to learn that these attacks do not mean that he gets what he wants as this will encourage him to behave in this way. Children always grow out of breath-holding attacks.

Broken bones
(*See* Fractures, page 295)

Bronchiolitis
Bronchiolitis is a viral infection of the bronchioles (the small breathing tubes in the lungs). It usually occurs in children under two years of age and is most common in the first year of life.

At the beginning of the illness the child may have symptoms of a cold (a runny nose and sneezing), but as the infection moves down to the lungs he develops other symptoms such as coughing, wheezing and rapid breathing. He may also have difficulty getting his breath (particularly when feeding) and his lips may go blue when he coughs.

Unfortunately there is no treatment for bronchiolitis, although sometimes the doctor will prescribe antibiotics to prevent any secondary infection. Bronchiolitis gets better by itself in a week or so.

Babies with bronchiolitis can develop feeding problems and

A-Z OF COMMON AILMENTS

quite severe breathing difficulties. If you notice these symptoms it is essential that you consult your doctor; he may suggest that the baby goes into the hospital for observation and treatment.
(*See* diagram, page 269)

Bronchitis
Bronchitis is an infection of the bronchi (the large breathing tubes in the lungs) which is usually caused by a virus. The child with bronchitis has a cough and fever. He may also be breathing faster than usual and wheezing. If your child shows these symptoms, you should consult your family doctor at once.

Antibiotics are sometimes used to prevent the development of secondary bacterial infection in bronchitis. Some children find cough mixtures soothing and occasionally an anti-wheeze drug, prescribed by the doctor, may be helpful. A child with bronchitis may lose his appetite, but it is important to see that he has plenty to drink. Bronchitis usually gets better over a few days and does not cause permanent lung problems.
(*See* diagram, page 269)

Bruises
Bruises occur where blood has leaked into the tissue under the skin. They are usually caused by a knock or fall and will gradually disappear over a week or so without treatment. If your child develops excessive bruising from a slight injury it is important that you consult your doctor as it may mean that there is something wrong with the clotting mechanism of the blood.
(*See also* Purpura)

Burns and scalds
(*See* Emergencies, page 294)

Car sickness
(*See* Travel sickness)

Catarrh
Catarrh is excessive production of mucus by the lining of the nasal passages in response to irritation. The most common form of irritation is a cold. Catarrh may last for several days but it usually clears up by itself. If it does persist, consult your doctor.

Celiac disease
This is an uncommon condition in which the lining of the small intestine is damaged. The damage, which is caused by gluten (a substance found in wheat, rye and oats), prevents the small intestine from absorbing food properly. Children with celiac disease frequently fail to thrive, develop mild diarrhea and may suffer from anemia and vitamin deficiencies. The condition only develops after the child has been exposed to foods containing gluten. If a child with celiac disease avoids all foods which contain gluten, the condition is completely cured and the damaged bowel returns to normal, but the special gluten-free diet must be followed throughout life.

Chest infections
(*See* Bronchiolitis, Bronchitis, Pneumonia)

Chickenpox
Chickenpox is an infectious disease caused by a virus. It is characterized by little "tear drop" spots which appear in groups on the body first, then the face and scalp and finally the limbs. The spots are itchy and easily broken, forming a crust or scab. When the rash begins, the child often has a fever which may last for three to four days. The doctor may suggest giving acetaminophen to reduce temperature. Aspirin should not be given due to an association with Reye syndrome. There is no specific treatment for the spots; just keep the child as comfortable as possible and try to stop him from scratching the spots as this can lead to secondary infection and scarring. The itching can

be reduced by dabbing the rash with calamine lotion, and a daily bath will prevent the spots from becoming infected. Any scars left after the illness can take a few months to disappear.
(*See also* Isolation)

Chilblains
Chilblains are small red itchy areas on the tips of the fingers or toes or at the tops of the ears. Severe cold causes the blood vessels in the exposed parts to constrict so that for a while the blood flow is reduced and they appear white or bluish. The chilblains appear later and are usually at their most painful or itchy when the child is warm. Once they have developed there is no treatment, but if they are severe the doctor may be able to give the child something to relieve the pain. Chilblains usually disappear over two to three weeks. To prevent chilblains, keep your child well wrapped up when he is out in the cold. If he is frequently troubled with them, despite being protected against the cold, you should consult your doctor.

Choking
(*See* Emergencies, page 294)

Circumcision
Circumcision is the surgical removal of part of the foreskin (prepuce) of the penis. It is usually performed for religious and social reasons, rather than for medical reasons. In the baby the foreskin is fused to the glans (the tip of the penis) and cannot be pulled back. As the penis grows during infancy the foreskin gradually separates from the glans so that it can be drawn back in most boys by early childhood. If the child has a very tight foreskin or suffers repeated infections underneath the foreskin such as balanitis, your doctor may advise circumcision.

Cleft lip
A cleft lip is a congenital abnormality of the lip which may occur with a cleft palate. It

can vary from a small notch in the upper lip to a complete cleft that extends into the nostril. Treatment involves surgery, usually within three months of birth.
(*See also* **Cleft palate**)

Cleft palate

A cleft palate, either alone or in association with a cleft or hare lip, is an abnormality which is present at birth. The palate makes up the roof of the mouth and separates the mouth from the nasal passages. When it is cleft there is a central gap in the part of the palate that lies at the back of the mouth. An untreated cleft palate causes feeding difficulties and speech problems. It is usually repaired by surgery in the first few months of life, once the baby is thriving and gaining weight satisfactorily.
(*See also* **Cleft lip**)

Clicking hip

(*See* **Congenital dislocated hip**)

Colds

These are infections of the nose and throat caused by a virus. The child has a runny or blocked nose, may cough, complain of a sore throat and become feverish. Small children with colds often stop eating for a few days. There is no known cure for a cold and antibiotics do not help. If there is fever your doctor may advise giving acetominophen to reduce temperature and ease the sore throat. In small babies the blocked nose can make feeding difficult so your doctor may prescribe nose drops.
(*See also* **Influenza**)

Cold sores

A cold sore is one or more clear spots with underlying red skin which typically occur on the lips or near the mouth. The spots, which may be painful, burst, crust over and heal without treatment within 10 days. They do not usually leave scars. Cold sores are caused by the herpes simplex virus and can recur when the child has a cold, a chest infection or has been in strong sunlight.

Colic

Colic is a type of unremitting crying. The cause is not known but some people think it is related to tummy ache occurring in spasms and due to gas. Infantile colic makes the baby draw his knees up and cry. It may occur a number of times a day but in between the baby feeds satisfactorily and appears quite well. This type of colic, which occurs in both bottle and breastfed babies, can be quite troublesome for the first three months or so of life. It may help to give the baby plenty of time on your lap or in your arms after a feeding. Occasionally your doctor wil prescribe some medicine.

Color blindness

Color blindness is not uncommon in boys but very rare in girls. The color-blind child has difficulty in distinguishing reds and greens but in other respects sees perfectly well. Color blindness is often only discovered when a child is tested with special color charts. Color blindness may run in families and there is no treatment for it, but it is not a serious disability.

Coma

Coma describes a state of unconsciousness from which it is not possible to rouse the

---

UPPER RESPIRATORY SYSTEM

1. Nasal cavity

2. Tongue **3.** Tonsils

4. Hard palate

5. Soft palate

6. Adenoids

7. Pharynx (throat)

8. Larynx (voicebox)

Air enters the respiratory system through the nose and mouth. It passes down the pharynx, into the larynx and into the lower respiratory system – the windpipe and lungs. The upper respiratory tract includes the nose, throat and larynx.

See **Adenoids, Colds, Laryngitis, Pharyngitis, Tonsillitis, Upper respiratory tract infection**

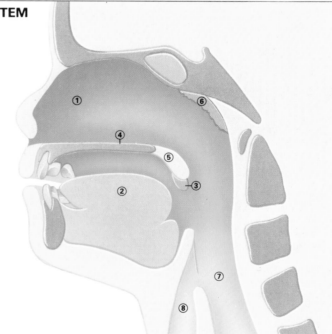

See Feeding your baby, page 96, for colic.

patient. It is a very serious condition and may be caused by a head injury, certain forms of poisoning, infections of the brain (meningitis or encephalitis) or a low sugar level in the blood. If your child becomes comatose you should lie him down on his side, so that if he vomits he will not inhale the vomit, and call an ambulance immediately. (*See also* **Head injuries, page 278**)

Concussion
(*See* **Head injuries, page 295**)

Congenital defects
These are abnormalities with which a child is born. They range from minor blemishes such as birthmarks to more serious abnormalities involving organs such as the heart, lungs or bowel. In such cases treatment will depend on the exact nature of the abnormality. (*See also* **Cleft lip, Cleft palate, Congenital dislocated hip, Heart disease**)

Congenital dislocated hip
The hip is a joint that works like a ball and socket, the top of the leg being the ball and part of the pelvis (hip bone) being the socket. In some babies the socket is rather shallow at birth and allows the leg bone to slip in and out. Although this is not visible at birth, a doctor can feel whether the hip moves in and out (dislocates) when he examines the baby. It is more common for the doctor to feel a click as he moves the hip, without it actually slipping out of the socket (a "clicking" hip). In this case all that is usually required is for the baby to be checked again, once or twice, to make sure the joint becomes completely stable over the first few months of life. Some doctors suggest using two diapers during these early weeks to secure the leg bone firmly in the socket. It is extremely unusual for a simple clicking hip to need more treatment than this.

If the baby's hip is dislocated, the doctor will recommend an early visit to an orthopedic surgeon (bone specialist) so that the hip can be placed in the best position for normal development. This may involve the baby wearing special splints and, very occasionally, an operation may be necessary. If congenital dislocated hips are left untreated they can lead to a limp and arthritis in later life.

Conjunctivitis
Conjunctivitis, or pink eye, is inflammation of the conjunctiva – the outer lining of the eyeball and the inner lining of the eyelids. It results in the white part of the eye appearing red. Sometimes there is a yellowish discharge and the eye feels itchy. There are a number of causes – a bacterial infection, a virus, an allergy to pollen, or a foreign body (such as a piece of dirt) in the eye. It is usual for both eyes to become inflamed but when conjunctivitis is caused by a foreign body only one eye is affected.

After consulting the doctor, the first thing to do is to wipe away any discharge with some absorbent cotton moistened in clean water and remove any grit from the eye. If it has caused an abrasion your doctor may prescribe antibiotic eye drops (*see* below) or cream. He may also prescribe these if he

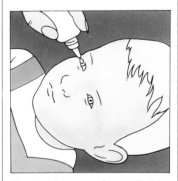

To administer **eye drops**, tilt the child's head back slightly and put the drops in the outer edge of the open eye. When the child blinks, the drops will flow over the eye.

suspects a bacterial infection.

Antibiotic creams should be applied, with clean hands, by pulling down the lower lid and placing a little cream on the eye. When the child blinks, the cream is spread over the affected area. For allergic conjunctivitis the doctor may suggest using some anti-allergic eye drops. If a child is suffering from infectious conjunctivitis give him his own towel and washcloth and keep them separate from those of the rest of the family. Keep the eye clean by washing it regularly with warm water.

A mild form of conjunctivitis, called sticky eye, is common in babies. This is often made worse because a baby's tear ducts are too small to drain the eye properly. The eyes should be bathed regularly with clean water and absorbent cotton; your doctor may prescribe antibiotic drops. (*See also* **Allergic rhinitis**)

Constipation
The number of times a day or week that a healthy child moves his bowels varies greatly. Constipation is when the stools are hard and difficult to expel. If your child is passing stools of soft or firm consistency infrequently and he does not strain unduly when doing so, he is not constipated. If, on the other hand, the stools are hard, passed with difficulty and are occasionally blood-streaked he is likely to be constipated. Blood streaking comes from anal fissures (little tears) which are caused by the passage of hard stools through the anus. In the vast majority of children constipation is a temporary problem which can be resolved by changes in diet. A young child can be given more water or a little prune juice on a spoon. An older child's diet should contain more fruit, vegetables and whole-grain cereals to increase the fiber content. If the problem persists your doctor may prescribe a laxative for a short period.

Some children become

constipated because they put off going to the toilet. This can happen when a child is away from home (perhaps on vacation) and takes a dislike to a strange toilet. It might help to encourage the child to go at set times every day, say after a meal.
(*See also* **Abdominal pain, Encopresis**)

Convulsions

Electrical activity occurs all the time in the brain and convulsions are caused by abnormal bursts of activity. As a result the convulsing child may have jerking limb movements, his eyes may roll back, he may become pale, be unresponsive or semi-conscious, and he may wet and soil himself. The vast majority of convulsions stop spontaneously after some minutes, but they are very frightening for parents.

There are many causes of convulsions, but by far the most common in infancy and childhood are those brought on by high fever. These are known as febrile convulsions and they occur in five per cent of normal healthy children between the ages of six months and five years. It is the raised temperature, often up to 40°C (104°F), which sets off the abnormal activity in the brain, so that the convulsion may occur at the beginning of an illness before the parents have realized that the child is sick. Infections of the ear, nose and throat are often responsible for the fever.

If a child has a convulsion consult your doctor at once. It may be necessary for the child to go to the hospital although the doctor may be happy to look after him at home, particularly if he has had convulsions before. If the fit is prolonged the doctor will give him an injection to stop it.

Once your child has had a febrile convulsion, he is likely to have another so you need to be aware of his temperature when he is sick. If he becomes feverish keep him cool, give

him acetominophen to reduce the temperature and call your doctor. The doctor may advise the use of regular anti-convulsant drugs in some children who have repeated febrile convulsions, but medical opinion is divided about this. Simple febrile convulsions do not cause brain damage and children grow out of them by the time they are four or five years old.

Much less common types of convulsions are those caused by infection of the brain (meningitis), low sugar or calcium level in the blood, or certain rare inherited diseases. If the doctor is uncertain about the cause of a convulsion he may recommend that the child is examined in the hospital.

Convulsions can sometimes occur in otherwise healthy children for no apparent reason. This is referred to as idiopathic epilepsy. In such cases the doctor may recommend that the child has regular anti-convulsant medication.
(*See also* **Meningitis, and First aid, page 297**)

Coughs

Coughing is a mechanism that allows the body to cope with inflammation or irritation in the throat or breathing tubes in the lungs. The action forces air out of the lungs at high pressure and thus expels any mucus, secretions or even an inhaled foreign body from the breathing tubes.

Coughs often occur in conjunction with colds as part of a viral infection of the upper airways and throat. In this situation no special treatment is needed, although your doctor may prescribe medicine to soothe the cough.

A cough is sometimes the result of an infection in the lungs, such as bronchiolitis, bronchitis or pneumonia. It may also occur with asthma or following accidental inhalation of a foreign body, such as a peanut. In these cases, the treatment that your doctor prescribes will depend on the

primary cause of the cough.
(*See also* **Croup, and Choking, page 294**)

Cradle cap

Cradle cap is greasy yellow scales and crusting over the top of a baby's scalp. Sometimes there are also patches of dry, red, itchy skin over the face, body and diaper area. This is a form of eczema known as seborrheic dermatitis. The scales on the scalp can be removed by daily shampooing, after they have been moistened overnight with an oily preparation such as olive oil. If the patches on the face or body are troublesome you may need to get a special cream or lotion from the doctor, although very often they will clear up spontaneously after a short time.

Crib death

Crib death is the unexplained death of a baby, usually while he is sleeping. It is also known as "sudden infant death syndrome." It is something that every parent dreads, but fortunately it is much less common than you might think. Many of the babies who die in this way are between two and six months of age and the majority appear perfectly healthy when put to bed. At present, research has not uncovered the cause, but a number of theories exist, including abnormal control of breathing, allergy or an infection.

Croup

Croup is caused by an infection around the larynx, or voice box. More usual in winter, it is most common in toddlers but can occur at any age in childhood. The croupy child has an unusual barking cough and noisy breathing which is often worse when he breathes in. He may also have a fever. These symptoms can develop quite suddenly and can be frightening for the child and parents. Humidified air may help the condition and this can be provided in the home by

See Common worries, page 129, for crib death.

steam from a gently boiling kettle (but do make sure that the child cannot pull the kettle over). However, it is essential that any child who develops croup is seen by a doctor. He may suggest that the child should go into the hospital for observation and for any necessary treatment.

Cuts and scratches
(*See* First aid, page 297)

Cyanosis
Cyanosis (blue attacks) refers to the blue appearance of lips, fingers and toes. The blueness is caused by reduced oxygen in the blood and tissues and occurs with some diseases of the heart and lungs. If cyanosis develops call your doctor immediately or take the child directly to a hospital emergency room.

Sometimes a child's hands and feet go blue with cold, but this is not serious and normal color will return as the child gets warm..

A child may go blue with a breath-holding attack, but normal color will return when he takes another breath.

Cystic fibrosis
Cystic fibrosis is one of the most common inherited diseases. It causes lung infections and difficulties with absorbing nutrients in food. Although both the parents of a child with cystic fibrosis are physically healthy, they each carry the abnormal cystic fibrosis gene and there is a one-in-four chance of them producing an affected child at each pregnancy. Unfortunately there is no way at present of identifying healthy people with the abnormal gene until they have a child with cystic fibrosis. The condition is diagnosed when the child fails to thrive or has recurrent chest infections. Regular medical treatment, physiotherapy and attention to the child's diet can help considerably.

Cystitis
(*See* Urinary tract infection)

D

Deafness
To understand the different types of deafness it is necessary to have a little knowledge of the ear and how we hear. Sounds are vibrations of the air which enter the outer ear and strike the ear-drum. On the other side of the drum, in the middle ear, are three tiny bones (the ossicles) through which the vibrations pass to reach the inner ear. This contains the organ of hearing – the cochlea – and within this are nerve fibers which detect the sounds and carry them to the brain. The Eustachian tube connects the middle ear to the back of the throat, thereby maintaining the air pressure in the middle ear.

Deafness can be caused by a blockage somewhere along the passage from the external ear canal to the cochlea (conductive deafness), or by a disorder which affects the cochlea or the nerves (nerve deafness). The two types of deafness can involve both ears or just one, and the degree of hearing loss may be variable. The most common cause of poor hearing in children is temporary conductive deafness due to a blockage in the Eustachian tube. As a result of the blockage fluid collects in the middle ear and prevents the proper conduction of sounds through to the inner ear. This type of deafness can occur with a common cold.

Conductive deafness can also be caused by glue ear, perforation of the ear-drum, otitis media or damage to the ear bones. Deafness caused by maldevelopment or damage to the cochlea or nerves is much less common and can result in partial or total deafness.

In childhood, hearing is essential for language development so any loss of

---

THE EAR

1. Outer ear   **2.** Ear canal
3. Ear-drum   **4.** Ossicles
5. Middle ear   **6.** Inner ear
7. Cochlea
8. Balancing apparatus
9. Auditory nerve
10. Eustachian tube

The ear is divided into 3 parts – the outer, middle and inner ear. Sound travels along the ear canal to the ear-drum and passes through the middle ear via 3 bones (ossicles) to the cochlea in the inner ear.

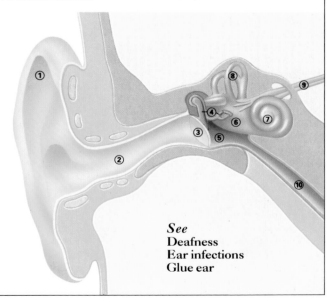

See
Deafness
Ear infections
Glue ear

hearing, however slight, should be recognized as soon as possible and treated promptly. Routine examination of a baby's hearing is carried out at a pediatrician's office and if any abnormality is detected the baby will be assessed by a specialist. However, if you think there is something wrong with your child's hearing at any time you should consult your doctor about it.
(*See* also Ear infections, Glue ear)

Dehydration
(*See* Diarrhea, Fever)

Dermatitis
(*See* Eczema, Diaper rash)

Diabetes
Diabetes results from a deficiency of insulin which controls the sugar level in the blood and tissues. The body fails to produce sufficient insulin and this results in a high blood sugar level. Because of this the diabetic child will feel thirsty, drink excessively and pass a lot of urine. He may also lose weight and feel generally unwell. If you notice these symptoms, consult your doctor. Once the diagnosis is made treatment with insulin injections is started and the blood sugar level returns to normal. Lifelong treatment is necessary and a special diet should be followed to help control the condition.

Diaper rash
This is a red blotchy rash in the diaper area which is very common in babies. It can be caused by a fungal infection, such as thrush, or by a reaction of the skin to wet and soiled diapers. To prevent or clear the rash, the baby's bottom should be kept as clean and dry as possible. This is best done by changing the diaper frequently and leaving it off whenever possible to expose the skin to the air. At each diaper change clean the baby's bottom and apply a barrier cream such as zinc oxide ointment. Waterproof pants should be

avoided as they tend to keep the skin moist and this will exacerbate the problem. If cloth diapers are used, avoid washing them with a strong detergent and always rinse them thoroughly at the end of the wash. If thrush infection is suspected your doctor will prescribe an antifungal cream.

Diarrhea
Diarrhea is the frequent passing of loose watery stools. In childhood it usually occurs with gastroenteritis, an infection of the bowel.

It is very important for a child with diarrhea not to become dehydrated. This will happen if he is losing more fluid in the diarrhea than he is taking by mouth. You should therefore cut out all solid food and give plenty of fluids. Small babies in particular need to be watched carefully as they can become dehydrated very easily. Sometimes your doctor will prescribe a special mixture of glucose and salt (Pedilyte) which you can make up with water. It is better to give small amounts of fluid frequently as your child is more likely to tolerate these than large amounts. When the diarrhea appears to be settling (usually over 24-28 hours), diluted milk and a light diet can be reintroduced. If the child remains well, a normal diet can gradually be given.

Less acute forms of diarrhea, with frequent loose movements, may relate to intolerance to certain foods and other problems of the bowel. In such cases the child does not usually become ill suddenly, but may fail to gain weight in the normal way. If your child develops these symptoms, consult your doctor.
(*See* also **Celiac disease, Gastroenteritis**)

Diphtheria
Diphtheria is a serious and highly infectious bacterial disease which causes inflammation of the nose and throat. This inflammation may become so severe that it

interferes with the child's breathing. Every child should be protected against diphtheria by immunization, which is part of the triple vaccine (diphtheria, tetanus and whooping cough) given in the first few months of life. As a result of immunization, there is practically no chance of catching it.
(*See* also **Immunization chart, page 127**)

Dislocations
(*See* **Congenital dislocated hip, and page 295**)

Dyslexia
Dyslexia is difficulty in reading or learning to read. It is sometimes accompanied by writing and spelling problems. Affected children do not show backwardness in other school subjects and many of them are of average or above average intelligence. Dyslexic children usually benefit from extra, specialized help with their reading and spelling.

Earache
Earache can be caused by infection in the outer ear (otitis externa) or inflammation of the middle ear (otitis media).
(*See* also **Ear infections**)

Ear infections
One of the most common illnesses of childhood is otitis media – inflammation of the middle ear. It is estimated to have occurred in 20 per cent of children by the time they are five years old. The illness can be caused by a bacterial infection or a virus and it may be accompanied by a cold or tonsillitis. The child with otitis media is often unwell and feverish and may complain of earache or headache; he may even appear to be slightly deaf. As the inflammation progresses the middle ear fills with fluid and this causes the pain and deafness to worsen. Sometimes the only indication of the infection in a small child is that

See Diaper changing, page 106, for diaper rash.

he repeatedly pulls or rubs his ear. If your child has any of these symptoms, consult your doctor. Treatment involves giving acetaminophen to relieve pain and fever, nasal decongestants to assist drainage of the infected area, and antibiotics to clear the infection. Sometimes the eardrum ruptures with the pressure of fluid. This relieves the pain and produces a discharge from the ear. Consult your doctor if this happens.

If a child has repeated attacks of otitis media the doctor may recommend that he is seen by an ear, nose and throat (ENT) specialist. Treatment may include the insertion of myringotomy tubes (tiny plastic tubes) to help drain the infected material from the ear, and removal of the adenoids.

Otitis externa is inflammation of the external ear canal. It is caused by a bacterial infection, a virus or a fungal infection. The inflammation may cause pain or itchiness in the ear canal and sometimes there is a discharge from the ear. If this occurs, consult your doctor. After examining the ear canal the doctor will probably prescribe ear drops. It is important that the ear canal is kept dry until the infection has cleared up so take care when washing the child's hair and do not allow him to go swimming.
(*See also* **Deafness, Glue ear, and diagram, page 278**)

Eczema

Eczema, or atopic dermatitis, refers to a group of skin complaints which are characterized by a red, itchy rash. The most common type is atopic, or allergic, eczema. This occurs more often in early childhood among children where there is a family history of asthma, eczema or hay fever.

Eczema often starts in the first four months of life and at this stage affects the body and face. As the child gets older it tends to involve the crook of the elbow, the back of the knee and the wrists and ankles.

Most children grow out of eczema in time. However, during its course it can be a very uncomfortable condition. Any child who suffers from it should avoid wearing tight-fitting, rough-fibered garments; loose, cotton clothing is best. You should consult your doctor about the use of special ointments, moisturizing preparations and mild bath oils. Eczema is sometimes made worse by certain foods, so your doctor may recommend that you leave these out of the child's diet.

Another type of eczema is seborrheic dermatitis which occurs with cradle cap in some babies and is treated similarly.
(*See also* **Cradle cap, Food allergy**)

Electric shock
(*See* **Emergencies, page 294**)

Encopresis

Encopresis, or fecal soiling, occurs when a child who is toilet trained starts to pass stools in his pants. In some cases it is due to a behavioral problem, in others it relates to chronic constipation and may be accompanied by a tummy ache. Neither problem is simple to cure and both require patient and sympathetic handling. If an emotional problem is the cause of the encopresis try not to scold the child. Show him that while you do not approve of what has happened you are trying to help by finding out what is upsetting him. If the problem persists you should consult your doctor who may be able to advise you or will refer you to a specialist.

If encopresis is due to chronic constipation the soiling is usually just a small amount of liquid stools which stain the underwear. This soiling occurs because soft, liquid stools from higher up in the bowel leak down around the hard stools which the child cannot pass. The child is unable to prevent these liquid stools seeping out, so there is no point in scolding

him. For this problem the doctor will probably recommend laxatives and stool softeners to relieve the constipation. If a child is frequently constipated it helps to introduce more fiber (fruit, vegetables, bran) to his diet.
(*See also* **Constipation**)

Enuresis
(*See* **Bed wetting**)

Epilepsy
(*See* **Convulsions**)

Eye infections
(*See* **Conjunctivitis, Styes**)

Eye injuries
(*See* **First aid, page 297**)

Fainting

Fainting is a brief loss of consciousness caused by a temporary upset in the blood supply to the brain. The fainting child may complain of a "whoosey" feeling in the head, become pale and floppy and be unable to stand alone. Fainting more often occurs in adults and adolescents, when it may be precipitated by standing for long periods in hot stuffy places, or by a shock or pain.

If a child feels faint make him lie down or sit with his head between his knees, and let some fresh air into the room. A sip of water may make him feel better. Do not try to hold a fainting child upright.

If a child who has fainted does not regain consciousness in a few seconds, call a doctor. A small child who faints for no apparent reason should be seen at once by a doctor as he may have had a convulsion.

Febrile convulsions
(*See* **Convulsions**)

Fecal soiling
(*See* **Encopresis**)

Fever

Fever occurs when the body temperature rises above normal

(37°C/98.6°F) and usually represents a reaction to infection. The infection that is causing the fever is often an obvious one, such as a cold, but it is advisable to have a feverish child examined by a doctor so that the cause can be established and treated.

While it may make the child feel unwell the high temperature is not usually harmful, except in a young child with a tendency to febrile convulsions. A feverish child will feel more comfortable if he is kept cool. Consult your doctor, who may prescribe an anti-fever medicine, such as acetaminophen, to bring down the child's temperature. A feverish child will not feel like eating and should not be forced to do so, but encourage him to drink as much as he can. His appetite will return as the fever subsides.
(*See also* Convulsions)

First Aid
(*See* pages 296-297)

Fits
(*See* Convulsions)

Flat feet
The feet of infants and small children are fatter, wider and flatter than those of older children and adults. In young children fatty pads create a fullness on the undersurface of the foot so that the arch is not visible. This is quite normal. As the child grows older this fatty pad disappears and the arch is revealed.

Fleas
(*See* Bites and stings, page 291)

Food allergy
Some children develop symptoms because of an abnormal reaction to certain foods. This reaction, which is often called food allergy, takes a variety of forms and affects different parts of the body.

Allergy or sensitivity to cows' milk may occur in infancy. Reactions sometimes follow a bout of gastroenteritis or the introduction of cows' milk to the baby's diet. In the former case, when the infection has settled down, the child continues to have diarrhea and/or vomiting when he drinks cows' milk. The doctor may advise you to cut out cows' milk and give a substitute, such as soy baby formula. After a few months the child usually loses his sensitivity and is able to drink cows' milk again, but it should be reintroduced carefully with your doctor's supervision.

Apart from diarrhea and vomiting, food allergy can produce urticaria or wheezing, and children already suffering from eczema may get worse. A variety of foods may be responsible for allergic reactions, although the most common are eggs, cows' milk and peanuts. When a single food produces an obvious reaction it should be excluded from the child's diet. A child with eczema – even if he shows no obvious reaction – may benefit from a diet which excludes certain foods. It is difficult to work out special elimination diets so it is essential that you consult your doctor before considering any alteration as the child's diet must be nutritionally balanced. At the present time much attention is given to the possible harmful effects of food additives and preservatives, but you should seek professional advice about this.
(*See also* Eczema, Urticaria)

Fracture
(*See* Emergencies, page 295)

Gastroenteritis
This is infectious diarrhea which is usually accompanied by vomiting. Most attacks are caused by a bacterial or viral infection of the bowel and they are not usually helped by antibiotics or medicine that slows down the frequency of bowel movements. The child may be generally unwell with a tummy ache and fever, so consult your doctor about treatment. It is most important to give the child plenty to drink to prevent him from becoming dehydrated.

Gastroenteritis usually clears up after a few days, but very occasionally a child who has a severe attack will be admitted to hospital for more intensive treatment of dehydration.

Gastroenteritis occurs less often in breastfed babies as the breast milk contains antibodies that help protect against infection.
(*See also* Abdominal pain, Diarrhea)

German measles
German measles, or rubella, is an infectious disease caused by a virus. It produces a red blotchy rash, a mild fever and enlargement of the glands at the back of the neck. It is not a serious disease in childhood and lasts for only a few days. Specific treatment is not required; just try to keep the child comfortable. However, if the disease is contracted during pregnancy (particularly in the first three months), it can damage the baby in the womb. Because of this very serious complication it is now recommended that all children receive immunization at 15 months of age (measles, mumps, rubella combined vaccine). Otherwise it should be given at an age up to adolescence. Any child with German measles is infectious to others who have not had it from a week before the rash appears to five days afterwards. If the child does come into contact with an unimmunized pregnant woman during this time you should advise her to consult a doctor immediately.
(*See also* Isolation)

Glue ear
Glue ear, or secretory otitis media, is a condition in which the middle ear chamber is filled with fluid. In time this fluid becomes thick and sticky, like glue, and prevents sound

vibrations passing through the middle ear. There is no associated pain or fever, but the child's hearing is impaired. Glue ear may affect one or both ears and usually follows an acute infection of the middle ear (otitis media) in association with a blocked Eustachian tube. This blockage is often caused by enlarged adenoids.

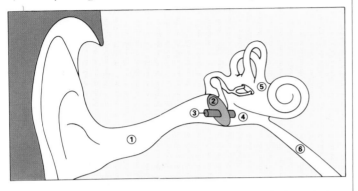

1. Ear canal   2. Ear-drum
3. Tube   4. Middle ear
5. Inner ear   6. Eustachian tube

A myringotomy tube is put in the ear-drum to drain the fluid which causes **glue ear**.

Treatment for glue ear includes antibiotics and nasal decongestants initially, but if these fail to cure the condition an operation may be necessary. The adenoids are removed, and the "glue" is sucked out through a slit made in the ear-drum. Tiny plastic tubes called myringotomy tubes are inserted into the slit to allow air to pass into the middle ear and the fluid to drain out. While a child has the myringotomy tubes in place he should keep his ears dry and avoid swimming. The myringotomy tubes usually fall out of their own accord after some months and the ear-drum heals with no further problem.
(*See also* **Deafness, and diagram, page 274**)

"Growing" pains
Children sometimes complain of pain in their legs and occasionally in their arms. These pains often seem to keep the child awake at night, although he is otherwise quite well, can move his limbs normally and has no bruising or swelling of the painful limb.

The cause of the pains is unknown, but it may relate to swelling of the muscles after a day of strenuous exercise or to hypertensible joints. Whatever the cause, the pains are not serious and will disappear in time. Often, massaging the limbs and putting a warm hot water bottle on or near them will ease the pain. If the pain persists or is associated with other problems, or if you are uneasy, consult your doctor.

H

Hay fever
(*See* **Allergic rhinitis**)

Headache
A headache is a common childhood complaint that has many possible causes. A child may have a headache with a fever, brought on by flu or an upper respiratory tract infection. Headache can also occur with earache or toothache. In such cases treating the complaint itself usually relieves the headache.

Recurrent headaches, when the child is perfectly well in between, also occur in childhood. They may have an emotional basis or they may be migraines, but you should consult your doctor.

A headache in conjunction with a temperature, vomiting, drowsiness and reluctance to look at the light may indicate a more serious disease, such as meningitis. If your child has these symptoms, consult your doctor immediately.
(*See also* **Meningitis**)

Head banging
Many normal children show repetitive movements at some stage of development – head banging, head rolling and rocking are examples of these. As long as it is a passing phase and does not interfere with the child's activities it can be regarded as normal and harmless.

Head rolling and rocking may be seen in the second six months of life. The baby will roll his head from side to side and may rock when he is put down in his crib on his back. Some children find these movements comforting and they generally stop after a while.

A child between the ages of one and two may bang his head on the side of the crib, the wall or the floor. This can be due to a temper tantrum or because the child wants attention. Kind and firm handling may help to prevent these episodes, but if they do occur the child should be placed where he cannot hurt himself. In fact it is very rare for children who head bang to do themselves any injury.

Frequent and persistent head banging is a cause for concern. If it becomes a problem you should consult your doctor; he may be able to offer some advice.

Head injuries
(*See* **Emergencies, page 295**)

Head lice
It is not uncommon for pre-school and schoolchildren to have head lice. They are transferred from child to child and their presence does not necessarily indicate a lack of hygiene. The eggs of the louse, called nits, are laid on the hair and appear as small grey-white specks which do not brush off. If you look carefully you may see a louse moving on the scalp. The lice cause the child

to scratch his scalp and this can lead to some secondary infection if left untreated. Consult your doctor about treatment; he will recommend a special shampoo. Other members of the family should be closely examined for nits and if there is any sign that they are infected they should be treated also.

Heart disease
Unlike in adults, heart disease in children is nearly always the result of a structural abnormality in the heart which has been present since birth. The majority of children with congenital heart disease appear perfectly well and the abnormality is only detected when a doctor listens to the child's heart with a stethoscope. However, there is sometimes other evidence of the problem, such as breathlessness or cyanosis (blueness of the lips).

Most heart defects in childhood are not serious and consist of a small hole between two of the chambers of the heart or an abnormality in one of the blood vessels. These abnormalities do not usually require any treatment and they will resolve themselves in time. However, if the problem is more complicated, the doctor may prescribe drugs, or an operation may be necessary. (*See also* Cyanosis)

Heart murmur
Murmurs are noises heard by a doctor when he listens to the heart with a stethoscope. They are caused by a disturbance in the flow of blood as it passes through the heart. This disturbance can be caused by some structural abnormality of the heart, as in congenital heart disease, or may just relate to the flow of blood itself. Some healthy children with perfectly normal hearts have a murmur caused by the blood flow. These are referred to as innocent murmurs; they are harmless and disappear as the child gets older. (*See also* Heart disease)

Hepatitis
(*See* Jaundice)

Hernias
A hernia is a protrusion of tissue through the wall of the cavity which contains it. Hernias in the groin (inguinal hernias) are not uncommon in small children. They produce a swelling in the groin which may be visible only when the child is crying or coughing. Any child who has such a swelling should be seen by a doctor as the minor operation which is needed to repair the hernia should not be delayed.

Umbilical hernias, which are swellings through the belly button, occur occasionally. They do not cause problems and need no treatment as they get smaller and disappear as the child gets older. Hernias do occur in other parts of the body, but these are uncommon. The majority require surgical treatment.

Herpes simplex
(*See* Cold sores)

Herpes stomatitis
(*See* Mouth infections)

Hiccups
Hiccups can occur in babies and children. They rarely last for longer than a few minutes and are not harmful.

Hives
(*See* Urticaria)

Hyperactivity
Many toddlers are extremely active and appear never to tire. These children are normal. Hyperactivity refers to those children who combine frenetic activity with an inability to focus on anything. Their behavior often appears impulsive and restless, they have poor concentration and are easily distracted. The hyperactive child may be prevented from concentrating at school, resulting in serious setbacks to learning. A small proportion of hyperactive children are mentally retarded, but the vast majority are otherwise quite well.

The cause of hyperactive behavior remains uncertain, although allergy to certain foods and food additives may play a part in some cases. If your child shows signs of being hyperactive, consult your doctor. Medicines and special diets are used in the treatment of some hyperactive children.

Whatever the cause, hyperactive children benefit from consistent, firm and kind handling within an orderly environment without distractions. The condition usually improves with age.

I

Immunization
Immunization, or vaccination, is a process by which protection against disease (immunity) is obtained by giving a small amount of the germ which causes the disease. The germ, or vaccine, which is either dead or inactive, stimulates the body to produce defense cells that can fight the disease without causing the illness itself. As a result, when the real infection occurs, a larger quantity of these defense cells are produced very quickly by the body and they prevent the disease from developing.

It is by the use of immunization or vaccination programs that many very serious diseases, such as tetanus, diphtheria and polio, have been almost eradicated. In order to maintain this situation children must be immunized at various stages of their development. Most health authorities give the triple DTP vaccine – diphtheria, tetanus and whooping cough – with the oral polio vaccine when the child is two months old. The aim of starting early is to protect against whooping cough which can be a very serious condition in babies.

The second and third DTP and oral polio vaccinations are given at about four and six

See Your baby's health, page 127, for immunization schedule.

A-Z OF COMMON AILMENTS

months of age. The child should receive a booster against diphtheria, tetanus and polio one year later and when he is about five years old. The MMR (measles, mumps and rubella) vaccination is generally given at 15 months and a diphtheria and tetanus between the ages of 14 and 16 years.

Occasionally there may be indications against immunization (contra-indications). For example, the doctor may advise postponing immunization if your baby has a bad viral infection. He should also be told if your child has had a convulsion, suffered brain damage at birth or if any close relative suffers from epilepsy. In such circumstances the doctor may decide to omit the whooping cough vaccine because of the increased risk of complications.
(*See also* **Isolation, Tuberculosis, Whooping cough,** and **Immunization chart, page 127**)

Impetigo

Impetigo is a skin disease caused by bacteria. It can occur anywhere on the body, but it usually begins on the face with red spots which rapidly become little blisters and then pustules. These spots weep and form yellow crusts. The infection can spread to other parts of the body as a result of the child scratching the spots, and it can also be passed on to other children very easily.

The doctor will suggest localized treatment, such as dabbing the crusts with an antiseptic solution three or four times a day to gently remove them. Washing with a medicated soap may also help, but the infection will clear more rapidly if treated with antibiotics.

Infantile paralysis
(*See* **Poliomyelitis**)

Influenza

Influenza, or flu, is a disease caused by the influenza virus. It is not normally a serious condition and usually lasts for about three or four days. Typical symptoms are fever, aches and pains, a headache and a cold. A child who has influenza will often stop eating.

There is no cure for the flu, but it will get better by itself over a period of days. Antibiotics have no effect against viruses but, if the child is feverish, acetaminophen will help to bring the child's temperature down and ease aches and pains. Aspirin should not be used due to its association with Reye Syndrome.

Insect bites
(*See* **Bites and stings, page 297**)

Isolation

Medical opinion is divided about the value or necessity of keeping a child in isolation. The isolation period of an illness is the time during which the infected person can pass the disease on to someone else, but as the most infectious stage is often before there are any outward signs it is very difficult to know when to isolate the child. In some cases it is necessary for other members of the family or friends to be protected from an infectious disease. Your doctor can advise you about this. The chart below gives isolation periods for the most common infectious diseases in childhood.

Jaundice

Jaundice is a yellow discoloration of the skin which is also visible in the whites of the eyes. It is the result of too much yellow pigment, called bilirubin, in the blood. Jaundice is common in newborn babies. It usually develops on the second or third day of life and disappears without treatment after about a week. There are many causes of jaundice at this age, but it most commonly occurs because the baby's body is adjusting to life outside the womb.

Jaundice in older children is quite uncommon and it is never normal. It can be an indication of infectious hepatitis and the

ISOLATION PERIOD FOR INFECTIOUS DISEASES

DISEASE	INCUBATION*	INFECTIOUS PERIOD
Chickenpox	1-3 weeks	The child is infectious from 2 days before the rash shows until all the spots have crusted.
German measles (rubella)	2-3 weeks	7 days before the onset of the rash until 5 days afterwards. If the child is in contact with a pregnant woman during this period, advise her to consult a doctor.
Measles	1-2 weeks	10 days before the rash appears until 5 days afterwards.
Mumps	2-4 weeks	10 days after the onset of the parotid swelling.
Whooping cough (pertussis)	1-2 weeks of catarrh and another 1-2 weeks until the cough appears.	The child is infectious for about 4 weeks after the onset of the cough.
*The incubation period of a disease is the time from exposure to the disease until the first symptoms show.		

jaundiced child should be seen by a doctor to establish whether any tests are necessary and how it should be treated.

K

Knock knees
This is when a child cannot put his ankles together while his knees are touching. Some toddlers have mild knock knees, which improve on their own by the time the child is six or seven years old. If the condition is marked and does not disappear with age, or it appears to be getting worse, you should consult your doctor. If necessary, the doctor will refer the child to an orthopedic surgeon (bone specialist) who will be able to advise on treatment.

L

Laryngitis
Laryngitis is inflammation of the larynx, or voicebox. In adults and older children it usually produces a hoarseness, and sometimes loss of voice; in young children, who have a smaller voicebox, the inflammation may lead to an attack of croup.
(*See also* **Croup, and diagram, page 271**)

Lice
(*See* **Head lice**)

Lymph glands
(*See* **Swollen glands**)

M

Measles
Measles is an infectious disease caused by a virus. Because it is such an unpleasant and often serious illness, children should be immunized against it, usually at 15 months.

The first symptoms of measles are sniffles, fever, conjunctivitis and a cough.

These symptoms are followed four to five days later by a red blotchy rash which begins on the face and then spreads to the body and limbs. As the rash spreads the fever often continues, but it usually settles a day or so after the rash appears on the legs. After this the rash also begins to fade.

Before and during the time that the rash is appearing, the child can feel miserable and sometimes develops a secondary chest or ear infection. There is no specific treatment for the rash but you should consult your doctor about treatment to relieve other symptoms. He may treat secondary infections with antibiotics, and suggest giving acetaminophen to reduce temperature. The child will feel like eating only a small amount, but should have plenty to drink.
(*See also* **Isolation, and Immunization chart, page 127**)

Meningitis
Meningitis is inflammation of the tissue which covers the brain and spinal cord. It is an uncommon but serious condition which can be caused by bacteria or a virus. A child with meningitis usually complains of a headache, vomits and is feverish. He may find that the light hurts his eyes, that it is painful to bend his neck and that he is drowsy. He may also have a convulsion. A baby with meningitis cannot complain of a headache, but he will have a temperature, may vomit, be irritable and disinterested in his feedings. In addition to this he may have a convulsion, and the fontanelle (the soft spot) on his head may be fuller than usual.

A sick child with these symptoms should be seen immediately by a doctor. The doctor will decide if the child needs to be admitted to hospital for tests, as it is only by examining the fluid around the brain and spinal cord that a diagnosis can be made. If the test shows that the child has

bacterial meningitis, a course of antibiotics should be started immediately. Some forms of viral meningitis also require treatment, but the less serious kind (such as mumps meningitis) will clear up by itself.
(*See also* **Mumps**)

Mites
(*See* **Scabies**)

Mouth infections
The most common mouth infection in babies is thrush, a yeast which produces white patches on the tongue and the inside of the cheeks. It can also occur on the baby's bottom and cause diaper rash.

Thrush is not a serious condition but it can cause discomfort to the baby when he is sucking or feeding. The infection may have been passed on by the mother at the time of birth, or have come from thrush on her nipples if she is breastfeeding. It can also arise if bottles are not sterilized properly. Your doctor will prescribe antifungal drops to clear the mouth infection.

Children occasionally develop mouth ulcers, which usually appear on the gums or the insides of the cheeks. They are caused by a virus and will disappear over a few days without treatment. However, if the ulcers are painful, the doctor may prescribe some soothing antiseptic cream.

Less commonly the herpes simplex virus, which also causes cold sores, may be responsible for a severe form of mouth ulcer called herpes stomatitis. The child who has this form of mouth ulcer will become unwell and feverish, developing small blisters in his mouth – on the tongue, gums, palate and insides of the cheeks – which burst to leave painful ulcers. Eating causes discomfort, but the child should be encouraged to drink as this will help to keep the mouth clean and prevent dehydration. The doctor may prescribe a soothing cream, but occasionally children with herpes stomatitis need to be put in the hospital because they require extra fluids. The condition usually clears after about 10 days.

Mouth ulcers
(*See* **Mouth infections**)

Mumps
Mumps is an infectious disease caused by a virus. The illness begins with pain and swelling in one or both of the parotid glands. These are saliva producing glands situated on either side of the face, just in front of and below the ear. The swelling usually reaches its peak two to three days later and then subsides over the next few days. Swelling of one gland may precede that of the other by one or two days. The child may also be feverish and feel very lethargic.

There is no specific treatment for mumps, but the child should be kept as comfortable as possible and given acetaminophen (as prescribed by the doctor) if he has a fever or the swelling is painful. The child is infectious for about 10 days after the onset of the parotid swelling.

Rare complications of mumps include a mild form of meningitis, which requires no treatment, or inflammation of the testes (orchitis). Orchitis may occur in boys about eight days after the parotid swelling. The testes become swollen and sore for about four days, but the inflammation will settle down without treatment after this time. In prepubertal boys no damage to the testes results, but if mumps is contracted by an adult male it can occasionally cause a degree of infertility.
(*See also* **Isolation**)

Nosebleeds
Nosebleeds are rare in small babies, but they are not uncommon in older children. The bleeding usually results

from an infection of the lining of the nose or because of persistent nose picking; it may be alarming but is rarely severe. Bleeding is best controlled by pinching the soft part of the nose so that the nostrils are closed off. The pressure should be applied for at least five minutes to allow a clot to form. The child should be sitting up and leaning forwards while this is done so that no blood drips down the back of the throat. Try to stop the child touching or blowing his nose after a nosebleed as this can lead to further bleeding. A child who has frequent nosebleeds should be examined by a doctor.

O

Obesity
Many babies who are overweight in the first months of life lose their extra weight in the second year when they become more mobile. However, fat or obese children are likely to become fat adults – a condition which significantly increases the risks of heart disease, high blood pressure and diabetes. It is therefore important that obesity is prevented in childhood and attention given to the quantity and quality of the food eaten. Avoid giving children too many heavy, high calorie foods such as ice cream, sweets, cakes, chips and sodas. If obesity is a real problem your doctor may be able to give you advice on an appropriate diet for the child.

Orchitis
(*See* **Mumps, Testes**)

Osteomyelitis
Osteomyelitis is bacterial infection of the bone. A child who has the condition will be generally unwell and feverish. He may complain of pain over the infected bone or be reluctant to use the affected limb. The painful area is sometimes swollen and tender. If a child develops these

symptoms, consult your doctor at once as early diagnosis and treatment are important to prevent the disease from developing further. Treatment is with antibiotics, which need to be given for several weeks, but sometimes surgery is necessary to clear out the infected area of bone.

Otitis externa
(*See* **Ear infections**)

Otitis media
(*See* **Ear infections**)

P

Perthes disease
Perthes disease is a condition in which the upper end of the thigh bone (where it forms the hip joint) is damaged. The cause of the damage is unknown. It is an uncommon disease which typically occurs in boys between the ages of four and ten. The initial symptoms may be pain in the hip, thigh or knee, and a limp. The child should be examined by a doctor and the diagnosis will be made by X-ray. Treatment involves resting the joint to allow the damaged bone to recover. This can be done by immobilizing the joint in a cast or by bed rest and traction.

Pertussis
(*See* **Whooping cough**)

Pharyngitis
Pharyngitis is inflammation of the pharynx, the wall at the back of the mouth and throat. It is usually caused by a virus and results in a sore throat and mild fever. A cough and a runny nose may also develop. It is not a serious condition and usually only lasts a few days. Treatment involves giving acetaminophen to relieve the sore throat and control fever. Occasionally, pharyngitis is caused by a bacterial infection, and the doctor will prescribe a course of antibiotics to clear it up.
(*See* **diagram, page 271**)

Phobias

A phobia is an irrational fear of something. For example, a child may have a fear of tigers or robbers in his bedroom at night, or he may be afraid of enclosed spaces, such as elevators. These fears are usually a passing phase with children and can be regarded as part of normal development. They are best handled with sympathy and reassurance. If a phobia persists for too long, mention it to your doctor as he may be able to give advice on how to handle the problem.

Pica

Normal infants and toddlers will put all sorts of unsuitable things into their mouths; they may even eat them. Such behavior is part of a natural exploration of the world, but it should be firmly discouraged as the child may inadvertently eat something that is harmful.

If dirt eating becomes a habit, it is referred to as pica, and should lead to concern about the child's general well-being. If you suspect that your child has pica, consult your doctor. Children with pica are at risk of lead poisoning.

Pigeon toes

This condition describes the position of the feet when they are turned inwards. As a result of pigeon toes the child may trip over his feet when he runs. Many toddlers are pigeon-toed, but this tends to correct itself as the child grows and has usually disappeared completely by the time he is six or seven. The most common cause of pigeon toes is inward turning of the shin or thigh bone. In most cases no treatment is required, but if the condition does not improve, or seems to be getting worse, you should consult your doctor. He may refer the child to an orthopedic surgeon (bone specialist) for advice.

Pink eye
(*See* Conjunctivitis)

Pinworms

There are a number of worms that can live as parasites in the bowels or intestines. The most common is the pinworm, which lives in the lower bowel and lays its eggs around the anus. These tiny little worms do not usually cause any abdominal symptoms, but they may make the child's bottom very itchy. The eggs are too small to be seen with the naked eye, but occasionally a worm may be seen around the anus or on the bedding; they are about ½ inch long and look like slender white threads. The infection is passed on by scratching the bottom, getting the eggs onto hands and then putting fingers into the mouth.

Pinworms may be suspected if a child has a very itchy bottom, but this can be confirmed by your doctor. The doctor may ask you to put some sticky tape over part of the child's bottom at night so that he can examine the tape the next day under the microscope and see if there are any worms or eggs. Pinworms are common in schoolchildren and can easily be eradicated with a special medicine.

Pneumonia

Pneumonia is an infection of the lungs, in particular of the small air-filled sacs (alveoli) at the end of the breathing tubes, and the surrounding tissue. It can be caused by a virus or a bacterial infection. A child with pneumonia will have a cough and fever; he may appear quite unwell and be breathing faster than normal. The illness can usually be diagnosed by the doctor when he listens to the child's chest, but he may refer the child to the hospital where confirmation can be obtained with a chest X-ray.

Treatment involves physiotherapy to clear the lungs of the infected secretions, acetaminophen to reduce fever, and antibiotics if the infection is caused by bacteria. Some cases of pneumonia can be nursed at home; others are managed better in the hospital.
(*See* diagram, page 269)

Poisoning
(*See* Emergencies, page 295)

Poliomyelitis

Polio is an infectious viral disease. It produces a mild febrile illness with lethargy and nausea, but it can also damage the nerves, causing permanent paralysis. Because of this very serious risk it is clearly essential for all children to be immunized against the disease. The vaccine is given during the first year of life. (*See also* **Immunization and Immunization chart, page 127**)

Prickly heat

Prickly heat is an itchy rash caused by blockage of the sweat glands in the skin. In a hot humid atmosphere the baby or child may develop tiny pin-point blisters of sweat, particularly on the face, neck and diaper area. No treatment is necessary as the rash will disappear by itself after a few days, but you can prevent prickly heat by making sure the child keeps cool in hot weather.

Purpura

This is a purplish rash caused by flecks of blood in the skin. It occurs because the blood is low in clotting cells (platelets) or because the tiny blood vessels in the skin are damaged and allow blood to leak out. Purpura can be caused by a number of diseases. Any child who shows the symptom should be seen by a doctor so that a diagnosis can be made.

Pyloric stenosis

Pyloric stenosis is a narrowing of the outlet of the stomach into the intestine. The narrowing is due to excessive muscular development which constricts the outlet and prevents milk and food from leaving the stomach. As the quantity of milk filling the stomach increases, the baby automatically vomits. In some cases vomiting is projectile (spurts out forcefully), which can be alarming for parents. The result of repeated

A-Z OF COMMON AILMENTS

vomiting is that the baby receives little nourishment from his food and begins to lose weight. Despite this, he usually feeds well.

Pyloric stenosis typically occurs in the first three months of life and is more common in boys than girls; the cause of the condition is unknown. The cure is a small operation to relieve the obstruction, after which the baby should have no further problems.

R

Rabies
Rabies is a very serious viral illness which affects the nervous system. It is transmitted by a bite from an infected animal (such as a dog, bat or fox). The rabies virus has infected animals in the United States and Canada and is present in other parts of the world, including northern Europe. If your child is bitten by an animal, make quite sure that he sees a doctor immediately.

Rash
(*See* Diaper rash, Eczema, Prickly heat, Urticaria)

Rickets
Lack of vitamin D in the diet is the most common cause of rickets. Vitamin D, which is present in many fatty foods such as milk, fish, liver and cod liver oil, controls the amount of calcium in the body. Calcium is important for building bones and strong teeth. As a result of calcium deficiency children with rickets have soft bones which may become deformed (for example, leg bowing) and there may be swelling at the wrists and ankles. Rickets is rarely seen today because of improved standards of nutrition, but if it is suspected consult your doctor. Treatment for rickets involves giving vitamin D supplements.

Ringworm
This condition is caused by a fungus, not a worm. It results in red scaly circles on the skin which may be very itchy. The scalp, body, groin, nails and feet may all be affected by the fungi. When it affects the feet it is known as athlete's foot.

Ringworm on the body is sometimes contracted from infected pets, but it is not a serious condition and usually disappears without treatment. However, if it proves troublesome it can be cleared more quickly with special ointment or tablets from the doctor. As ringworm is highly contagious, your doctor may suggest that the child stays away from public places, such as swimming pools, until the infection has cleared up.

Rubella
(*See* German measles)

S

Scabies
This is a highly contagious infection caused by the scabies mite, which burrows painlessly into the upper layers of the skin to lay its eggs. The burrows are usually found between the fingers and on the hands and wrists, but they may also show on the body and limbs. They produce a rash which is extremely itchy, particularly at night.

Scabies is acquired through direct contact with an infected person, so if a child has the condition everyone else in the family should be carefully examined. The condition is readily cured with a special lotion, which your doctor can prescribe; it is best to apply this after a bath. Once the treatment is finished the child should be given clean night clothes and bed linen.

Scalds
(*See* Emergencies, page 294)

Scoliosis
Scoliosis is abnormal curvature of the spine. It is an uncommon condition which may be caused

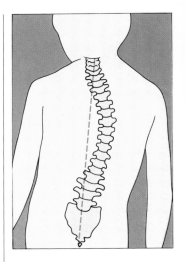

Scoliosis *is an abnormal sideways curvature of the vertebral column (spine).*

by abnormality of the bones, nerves or muscles of the back, although in some cases no underlying cause is found. A child with scoliosis will probably be referred by your doctor to an orthopedic surgeon (bone specialist) who will give advice on how to manage the condition.

Seborrheic rash
(*See* Cradle cap)

Shock
(*See* page 295)

Sickle cell disease
Sickle cell disease is an inherited blood condition which affects some people of West African origin. It results in chronic anemia and episodes of pain due to blockage of the blood vessels. A child with sickle cell disease has two abnormal sickle cell genes. If a child has a single abnormal sickle cell gene (sickle cell trait) he will only suffer from mild anemia and is unlikely to have problems.

There is no cure for sickle cell disease, but blood transfusions will correct the anemia and prompt medical treatment may relieve the painful crises. A child with sickle cell disease has inherited an abnormal gene from each of his parents and they have a one-in-four chance of having a similarly affected child at each subsequent pregnancy.

Sinus infection

The sinuses are air-filled spaces in the bones of the face which are connected to the nose. A sinus infection (sinusitis) is inflammation of one of these areas, usually caused by a bacterial infection. It is often accompanied by a cold, temperature and pain in the infected area, which may be beside the nose or above the eyes. The sinuses are not fully developed in young children, so sinusitis is rarely a problem under the age of six. Treatment for sinus infection involves giving decongestants and antibiotics.

Sleep walking

Sleep walking is more likely to occur in children of school age than younger children. The cause is unknown, but it may be associated with periods of stress, such as starting school. A child found sleep walking should be gently directed back to bed.

Children who walk in their sleep rarely harm themselves, but do use your common sense. If a child has a tendency to sleep walk make sure that there are no immediate dangers (for example, an open window). The problem disappears spontaneously as the child gets older.

Smothering
(*See* Emergencies, page 295)

Sore throat

A sore throat is a common childhood complaint that usually occurs with an upper respiratory tract problem, such as a cold, cough, pharyngitis or tonsillitis. A child with a sore throat should be given plenty of fluids and, if he seems to be generally unwell, consult your doctor.
(*See* diagram, page 271)

Speech disorder
(*See* Stuttering)

Spitting up
(*See* Vomiting)

Splinters
(*See* First aid, page 297)

Sprains
(*See* First aid, page 297)

Squint

A squint is when the eyes do not look in exactly the same direction. It may result from short sightedness in one eye or an imbalance in the control of the eye movements. Newborn babies sometimes have a temporary squint which they quickly lose as control of the eyes develops. However, a persistent squint may prevent proper development of vision, so any child or baby who appears to have one should be seen by a doctor, who may refer him to an ophthalmologist (eye specialist). The treatment which the specialist

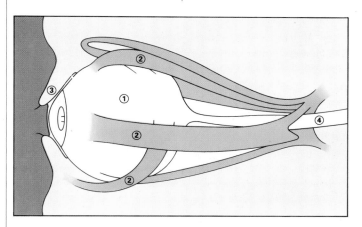

1. Eyeball
2. Muscles **3.** Eyelid
4. Optic nerve

*A **squint** results when the muscles controlling each eye fail to coordinate the eye movements.*

recommends will depend on the underlying cause of the squint, but may involve patching of the good eye to encourage the squinting one to work harder, or perhaps a recommendation that the child wears glasses. Very occasionally the problem requires surgical correction.

Stammering
(*See* Stuttering)

Sticky eye
(*See* Conjunctivitis)

Stings
(*See* First aid, page 297)

Stomach upsets
(*See* Gastroenteritis)

Stuttering

Children between the ages of three and four will often stumble or stutter over words when they are excited or trying to describe something that has just happened. This is a normal phase of language development which generally disappears by the time the child goes to school. Faltering speech is not helped by an authoritarian attitude, so it is better not to tell the child to slow down and repeat what he is saying because this may frustrate and inhibit him. If he does stutter, listen to him patiently and try not to draw attention to it.

Should the problem persist, consult your doctor who may refer you to a speech therapist.

Styes

A stye is a pimple, or tiny boil, at the base of the eyelash. The doctor will prescribe an antibiotic ointment but you can soak absorbent cotton in warm water and apply it to the stye to alleviate discomfort. Styes usually heal in a few days.

Sunburn

Babies and young children have delicate skin and they can become sunburnt very easily. It is therefore important not to expose a young child to too much direct sunlight. If the child is out in the sun for any length of time, you may want to protect him with a sun hat and sunscreen. A carriage canopy or stroller umbrella can provide protection for a baby who is outside in hot weather.

If sunburn does occur it may not be noticeable right away, but will appear some hours later in the form of reddened tender skin and possibly blisters. Cool water and calamine lotion will soothe slightly sunburnt skin, but if the sunburn is severe you

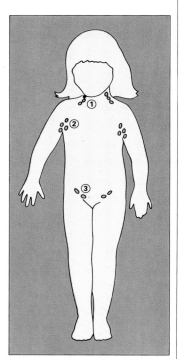

1. Cervical lymph glands
2. Axillary lymph glands
3. Inguinal lymph glands

Although they are part of the body's defense system, the **lymph glands** *can themselves become swollen due to infection. The main groups of glands are in the neck (cervical), the armpits (axillary) and the groin (inguinal).*

should give the child plenty of fluids and consult your doctor immediately.

Swallowed objects
(*See* **First aid, page 297**)

Swollen glands

The lymph glands are part of the body's defense against infection. They are situated throughout the body, but most of them are in the groin, armpits and neck. They are not normally easy to feel, but sometimes they become swollen in response to an infection. For example, with a sore throat the neck glands become enlarged and they can be felt as small, rubbery lumps under the skin. As the infection disappears the glands gradually return to their normal size. If your child has persistent enlarged glands he should be examined by a doctor so that the cause can be established.

Temperature
(*See* **Fever**)

Testes

The testes are the male sexual glands which develop in the abdomen prior to birth. While the baby is still in the womb, the testes move down from the abdomen into the scrotum. Occasionally this descent is incomplete at the time of birth so that one or both of the testes are undescended and cannot be felt in the scrotum.

Most undescended testes come down into the scrotum during the first year, but in cases where this does not happen, a small operation may be necessary; this allows the testes to become fixed in the scrotum where they can develop normally.

A retractile testis is one that is intermittently pulled up from the scrotum into the groin. It differs from an undescended testis in that it can be coaxed down into the scrotum with gentle pressure. A retractile

testis requires no treatment as it will remain permanently in place in time.

Torsion of the testis occurs when it twists on its stalk. This causes sudden pain in the testis and the child may feel sick and vomit. The testis may be swollen and tender. If a child has these symptoms, consult your doctor at once. The condition will have to be treated surgically.

Orchitis, or inflammation of the testes, is not common before puberty but may be a complication of mumps and some other infectious diseases. The scrotum becomes swollen and painful and the child may have a temperature. Consult your doctor; treatment will depend on the cause.
(*See also* **Mumps**)

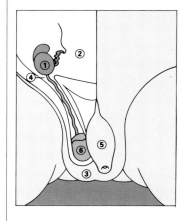

1. Undescended testis
2. Abdomen   **3.** Scrotum
4. Inguinal canal
5. Penis   **6.** Testis in correct position

Tetanus

Tetanus is a very serious illness caused by a type of bacterium that lives in soil, dust and water. The bacteria gain access to the body through open wounds and produce a toxic substance which puts the muscles of the body into spasm. The condition can be prevented by tetanus immunization, which all children should have during the first year of life. A tetanus booster is given at the age of five, or to any child who

sustains a dirty injury and has not had a booster for the past five years.
(*See also* **Immunization chart, page 127**)

Thalassemia

Thalassemia is an inherited blood condition which affects the blood cells and results in chronic anemia. The thalassemia gene is found quite frequently in people of Mediterranean or Asian extraction. A single abnormal thalassemia gene (thalassemia minor) does not cause significant anemia, but if a child has two abnormal genes (thalassemia major) he will develop anemia and require regular blood transfusions and therapy. A child with thalassemia major has inherited one abnormal gene from each parent and they will have a one-in-four chance of producing another affected child at each subsequent pregnancy.

Thrush
(*See* **Diaper rash, Mouth infections**)

Tongue tie

Sometimes the tissue that joins the tongue to the floor of the mouth extends to the tip of the tongue and stops it from protruding normally. In the vast majority of cases this presents no problem to the child and it will improve as he gets older. Very rarely a tongue tie may be tight enough to prevent a child from making certain sounds properly. In this situation a simple operation is needed to release the tongue.

Tongue tie is often thought – quite wrongly – to be the cause of feeding problems and speech difficulties. Don't be misled; seek proper advice if your child has difficulty with either of these problems.

Tonsillitis

The tonsils are a pair of glands situated on either side of the back of the throat. Tonsillitis occurs when the tonsils become inflamed due to a bacterial infection or virus. The child with tonsillitis will have a sore throat and fever, and may feel generally unwell and not be eating. The glands under the chin and neck, which drain the tonsils, become enlarged also. If bacterial tonsillitis is suspected the doctor will prescribe antibiotics; otherwise the treatment involves giving acetaminophen to relieve the fever and sore throat, and plenty to drink. Tonsillitis usually gets better over three to four days.

Removal of the tonsils used to be carried out very often, but it is now considered to be an unnecessary operation in many cases. However, children who have recurrent attacks of tonsillitis, and are repeatedly missing school as a result, may benefit from having their tonsils removed. This minor operation is called a tonsillectomy. The decision to do this will be made by the ear, nose and throat (ENT) specialist who performs the operation. Very occasionally the tonsils become so enlarged that they interfere with normal breathing – this also means that a tonsillectomy has to be performed.

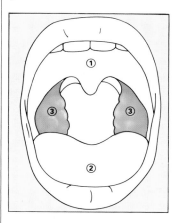

1. Palate
2. Tongue
3. Inflamed tonsils

*The **tonsils** are two pieces of lymphoid tissue which may become swollen and inflamed due to infection.*

Toothache

Toothache can be caused by decay of a tooth (caries), inflammation of the root of a tooth (a tooth abscess) or a gum infection. Sometimes pain caused by inflammation of the ear or jaw-bone can feel like toothache. A child with toothache should be seen by a dentist first, but if nothing is wrong with the child's teeth you should consult your doctor about the pain.

Travel sickness

Travel or motion sickness is a tendency to feel sick and vomit while traveling. It is the movement which causes the sickness, so it can occur in a plane, boat, car or even on a merry-go-round. If your child readily vomits in such situations he should be encouraged to sit still during the journey, preferably by the window so that he can get some fresh air. Some children find that reading while traveling can precipitate motion sickness and this should be avoided. Antihistamines may be helpful in preventing travel sickness, but they should be taken at least half an hour before the start of the journey. Most children grow out of motion sickness in time.

Tuberculosis

Tuberculosis (TB) is a bacterial disease which primarily causes inflammation of the lungs. However, it can affect other parts of the body, such as the brain, neck glands, bones and kidneys. Treatment for the disease is with antibiotics and therapy has to be continued for some months.

During the early part of this century it was a relatively common disease in the US, but it now occurs much less. It is acquired either through close contact with someone who has TB of the lung or by drinking milk that has come from infected cattle.

Typhoid
(*See* **Illness on vacation, page 265**)

U

Ulcers
(*See* Mouth infections)

Unconsciousness
(*See* Head injuries, page 295, and Coma)

Upper respiratory tract infection
Infections of the upper respiratory tract, or URI, include coughs, colds, tonsillitis, pharyngitis and otitis media. These infections are frequently caused by viruses and are generally less serious than those of the lower respiratory tract, such as bronchitis, bronchiolitis and pneumonia.
(*See* diagram, page 271)

Urinary tract infections
The urinary tract includes the kidneys, the ureters, the bladder and the urethra. An infection can involve all or part of this system. When the kidneys are primarily involved the condition is called pyelonephritis; when the infection is mainly in the bladder it is cystitis.

Urinary infections are caused by bacteria. The symptoms are many and may include fever, pain on passing urine, passing urine more frequently than usual, hematuria (blood in the urine), abdominal pain, vomiting, irritability, unwillingness to eat, loose bowel movements, or weight gain due to fluid retention. To diagnose a urinary tract infection, a urine sample is taken and examined for signs of infection. If the child is very young, the doctor will provide a special bag for collecting the urine sample.

If urine infection is confirmed, the child should be given plenty of fluid to help wash out the infection, which is treated with the appropriate antibiotics. When the course of antibiotics is finished a urine sample should again be checked to make sure that the infection has been eliminated. The child should also be examined to make sure that there is no underlying urinary tract abnormality. An infection that has been inadequately treated can cause permanent damage to the kidneys.

Urticaria
Urticaria (also known as hives) is an allergic skin reaction which results in itchy welts and blotches. The rash usually clears up over a few days, but calamine lotion may be soothing and sometimes antihistamines, prescribed by the doctor, will reduce the itchiness. Urticaria can be caused by an allergy to certain foods, by stinging nettles, various pollens, drugs, infections, flea bites and by physical factors, such as water or cold weather.

V

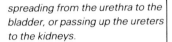

Vaginal infection
A vaginal discharge of thick white mucus is quite normal in newborn baby girls; occasionally it is accompanied by a small amount of blood staining. Both symptoms result

---

URINARY SYSTEM

Urine is filtered by the kidneys and passed to the bladder, where it is expelled from the body via the urethra. From here it passes out of the body. Urine infection is sometimes caused by bacteria spreading from the urethra to the bladder, or passing up the ureters to the kidneys.

1. Kidneys **2.** Ureters
3. Bladder **4.** Urethra

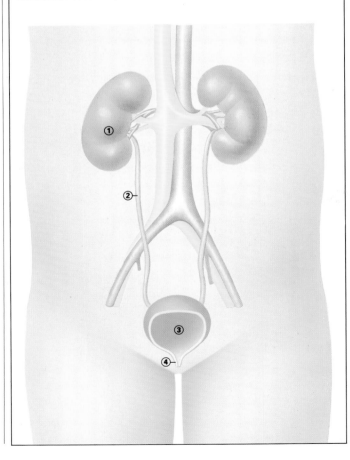

from the effect of the mother's hormones on the glands of the baby's cervix, but they usually disappear in the first two weeks of life.

In young girls the skin of the vulva and vagina is very delicate so that irritation or infection can easily cause inflammation and a discharge. Tight trousers and rough textured tights should be avoided as they rub against the skin. Some types of bubble bath also cause irritation. Occasionally the bottom scratching associated with pinworms can damage the vulval skin and cause a slight infection. If a child has a sore vulva, with or without a discharge, it may be helpful to use mild soap for washing, avoid bubble bath and see that she wears loose cotton pants. Your doctor may prescribe a hormone cream to increase the skin's resistance to irritation. If the discharge is due to a bacterial infection, antibiotics will be prescribed.

Occasionally little girls push small objects into their vaginas. This can result in persistent infections and discharge, which will only clear when the object is removed. Your doctor may recommend that this is done while the child is under a general anesthetic.
(*See also* **Pinworms**)

Vomiting

Vomiting is the expulsion of the stomach contents through the mouth as a reaction to an infection, or because of an obstruction to the passage of food in the bowel. Sometimes it is not significant and may relate to a minor infection such as a cold or tonsillitis, but if vomiting is persistent and occurs with abdominal pain, headache, diarrhea or feeding difficulties, or your child seems generally unwell, you should consult your doctor.

Vomiting should not be confused with spitting up, which is when babies regurgitate a small amount of excess milk after a feeding. This is perfectly normal.

Warts

These are small skin growths caused by a virus. They are very common in childhood and are not serious, although they may be uncomfortable and unsightly. Warts are usually found on the fingers, hands and elbows, and there may be one or more. Consult your doctor about treatment. Chemical paints or freezing with carbon dioxide snow may get rid of the warts, but sometimes they recur after treatment. If left alone they will disappear by themselves, but this often takes some months.

A plantar is a wart on the sole of the foot. Because of its position in the thick skin under the foot it produces a small, hard lump. The plantar wart is painless, except when the child is standing or walking, when it presses into the foot and may feel like a pebble in the shoe. Plantar warts can be treated in the same way as other warts, but the doctor may also pare down the lump of hard skin so that it does not press into the foot.

Wax in ears

It is quite natural for a certain amount of yellow wax to be formed in the ear canals. Its function is to cleanse the ear of dust particles. When cleaning your child's ears it is only necessary to wipe wax from the outside. Do not poke deep into the ear with the corner of a towel or a cotton swab as you could damage the eardrum.

Wheezing
(*See* **Asthma, Bronchitis**)

Whooping cough

Whooping cough, or pertussis, is a respiratory disease caused by bacteria. It generally begins with the symptoms of a cold, followed a few days later with a cough that is characterized by a whooping sound as the child catches his breath. The cough comes in spasms and usually makes the child red in the face. He may also vomit after an episode of coughing. The number of coughing bouts per day varies and the condition may continue for several weeks. The child is infectious for up to four weeks after the cough begins.

Whooping cough is particularly dangerous in small babies because the coughing spasms interfere with normal breathing. If you notice any of these symptoms, consult your doctor immediately. Once whooping cough is established, antibiotics will not alter its course, although they may make the child less infectious.

Whooping cough can be prevented by immunization. The child should be immunized on three occasions, separated by several weeks. Whooping cough immunization is usually administered with diphtheria and tetanus immunization in the triple vaccine, but it may not be recommended if your baby suffers from fits or has brain damage. If you have any doubts about whether your child should be immunized against whooping cough you should consult your doctor.
(*See also* **Immunization chart, page 127**)

Worms
(*See* **Pinworms**)

Safety around the house

GENERAL SAFETY POINTS

● Keep all open, gas or electric fires guarded, preferably with a guard which attaches to the wall.
● Never dry clothes over a firescreen.
● Put safety film over glass or fit safety glass.
● Fit safety covers to electric sockets not in use.
● Remove all ashtrays and matches to discourage visitors from smoking.
● Never leave plastic bags lying around.
● Fit safety catches to all windows.

Accidents are now the major cause of death for young children, and accidents in the home are second only to road accidents. Thinking ahead and planning how to organize your home before your child gets to the next stage of his development is essential – you may not know that he can crawl until the day he reaches out for the electric heater, or that he can stand up until he pulls the oven door down on top of his head.

Take precautions to avoid anything that could burn or scald your child – always make sure fires are properly guarded; turn all saucepan handles inwards out of reach; never leave teapots and hot drinks within reach. All poisonous substances, like medicines, bleaches, household cleaners and garden pesticides, should be safely locked away. You should make sure that your child's equipment and all toys are safe and of a reputable make, that you keep your active baby harnessed in carriages, strollers and highchairs and that you put away breakable objects which could cut. Avoid loose cords with which a child could pull a heavy object down on top of him, and see that all electrical

GARDEN

● Always lock up sheds and garages where you keep garden chemicals and dangerous tools. Don't leave gardening tools around.
● Make sure you don't have any poisonous plants.
● Teach your child not to eat anything from the yard.
● Cover pools securely and never leave buckets of water around.
● Supervise water play all the time.
● Fit a child-proof latch to the gate to your yard.
● Make sure that children do not play with the excrement of dogs or cats. Keep sandboxes covered.
● Make sure that climbing frames, swings and all outdoor play equipment are in good order.
● Always use a carriage net.

BATHROOM

● Keep all medicines, cosmetics, household cleaners and razor blades well out of reach, preferably in a cupboard with a child-proof lock.
● Run the bath before your child gets in and always check that the water is not too hot. Never leave your child unattended in the bath as he can drown even in a few inches of water.
● Never use a portable electric space heater in the bathroom.
● Avoid having excessively hot water in the taps.

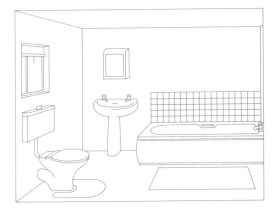

LIVING ROOM

Keep all breakable objects out of reach.
● Use clips to secure trailing cords.
● Disconnect your television when not in use.
● Don't put hot drinks on low tables. Keep alcohol out of a child's reach.
● Never hold or pass hot drinks over your baby.
● Make sure that rugs cannot slip under your feet and that loose fringes won't trip you up.
● Make sure shelves and bookcases are secure and can't be pulled over or used as a climbing frame.

appliances are safely switched off and put away. Remember that a child will get an electric shock if he half pulls out a plug that is attached to a working appliance and then touches the pins of the plug.

Always make sure that equipment for your child has been checked for safety. If any toy or equipment proves unsafe, report it to the U.S. Consumer Product Safety Commission (**see** Useful addresses, page 298). Keep all equipment like strollers and swings in good condition.

HALLWAYS AND STAIRS

● Keep hallways well lit. Never leave toys or other objects lying around where you could trip over them.
● Hold on to the banister while carrying a child downstairs. Check that the carpet is securely fitted.
● Check that banisters are secure and that a small child can't get between the rails.
● Always use a safety gate on the stairs until your child is completely safe.
● Don't let your child walk around with things like scissors or sharp pencils in case he falls on them.

BEDROOMS

● Don't leave cosmetics, perfumes, breakables, nail scissors etc. within a child's reach.
● Make sure that closet doors can be opened from the inside in case your child gets shut in. Make sure cupboards are not top-heavy and can't be pulled over.
● Don't leave an electric blanket on if a child is on his own in the room.
● Disconnect any electrical equipment, such as hairdryers, when not in use.

CHILDREN'S ROOM

● Keep the room free of breakable or harmful objects.
● Make sure that all the equipment is stable and all the toys are safe.
● Never use a pillow for a baby under one year old.
● Never put your child to sleep in his bib or in clothes with ribbons or drawstrings around the neck – they could catch on something and strangle him.
● Remove hot water bottles before you put your baby or child to bed.
● Nightwear should not be made of flammable fabric.

A B C D E F G H I J K

KITCHEN

● Keep all bleach, household cleaners and detergents well out of reach, preferably in a locked cupboard. Never keep then in unlabeled containers.
● Turn all saucepan handles inwards. Don't let your child play with the knobs of the stove.
● Never leave a fry pan unattended.
● Make sure your child is sitting at the table or harnessed in his highchair before you dish up hot food.
● Make sure your child can't get at the garbage can.

● Always disconnect electrical appliances when not in use.
● Avoid highly polished floors and loose rugs. Wipe up spills immediately.
● Don't use long tablecloths which a child can pull.
● Keep knives and other sharp tools out of reach.
● Keep a fiberglass cloth or a fire extinguisher to smother any fire.
● Never leave an iron where a child can pull it down.

SAFETY AROUND THE HOUSE

Emergencies

As a parent, there may be a time when quick and knowledgeable action on your part could save your child's life. Learning first aid skills from a book is not easy, particularly with special techniques such as CPR and heart massage for which you really need detailed instruction and practice. Find out who runs first aid courses locally and take the trouble to go along. The American Red Cross organizes such courses (**see** Useful addresses, page 298). You could also check with the rescue and first aid squads, as well as the hospital in your area. Many public swimming pools run special classes to teach young children to swim. These can be great fun, as well as giving your child a skill which could save his life.

A child should always be taken to hospital after an accident if he is unconscious, drowsy or vomiting, has bleeding or discharge from the ears or nose or has lost a lot of blood. Find out where your nearest emergency room is and plan how you'd get there in the event of an accident.

CPR (CARDIO PULMONARY RESUSCITATION)

If your child has stopped breathing, CPR (the 'kiss of life') should be given immediately. Do this even if you think it is too late – it may not be.

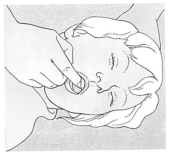

1 Lie the child on his back. Clear his mouth of any foreign bodies, blood or vomit.

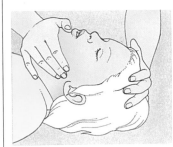

2 Gently tilt the child's head back with one hand and lift the chin up and forward with the other so that his tongue is not blocking his throat.

3 Pinch the child's nostrils to close off the nasal airway and seal your mouth over his open mouth (for small children and babies, cover their mouth **and** nose). Give four quick breaths into the child's mouth and check that the chest rises and falls.

4 Give one breath every three seconds – a little faster for a baby – and keep on until the child starts to breathe again, or professional help arrives.

5 When the child is breathing again, gently turn him over and place him in the **recovery position** (see right).

HEART MASSAGE

If after the first attempts at CPR the child is very pale or a blue-grey color and not breathing, the heart may have stopped.

Check the carotid pulse in the child's neck (just below the jaw bone and in line with the earlobe) and, if it is absent, give heart massage as well as CPR.

Lie the child on his back and kneel beside him.

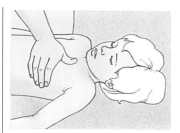

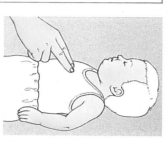

1 For a child of two years or more, press gently but firmly on the lower part of his breastbone (center of the chest, between the nipples) with the heel of your hand. Press about once every second (about 60-80 compressions per minute).

2 After five compressions, give CPR. If there is someone with you, one of you can do heart massage, stopping after five compressions for the other to breathe into the child's lungs. Check for a pulse at least every three minutes.

1 For a baby, use two fingers and less pressure, and press a little faster (about 100 compressions per minute).

3 Once you can feel the child's pulse, stop heart massage. Carry on with CPR until breathing starts, or a doctor or ambulance arrives to take over.

THE RECOVERY POSITION

It is dangerous for someone who is unconscious to be left lying on their back, as the throat can be blocked by the tongue or by vomit. If the child is unconscious or very drowsy, but is breathing, place him in the recovery position.

1 Kneel beside the child, turn his head towards you and place his nearest arm under his bottom, palm of the hand upwards. Place his other arm across his chest. Bend the leg furthest from you over the near leg. Supporting the child's head, pull his body towards you and lower him onto his stomach.

2 Bend his arm and leg nearest to you to help support the body, turning his head slightly to one side and well back so that he can breathe easily. Never leave the child alone – unless you have to get help – as he could choke or stop breathing.

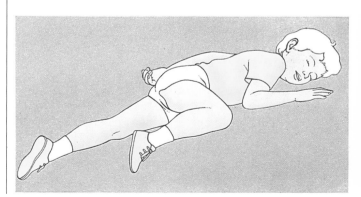

293

BURNS AND SCALDS

A burn can be caused by fire, chemicals, electricity or by coming into contact with a very hot object. A scald is caused by steam or hot liquid.

A burn or scald is serious if it covers a large area, is very deep or is on the face or any other particularly sensitive part of the body. The danger with serious burns or scalds is that too much fluid (plasma) can be lost from the skin. This is particularly serious with children, when the condition can rapidly lead to **shock** (see opposite page).

1 Immerse the burnt or scalded area in cold water for at least 10 minutes to take some of the heat out of the skin.

2 Take off tight clothes as the skin will swell up.

3 Call the doctor or take the child to the hospital without delay.

● For minor burns or scalds, put a clean white cotton cloth or piece of gauze over the burn to stop it from becoming infected.

Clothes on fire

If there is plenty of water at hand, douse the child's clothing with it. If not, get him onto the ground and smother the flames by covering him with a heavy rug, blanket, towel or coat. **Don't** use synthetic fabrics which could cause worse damage.

As a last resort, use your own body to smother the flames. However, make sure there is no gap between your bodies where air might get through and fan the flames. When you have smothered the flames, immerse the burnt area in cold water. If clothes are stuck to the skin, **don't** try to pull them off and **don't** burst any blisters. Give the child sips of water and take him to the hospital immediately.

CHOKING

1 For a child, lie him over your knee, with his head down (or hold him upside down by his legs). Give him four sharp slaps between the shoulder blades to dislodge the object.

1 For a baby, hold him face down over your arm (or pick him up by his legs and hold him upside down) and give him four sharp slaps between the shoulder blades.

2 You may need to scoop the object on which he choked out of his mouth to prevent the same thing happening as soon as you put him the right way up. **Don't** try to scoop an object out if it's at the back of the child's throat as you may wedge it in even further.

● If this doesn't work, as a last resort stand or sit the child in front of you, facing away. Using two fingers of each hand, give four short sharp thrusts to the upper abdomen (between the navel and breastbone). This should force the child to breathe out and dislodge the object. However, be prepared to give **CPR** if the child stops breathing.

DROWNING

Get your child out of the water, if possible. If not, you will have to give emergency first aid in the water.

1 Empty the child's mouth and, if his breathing has stopped, give **CPR**.

2 Send someone to call a doctor or ambulance and carry on with CPR until help arrives. Be prepared to start **heart massage**.

The child will cough up water when he starts to breathe again.

ELECTRIC SHOCK

Don't touch the child as the shock can be transmitted to you.

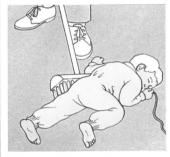

1 Switch off the electricity at the main immediately or pull out the plug. If this is not possible, break the electrical contact with something which does not conduct electricity, such as a wooden broom or chair, or a plastic object, and push your child away from the wire or socket. If there is water around, be very careful not to stand in it as water conducts electricity.

2 Check your child's breathing and, if he is breathing, but unconscious, place him in the **recovery position** (see previous page).

Your child may need to be treated for burns or for **shock** (see opposite page) so take him to the nearest hospital with an emergency room or call a doctor without delay.

● If the electric shock is minor, comfort the child until he is feeling better.

FRACTURES AND DISLOCATIONS

A fall or injury may cause a bone to fracture or dislocate. A fracture is when a bone is broken or partly broken; a dislocation occurs when the bone is wrenched out of its socket at a joint (such as the knee, elbow or thumb). It may be difficult to distinguish between a fracture and a dislocation, so you should follow the same emergency procedure for both.

Don't move the child from where he is unless you have to, especially if you think he might also have injured his back or neck. Make him comfortable and get medical help. Watch for signs of **shock** (see right).

If you have to move the child, immobilize the affected limb.

For a broken leg, place some padding between the legs and tie the injured leg gently but firmly to the other leg with bandages.

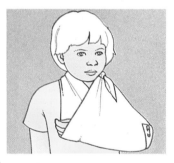

For a broken arm, use a triangular bandage (or a square folded in half) to make an emergency sling. Gently bend the injured arm across the chest and slide one end of the bandage between the elbow and the chest and over the shoulder. Bring the other end of the bandage over the arm and wrist, and tie the two ends at one shoulder. Pin the excess bandage at the elbow.

HEAD INJURIES

Bangs on the head are very common in childhood and usually cause no lasting harm. If the child remains conscious and screams loudly you almost certainly have nothing to worry about. However, consult your doctor if you think your child is ill or behaving strangely in any way after a blow to the head, even if it is hours later.

Take your child to the hospital immediately if he shows any of the following signs: vomiting, drowsiness, complains of a severe headache, or has a discharge from nose or ear.

● If the child's condition changes, especially if he becomes unconscious (which could lead to coma), make sure he is seen by a doctor at once. The child may be concussed or have had a fit which caused the fall.

HEAVY BLEEDING

Major loss of blood from a wound is serious and must be controlled quickly.

1 Take any piece of clean cloth (such as a laundered handkerchief) – or use your hand – and press firmly on the wound. At the same time, raise the affected area to help stop the bleeding. Keep the child still.

● If there's a bone protruding, or a piece of glass or sharp object in the wound, press around the edges of the wound, not directly onto it. **Don't** remove anything from a wound as it may be acting as a plug to stop the bleeding.

2 To prevent infection, cover the wound with a bandage. If there is anything protruding, **don't** press down on the wound. Make sure your child is seen by a doctor as soon as possible as the wound may need stitches.

3 Comfort your child and watch for signs of **shock** (see right).

POISONING

If you suspect that your child may have swallowed something poisonous, take him to the hospital immediately. If you can find out what your child has swallowed, take the container to the hospital too so that they know what kind of poison it is and how to treat it.

If the child is vomiting, hold him with his body bent forward so that he can't choke.

Don't try to make the child sick by giving salty drinks, or by any other method – you could cause more harm, especially if what he's swallowed is corrosive.

● If you are sure that the child has swallowed a household chemical, such as turpentine, paraffin, kerosene, caustic soda or bleach, give him milk to dilute the poison and cool the burning – it also lines the stomach and may protect it.

SMOTHERING/SUFFOCATION

1 Quickly remove whatever has smothered the child.
2 If he has stopped breathing, give him **CPR**.

SHOCK

If a child is pale, sweating and unwell after an accident, he may be suffering from shock, which can be a serious condition. Other signs of shock are:
● faintness and nausea
● rapid pulse and breathing
● delirium

Make the child lie down with his head turned to one side. Loosen clothing and raise his legs. Keep him warm but not too hot (for example, lightly cover him with a blanket but don't give him a hot water bottle). If the child becomes unconscious, place him in the **recovery position** and seek medical help at once. If the child is conscious, but remains shaken, consult your doctor.

First aid treatment

The entries on these pages cover the less serious injuries and scrapes of childhood. It is a good idea to keep a first aid box in your home for such eventualities, so that you can act at once if your child is hurt. You can buy a first aid box or kit from most large drug stores, or you could assemble your own (*see* left) and keep it in a tin or airtight container. The box should be kept in a safe place, out of reach of children, but not locked away where you might not be able to get it easily when you're in a hurry. Make sure you check the contents of the box regularly and replace any items you have used.

Take the first aid box with you in the car when you go out (or keep another kit there), and take a modified first aid kit with you on vacation (*see* Vacation checklist, page 265).

Animal bites
If the bite is superficial, clean the wound with warm water, and apply a sterile dressing if necessary. If it's a serious wound, or on your child's face, take him to a doctor at once. For both minor and more serious wounds, your child may need a tetanus booster, if he has not had one recently. *See also* Snake bite, and Rabies, page 283.

Blisters
Blisters usually occur as a result of friction or a burn. Never prick a blister as it forms a protective layer between the skin and damaged area which protects against infection. Cover the blister with a small piece of gauze kept in place with adhesive strips. It will go down of its own accord and the hard dry skin will change color and fall off in a few days. If the blister does burst, keep it clean and dry.

Convulsions
Never leave a child during a convulsion, or fit, in case he vomits and chokes. Put him in the **recovery position** (page 293) and loosen his clothing. *Don't* try to restrain him.

When the convulsion is over the child may be confused, or even drift off to sleep. Always seek medical advice.

Convulsions in small children are often caused by a high temperature or fever (when they are referred to as febrile convulsions). If your child is prone to convulsions, try to ensure that he doesn't run a high temperature by giving him acetominophen when he's ill and sponging him with tepid water to keep his fever down.

Crushed fingers
This is a fairly common accident with small children who haven't yet learned how doors and drawers work and may inadvertently trap their fingers in one.

Comfort your child – the wound will be painful – and run his hand under cold water, or apply a cold compress, to help ease the pain and swelling. Painkillers are not necessary, but you could cover the hand loosely with a clean handkerchief to protect it from further knocks.

If the pain doesn't subside after a few hours, or if there is any damage to the fingers consult your doctor.

Cuts and scratches
If a wound is deep or bleeding profusely, follow the advice for heavy bleeding (page 295).

Minor cuts and scratches can be treated at home. Clean the wound with warm water, wiping from the middle outwards. Use each swab once only to help prevent cross infection. Pat the skin dry and apply a mild antiseptic cream.

Cover with a dressing or Band-Aids to keep the wound clean.

Eye injuries

Small objects, such as grit or dirt, can usually be washed out of the eye by bathing with water. If you can see a foreign body in the eye, remove it gently with the tip of a clean tissue or handkerchief before bathing. *Don't* let your child rub the eye, especially if you think something sharp has gone into it.

If your child's eye has been injured in any way, take him to the doctor or to the hospital emergency room.

If the injury has been caused by a chemical, put the child's head on one side and flush the eye with cold water. Be sure to wash from the inside corner of the eye outwards. This ensures that chemicals are not washed across the face and possibly into the other eye. Apply an eye pad and take the child to the hospital at once.

Foreign body in the ear

Don't try to remove the object yourself as you may wedge it in more firmly. Take the child to the doctor or local hospital – a nurse or doctor will probably syringe the ear to get the foreign body out.

If an insect has gone into the ear, lie the child on his side and gently pour warm water into it so that the insect floats to the surface. If this doesn't work, get medical help.

Don't pour water into the ear if the child has myringotomy tubes fitted, or if there is a foreign body other than an insect, as it could cause the object to swell.

Foreign body in the nose

An unpleasant discharge from one nostril is often a sign that something has been pushed into the nose. Tell the child to blow through the affected nostril, while you cover the other one. If this is not successful in dislodging the object, take the child to the hospital or the doctor's office.

Heatstroke

Never let small children or babies become too hot – they should not be in full sunlight for any length of time or left in a closed car in the summer.

Heatstroke can be a serious condition, so watch out for signs of overheating. For example, if your child becomes restless, very hot or flushed and is unwell with a raised temperature, seek medical advice as soon as possible. In the meantime, keep the child cool and still – remove clothes, sponge the body with cool or tepid water, fan the child by using a towel or electric fan, and give him sips of cold water to drink.
See also Sunburn, page 285.

Insect bites and stings

Insect bites (such as mosquito or flea) can be soothed with calamine lotion or an antiseptic cream. It may help to cover bites to prevent your child scratching, as this only makes the irritation worse.

A bee or wasp sting can be very painful and alarming. If you can see the sting, pull it out with a pair or tweezers, but if you can't – or it's too deep – *don't* try to squeeze it out or you'll cause more pain and inflammation. A piece of absorbent cotton soaked in a solution of bicarbonate of soda (diluted vinegar for a wasp sting) and held over the sting is a good household remedy. A cold compress will help to reduce pain and swelling.

If the child has been stung in the mouth there may be a lot of swelling. Call your doctor immediately, and, while you are waiting for him, get the child to rinse his mouth out with a solution of bicarbonate of soda and give him a lump of ice or a popsicle to suck. Watch for signs of **shock** (page 295).

Snake bite

If your child has been bitten by a snake, lie him down and keep him as still as possible to help prevent the poison from spreading through the body.

Don't raise the affected limb. Clean the wound and apply a sterile dressing. Send for medical help without delay, and reassure your child as he may be frightened. It will help if you can remember what the snake looked like, and tell the doctor, so that the right anti-venom can be given.

Splinters

Small splinters may work their way out of their own accord, but if there's a bit of the splinter sticking out, you can pull it out with a pair of tweezers. A splinter under the skin can be squeezed and taken out with a sterilized needle (that has been passed through a flame and cooled). Calm and reassure your child as you remove the splinter – it is likely to be painful. *Don't* try to pull out a splinter of glass or metal yourself – leave this to the doctor.

If the area of skin becomes infected, bathe it in warm water, apply antiseptic cream and take the child to the doctor.

Sprains

Get your child to take his weight off the sprained limb and rest in a comfortable position. Apply a cold compress to ease the swelling. Bind the affected joint with a pad of absorbent cotton and an elastic bandage, but make sure it is not too tight. If pain and swelling are severe, consult your doctor.

Swallowed objects

Small children are always putting small objects into their mouths and they may inadvertently swallow them. This is not an emergency unless the object was sharp or the child chokes (*see* Choking, page 294). Many objects simply pass through the digestive tract and come out at the other end. However, the object may cause an obstruction so if you are worried or in any doubt that it has come out, take your child to the doctor.

FIRST AID TREATMENT

Useful addresses

When writing for information please enclose a stamped, self-addressed envelope. All addresses are correct at the time of going to press.

PRENATAL CARE AND BIRTH

American Academy of Husband-Coached Childbirth
PO Box 5224
Sherman Oaks
CA 91413-5224
1-800-423-2397 (toll-free hotline for all states except California) 1-800-42-BIRTH (toll-free in California)
Information and support for those seeking natural childbirth (Bradley method).

American College of Nurse-Midwives (ACNM)
1522 K Street NW
Suite 1000
Washington, DC 20005
202-289-0171
Supplies lists of practicing nurse-midwives as well as lists of publications of interest.

Association for Childbirth at Home, Intnl. (ACHI)
PO Box 430
Glendale
CA 91209
213-663-4996
Support to parents seeking home birth.

C/SEC
22 Forest Road
Framingham, MA 01701
508-877-8266
Support and information on cesarean birth.

Cesarean Prevention Movement, Inc. (CPM)
PO Box 152
Syracuse, NY 13210
315-424-1942
Information about avoiding unnecessary cesareans.

Childbirth Education Foundation (CEF)
PO Box 5
Richboro, PA 18954
215-357-2792
Information on childbirth, newborn care and parenting.

Couple to Couple League (CCL)
PO Box 111184
Cincinnati, OH 45211
513-661-7612
Teaches natural family planning

Informed Homebirth/ Informed Birth and Parenting
PO Box 3675
Ann Arbor, MI 48106
313-662-6857
Information on alternatives in childbirth methods, parenting and education.

National Association of Childbearing Centers (NACC)
3123 Gottschall Road
Perkiomenville
PA 18074
215-234-8068
Information on where to find birth centers and how to start one.

SHARE
St. Elizabeth's Hospital
211 S 3rd Street
Belleville, IL 62222
Support for parents who have lost a newborn through miscarriage, stillbirth, or early infant death

POSTNATAL SUPPORT

Center for Study of Multiple Births (CSMB)
333 E. Superior St
Suite 464
Chicago, IL 60611
312-266-9093
Provides information on caring for twins and multiple birth children.

Depression After Delivery
PO Box 1282
Morrisville, PA 19067
215-295-3994
Self-help mutual aid group to support mothers with post-partum depression.

La Lèche League International
9616 Minneapolis Ave
Franklin Park, IL 60131
312-455-7730
Breastfeeding advice and support (Check phone directory for local chapter or write to the above address).

National Center for Education in Maternal and Child Health
38th and R Streets, NW
Washington, DC 20057
202-625-8400
Information on genetics, chronic illness/disability, pregnancy and nutrition.

National Organization of Mothers of Twins Clubs Inc. (NOMOTC)
12404 Princess Jeanne, NE
Albuquerque, NM 87112-4640
505-275-0955

Parent Care
101 1/2 S Union Street
Alexandria, VA 22314
703-836-4678
Information and support for parents of premature and high-risk infants.

SUPPORT AND INFORMATION FOR PARENTS

Adoptive Parents' Education program
PO Box 32114
Phoenix, AZ 85064
Information and referrals on adoption; videos, tapes.

Adoptive Services Information Agency
7720 Alaska Ave NW
Washington, DC 20012
202-725-7193
Information on international adoption

American Association of Marriage and Family Therapy
1100 K St., NW, 10th floor
Washington, DC 20036
202-452-0109
Provides lists of members in your home area.

Childhelp U.S.A.
6463 Independence Ave.
Woodland Hills, CA 91370
1-800-4-A-CHILD
24 hour hotline for victims of child abuse, parents who think they might abuse their children, and anyone reporting suspected child abuse.

Compassionate Friends
PO Box 3696
Oak Brook, IL 60522-3696
708-990-0010
Support for families over the death of a child.

Family Resource Coalition
230 N. Michigan Ave.
Chicago, IL 60601
312-726-4750
Provides lists of parent education groups in each state.

Fatherhood Project
C/o Families and Work Institute
330 7th Avenue, 14th floor
New York, NY 10001
212-268-4846
Support for men in childrearing roles

National Committee for Prevention of Child Abuse (NCPCA)
332 South Michigan Ave.,
Suite 1600
Chicago, IL 60604-4357
312-663-3520
Publishes material about child abuse and parenting.

National Foundation – March of Dimes Birth Defects Foundation (MDBDF)
1275 Mamaroneck Ave.
White Plains, NY 10605
914-428-7100
Provides information on prenatal care and prevention of birth defects.

National Sudden Infant Death Syndrome Foundation (NSIDSF)
10500 Little Patuxent
Pkwy, No 420
Columbia, MD 21044
301-964-8000
Refers to local chapters which provide support and information to parents.

OURS, Inc.
3307 Highway 100 North,
Suite 203
Minneapolis, MN 55422
612-535-4829
Support and information to adoptive parents and children in need of permanent families.

Parents Anonymous
6733 South Sepulveda
Boulevard, Suite 270
Los Angeles, CA 90045
213-410-9732
Counselling for parents who have or who are tempted to abuse their children. (Check directory for local chapter or write to the above address.)

Parents Without Partners
8807 Colesville Road
Silver Spring, MD 20910
301-588-9354
Mutual support group for single parents and their children.

Rehabilitation Information Round Table
C/o Phyllis Quinn
American Physical Therapy Association
1111 N. Fairfax St.
Alexandria, VA 22314
703-684-2782

Stepfamily Association of America
215 Centennial Mall S
Suite 212
Lincoln, NE 68508
402-477-7837

Visiting Nurse Associations of America
3801 E Florida
Suite 806
Denver, CO 80210
303-753-0218

SERVICES FOR ALL CHILDREN IN NEED

Catholic Charities U.S.A.
1319 F St., 4th Floor, NW
Washington, DC 20004
202-639-8400
Provides a wide range of services through local bureaus to families suffering from child abuse and/or neglect, including material assistance.

Legal Services Corp.
400 Virginia Ave., SW
Washington, DC 20024
202-836-1843
*Offers free legal assistance
in such areas as welfare
and family matters.*

Salvation Army
National Headquarters
799 Bloomfield Avenue
Verona, NJ 07044
201-239-0606
*Provides a wide range of
social services, including
running day care centers
and nursery schools.*

United Way of America
701 N. Fairfax
Alexandria, VA 22314
703-836-7100
*Several thousand United
Way offices throughout the
country provide
information and referrals to
health and human care
services.*

CHILDCARE, PLAY AND EDUCATION

Children in Hospitals
31 Wilshire Park
Needham, MA 02192
617-482-2915
*Offers help and advice on
negotiating with hospital
staff in order to minimize
the trauma of
hospitalization.*

**Child Welfare League
of America – Research
Center**
440 1st St., NW,
Suite 310
Washington, DC 20001
202-638-2952
*Information on day care in
centers and homes.*

**National Association for
Education of Young
Children**
1834 Connecticut Avenue,
NW
Washington, DC 20009
202-232-8777

**Nova University Family
Center**
3301 College Ave.
Fort Lauderdale, FL 33314
305-475-7670
*Programs, services and
publication for parents with
infants and young children.*

**Parent Cooperative Pre-
Schools International**
PO Box 90410
Indianapolis, IN 46290
317-849-0992
*Provides information on
setting up parent
cooperative preschools.*

**U.S.A. Toy Library
Association (USATLA)**
1800 Pickwick Ave.
Glenview, IL 60025
312-724-7700
*Information on the
importance of play and the
development of toy
libraries.*

CHILDREN WITH SPECIAL EDUCATIONAL NEEDS

**Association for Learning
Disabilities of America**
4156 Library Road
Pittsburgh, PA 15234
412-341-1515
*Information and referral
center.*

**National Association for
Gifted Children (NAGC)**
1155 15th St., NW, No
1002
Washington, DC 20005
202-785-4268

**National Information
Center for Children and
Youth with Handicaps**
Box 1492
Washington, DC 20013
703-893-6061
*Provides information
concerning educational
rights to parents of children
with physical, mental and
emotional handicaps.*

**Orton Dyslexia Society
(ODS)**
724 York Road
Baltimore, MD 21204
1-800-ABCD-123 (toll-free)

CHILDREN WITH HANDICAPS OR PARTICULAR PROBLEMS

**American Celiac Society/
Dietary Support
Coalition**
58 Musano Court
West Orange, NJ 07052
201-325-8837

**American Cleft Palate/
Craniofacial Association**
1218 Grandview Avenue
Pittsburgh, PA 15211
412-481-1376
1-800-242-5338 (toll-free –
all states except
Pennsylvania)
1-800-232-5338 (toll-free in
Pennsylvania)
*For information and
support groups.*

**American Council of the
Blind (ACB)**
1155 15th St., NW
Suite 1100
Washington, DC 20005
202-467-5081
1-800-424-8666 (toll-free)
*Support and outreach to
sighted parents of blind
and visually impaired
children; blind and visually
impaired parents.*

**American Diabetes
Association (ADA)
National Service Center**
1660 Duke Street,
Alexandria, VA 22314
703-549-1500
1-800-ADA-DISC (toll-free
to get number of local
affiliates)

**American Juvenile
Arthritis Organization
(AJAO)**
1314 Spring St., NW
Atlanta, GA 30309
404-872-7100

**Association of Birth
Defect Children (ABDC)**
5400 Diplomat Circle
Suite 270
Orlando, FL 32810
407-629-1466

**Association for Retarded
Citizens of the United
States**
PO Box 6109,
Arlington, TX 76005
817-640-0204
*Provides services and
information for mentally
retarded children and their
families; referrals to local
and state chapters.*

**Cystic Fibrosis
Foundation (CFF)**
6931 Arlington Rd.
Bethesda, MD 20814
301-951-4422

**Epilepsy Foundation of
America (EFA)**
4351 Garden City Drive,
Landover, MD 20785
301-459-3700
1-800-332-1000 (toll-free
for all states except
Maryland)

**Human Growth
Foundation (HGF)**
7777 Leesbug Pike
Falls Church, VA 22043
703-883-1773
*Provides information for
families of children with
physical growth problems.*

**Muscular Dystrophy
Association (MDA)**
810 Seventh Ave.
New York, NY 10019
212-586-0808

**National Association for
Hearing and Speech
Action (NAHSA)**
10801 Rockville Pike
Rockville, MD 20852
1-800-638-TALK (toll-free
hotline)

**National Association for
Sickle Cell Disease, Inc.
(NASCD)**
3345 Wilshire Boulevard
Suite 1106
Los Angeles, CA 90010-
1880
213-736-5455 (for
California residents)
1-800-21-8453 (toll-free for
all states except California)

**National Down
Syndrome Congress**
1800 Dempster St.
Park Ridge, IL 60068
312-823-7550
1-800-232-6372 (toll-free
national and international)

**National Reye's
Syndrome Foundation**
PO Box 829
Bryan, OH 43506
419-636-2679

**Osteogenesis Imperfecta
Foundation**
PO Box 14807
Clearwater, FL 34629
813-855-7077
*Information about this
hereditary bone disorder.*

**Play Schools Association
(PSA)**
9 E. 38th St., 8th floor
New York, NY 10136
212-725-6540
*Develops programs for
latch-key children and for
children who are
emotionallly and physically
handicapped, brain injured
or hospitalized.*

Recording for the Blind
20 Roszel Rd.,
Princeton, NJ 08540
609-452-0606
*Cassette library for blind
and handicapped.*

**Spina Bifida Association
of America (SBAA)**
1700 Rockville Pike, Suite
540
Rockville, MD 20852
301-770-7222
1-800-621-3141 (toll-free)

**United Cerebral Palsy
Associations**
7 Penn Plaza, Suite 804
New York, NY 10001
212-268-5962
1-800-872-1827 (toll-free,
all states except New York)

INFORMATION ON HEALTH, SAFETY AND FIRST AID

Amercan Red Cross,
National Headquarters
17th and D Sts,
NW Washington, DC
20006
202-737-8300

**National Fire Protection
Association (NFPA)**
1 Batterymarch Park,
Quincy, MA 02269-9101
671-770-3000
*Conducts fire safety
education programs*

**National Highway Traffic
Safety Administration**
U.S. Department of
Transportation
400 7th St., NW
Washington, DC 20590
1-800-424-9393
*Hotline for information
about car seats and
automotive safety.*

National Safety Council
444 N. Michigan Ave.
Chicago, IL 60611
312-527-4800
*Publishes material on safe
toys and furniture, safety
restraints, etc.*

**U.S. Consumer Product
Safety Commission**
1750 K Street, NW
Washington, DC 20207
1-800-638-2772
*Toll-free for complaints
about faulty items and
information on safe ones.*

Index

Acknowledgments

The publishers would like to thank the following for their help in the preparation of this book –

All the children – and their parents – who took part in the photography:
Kazuko Ali; Sally Avelas; David Bates; William Booth-Dorling; Eileen and Ron Burnham; Pat and Richard Burnham with Hayley and Nicole; Helen Cluff; Anna Crawford; Sue Eziefula with Nicky and Daniel; Carla Freeman; Vanessa Gallwey with Lucy and Emma; Mrs Gervais with Laurine; Katie and Joe Gordon; Katie Gotla; Lucy Gregory; Sheila Gregory with Edward and Oliver; Jade Hansbury; Susannah and Elizabeth Hill; Emma Johnson-Gilbert with Cordelia and Jemima; Katie and William Joll with Harry and Flora; Teresa and John Jones with Chloe; Judith and Philip Kaye with Oliver; Liz Lazenby with Katharine; Philippa Mason with Emily; Iain Mathieson; Martha McAlpine; Joanna Munday; Jane and Patrick O'Shea with Megan, Emily and Madeleine; Stewart Paveley; Louise and Tony Power with Olivia; Hannah Ross-Tatum; Gilda and Simon Russell with Edward; Geraldine Scott and Adrian Payne with Charlene; Thida Sheldon; Mrs Simser with Nural; Ben Smith; Jo and Simon Thackray with Jemima and Thomas; Lindy Tristram with Louis; Yvonne and Eugene Trowers with Danielle; Sebastian and Alexander Vencken; Elaine Walker and Steve Elsworth with Daniel; Barbara Wilson with Adam; Thomas Woolley; Vicky Zentner with Jamie Butcher.

All those who helped with particular aspects of the book:
Dr Maureen A. Fee, for her help with the American edition; Carole Ash and Gillian Della Casa for design help; Christine Parlane, Sarah Riddell and Vicky Robinson for editorial help; Gill McCormick, home economist; The British Red Cross Society; Staff Nurse Deborah Libby; the teachers and children at Wyndham Nursery School, Richmond, Surrey, and at St Clements and St James Nursery Class, West London; Sister Bayley, Sister Eagle, Staff Midwife Lim, Sister Poynton, Mrs Margaret Brant and the staff in the maternity unit at University College Hospital, London.

For photographs taken especially for Conran Octopus:
Cover by Sandra Lousada
Colin Burnham 156, 169 center, 171 center, 214, 246; Sandra Lousada 11, 24-5, 30-63, 66, 67 above and below left, 68, 82-98, 101, 113, 115-25, 130-1, 132 right; 134, 138, 139 left, 144-7, 150-5, 157-68, 169 above, 170, 171 below, 175-7, 180-1, 188-92, 193 above, 196-9, 202, 204-13, 215-22, 226-7, 230, 235-6, 238-44, 247-53, 258, 262-3; Ray Moller 1-5, 8-9, 64-5, 107, 114, 132 left, 135, 136-7, 139 right, 178-9, 200-1, 224-5, 234, 237, 256, 259, 260-1, 304; John Russell 99, 149, 193 below, 231.
For their kind permission to reproduce photographs:
Arcaid/Richard Bryant 229 below; Camera Press 71, 183, 229 centre; 'A Child is Born' by Lennart Nilsson, published by Faber & Faber Ltd, London 18, 20; La Maison de Marie Claire 10; Terry Sims 174; Lois Thurston 26, 67 below right; Elizabeth Whiting & Associates/Julian Nieman 228; Jennie Woodcock 126; Tim Woodcock 203; Zefa Picture Library 223.